YEAR A ▪ 2005

workbook

FOR LECTORS AND GOSPEL READERS

Martin Connell

LTP

LITURGY
TRAINING
PUBLICATIONS

New American Bible readings are taken from *Lectionary for Mass for Use in the Dioceses of the United States of America, second typical edition* © 1998, 1997, 1970 by the Confraternity of Christian Doctrine, Washington, D.C., and are reproduced herein by license of the copyright owner. All rights reserved. No part of *Lectionary for Mass* may be reproduced in any form without permission in writing from the Confraternity of Christian Doctrine, Washington, D.C.

WORKBOOK FOR LECTORS AND GOSPEL READERS 2005, UNITED STATES EDITION © 2004 Archdiocese of Chicago. All rights reserved.

Liturgy Training Publications
1800 North Hermitage Avenue
Chicago, IL 60622-1101
1-800-933-1800
fax 1-800-933-7094
orders@ltp.org
www.ltp.org

Editor: Paul A. Zalonski
Production editor: Audrey Novak Riley
Typesetter: Jim Mellody-Pizzato
Original book design: Jill Smith
Revised design: Anna Manhart and
Jim Mellody-Pizzato
Cover art: Barbara Simcoe
Interior art: Steve Erspamer, SM

Printed in Canada.

ISBN 1-56854-481-2
WL05

CONTENTS

The Author

Martin Connell received the sacraments of initiation in the Archdiocese of Philadelphia in the years bracketing the Second Vatican Council, with his Baptism before the Council, when he was ten days old, and his First Eucharist and Confirmation a few years after the Council. His life-long celebration and study of the sacraments is a fruit of God's grace mediated by the faith of his family — of his Irish-American father, Bill (+1996); his daily-Mass-going, Italian-American mother, Rose Marie Santore; his brother, Bill and his wife, Janeen, and children Kim and Krissy; and his sister, Maureen and her husband, Charles, and children Kelli and Kevin.

Martin is a professor of liturgical studies at Saint John's University in Collegeville, Minnesota, where he teaches the history of the liturgy, the sacraments of initiation and Eucharist, the liturgical year, and the writing of prayers. His most recent books are *Church and Worship in Fifth-Century Rome: The Letter of Innocent I to Decentius of Gubbio,* Joint Liturgical Studies #52 (London: Alcuin/GROW, 2002), and *New Proclamation, Year B 2003,* with Frederick Houk Borsch, James M. Childs Jr., and Philip H. Pfatteicher (Minneapolis: Augsburg/ Fortress, 2002). His recent articles have appeared in *America, Worship, Studia Liturgica, Theological Studies,* and *U.S. Catholic.* By God's grace, the ideas for such works usually come to him while he is jogging long distances or knitting.

Dedication

The author dedicates this work to the memory of his godfather, Joseph Connell (+1986), and to his godmother, Marcella Houck, a minister of the word at Saint George's Parish, in Glenolden, Pennsylvania.

Introduction

As time goes by, the celebration of the Liturgy of the Word in Roman Catholic worship is a conservator of an important human value. Humanity is shaped by social dynamics, and you, as a minister of the word in the Church and the world, are one of humanity's life preservers in a period of unprecedented change in social communications.

This change in social communications is abetted by computer use and the type of human contact that is mediated through computers. The emergence of computerization might seem only positive for the development of social, educational, economic, and political life. And it might also seem only positive that more of the world's people can communicate with other people who live in places they will never be able to visit. But the news is not all good news.

With the ever-increasing amount of time people spend in front of glowing computer screens, much of our social experience is removed from actual human touch, hearing, and speech. It is a disembodied way to connect.

As I work on this edition of *Workbook for Lectors and Gospel Readers*, I live in Buenos Aires, the capital of Argentina, on the Atlantic coast of South America. At present many people in this huge, well-wired city use public computers in public places. They sit in huge rooms with other real, live, and, one supposes, loving people, yet in these places, they have little or no interaction with the people sitting to their right and left. People converse by e-mail and Internet, engaging in relationships without flesh, interacting as if they existed without bodies, without faces, without voices.

Human Bees in their Cells?

The Church has not been silent about the gifts and dangers of computers and the Internet. The Pontifical Council for Social Communications issued its "Ethics in Social Communications" in 2000. Among the radically new consequences the Internet might bring, the teaching lists "a certain discouragement of interpersonal relationships." Considering the Internet's potential to "separate and isolate," it raises the "inescapable question": "Will the audience of the future be a multitude of audiences of one?" with each person staring at a screen rather than experiencing another person directly. A prescient metaphor describes those who use the Internet for much of their work and communication: "Might the 'web' of the future turn out to be a vast, fragmented network of isolated individuals—human bees in their cells—interacting with data instead of with one another?"

The Church teaching raises a serious question about the quality of human relationships shared electronically: "What would become of love . . . in a world like this?" These new media have changed the world, but "they do not make the reaching out of mind to mind and heart to heart any less fragile, less sensitive, less prone to fail."

Given our fragility in this new electronic world, we thank God for the gift of the Liturgy of the Word in the Sacred Liturgy in which you are a servant of God and of the Church. Sunday Mass and its scriptural proclamations cannot happen without human relationships at their most incarnate. By its interplay of speaking and hearing, of movement and seeing, of processing and proclaiming as prescribed by the rites of the Church, the Liturgy of the Word has always preserved the sensory aspect of human relationships. Coming together week after week until the end of time, meeting our fellow believers face to face, voice to voice, hand to hand, meeting our Lord together in the scriptures and the sacraments, is a guard against the snares of this new world of computers and electronic communications.

These sensory foundations of our sacramental life are as fundamental as the conception of Jesus in the flesh in Mary's womb. While we might learn a lot about the sacraments via the Internet, a computer can never make someone a member of the body of Christ or make bread and wine Christ's body and blood. The tangibility of the members of the assembly greeting one another, proclaiming and hearing the Word of God, exchanging the kiss of peace, and receiving the body and blood of Christ is an important measure against which we can weigh our experience of life mediated by the Internet.

The Liturgy of the Word as Relational

In spite of the nearly universal lack of knowledge of the Bible in Roman Catholic parish life for centuries before Vatican II, the ritual traditions of the Word endured. These traditions sustained important human experiences and cardinal ecclesial values. The printed text of the Bible is the word of God, but a Bible sitting on a desk or a table or at one's bedside is not a sacrament. Reading the Bible alone, in silence, is formative, spiritual, and meditative, but it is not a sacrament. The word of God is realized in the sacramental experience of the Church in the communal celebration of the Word. There is a primary power to the sensory experience that requires not "one," but "two or three gathered in my name" (Matthew 18:20).

As Catholics we have learned a great deal about the Scriptures from our separated brothers and sisters, the followers of the Reformation, whose study and research and prayer of the scriptures have enriched all Christians. As Catholics, we understand our lives through the lens of both scripture and sacrament, in the liturgy and the assembly of the baptized.

The Catholic Mass and Liturgy of the Hours with their respective celebrations of the Liturgy of the Word have had a significant influence on the worship of many Protestant churches. The three-year Lectionary that was born in the Catholic Church after Vatican II—with Year A for the Gospel of Matthew, Year B for Mark (and a portion of John), and Year C for Luke—has been taken as a model by many other churches who use the Revised Common Lectionary. Our Catholic liturgical practices have aided these ecclesial communities in developing a keener sense of the ritual and liturgical theology of the sensory experience of the proclamation—the seeing, hearing, and even touching—which enhance the worship of God. These are signs of the grace of God in our lives.

Christ, the Samaritan Woman, and You

The experience of the proclamation of the word has been part of the Church's life from its earliest days. In its first words, the Gospel of John describes Christ as the Word: "In the beginning was the Word, and the Word was with God, and the Word was God" (1:1). This Gospel was written by the Evangelist decades after Jesus' death, so when John wrote about Jesus as the Word, the Church with whom he worshiped was regularly proclaiming and hearing the scriptures, just as the Church continues to do millennia later. In the same way, the author of the First Letter of John wrote about the "word of life," and the writer was attentive to human senses in the letter's opening: "We declare to you . . . what we have *looked at* and *touched* with our *hands*" (1:1). And the author repeats: "We declare to you what we have *seen* and *heard* so that you also may have communion with us" (1:3). This is the Word of God, the Word who is our life.

In the *Workbook* you hold, there are readings from the Gospel of John especially during Lent and the Easter season. Among the readings of this Year A, you will find the story of Jesus and the woman at the well—the Samaritan woman as she is often called, because the author never tells us her name. For centuries, this story has been proclaimed during Lent, and you will find it here on the Third Sunday of Lent (pages 71–76). The narrative begins with Jesus, whom the Evangelist had already identified as the Word, the living, incarnate presence of God in the world, asking the woman for a drink of water. There are many fascinating aspects to the conversation between Jesus and the Samaritan woman, but as a lector you might be particularly interested in the end of the story.

The woman gradually becomes more engaged with Jesus, transformed into a new person and converted to the faith that changes her life. At the end of the story, the Evangelist reveals that "many Samaritans from that city believed in him because of the woman's testimony." Without recourse to the original Greek, one might not realize that the word translated as "testimony" here is the same one that had been used of Jesus Christ himself in the prologue of the gospel. The Samaritans believed because of the woman's *logos*, the same word used in the gospel's first verse, "In the beginning was the *Word*." The Evangelist's choice of *logos* for her testimony unites the witness of the woman to the person of Christ. She is doing Christ's work.

As you begin your preparation for proclaiming the Sacred Scriptures during this liturgical Year A, you take your place in the long line of bearing witness to God's presence in that *logos*, in that Word. Jesus Christ is the living Word of God. He ministered to the Samaritan woman, who testified to her experience of Christ and converted many to the faith by her ministry of the Word. Now you, millennia later, take part in this witness of the Word to the Church, testifying as she did for the conversion and salvation of many. Your work is Christ's work, the Word of God living and active in the Church. You are contributing to the sacramental tradition that preserves the Church's prophetic role as a sign of contradiction in the wired world. Your work calls for training and ongoing practice, and the *Workbook* you hold is a sign of your resolve to be well prepared for your ministry.

The Theology of the Ministry of the Reader

The Order for the Blessing of Readers in the *Book of Blessings* blesses those who serve as ministers of the word in parishes and communities. The text of the Blessing of Readers offers the Church's view of the importance of this ministry in its life. So as you open this *Workbook for Lectors and Gospel Readers*, set your mind and heart on the tradition of the Church at prayer in blessing its readers. The celebration makes a mindful dedication of the ministers to their work in the body of Christ.

The Introduction to the Order for the Blessing of Readers and the Introduction to the *Lectionary for Mass* make it clear that bishops and pastors are to pay special attention to the formation of those who serve the Sacred Liturgy. The Introduction to the Lectionary notes that a reader has a proper function in the celebration and should exercise this even when the ordained are present; that the ministry of reader is conferred in a liturgical rite; that the reader may assist in the arrangement of the Liturgy of the Word in terms of preparing other members of the faithful who may be assigned to read. While some readers are not instituted for service, the Sacred Liturgy requires the service of those who are capable. Clearly, it is the mind of the Church that "Proper measures must therefore be taken to ensure that there are certain suitable laypeople who have been trained to carry out this ministry. Whenever there is more than one reading, it is better to assign the readings to different readers, if available" (Introduction to the *Lectionary for Mass*, 52).

Your work in the Church is not simply what takes place in the Sunday liturgy; that is only the most visible part of a work that has formed you throughout your life. All that God has given you contributes to your formation in service to the Church. Here we consider the ministry of the reader as it is confirmed in the words of the Order for the Blessing of Readers.

Theology of the Ministry of the Reader

The rite for the blessing within a celebration of the Word of God includes this wonderful explanation of the theology of the proclamation of the scriptures in the assembly.

The word of God, proclaimed in the sacred Scripture, enlightens our minds and hearts. When the Scriptures are read in the liturgical assembly, God speaks to us and calls us to respond in faith and love. The ministry of the reader, then, is important to the life of the Church, for the reader proclaims God's living word.

The Church is clear that by your ministry in the assembly, "God speaks to us and calls us to respond in faith and love," a beautiful revelation of the importance of the word and the ministry in the life of the Church (ICEL, *Book of Blessings* [Washington: 1989], chapter 61).

The intercessions included in the Order of the Blessing of Readers also contribute to this theology of the word, and offer insights into some of the responsibilities that the reader bears in the community of faith to which he or she belongs.

The word of God calls us out of darkness into the light of faith. With the confidence of God's children let us ask the Lord to hear our prayers and to bless these readers:

For the Church, that we may continue to respond to the word of God which is proclaimed in our midst.

For all who listen as the Scriptures are proclaimed, that God's word may find in them a fruitful field, we pray to the Lord.

For those who have not heard the message of Christ, that we may be willing to bring them the good news of salvation, we pray to the Lord.

For our readers, that with deep faith and confident voice they may announce God's saving word, we pray to the Lord.

This strong theology of the word also prompts the Church to recognize how important it is for the ministry to choose people whose lives reflect the scriptures that they proclaim. How the ministry and your witness to it will unfold throughout the liturgical year is God's gift, and your life of prayer in the Holy Spirit brings the light of faith into a world that at times can be filled with darkness and confusion. The rite poignantly prays that ministers of the word will be confident in the Church's witness in the world and in their own place in that witness. In your work you will "bring the good news of salvation" to those who have not heard it and "with deep faith and confident voice," you will "announce God's saving word."

The Order of Blessing closes with this prayer:

Everlasting God,
when he read in the synagogue at Nazareth,
your Son proclaimed the good news of salvation
for which he would give up his life.

Bless these readers.
As they proclaim your words of life,
strengthen their faith
that they may read with conviction and boldness,
and put into practice what they read.

Each exercise of this ministry of the word is an opportunity for the conversion of the Church at large and of your own life, little by little, into the Paschal Mystery borne in the life of Jesus himself and in his followers such as the Samaritan woman.

As a minister of the word, you are encouraged to "meditate on [the word] constantly," and allow it to form you in faith. When you have an opportunity to study the scriptures—in a high school or college classroom environment or in the parish—take advantage of it. Your proclamations will be strengthened the more you come to know the history of the people of Israel in the Old Testament, the life of Jesus Christ in the Gospels, and the life of the early Church in the Acts of the Apostles and in the letters of the New Testament.

The Proclaimer and the Listener

The Liturgy of the Word is the Church's proclamation of God's life in us, and it is mediated by the gifts you have (or will learn) as a good and effective minister of the Word. Whether you have been in the ministry for a long time or are relatively new to it, you can always work on your ability to proclaim. It is difficult to prescribe the best way to proclaim, for many of the tools of proclamation are unique to each person as a unique creation of God. But there are guidelines that you can attend to as a newcomer or as a renewed comer.

Aelred Rosser, an eminent teacher of proclaiming the word and former author of the *Workbook*, wrote of the characteristics of human speech and the vocal variety that helps hearers attend to the proclamation of the Scriptures. Among the qualities you can consider and practice are melody, rate, pause, volume change, and articulation. Each minister employs such qualities

differently, uniquely, and each minister can benefit from the help of others by having them listen to proclamations and evaluate them. The characteristics of bad proclamation are easier to identify than those of good ones. Bad proclamations are dull, monotonous, hasty, inaudible, unclear, mumbled, and easily forgettable, or stiff, stagey, pompous, exaggerated, and annoying. That is not what the Church seeks in its proclamation of God's word! The most important recommendation is that you ask for advice from trained proclaimers, from those whose proclamations you yourself find strong and convincing, from those whose readings have a balance of the power of faith and strength of delivery, from those who can give criticism that is both gentle and direct.

We have all proclaimed the word and come away thinking that we could have done a much better job, only to find that it was one of the most well-received reading we had ever proclaimed. At the same time, we can remember times when we had studied the passage closely, rehearsed well, dressed appropriately for the task, and proclaimed the text without mistake or impediment, only to find that no one seemed to have noticed. The work of the ministry is a process, one that takes time and attention, and having the *Workbook* in hand, as you do, is a good start.

Whether the assembly to whom you proclaim has the printed text of the scriptures to read as you proclaim, you need to prepare and proclaim as if no one in the assembly has the text before them. Indeed, your proclamation should be so sharp and so effective that those who picked up the booklet when they came in will never glance at it because your delivery is so clear and animated.

Practical Matters of the Word and its Delivery

In addition to your own natural instrument, your voice, there are the practical tools of your church building. You need to be comfortable with the sound system, with the right position for the microphone, with the height of the bookstand, as well as with the Lectionary itself. If the church is relatively small, perhaps it does not have a sound system; in this case, you should ask a friend to help you determine the volume

you need to use so that people in the last places can hear your proclamation clearly. If your parish does not routinely offer help in acclimating you to these practical matters, you can and indeed must ask.

Moreover, in addition to the practical matters, the text that you will be proclaiming calls for a different voice than everyday speech. The Bible is a complex book. In fact, it is not merely *a* book, but a *library* of books, with many different authors, who wrote in many different genres and styles, from many different places and different centuries. Part of your task in taking on the ministry of the reader is to engage in Bible study. This will give you tools that will help you with the readings you are assigned. It is important that your proclamation be confident and convincing, and these qualities come from your own understanding of the word and its intricacies. The *Workbook* is one tool, and there are many others that you can consult. (The list in "Recommended Works," below, offers some suggestions.)

A final practical note about what you should wear for your service as reader. In a place as large and varied as North America it is virtually impossible to speak

specifically about what a reader should wear or not wear, but some general guidelines might help as you stand in front of the closet on Sunday morning wondering what to wear. It is not necessary to wear the color of the liturgical season or day, but do your best not to choose a color that contradicts the liturgical color of the season or day. For example, since purple is the color for Lent, purple is not a good choice for the Easter season. Similarly, since the liturgical color of Advent is purple, wearing purple during the season of Christmas would be a little odd at best, contradictory at worst. Black is relatively neutral, but during the Easter season, when white is the liturgical color, black might look out of place.

As a minister, your apparel should be dignified, perhaps a step up in formality from the ordinary dress for the members of the assembly. Ministers of the word should not proclaim the word in outdoor clothes. Even if there is no place for the members of the assembly to hang their coats, you should not proclaim the word wearing yours. Ultimately, we recommend that you follow the guidelines established by your bishop and your pastor about the type of clothing to be worn while serving the Sacred Liturgy in light of the prescription of the *General Instruction of the Roman Missal* (194) which says, "the lector, wearing approved attire. . . ." Attention to the dignity of serving as a lector is not merely aesthetic; it honors the revelation of God.

Pronunciation Key

Most consonants in the pronunciation key are straightforward: The letter B always represents the sound B and D is always D, and so on. Vowels are more complicated. Note that the long I sound (as in kite or ice) is represented by $\bar{i}$ while long A (as in skate or pray) is represented by *ay*; long A followed by an R (as in prayer or Samaritan) is represented by *ai*. Long E (as in beam or marine) is represented by *ee*; long O (boat, coat), *oh*; long U (sure, secure) by *oo* or *yoo*. Short A (cat), E (bed), I (slim), and O (dot) are represented by *a*, *e*, *i*, and *o* except in an unstressed syllable, when E and I are signified by *eh* and *ih*. Short U (cup) is represented by *uh* or sometimes *u*. An asterisk (*) indicates the *schwa* sound, as in the last syllable of the word "stable." The letters *oo* and *th* can each be pronounced in two ways (as in *cool* or *book*; *thin* or *they*); underlining differentiates between them. Stress is indicated by the capitalization of the stressed syllable in words of more than one syllable.

bait = bayt	finesse = fih-NES
cat = kat	thin = thin
sang = sang	vision = VIZH*n
father = FAH-<u>ther</u>	ship = ship
care = kair	sir = ser
paw = paw	gloat = gloht
jar = jahr	cot = kot
easy = EE-zee	noise = noyz
her = her	poison = POY-z*n
let = let	plow = plow
queen = kween	although = ahl-<u>THOH</u>
delude = deh-L<u>OO</u>D	church = cherch
when = hwen	fun = fun
ice = īs	fur = fer
if = if	flute = fl<u>oo</u>t
	foot = foot

Recommended Works

Guides for Proclaiming God's Word

Martin Connell, *Guide to the Revised Lectionary* (Chicago: LTP, 1998).

Charlotte Lee and Frank Galati, *Oral Interpretation* (Boston: Houghton Mifflin, 1997).

Susan E. Myers, *Pronunciation Guide for the Sunday Lectionary* (Chicago: LTP, 1998).

Aelred R. Rosser, *A Well-Trained Tongue: Formation in the Ministry of Reader* (Chicago: LTP, 1996).

Biblical Studies

Raymond E. Brown, *Introduction to the New Testament* (Anchor Bible, 1997).

Pheme Perkins, *Reading the New Testament: An Introduction* (Paulist Press, 1988).

John A.T. Robinson, *Redating the New Testament* (John Knox Press, 1977).

1ST SUNDAY OF ADVENT

Lectionary #1

READING I   Isaiah 2:1–5

Isaiah = i-ZAY-uh

This verse identifies the prophet.
Amoz = AY-muhz
Judah = JOO-duh
Jerusalem = juh-ROO-suh-lem

Proclaim this as if you are envisioning this glorious future time. Deliver it with confidence.

The previous verse tells us who will come, and here is what they will say. The quotation marks set off their words.
Jacob = JAY-kub

Zion = ZI-ahn

Emphasize these metaphors of swords and plowshares, spears and pruning hooks.

Deliver the closing lines with a note of invitation.
Pause slightly before the final acclamation.

A reading from the Book of the Prophet Isaiah

This is what **Isaiah**, son of **Amoz**,
    saw concerning **Judah** and **Jerusalem**.

In days to come,
the **mountain** of the LORD's house
    shall be established as the **highest** mountain
    and raised above the hills.

All nations shall **stream** toward it;
    many peoples shall come and say:
"**Come**, let us climb the LORD'S mountain,
    to the house of the God of Jacob,
that he may **instruct** us in his **ways**,
    and we may **walk** in his **paths**."

For from **Zion** shall go forth instruction,
    and the **word** of the LORD from **Jerusalem**.
He shall judge between the nations,
    and impose terms on many peoples.
They shall beat their **swords** into **plowshares**
    and their **spears** into **pruning** hooks;
one nation shall **not** raise the **sword** against **another**,
    nor shall they train for war again.

O house of Jacob, **come**,
    let us **walk** in the **light** of the **Lord**!

READING I   This reading from Isaiah is apt for the start of Advent and of the liturgical year, as well as for anticipating the coming of the Lord at the end of time. The prophet proclaimed it for the ancient Israelites, but it has long been a traditional reading for the Church's season of waiting for the Lord.

In this text we discover that the Lord's coming is signaled not only by the appearance of a newborn infant in swaddling clothes, but also by conversion among humanity: Enemies will become friends.

Weapons will be recast as gardening tools and farming implements, and former warriors will raise up beauty and abundance from the earth.

In your parish there are two groups of people whom you might keep in mind as you prepare this proclamation. First, gardeners and farmers. Think of them and of their work that brings beauty and nourishment to the world. For them, take your time over the part of the reading that will be a consolation to the "green thumbs" in your assembly. Second, there might be some who are inclined toward violence and hatred. The

text points out that violence is contrary to the will of God. Be clear and persuasive in your delivery so that you might encourage those to whom this word is addressed.

The opening verse is simply a biographical jot about the prophet, connecting the word to his ancestry and to the land of Israel. The final verse is addressed to believers. Practice delivering it so that your assembly will recognize the season of Advent as a communal journey toward the realization of the Lord's presence among us: "Let us walk in the light of the Lord!" The

Romans = ROH-munz

Paul addressed the Christians in Rome as "brothers and sisters," and by right of our baptism, so do you address the assembly to whom you minister the word.

Here Paul invites believers to let the coming of the Lord make a difference in how we live our lives.

These imperatives exhort the Church to "wear" Christ as we were "clothed" with Christ by the white garment at our baptism.

READING II   Romans 13:11–14

A reading from the Letter of Saint Paul to the Romans

Brothers and sisters:
You know the **time**;
    it is the hour **now** for you to **awake** from **sleep**.
For our salvation is **nearer now** than when we first believed;
    the night is advanced, the **day** is **at hand**.
Let us then **throw off** the works of darkness
    and **put on** the **armor** of **light**;
    let us conduct ourselves properly as in the day,
    not in orgies and drunkenness,
    not in promiscuity and lust,
    not in rivalry and jealousy.

But **put on** the **Lord** Jesus **Christ**,
    and make **no** provision for the **desires** of the **flesh**.

assembly should be able to hear the exclamation point in the joy with which you invite them into this precious season at the beginning of the liturgical year.

READING II Neither the apostle Paul nor the Christians in Rome—to whom he addressed this letter a few decades after the death of Jesus—could have imagined that almost two millennia later we would still be proclaiming these urgent messages: "salvation is nearer now than when we first believed," and "the day

is at hand." The urgency has not abated in the Church's seeking to receive God's presence in our midst.

The first reading addressed how the coming of the Lord would make a difference in terms of society, peace, and justice. This reading takes up the realization of God's presence among us in terms of darkness and light, night and day. The apostle clarifies that this will make a difference in how we live in society, not in terms of war and peace, but in terms of the desires of the flesh.

It might feel a little awkward to be preaching to your friends, family members,

neighbors, and fellow parishioners against "orgies and drunkenness," "promiscuity and lust," "rivalry and jealousy." But your ministry calls you to stand in the shoes of the apostle and bring to life the words he wrote so long ago. The word of the Lord is living and active these many centuries later, and your vocation entails an earnest proclamation of the word, even if it does make you squirm a bit.

Make clear the parallel between the two uses of the verb "put on," even though there is some distance between them. See

GOSPEL   Matthew 24:37–44

A reading from the holy Gospel according to Matthew

Jesus said to his **disciples**:
"As it was in the days of **Noah**,
  so it will be at the **coming** of the **Son** of Man.
In those days before the flood,
  they were **eating** and **drinking**,
  marrying and **giving** in marriage,
  up to the day that Noah entered the **ark**.
They did not know until the **flood** came
    and carried them all away.
So will it be **also** at the **coming** of the **Son** of Man.
Two men will be out in the field;
  one will be taken, and **one** will be left.
Two women will be grinding at the mill;
  one will be taken, and **one** will be left.

"Therefore, stay **awake**!
For you **do not know** on which day your Lord will **come**.
Be **sure** of this: if the master of the house
  had **known** the **hour** of night when the **thief** was **coming**,
  he would have **stayed awake**
  and not let his house be broken into.
So too, **you also** must be prepared,
  for at an **hour** you do **not** expect, the **Son** of Man will **come**."

Pause after introducing the reading so that the assembly will be poised to hear these opening few words identifying Jesus and the disciples as the speaker and hearers.

This summary of the familiar story will find the assembly picturing Noah, his family, and the animals in the ark. Your proclamation will need to keep their attention.

This sobering theology—one taken, one left behind—is not easy to proclaim.

This final verse's warning of the unexpected time of the Son of Man's coming is the eschatological element characteristic of the First Sunday of Advent.

if you might proclaim the verb in a way that makes the assembly hear the echo, even if only unconsciously. Practice the reading and proclaim it with authority.

GOSPEL   During Advent, the liturgy's theological emphasis moves from the end of the world (on the First Sunday of Advent) to the imminent birth of the Messiah (on the Fourth Sunday of Advent). Theologians call the end of the world and the glorious coming of the Son of Man the *eschaton,* from the Greek word

meaning the "last thing," and the related theology is "eschatology."

This Sunday's eschatological emphasis reminds the Church that anticipating the end of the world is as deep in our theology as looking for the infant in swaddling clothes, even though it is not as consoling. Vigilance for the Second Coming should be part of our theology at all times, though today's reading from Matthew is not the most comforting in its warning to "stay awake"!

Here Matthew's Gospel reflects his community's expectation that the world was going to end sooner rather than later. The

images in this ominous passage are chilling because the final judgment feels so arbitrary, as if for no apparent reason "one will be taken, and one will be left."

The Church's scriptural tradition has a good balance of consolation and warning. Your ministry of proclaiming the Gospel does not include picking and choosing what is to be read; it calls those assembled to appreciate the broad spectrum of God's word and the theology of this Advent time of the liturgical year. Be forward with it, discomfiting though it may be.

2ND SUNDAY OF ADVENT

Lectionary #4

READING I   Isaiah 11:1–10

Isaiah = ī-ZAY-uh

Emphasize the opening phrase: "On that day."

The phrase "the spirit" or "a spirit" begins each of the next four lines; pause before each to highlight this parallel structure.

Pause at the breaks.

Consider your mental image of the Messiah, for the vividness of that image will come through.

Similarly, imagine these pairs in the created world: wolf-lamb, leopard-kid, calf-lion, and so on, so that, as with the image of the Messiah, your imagination will animate the words as you proclaim them.

A reading from the Book of the Prophet Isaiah

On **that** day, a **shoot** shall sprout from the **stump** of Jesse,
    and from his **roots** a **bud** shall **blossom**.
The **spirit** of the Lord shall rest upon him:
    a spirit of **wisdom** and of **understanding**,
a spirit of **counsel** and of **strength**,
    a spirit of **knowledge** and of fear of the **Lord**,
    and his **delight** shall be the fear of the **Lord**.

Not by **appearance** shall he judge,
    nor by **hearsay** shall he decide,
but he shall **judge** the **poor** with **justice**,
    and decide aright for the land's **afflicted**.
He shall **strike** the **ruthless** with the **rod** of his mouth,
    and with the **breath** of his lips he shall **slay** the wicked.
Justice shall be the **band** around his waist,
    and **faithfulness** a **belt** upon his hips.

Then the **wolf** shall be a **guest** of the **lamb**,
    and the **leopard** shall lie down with the **kid**;
the **calf** and the **young lion** shall browse together,
    with a **little** child to guide them.

READING I   Like many of the first readings in Advent, today's comes from the prophet Isaiah. It has four basic parts. Parts one and four have common elements, forming a kind of semantic embrace. The most noticeable common part is the phrase "on that day." Put some weight on that phrase because it looks ahead to the day of God's vindication and bringing of peace, characteristic of Advent's theology.

After the mention of Jesse and the shoot that will sprout from the stump, be careful about the pronouns "him," "his," "he." These might be a little confusing: Grammatically, they could refer to Jesse, the ancestor of the coming Messiah. But they are actually referring to the Messiah, in the guise of the metaphors "shoot" and "bud." Your verbal emphasis on "shoot" will help the assembly's understanding.

The second part of the reading describes how the Messiah will judge the people of the earth. It is a lovely passage in which the poor and the meek are held up in righteousness and the wicked come to a bad end. Proclaim this with conviction, and use your imagination, particularly where the gifts of the Messiah are described as pieces of clothing, a unique and memorable literary device of the prophet Isaiah.

One of the most beautiful, poetic, and hope-filled passages of the entire Bible is the third part of this Advent reading from Isaiah. Rather than simply talking about peace and justice in abstract terms, the prophet paints a lovely picture of animal enemies living together in peace. Take your time with this beautiful portrait of the world as God would have it. Stand confidently in Isaiah's shoes as you proclaim this vision to your assembly.

The **cow** and the **bear** shall be neighbors,
    together their **young** shall rest;
    the **lion** shall eat hay like the **ox**.
The **baby** shall play by the **cobra's** den,
    and the **child** lay his hand on the adder's lair.
There shall be **no harm** or **ruin** on **all** my holy mountain;
    for the earth shall be **filled** with **knowledge** of the **Lord**,
    as water covers the sea.

On **that** day, the **root** of Jesse,
    set up as a **signal** for the **nations**,
the **Gentiles** shall seek out,
    for his **dwelling** shall be **glorious**.

Again emphasize the phrase "on that day."

READING II   Romans 15:4–9

Romans = ROH-munz

A reading from the **Letter of Saint Paul to the Romans**

Brothers and sisters:
Whatever was written **previously** was written for our **instruction**,
    that by endurance and by the encouragement of the Scriptures
    we might have **hope**.
May the God of **endurance** and **encouragement**
    grant you to think in **harmony** with one another,
    in keeping with Christ **Jesus**,
    that with **one** accord you may with **one** voice
    glorify the **God** and **Father** of our **Lord** Jesus **Christ**.

Paul is pointing the first-century church in Rome to the Hebrew Scriptures, but his advice is as applicable to the twenty-first-century church to whom you are proclaiming these words today.

Take your time here and proclaim with conviction that the coming of God *will* bring about harmony among believers.

READING II Saint Paul had a particular pattern of opening and closing his letters, and the Letter to the Romans is no exception. What is exceptional about this letter's closing is its length. Here we find the beginning of the letter's closing. Nearly 60 verses from the end we get the sense that he is giving the believers in Rome some last advice about how to get along.

Some of the text is clearly referring to the tensions between the followers of Christ and the Jews. Such tensions are not as striking today as then, particularly since the Second Vatican Council. The Commission of the Holy See for Religious Relations with Jews aims at "underlining the eschatological dimension of Christianity [where] we shall reach a greater awareness that the people of God of the Old and the New Testament are tending towards a like end in the future: the coming or return of the Messiah—even if they start from two different points of view." How each particular community faces divisions and resolves contentions is ever important, so there is an effective Advent message to be heard in Paul's words today.

Paul's final advice encourages believers to live "in harmony" so that together, with one voice, they might glorify God. Though this letter was written to a particular church in Rome, Paul's advice here is as relevant for ecclesial life today as you minister as it was nearly two millennia ago when the apostle posted it to that ancient community in Italy.

The division of Jews and Gentiles does not bear on Church life as it did when Paul wrote, but Paul's point is still valid: Just as Christ welcomes all people for the glory of God, so should we.

Welcome one another, then, as Christ **welcomed** you,
  for the glory of God.
For I say that **Christ** became a **minister** of the **circumcised**
  to show God's **truthfulness**,
  to confirm the promises to the **patriarchs**,
  but so that the **Gentiles** might **glorify** God for his **mercy**.
As it is written:
  *Therefore, I will praise you among the **Gentiles***
  *and sing **praises** to your **name**.*

Judea = joo-DEE-uh

Be careful with the quotation marks in these opening verses. Understand the layers of the text so that you can proclaim it clearly and without confusion.
Isaiah = ī-ZAY-uh

Imagine how John looked and sounded in his baptizing and preaching, so that your image of him will come alive at your proclamation.
Jerusalem = juh-ROO-suh-lem

GOSPEL Matthew 3:1–12

A reading from the holy Gospel according to Matthew

John the **Baptist** appeared, preaching in the desert of **Judea**
  and saying, "**Repent**, for the kingdom of **heaven** is at hand!"
It was of him that the prophet **Isaiah** had spoken when he said:
  *A voice of one **crying out** in the desert,*
  ***Prepare** the way of the **Lord**,*
  *make straight his **paths**.*

John wore **clothing** made of camel's hair
  and had a leather **belt** around his waist.
His food was **locusts** and wild **honey**.
At **that** time **Jerusalem**, all **Judea**,
  and the **whole** region around the Jordan
  were going out to him
  and were being **baptized** by him in the Jordan River
  as they **acknowledged** their **sins**.

Because of these timeless issues of Church life and the timeless recommendations of Paul, you, as minister of God's word, are the apostle of the Good News to the community in which you serve. Be confident in your vocation and proclaim this advice with clarity and conviction. This is God's word through the apostle, and your call brings this word to life in this season of Advent.

GOSPEL Scripture scholars posit that the infancy narrative of Matthew's Gospel (chapters 1 and 2) might have been written down later than the rest of the Gospel. If so, the verses assigned to today's Gospel would have been the beginning of the whole story of Jesus. (In Mark's Gospel, for example, this is the opening narrative.) Therefore, proclaim it with the excitement of the beginning of a story, anticipating an event for which we are longing.

Notice that, though we as a Church are anticipating the celebration of the *infant* Messiah, the scriptures here on the Second Sunday of Advent have John the Baptist preaching preparation and repentance in anticipation of the coming of the *adult* Messiah. In the early life of the Church, Advent might have been a period of preparation for Baptism. Only later, when Christmas found its place in the calendar, did Advent develop into a season of preparation for

When he saw many of the Pharisees and Sadducees
    coming to his baptism, he said to them, "You brood of **vipers**!
Who **warned** you to flee from the coming wrath?

"Produce **good fruit** as **evidence** of your **repentance**.
And do not presume to say to yourselves,
    'We have **Abraham** as our **father**.'
For I tell you,
    God can raise up children to Abraham from **these stones**.
Even now the **ax** lies at the **root** of the trees.
Therefore every tree that does not bear **good fruit**
    will be cut **down** and thrown into the **fire**.

"**I** am baptizing you with **water**, for **repentance**,
    but the one who is coming **after** me is **mightier** than I.
I am not worthy to carry his **sandals**.
He will baptize you with the **Holy Spirit** and **fire**."
His **winnowing** fan is in his **hand**.
He will clear his **threshing** floor
    and gather his **wheat** into his **barn**,
    but the **chaff** he will **burn** with unquenchable **fire**."

Take your time with John's description of Jesus' ministry of baptism.

Christmas. So the exhortations to "Repent!," "Prepare!," "Make straight!" in this reading, which has been part of Advent for centuries, might be echoes of that ancient preparation for Baptism. They are no less exhortatory for your own community, so read them with power and dynamism.

For those to whom you proclaim, whether or not they were conscious of it at the time, Baptism was the occasion for the birth of Christ in their lives, as it is for all the baptized. Therefore, as the priest or deacon who will proclaim the Gospel, you might imagine the assembly in preparation for the sacrament, thirsting for the waters of baptism. In this way, your proclamation will be vivid, like that of John the Baptist's a long time ago. Your proclamation is one in which the Church is changed by the power of the word.

Today's Gospel reading is a long narrative with some difficult descriptions. You might spend some time pondering some of the many works of art that depict the ascetic John the Baptist so that you will have an image in your mind as you describe John's ministry to your assembly.

IMMACULATE CONCEPTION

Lectionary #689

READING I   Genesis 3:9–15, 20

A reading from the Book of Genesis

Genesis = JEN-uh-sis

After the man, **Adam**, had eaten of the **tree**,
  the LORD God **called** to the man and **asked** him,
    "Where **are** you?"
He answered, "I **heard** you in the garden;
  but I was **afraid**, because I was **naked**,
  so I **hid** myself."

Pause after each of the two exchanges between God and Adam.

Then he asked, "Who **told** you that you were **naked**?
You have eaten, then,
  from the **tree** of which I had **forbidden** you to eat!"
The man replied, "The **woman** whom you put here with me—
  she gave me **fruit** from the **tree**, and so I **ate** it."
The LORD God then asked the **woman**,
  "Why did you **do** such a thing?"
The **woman** answered, "The **serpent** tricked me into it,
    so I ate it."

Pause again after the exchange between God and the woman.

Then the LORD God said to the **serpent**:
  "Because you have **done** this, you shall be **banned**
  from **all** the animals
  and from **all** the wild **creatures**;
  on your **belly** shall you **crawl**,
  and **dirt** shall you **eat**
  all the **days** of your **life**.

Proclaim these words clearly so that the imaginations of those in the assembly will be caught by the description of the serpent crawling on its belly and eating dirt.

READING I   **For the solemnity of the Immaculate Conception, the** first reading is a familiar passage from the beginning of the Bible. This is a narrative with a number of characters, and three of them—God, the man, and the woman—have speaking parts. The fourth character in the story, the serpent, does not have a speaking part, but does have a significant role.

Keep the difference between *dramatic reading* and *proclamation* in mind as you prepare for this proclamation. If this were a dramatic reading, you would work at finding

a unique voice for each of the speaking characters, and you would say all the words of a particular character in that unique voice, as in a play on stage. With the ministry of the word, however, dramatic reading is not the goal. The liturgy is not a re-enactment of something that happened in the past; rather, God is living and active in the lives of human beings as much in our own day as in the past, even, perhaps especially, in the reading of the scriptures.

For this reason, then, this is a *proclamation*, a reading that is not merely a reminder of a past (though it is that, to some

degree); it is a communal experience in which the hearts and minds of those in the assembly are engaged in a common experience of hearing a text. You are the minister of the word, and for this feast your ministry is to bring the word of God to life in the community of faith by a well-prepared and well-proclaimed text.

This particular reading will take some attention to preparation because it is fairly complex. You might mark or highlight in this *Workbook* the words of the three different

This passage about the enmity between the woman and the serpent is why this reading is assigned to the Immaculate Conception. Mary is the "new Eve," so this description of Eve in relation to the serpent is important to the theology of the day and of Mary's place in Catholic tradition.

I will put **enmity** between **you** and the **woman**,
and between **your** offspring and **hers**;
he will strike at your **head**,
while **you** strike at his **heel**."

The man called his wife **Eve**,
because she became the **mother** of **all** the **living**.

Ephesians = ee-FEE-zhunz

This reading is only three sentences long, but each one of them is complex. The first one is a blessing, praising God but not addressed directly to God. You are proclaiming praise on behalf of the assembly.

The familial image in the middle of this passage—"adoption"—is engaging and theologically potent. Proclaim it with clarity.

READING II   Ephesians 1:3–6, 11–12

A reading from the Letter of Saint Paul to the Ephesians

Brothers and sisters:
Blessed be the **God** and **Father** of our **Lord** Jesus **Christ**,
who has **blessed** us in **Christ**
with **every** spiritual blessing in the **heavens**,
as he **chose us** in him, before the foundation of the world,
to be **holy** and without **blemish** before him.

In **love** he destined us for **adoption** to himself
through Jesus **Christ**,
in accord with the **favor** of his **will**,
for the **praise** of the **glory** of his **grace**
that he granted **us** in the **beloved**.

In **him** we were **also** chosen,
destined in accord with the **purpose** of the One
who accomplishes **all** things according to the intention
of his **will**,
so that we might **exist** for the praise of his **glory**,
we who **first hoped** in **Christ**.

speakers with different colors, one color for what is said by the Lord God, another for what is said by the man, and the third for what is said by the woman. The largest part is that of God, who speaks to the man, the woman, and the snake. Next is the man, who speaks only to the Lord, but does so for a number of sentences. The woman has the briefest part—one line, "The serpent tricked me into it, so I ate it"—but it is one line about which theologians have used a great deal of ink over the centuries.

Your task is to make the story engaging, and you can do that best by being animated in proclaiming the well-known tale to the assembly on this day of the Immaculate Conception.

READING II This passage starts with a hymn of praise to God, a beautiful and theologically powerful hymn that opens the Letter to the Ephesians as a whole. The reading has three basic parts: the first is the blessing; the second and third parts speak, respectively, of how Christians

have become God's children by Christ, the "beloved," and of how as God's children we have gained an inheritance in Christ.

This passage is rich in theology, and therefore quite dense with relevant content for this solemnity of Mary. What you can most fruitfully emphasize in your proclamation is what humanity has gained by the saving life of Christ, which came through Mary's cooperation with grace and in which believers share. You are minister to a particular community of faith, one in which the

A reading from the holy Gospel according to Luke

The angel **Gabriel** was sent from **God**
    to a town of **Galilee** called **Nazareth**,
    to a virgin betrothed to a man named **Joseph**,
    of the house of David,
    and the virgin's name was **Mary**.
And coming to her, he said,
    "**Hail**, full of **grace**! The **Lord** is with you."

But she was greatly **troubled** at what was said
    and **pondered** what sort of greeting this might be.
Then the angel said to her,
    "Do not be **afraid**, **Mary**,
    for you have found **favor** with God.
Behold, you will conceive in your womb and bear a **son**,
    and you shall **name** him **Jesus**.
He will be **great** and will be called **Son** of the Most **High**,
    and the Lord God will give him the **throne** of **David** his father,
    and he will **rule** over the house of **Jacob forever**,
    and of his Kingdom there will be **no end**."

But **Mary** said to the **angel**,
    "How can this **be**,
    since I have **no** relations with a **man**?"

This is one of the most beloved stories in the tradition, so proclaim it with loving care.
Galilee = GAL-ih-lee
Nazareth = NAZ-uh-reth

This is the scriptural source of the beginning of the familiar prayer, "Hail, Mary, full of grace, the Lord is with thee."

Take your time here and let the assembly glean the theology of Advent in this passage.

adoption and inheritance are manifest. So you might keep in mind as you proclaim that you are in fact ministering to the living Body of Christ, and that this assembly—however great or small, however lively or quiet, however active or passive in the celebration of the Lord's Supper—is made up of the children adopted by God because of Christ's life. If you know and trust this to be so by God's love, your proclamation will reveal this with freshness in your words. Depend with faith on the words of the reading so that the assembly can, in turn, trust your living words

mediating the scriptures to them, the living Body of Christ.

It might seem a little odd to have a second reading on a solemnity of Mary in which Mary is not even mentioned. Yet because Mary is the Mother of God, she is also the mother of the Church. In its teaching on the Church, Vatican II found in Mary a model for the Church. So what you proclaim here about believers as sharing in the adoption and inheritance of Christ does have a revelatory theology about Mary, though it is not explicit. The letters of the New Testament do not highlight Mary's role in the same way

that the Gospels do. Your task in the passage is to proclaim the Church as the children of God, as those who have inherited God's grace from Christ's purpose and life.

GOSPEL This is one of the most familiar passages of the Christian Scriptures. Many believers do not understand what is celebrated on the Solemnity of the Immaculate Conception, thinking that it celebrates the conception of Jesus in the womb of Mary. But the feast is actually celebrating the conception of Mary in the

Mary's connection with her relative Elizabeth is another beloved facet of the biblical story. Proclaim this part with care.

And the angel said to her in reply,
 "The **Holy Spirit** will come upon you,
  and the **power** of the Most **High** will **overshadow** you.
Therefore the **child** to be **born**
  will be called **holy**, the Son of **God**.
And **behold**, **Elizabeth**, your relative,
  has **also** conceived a son in her old age,
  and this is the **sixth** month for her who was called **barren**;
  for **nothing** will be **impossible** for **God**."

Mary said, "**Behold**, I am the **handmaid** of the Lord.
May it be **done** to me according to your **word**."
Then the angel **departed** from her.

womb of her mother. (According to tradition, Mary's mother is named Ann and her father Joachim; their names are not mentioned in the New Testament.)

The narrative has two parts: the setting of the context and the conversation between Gabriel and Mary. The first part introduces the characters—Gabriel, Mary—and places the story in Nazareth. Take your time with this, for it can be both a blessing and a burden to proclaim a narrative like this that is so familiar to almost all in the assembly.

The second part of the reading is the dialogue between the angel and the mother-to-be, each of them having two speeches, though both of Gabriel's are considerably longer than those of Mary. Between the parts of the dialogue, there are identifying interjections. The assembly's grasp of the scene and its implications depend on your clear pronunciation of the proper names. Since you have the punctuation marks before

you, you can distinguish discourse from narrative. From your voice, hearers without the text should be able to know where the quotations are as clearly as if they were reading along with you.

The Gospel passage for this solemnity is fitting for Advent even apart from the Immaculate Conception. You can be emphatic near the end of the reading, with the Evangelist's details about the Holy Spirit's role in the conception of Jesus in his mother's womb and about Elizabeth's conceiving in old age.

3RD SUNDAY OF ADVENT

Lectionary #7

READING I — Isaiah 35:1–6a, 10

Isaiah = ī-ZAY-uh

Imagine these nature images as you prepare and as you proclaim.

A reading from the Book of the Prophet Isaiah

The **desert** and the **parched** land will **exult**;
    the **steppe** will **rejoice** and **bloom**.
They will bloom with **abundant** flowers,
    and **rejoice** with **joyful** song.

These place names might be distracting for an assembly unfamiliar with them, so don't put too much emphasis on them.

The **glory** of Lebanon will be given to them,
    the **splendor** of Carmel and Sharon;
they will see the **glory** of the **Lord**,
    the **splendor** of our **God**.

Strengthen the hands that are **feeble**,
    make **firm** the knees that are **weak**,
say to those whose **hearts** are **frightened**:
    Be strong, fear not!
Here is your God,
    he comes with **vindication**;
with **divine** recompense
    he comes to **save you**.

The imagery here is delightful. Proclaim it with joy and enable the assembly to realize the power of God's coming.

Then will the **eyes** of the **blind** be **opened**,
    the **ears** of the **deaf** be **cleared**;
then will the **lame leap** like a **stag**,
    then the **tongue** of the **mute** will **sing**.

READING I — Now the Church is in the middle of our season of anticipation, two weeks from the beginning of Advent and two weeks from the great solemnity of Christmas. And, as is characteristic of the season, the first reading comes from the prophet Isaiah, the Old Testament consoler of the people, and the prophet of Israel whose words are often taken up in the theology of Advent. His words of consolation and of anticipation of the future glory of the Lord, proclaimed to the people of Israel during difficult times, are fitting for this season during which we recall the past and anticipate the future glory at the end of time. Your proclamation, too, does this for the community in which you minister, looking back at God's actions in the past and anticipating the glory of the Lord for which we wait. As you prepare, bear in mind that the season of Advent is not merely about remembering and waiting for the birth of the Savior, but also about anticipating the Second Coming, part of Isaiah's message here.

The nature images at the start of the passage anticipate the healing images a few verses later, and the nature images are beautiful. Have you ever seen (even if only in photographs) the desert blooming in the spring? Call that to mind as you proclaim, so that the beauty of the prophecy will come to life in the vividness of your words.

The healing prophecy is quite inspirational for the Church in Advent. If you look ahead to the Gospel reading for this Sunday, you will find that it would be appropriate for you to emphasize these verses because they are nearly identical to what will be heard

Those whom the Lord has ransomed will **return**
    and **enter** Zion **singing**,
        crowned with **everlasting joy**;
they will meet with **joy** and **gladness**,
    sorrow and **mourning** will **flee**.

Zion = ZĪ-ahn

READING II James 5:7–10

A reading from the Letter of Saint James

Be **patient**, **brothers and sisters**,
    until the **coming** of the **Lord**.
See how the **farmer** waits for the precious fruit of the **earth**,
    being **patient** with it
    until it receives the **early** and the **late** rains.
You **too** must be patient.
Make your hearts **firm**,
    because the coming of the **Lord** is at **hand**.

Do not **complain**, brothers and sisters, about one another,
    that you may not be **judged**.
Behold, the Judge is standing before the **gates**.
Take as an example of **hardship** and **patience**, brothers
        and sisters,
    the **prophets** who spoke in the name of the **Lord**.

Emphasize "the coming of the Lord" in this line, for it sets the passage in Advent.

This is a unique image; perhaps imagine yourself standing in your fields, looking down at the earth and up at the sky, waiting.

Again emphasize "coming of the Lord."

The text moves in a new direction here, so pause before the shift.

Close the final sentence gently.

---

in Matthew's chapter 11. Therefore, slow down and be deliberate in your proclamation of this part, for it is wonderfully poetic. (Your proclamation might have the hearts of the assembly leaping like the deer in the lyrical passage!)

The reading ends on a positive note: "they will meet with joy and gladness, / and sorrow and mourning will flee." Be buoyant as you end the reading so that the optimism of the prophet is captured in your tone, so fitting now as we move toward the end of the season of Advent.

READING II This reading from the Letter of James has two parts, the first drawing on agricultural imagery, and the second on a theology of judgment.

Since it is the middle of December, the farm imagery will be out of season, but if many of the members of your community live on farms or grew up in farm country, this passage will be appealing for them. If the community is in a more urban setting, your hearers might draw from their imagination of life on a farm.

The key phrase in the first part of the reading is "the coming of the Lord," which

appears at the beginning of verse 7 and the end of verse 8, embracing the image of the farmer waiting for the "precious fruit." Be deliberate in your emphasis of this coming. The virtue of the patience of the farmer is the heart of the message here, for, though we celebrate this Advent season with vigor, the Church has been waiting for two millennia for the second "coming of the Lord," and it has not yet been manifest fully.

The second part of the passage is about judgment. On the human level of life in a church almost two thousand years ago,

GOSPEL   Matthew 11:2–11

A reading from the holy Gospel according to Matthew

When John the **Baptist** heard in **prison** of the works of the **Christ**,
  he sent his **disciples** to Jesus with this **question**,
  "Are **you** the one who is to **come**,
  or should we look for **another**?"
Jesus said to them in reply,
  "Go and tell John what you hear and see:
  the **blind** regain their **sight**,
  the **lame walk**,
  lepers are **cleansed**,
  the **deaf hear**,
  the **dead** are **raised**,
  and the **poor** have the good news **proclaimed** to them.
And **blessed** is the one who takes **no** offense at me."

Pause before proclaiming the opening verse; it establishes that John is in prison when he sends the inquiry to Jesus.

This Gospel passage has three portions. This first part has a connection with the first reading from Isaiah. Proclaim it so that the link is clear.

James orders that the community not grumble against one another, so that they themselves may not be judged. From this the text moves to the "Judge," the Lord himself. It still stands as good advice today.

The last verse of this reading feels like the beginning of a reflection on the "example" of the prophets, rather than the end of a thought. But because it is the last part of the reading, it needs to be proclaimed as a closing. Practice it to get the right feeling.

GOSPEL   The tradition has always highlighted John the Baptist during the season of Advent. In fact, his common title as the "forerunner" of Christ comes from his role as the one whose coming anticipated the coming of Jesus himself.

Apart from the role of the Baptist throughout the passage, this Gospel reading does not have a solid rhetorical coherence. Some of the difficulty is with the middle section, with "someone dressed in fine clothing," and "those who wear fine clothing are

in royal palaces." This does not appeal to the imagination now as it did when Matthew wrote the Gospel. The parts before this and after this are strong, so the message of the Gospel in Advent is not dimmed by the brief middle section.

There is coherence throughout in the steady concentration on the Baptist, which in this passage has three basic elements. First, there is the long-distance exchange between John and Jesus himself. John is imprisoned and he passes along an inquiry to Jesus by way of his disciples.

This part is enigmatic. Since it is not likely to be the heart of the homily, you need not stress it. The first and third parts can bear the main message.

As they were going off,
   Jesus began to speak to the crowds about John,
      "**What** did you go out to the desert to **see**?
A reed swayed by the **wind**?
Then **what** did you go out to **see**?
Someone dressed in fine clothing?
Those who wear fine clothing are in **royal palaces**.
Then **why** did you go out? To see a **prophet**?
Yes, I tell you, and **more** than a prophet.
This is the one about whom it is written:
   *Behold, I am sending my **messenger** ahead of you;*
   *he will **prepare** your **way** before you.*

"**Amen**, I say to you,
   among those born of **women**
      there has been none **greater** than John the **Baptist**;
      yet the **least** in the kingdom of **heaven** is **greater** than **he**."

Practice the final verse so that your reading will render it most effectively for the assembly to which you minister.

Jesus' answer is the second part. Jesus tells the disciples to tell John what their senses reveal to them, "what you hear and see." The tradition has always held to the expectation of healing at the Lord's arrival, and the sacrament of the anointing of the sick is quite pointed in its prayer for healing. Yet for most of us, such healing is not often seen.

In the third part is the familiar designation of John as the "messenger ahead of you" and the greatest "among those born of women." That last verse is powerful, for in it Jesus makes John the Baptist the greatest among all those born, yet even the least in the kingdom of heaven is greater than John. Take your time with this final verse. Its message is potent, but its form is not easy to proclaim.

4TH SUNDAY OF ADVENT

Lectionary #10

READING I   Isaiah 7:10–14

Isaiah = i-ZAY-uh

Ahaz is not a well-known Bible character; pronounce his name with clarity.
Ahaz = AY-haz

A reading from the Book of the Prophet Isaiah

The LORD spoke to **Ahaz**, saying:
Ask for a **sign** from the LORD, your **God**;
   let it be **deep** as the netherworld, or **high** as the sky!
But **Ahaz answered**,
   "**I** will not ask! I will **not** tempt the LORD!"

Then **Isaiah** said:
   Listen, O **house** of **David**!
Is it not **enough** for you to weary **people**,
   must you **also** weary my **God**?
Therefore the LORD himself will give you **this sign**:
   the **virgin** shall **conceive**, and bear a **son**,
   and shall name him **Emmanuel**.

This prophecy of Isaiah is fulfilled in the passage from the Gospel of Matthew that will be proclaimed later today.
Emmanuel = ee-MAN-yoo-el

READING I This brief passage from Isaiah has caused no small amount of theological and scriptural contention over the centuries. The Hebrew word *almah* is rendered as "young woman" in some translations of the Bible and as "virgin" in others. The Hebrew word might have meant either of these, which is the license for the disagreements. That does not cast doubt on the Christian theological doctrine of the virginity of Mary, since in the original Greek of the Gospel of Matthew, the quotation of Isaiah 7:14 *almah* is rendered as "virgin" without ambiguity.

In spite of this contentious history, on this final Sunday of Advent, this passage is here for the delight of the community of faith gathered in anticipation of the coming of God. Read it with confidence and joy.

READING II This is a tough passage! Even though this reading from the Letter to the Romans is only three sentences long, the Bible divides it into *seven* verses. Its message is clearly quite complex. In order to proclaim it clearly, you need to understand about what the passage is saying and how the apostle presented what he included in it.

READING II   Romans 1:1–7

A reading from the Letter of Saint Paul to the Romans

Paul, a slave of Christ **Jesus**,
    called to be an **apostle** and set apart for the **gospel** of God,
    which he promised **previously** through his **prophets**
        in the holy Scriptures,
the **gospel** about his Son, descended from David
        according to the **flesh**,
    but established as Son of **God** in **power**
    according to the Spirit of **holiness**
        through resurrection from the **dead**, Jesus **Christ** our **Lord**.

Through him we have received the **grace** of **apostleship**,
    to bring about the **obedience** of **faith**,
    for the sake of his name, among **all** the Gentiles,
    among whom are you also, who are called to belong
        to Jesus **Christ**;
    to **all** the **beloved** of God in **Rome**, called to be holy.

Grace to you and **peace** from **God** our **Father**
    and the **Lord** Jesus **Christ**.

Romans = ROH-munz
This is a long and complex sentence, describing, in turn, "Paul," the "gospel," and the "Son." Pause slightly after each of these identifiers so that the assembly can follow the apostle's rhetoric.

Here is the theological crux of the whole Letter to the Romans.

Gentiles = JEN-tils

Notice that this last part identifies the members of the Church as those "called to be holy."

In your proclamation, offer this "grace and peace" to the members of your church as lovingly as Paul offered it to the church in Rome those many, many years ago. The offering is no less powerful in your time and place than it was in Paul's.

It will help your understanding and your proclamation if you take apart the first section so that you can recognize what is modifying what.

Gather three markers or highlighters in different colors. In this *Workbook* (not the Lectionary!) use the first marker to highlight from "Paul, a slave" to "the gospel of God." Take the second marker and highlight from "which he promised" to "about his Son." Take the third marker and highlight from "descended from David" to "Jesus Christ our Lord."

The first part identifies the apostle. Then the second part describes the Gospel. (The phrases "gospel of God" and "gospel about the Son" form an embrace around what is between them.) Then the third part describes the "Son." Here there is also an embrace, opening with the phrase "his Son" and closing with the equivalent identifying phrase, "Jesus Christ our Lord."

After you have teased out the sections of this long sentence, you should be able to prepare and then proclaim the passage more easily.

The middle section of the reading introduces some of the theological and social issues that Paul discusses fully in the rest of the Letter to the Romans.

The final words of the passage are about the believers in Rome, whom Paul identifies as "called to be holy." As a minister of the word in your church, you, like Paul, are addressing the local saints (all the baptized), those "called to be holy," in your parish.

GOSPEL   Matthew 1:18–24

A reading from the holy Gospel according to Matthew

This is how the **birth** of Jesus Christ came **about**.
When his mother **Mary** was betrothed to **Joseph**,
    but **before** they lived together,
    she was found with **child** through the Holy **Spirit**.

Joseph her **husband**, since he was a **righteous** man,
    yet unwilling to expose her to **shame**,
    decided to divorce her **quietly**.

Such was his intention when, **behold**,
    the **angel** of the **Lord appeared** to him in a **dream** and said,
    "**Joseph**, son of David,
    do **not** be afraid to take **Mary** your **wife** into your **home**.
For it is through the Holy **Spirit**
    that this **child** has been **conceived** in her.
She will bear a **son** and you are to name him **Jesus**,
    because he will save his people from their sins."

All this took place to fulfill what the Lord had said
        through the **prophet**:
    Behold, *the* **virgin** *shall* **conceive** *and bear a* **son**,
    and they shall name him **Emmanuel**,
    which means "God is with us."
When **Joseph** awoke,
    he **did** as the angel of the Lord had **commanded** him
    and **took** his **wife** into his **home**.

Start this proclamation as if it were the beginning of the whole New Testament. Be bold and fresh in your words.

Pause after you read that Joseph was about to divorce Mary, so that you can relate this new beginning as the surprise it must have been: "Such was his intention when, behold. . . ."

Here are the words of the angel explaining to Joseph just what will take place.

Here are the words of the prophet Isaiah, fulfilled in Mary's virgin pregnancy. Emmanuel = ee-MAN-yoo-el

Pause after "God is with us" so that the resolution of the narrative is heard as a fitting end to this story.

GOSPEL   Year A concentrates throughout on the Gospel of Matthew. On the first three Sundays of Advent, the Gospel readings came from the middle of Matthew's Gospel, centering primarily on texts where Jesus speaks of the coming of God into the world, an "advent" different from what we ordinarily think of in the weeks before Christmas.

Today is the first Gospel of the liturgical year that draws from the infancy tradition of the Gospel of Matthew. Notice that the passage begins not at Matthew 1:1, but at 1:18, for the genealogy of Jesus, Mary, and

Joseph takes up the first section of this Gospel; indeed, today's reading is the first section of the whole New Testament since Matthew is the first book therein. (The family tree is the Gospel reading on the vigil of Christmas [pages 19–23].)

Of the two infancy narratives in the New Testament, one has Mary in the foreground (the Gospel of Luke) and the other features Joseph (the Gospel of Matthew). Matthew links Joseph to the Joseph of the Book of Genesis (chapters 38–50). The appearance of the angel in a dream is part

of Matthew's way of linking the Genesis Joseph to the Joseph of the Gospel.

The first reading is the passage from Isaiah that is explained in the Gospel. For this reason, it is important for you to highlight these two verses so that they are heard in all their prominence in the infancy narrative in particular and in the Christian story as a whole. Proclaim the text with joy, for Christmas is at hand.

CHRISTMAS VIGIL

Lectionary #13

READING I   Isaiah 62:1–5

A reading from the Book of the Prophet Isaiah

Proclaim this pronoun, "I," as if the words were written to those to whom you proclaim, who are the "you" and "your" of the passage.
Isaiah = ī-ZAY-uh
Zion = ZĪ-ahn
Jerusalem = juh-ROO-suh-lem

For **Zion's** sake I will **not** be silent,
　for **Jerusalem's** sake I will **not** be quiet,
until her **vindication** shines forth like the dawn
　and her **victory** like a burning **torch**.

Nations shall **behold** your vindication,
　and **all** the kings your **glory**;
you shall be called by a **new** name
　pronounced by the mouth of the LORD.
You shall be a **glorious crown** in the hand of the LORD,
　a **royal** diadem held by your **God**.

Work at enunciating the phrases as if they are names. It might be helpful to imagine the third one as "My-Delight."

No more shall people call you "**Forsaken**,"
　or your land "**Desolate**,"
but you shall be called "My **Delight**,"
　and your land "**Espoused**."
For the LORD **delights** in you
　and makes your land his **spouse**.

Proclaim the marriage and wedding images so that their theology comes through clearly.

As a **young man** marries a **virgin**,
　your **Builder** shall marry **you**;
and as a **bridegroom** rejoices in his **bride**
　so shall **your** God rejoice in **you**.

READING I Every Advent the prophet Isaiah guides our anticipation of the Solemnity of the Nativity of the Lord. Even on the solemnity itself, the prophet has the first word from Sacred Scripture, and this is so through all four Masses of Christmas Day—at the vigil, at midnight, at dawn, and Christmas Day. Such a preponderance of the prophet Isaiah's words is evidence of how much this book of the Old Testament has contributed to the Gospel tradition about the birth of Jesus, and also

reveals how much the prophet has shaped the liturgical traditions for this great feast.

　This section of the prophet's message is a weighty and beautiful text, but its literary style and devices were more familiar to the Israelites than they are for your assembly today. You might have to practice this passage a number of times so that you can proclaim it as well as its meaning deserves.

　Take your time and be clear with the middle verse, "You shall be a glorious crown," and then again toward the end of the passage, for the last part is striking. In it the relationship between God and the

Church is compared to the intimate union of bride and groom. The intimacy suggested by the prophet for this celebration of the Incarnation is poignant; God does indeed know us this well.

　For yourself as the minister and medium of this beautiful scripture message, perhaps it would be make for a more vivid proclamation if you, like the prophet, call to mind the love between yourself and your own beloved. How much like home is it for you to be in the presence of your beloved? So is it to be in the Lord's presence, particularly at

READING II   Acts 13:16–17, 22–25

A reading from the Acts of the Apostles

When **Paul** reached **Antioch** in Pisidia and entered
      the **synagogue**,
   he **stood** up, **motioned** with his hand, and **said**,

"Fellow **Israelites** and you others who are God-fearing, **listen**.
The God of this people **Israel** chose our ancestors
      and exalted the people during their **sojourn**
         in the land of **Egypt**.
With **uplifted** arm he **led** them out of it.

"Then he removed **Saul** and raised up **David** as king;
   of him he **testified**,
      'I have found **David**, son of **Jesse**, a **man** after my own **heart**;
      he will carry out my **every** wish.'

"From this man's **descendants** God, according to his promise,
      has brought to Israel a **savior**, **Jesus**.
John heralded his coming by **proclaiming** a **baptism** of **repentance**
      to **all** the people of **Israel**;
   and as John was completing his course, he would say,
      '**What** do you suppose that I **am**? I am **not** he.
Behold, one is coming **after** me;
   I am not **worthy** to unfasten the **sandals** of his **feet**.'"

This opening sets the stage for what follows.
Antioch = AN-tee-ahk
Pisidia = pih-SID-ee-uh
synagogue = SIN-uh-gog

From here forward it is Paul's speech to the assembly in the synagogue.
Israelites = IZ-ree-uh-lits

This section gives the passage a hint of Christmas.

This is familiar to us from the Gospels, where we hear John use this image of the sandals.

this time of celebrating the Incarnation, the Word made flesh and dwelling with us.

READING II   As the proclaimer of this passage from Acts, you have two tasks. First, you are setting the scene for Paul's speech to his fellow Israelites. Second, and for the majority of the reading, you stand in Paul's shoes and proclaim the words that the apostle himself spoke in that ancient assembly of the synagogue. Although

you want your assembly to hear the identification of character and place clearly, you might be even more animated, engaged, and engaging when you move to the speech itself.

Recall here that Paul was a Jew himself. (You might remind yourself of how deeply rooted he was in the tradition and practice of Judaism by reading Galatians 1:11–24.) The passion with which you deliver the passage can be enriched by this realization.

The reading might resonate at a number of levels. First, on the theological level, we can be reminded that the infancy narratives—that is, the Christmas story—were added to the Gospels long after the historical birth of Jesus. The infancy narratives actually reveal more about the theological birth of God-made-flesh in the Church and its worship than they do about the historical birth of Mary's child. So Paul's speech here is more appropriate for the Christmas solemnity than one might at first realize, for

GOSPEL   Matthew 1:1–25

A reading from the holy Gospel according to Matthew

The book of the **genealogy** of Jesus **Christ**,
	the son of **David**, the son of **Abraham**.

Abraham became the father of **Isaac**,
	Isaac the father of **Jacob**,
	Jacob the father of **Judah** and his brothers.
Judah became the father of **Perez** and **Zerah**,
	whose **mother** was **Tamar**.
Perez became the father of **Hezron**,
	Hezron the father of **Ram**,
	Ram the father of **Amminadab**.
Amminadab became the father of **Nahshon**,
	Nahshon the father of **Salmon**,
	Salmon the father of **Boaz**,
	whose **mother** was **Rahab**.
Boaz became the father of **Obed**,
	whose **mother** was **Ruth**.
Obed became the father of **Jesse**,
	Jesse the father of **David** the king.

David became the father of **Solomon**,
	whose **mother** had been the **wife** of **Uriah**.
Solomon became the father of **Rehoboam**,
	Rehoboam the father of **Abijah**,
	Abijah the father of **Asaph**.
Asaph became the father of **Jehoshaphat**,
	Jehoshaphat the father of **Joram**,
	Joram the father of **Uzziah**.

This is perhaps the most difficult passage of the whole Lectionary to proclaim because of the many difficult names. Practice them so that you can proclaim them with ease.
Abraham = AY-bruh-ham
Isaac = Ī-zik
Jacob = JAY-kub
Judah = JOO-duh
Perez = PAIR-ez
Zerah = ZEE-rah
Tamar = TAY-mar
Hezron = HEZ-run
Amminadab = uh-MIN-uh-dab
Nahshon = NAH-shun
Salmon = SAL-mun
Boaz = BOH-az
Rahab = RAY-hab
Obed = OH-bed

Solomon = SOL-uh-mun
Uriah = yoo-RĪ-uh
Rehoboam = ree-huh-BOH-um
Abijah = uh-BĪ-juh
Asaph = AY-saf
Jehoshaphat = jeh-HOH-shuh-fat
Joram = JOR-um
Uzziah = uh-ZĪ-uh

---

the birth of Christ in people of attentive faith is as vibrant an aspect of the Incarnation as the birth to Mary and her husband Joseph. Both are God's gifts, as Paul would have had uppermost in mind and heart.

On the historical level, this speech can be taken as an anticipation of the Gospel genealogy that will follow. Paul's mention of God's mighty works among the Jews—that God "chose our ancestors," and "exalted the people during their sojourn in the land of Egypt," who "raised up David as king," and so on—these are parts of the story of Israel that is raised in the list of names in the Gospel.

As you review this reading and anticipate your ministry on Christmas Eve, be decisive about how you will stand in Paul's place and recount the history of God's promise to the Jews and how you will stand in the place of the Baptist, saying, "I am not worthy," and so on. This is a key reading at a very solemn moment of the liturgical year. You, like Paul, stand in an assembly of faith to deliver an important message.

GOSPEL   In the middle of this reading from Matthew there is a little arithmetic lesson. The genealogy is divided into three sections of fourteen generations—the first from Abraham to David, then from David to the Babylonian deportation, then from the captivity to Jesus, who is called the Christ. You might divide up the list in the same way as you practice. Get comfortable with the first set before you move on to the second, and so on to the third. It is important that you become familiar with

Jotham = JOH-thum

Ahaz = AY-haz

Hezekiah = hez-eh-KĪ-uh

Manasseh = muh-NAS-uh

Amos = AY-muz

Josiah = joh-SĪ-uh

Jechoniah = jek-oh-NĪ-uh

Babylonian = bab-ih-LOHN-ee-un

Shealtiel = shee-AL-tee-el

Zerubbabel = zuh-ROO-buh-b*l

Abiud = uh-BĪ-ud

Eliakim = ee-LĪ-uh-kim

Azor = AY-zor

Zadok = ZAY-dok

Achim = AH-kim

Eliud = ee-LĪ-ud

Eleazar = el-ee-AY-zer

Matthan = MATH-un

Jacob = JAY-kub

Slow down here so that any whose attention may have wandered during the names
will perk up and realize the Evangelist's
point about God's plan.

Uzziah became the father of **Jotham**,
 Jotham the father of **Ahaz**,
 Ahaz the father of **Hezekiah**.
Hezekiah became the father of **Manasseh**,
 Manasseh the father of **Amos**,
 Amos the father of **Josiah**.
Josiah became the father of **Jechoniah** and his brothers
 at the time of the **Babylonian exile**.

After the **Babylonian exile**,
 Jechoniah became the father of **Shealtiel**,
 Shealtiel the father of **Zerubbabel**,
 Zerubbabel the father of **Abiud**.
Abiud became the father of **Eliakim**,
 Eliakim the father of **Azor**,
 Azor the father of **Zadok**.
Zadok became the father of **Achim**,
 Achim the father of **Eliud**,
 Eliud the father of **Eleazar**.
Eleazar became the father of **Matthan**,
 Matthan the father of **Jacob**,
 Jacob the father of **Joseph**, the **husband** of **Mary**.
Of her was born **Jesus** who is called the **Christ**.

Thus the **total** number of generations
 from **Abraham** to **David**
 is **fourteen** generations;
 from **David** to the **Babylonian exile**,
 fourteen generations;
 from the **Babylonian exile** to the **Christ**,
 fourteen generations.

the names so that the messenger (you) will not distract from the message (the word of God). As you prepare, take one of these periods at a time and practice it until you can proclaim even the most difficult names without stumbling.

This is surely one of the most difficult and beautiful Gospel passages in the Lectionary. Most readers will opt for the shorter version, presuming that the assembly will be bored with the proclamation of

this long list of ancestors. But stop for a moment and think about the quirky and odd and unique characters in your own family's history. Though the list of names in this Jewish genealogy might sound dull, even a little searching for the characters and stories behind the names will reveal that God chose to have his Son born into a family as real and varied and colorful as any of our own!

There are some well-known figures of Israel's history here, with Abraham, Isaac, Jacob, Solomon, and David, and these you need to pronounce accurately, or course. But most of the people named here are not familiar, and with these, it is as important that you proclaim their names confidently as that you proclaim them accurately. The women in the genealogy are very important: Tamar, Rahab, Ruth, the wife of Uriah, and of course, Mary, Jesus' mother. Scripture

Be emphatic with this line that establishes the narrative setting.

Now **this** is how the **birth** of Jesus Christ came about.
When his mother **Mary** was betrothed to **Joseph**,
but **before** they lived together,
she was found with **child** through the Holy **Spirit**.

Joseph her **husband**, since he was a **righteous** man,
yet unwilling to expose her to **shame**,
decided to divorce her quietly.
Such was his intention when, **behold**,
the **angel** of the Lord **appeared** to him in a **dream** and said,
"**Joseph**, son of **David**,
do **not** be afraid to take **Mary** your **wife** into your home.
For it is through the Holy **Spirit**
that this child has been **conceived** in her.
She will bear a **son** and you are to name him **Jesus**,
because he will save his **people** from their **sins**."

Matthew models his Joseph upon the Old Testament Joseph, from the end of Genesis.

Emphasize the Holy Spirit.

All this took place to **fulfill**
what the **Lord** had said through the **prophet**:
Behold, *the* **virgin** *shall* **conceive** *and bear a* **son**,
and they shall name him **Emmanuel**,
which means "**God** is **with** us."

Because so much of our Christmas hymnody uses the name Emmanuel and its meaning, "God is with us," proclaim this part of the reading clearly. Emmanuel = ee-MAN-yoo-el

When Joseph **awoke**,
he did as the angel of the Lord had **commanded** him
and took his wife into his home.
He had **no** relations with her until she bore a **son**,
and he **named** him Jesus.

The ending is a quiet resolution to a mysterious yet familiar narrative.

[Shorter: Matthew 1:18–25]

scholar Rev. Raymond Brown suggests several reasons for their appearance in the list: because their marriages were somehow irregular or extraordinary, or perhaps because they demonstrated initiative as instruments of God's plan of salvation, or even because these women were Gentiles or associated with Gentiles, thus demonstrating that God goes outside the expected boundaries. Whatever the combination of reasons for their place, do them justice in highlighting their role in salvation according to the family tree leading up to Jesus.

CHRISTMAS MIDNIGHT

Lectionary #14

READING I   Isaiah 9:1–6

Isaiah = ī-ZAY-uh

The metaphors of light and darkness are important to the liturgy and theology of Advent and Christmas.

A reading from the Book of the Prophet Isaiah

The people who walked in **darkness**
    have seen a great **light**;
upon those who **dwelt** in the land of **gloom**
    a **light** has **shone**.
You have brought them **abundant** joy
    and great **rejoicing**,
as they **rejoice** before you as at the **harvest**,
    as people make **merry** when dividing spoils.

For the **yoke** that **burdened** them,
    the **pole** on their **shoulder**,
and the **rod** of their **taskmaster**
    you have **smashed**, as on the day of Midian.

For **every** boot that tramped in battle,
    every cloak rolled in blood,
    will be burned as **fuel** for **flames**.
For a **child** is **born** to us, a **son** is **given** us;
    upon his shoulder **dominion** rests.
They name him Wonder-**Counselor**, God-**Hero**,
    Father-**Forever**, Prince of **Peace**.
His dominion is **vast**
    and forever **peaceful**,

This part of Isaiah's prophecy is foundational for much of what is central to the Christian tradition's theology of the Savior.

READING I The lights of Christmas trees are reflections of the theology of light at the heart of this great solemnity of the liturgical year; that theology is indeed part of the Christian tradition at all times. (Recall Jesus' words about himself in the Gospel of John, "I am the light of the world.") The many lights are images of the one great Light of our lives, the gift of God's life in us, Emmanuel, God-with-us. This is the gift of grace in the incarnate life of Jesus, the light of the world.

The opening prayer for this Mass at midnight or Mass during the night asks of God, "Father, you make this holy night radiant with the splendor of Jesus Christ our Light," and at all the liturgies of this great feast the image of light is central.

Christmas found its place in the calendar because it is a consolation at the darkest time of the year, near the winter solstice (December 21); when the days are shortest, the Church looks for its light in the lengthening of the days and in the coming of Christ. Calendar and theology work together, at least in the northern hemisphere, where the feast falls near the shortest days.

The first reading from the prophet Isaiah draws on this same metaphor of light: "The people who walked in darkness have seen a great light." If you are familiar with Handel's great *Messiah,* you will recognize the last part of this reading from Isaiah as central to that eighteenth-century oratorio.

From a historic point of view, one might think of this deed of salvation as already accomplished, which is so, but the Gospel needs to be proclaimed and heard and taken to heart again and again, year after year, in each community of faith and in each

from David's throne, and over his kingdom,
   which he confirms and sustains
by **judgment** and **justice**,
   both **now** and **forever**.
The **zeal** of the LORD of **hosts** will **do** this!

READING II   Titus 2:11–14

A reading from the Letter of Saint Paul to Titus

Beloved:
The **grace** of **God** has **appeared**, saving **all**
   and training us to reject **godless** ways and **worldly** desires
   and to live **temperately**, **justly**, and **devoutly** in this age,
   as we await the **blessed** hope,
   the **appearance** of the **glory** of our great **God**
   and savior Jesus **Christ**,
   who gave himself for us to **deliver** us from all **lawlessness**
   and to **cleanse** for himself a people as his own,
   eager to do what is **good**.

GOSPEL   Luke 2:1–14

A reading from the holy Gospel according to Luke

In those days a **decree** went out from Caesar **Augustus**
   that the whole **world** should be **enrolled**.
This was the **first** enrollment,
   when **Quirinius** was governor of **Syria**.

Titus = TĪ-tus

Emphasize "appeared" for its Christmas significance.

Another strong phrase for the theology of the feast is this "appearance of the glory of our great God and savior."

There are many proper names in these few verses; do not rush through them.
Caesar = SEE-zer
Augustus = aw-GUS-tus
Quirinius = kwih-RIN-ee-us
Syria = SEER-ee-uh

Christian life. Your ministry as reader is part of this hearing and manifestation of Christ.

The reading from the prophet is not only key to the Christmas tradition, it helped shape that tradition. It is part of the Hebrew Scriptures that influenced the writers of the Gospels. Your clear and confident proclamation can also shape and revive the hearts of the assembly.

READING II   We do not often hear much about the Letter to Titus. The Lectionary includes passages from this text only a few times over its three-year cycle.

No one named Titus is mentioned in the Acts of the Apostles, but Titus is mentioned as a companion of Paul in the Letter to the Galatians (2:1–3) and the Second Letter to the Corinthians (7:6–7, 13–14; 8:6, 16).

Because the feast and context are so grand and this passage is so short, be thoughtful about how you begin and end the reading. Stand still at the ambo and wait a moment for the assembly's attention before you begin. Announce the text—"A reading from the Letter of Saint Paul to Titus"—and

pause again. Then proclaim the short passage. Pause and look at the assembly, and then proclaim the closing—"The word of the Lord"—with deliberate dignity. Your deliberate and dignified announcement and proclamation will ensure that the short passage receives the attention it deserves.

This brief text is very fitting for the celebration of Christmas, and the exalted theology and exhortation to the liturgical assembly are as appropriate in our time as it was when written many centuries ago. It makes a connection between the "appearance" of the glory of God and the moral life, between

Pause here to allow for the transition from the universal to the particular in the persons of Joseph and Mary.
Galilee = GAL-ih-lee
Judea = joo-DEE-uh

So all went to be enrolled, each to his own town.
And **Joseph** too went up from **Galilee** from the town of **Nazareth**
 to **Judea**, to the city of **David** that is called **Bethlehem**,
 because he was of the house and family of **David**,
 to be enrolled with **Mary**, his **betrothed**, who was with **child**.

While they were there,
 the **time** came for her to **have** her child,
 and she gave **birth** to her **firstborn son**.
She **wrapped** him in **swaddling** clothes and **laid** him in a **manger**,
 because there was **no room** for them in the **inn**.

As described below, the shepherds are important characters in the story of Christmas.

Now there were **shepherds** in that region living in the **fields**
 and keeping the **night** watch over their **flock**.
The **angel** of the Lord **appeared** to them
 and the **glory** of the Lord shone **around** them,
 and they were struck with great **fear**.
The **angel** said to them,

This is the narrative and theological hub of the feast, so proclaim this announcement of the angel with clarity and without haste.

 "Do **not** be **afraid**;
 for **behold**, I proclaim to you **good news** of **great joy**
 that will be for **all** the **people**.
For **today** in the city of **David**
 a **savior** has been born for you who is **Christ** and **Lord**.
And **this** will be a **sign** for you:
 you will find an **infant** wrapped in **swaddling** clothes
 and **lying** in a **manger**."

And **suddenly** there was a multitude of the heavenly **host**
 with the angel,
 praising **God** and saying:
 "**Glory** to God in the **highest**

Take your time here and be clear, for the connection between this verse and the liturgical hymn of "Glory to God in the highest" can be very effective.

 and on earth **peace** to those on whom his favor rests."

the gift of salvation in Christ and the transformation of human ways. The word "temperately" does not often come to mind when thinking of the celebration of this holiday, but this is among the words from the letter to Titus that you will proclaim.

 Proclaim Paul's words of the appearance of God's glory in our savior Christ with profound joy.

GOSPEL The Evangelist Luke included the details about the emperor's decree to emphasize the universal significance of the birth of this child. This

emphasis anticipated the attractiveness of the faith, for the story of Jesus has indeed spread to "the whole world." From the universality at the start of the passage, the story narrows down quickly to the main characters: Joseph, Mary, and the child.

 One of the wonderful literary qualities of many of the stories throughout the Gospels, including the Christmas story, is that hope or joy is often set next to something frightening or grim. Here, the joy of the birth is set in contrast to the homelessness of the couple. The shepherds are at first terrified by the angel; then the angel brings the

good news of the birth. The greatness of the savior's appearance is heightened by the lowliness of his cradle, the manger, which is a feeding trough for animals.

 In all, this is a great story, and your proclamation of the Gospel is very important for this feast as well as for the seasons of Advent and Christmas that precede and follow. The climax of the passage is the song of the heavenly host, and as proclaimer you stand in the place of that host of angels. End your proclamation with joy in the Gospel.

CHRISTMAS DAWN

Lectionary #15

Isaiah = ī-ZAY-uh

Proclaim with joy and glory what the Lord "proclaims" to the world.

Zion = ZĪ-ahn

The last sentence might be tricky. See the recommendation below on how to deal with this verse.

READING I   Isaiah 62:11–12

A reading from the Book of the Prophet Isaiah

See, the LORD proclaims
    to the **ends** of the **earth**:
say to daughter **Zion**,
    your **savior** comes!
Here is his **reward** with him,
    his **recompense** before him.

They shall be called the **holy** people,
    the **redeemed** of the LORD,
and you shall be called "**Frequented**,"
    a city that is **not forsaken**.

READING I Throughout the season of Advent and at each of the liturgies of this great solemnity of Christmas, the first reading is from the prophet Isaiah. Unlike most of those readings, however, today's is short, only two verses, so you will need to communicate its message as clearly as possible, without rushing.

The brevity of the passage calls you to pause after the identification—"A reading from the Book of the prophet Isaiah"—so that the assembly is poised to listen right from the start of the biblical word.

The meaning of the passage is not readily clear, so study its theology first before you consider it as a text to be spoken and proclaimed well. The last sentence is the one that is a little tricky. The prophet is telling the ancient people in exile that the coming of the Lord will change the fortunes of the nation (personified as daughter Zion), and as a result the beloved, defeated city itself will be seen in a new way. Their city had been abandoned and forsaken, but with the coming of the Lord, it would become "Frequented."

Don't be distracted by the capitalization there; it merely signifies that the coming of the Lord will give the city a new name, just as people whose lives had been changed by the Lord received new names: Abraham, for example. The capitalization signifies that this word is a name, not just a description.

READING II We do not often hear the Letter of Paul to Titus in the Lectionary. Titus is not mentioned as one of the apostles either in the Gospels or in the

Titus is unfamiliar to many; be clear as you read the name of the book.
Titus = TĪ-tus

Stress this mention of Baptism, so important to the mission of the Church and to the theology of this solemnity of Christmas.

READING II   Titus 3:4–7

A reading from the Letter of Saint Paul to Titus

Beloved:
When the **kindness** and **generous** love
  of God our savior **appeared**,
not because of any righteous deeds **we** had done
  but because of his **mercy**,
he **saved** us through the **bath** of rebirth
  and **renewal** by the Holy **Spirit**,
whom he **richly** poured out on us
  through Jesus **Christ** our **savior**,
so that we might be **justified** by his grace
  and become **heirs** in **hope** of eternal **life**.

Acts of the Apostles, but there is a Titus mentioned as a companion of Paul in the Letter to the Galatians (2:1–3) and also in the Second Letter to the Corinthians (7:6–7, 13–14; 8:6, 16).

Because this passage is so short, be mindful of how you begin the reading so that the liturgical assembly is poised to hear the word from the start.

The wonderful aspect of this reading is that it makes explicit the connection between "the kindness and generous love of God our savior appeared" and the "bath of rebirth," clearly a reference to Baptism. Not

many Christians think of their own baptism as participating in the Paschal Mystery in as serious a way as the birth of Jesus, or that their baptism has salvific consequences for themselves or for the world around them. Since the text makes this link, make the most of this mention of Baptism on the solemnity of Christmas.

The Letter to Titus, moreover, emphasizes the role of the Spirit in the appearance of Christ and in our salvation. Recall what the angel says to Mary in the Gospel of Luke: "The Holy Spirit will come upon you." So the Spirit was sent to begin the incarnation of

the Savior in his mother, and according to today's scripture, so is the Spirit poured out on each of us at our baptism, and on the Church at this feast of Christmas as a continuation of God's saving work.

GOSPEL   Each of the Christmas liturgies—vigil, night, dawn, and day—has its own Gospel narrative, and in the dawn liturgy at which you will proclaim the Gospel, the shepherds in the fields are featured. People who live in places where there are no sheep and no shepherds

GOSPEL   Luke 2:15–20

A reading from the holy Gospel according to Luke

When the **angels** went away from them to **heaven**,
    the **shepherds** said to one another,
    "Let us go, then, to **Bethlehem**
    to see this thing that has taken place,
    which the **Lord** has made known to us."

So they went in haste and found **Mary** and **Joseph**,
    and the **infant** lying in the **manger**.
When they saw this,
    they made known the **message**
    that had been told them about this **child**.
All who heard it were **amazed**
    by what had been told them by the **shepherds**.

And **Mary** kept all these things,
    reflecting on them in her **heart**.
Then the **shepherds** returned,
    glorifying and **praising** God
    for all they had **heard** and **seen**,
    just as it had been told to them.

Insert pauses between the various elements of the narrative to let the ingredients of the story be appreciated.

Since the mother of Jesus is so dear in the tradition and this passage reflects her feelings, emphasize this sentence.

can imagine the shepherds as romantic characters. But tending sheep was not then and is not now a romantic business, and, for Luke's original audience, the shepherds would not have been romantic in the least. But that is their significance. Like so many characters the adult Jesus will appeal to in the Gospels, the shepherds are outsiders.

The nativity sets and crèches in our homes are often set up with the shepherds already present, but the narrative of the Gospel here reveals that the angels tell the shepherds of the great event only after it has taken place.

The Christmas Gospel is a very familiar narrative, so make it your goal in preparing and in proclaiming to offer it to the liturgical assembly with freshness, so that those attending might hear it as if for the first time.

The passage has four basic elements: the shepherds talk about what they have heard and set out; they find the family and report what the angel told them; Mary takes all this to heart; and the shepherds return, praising God. That's a lot of action for such a short passage, so take your time and proclaim it with joy.

CHRISTMAS DAY

Lectionary #16

READING I   Isaiah 52:7–10

Isaiah = ī-ZAY-uh

The phrases beginning with "announcing," "bearing," "announcing," and "saying" are describing the messenger. Do not rush through these even though they are grammatically similar; make each a clear description.

Zion = ZĪ-ahn

This part connects well with the announcement of the messenger.

Continue the positive tone. The ruins are being called to sing for joy.

Jerusalem = juh-ROO-suh-lem

A reading from the Book of the Prophet Isaiah

How **beautiful** upon the **mountains**
    are the **feet** of him who brings glad **tidings**,
announcing **peace**, bearing good **news**,
    announcing **salvation**, and saying to **Zion**,
    "Your God is **King**!"

Hark! Your **sentinels** raise a cry,
    together they shout for **joy**,
for they see **directly**, before their eyes,
    the LORD **restoring** Zion.

Break out together in **song**,
    O **ruins** of Jerusalem!
For the LORD **comforts** his people,
    he **redeems** Jerusalem.
The LORD has **bared** his holy arm
    in the sight of all the nations;
all the **ends** of the **earth** will **behold**
    the **salvation** of our **God**.

READING I   This reading gives a boost to ministers like yourself, that is, to ministers of the word. For it begins with this: "How beautiful upon the mountains are the feet of him who brings glad tidings, announcing peace," and so on. Though you do not stand upon the mountains as you proclaim, you do bring good news and announce salvation. Take that to heart for this Christmas liturgy.

The joy and good news did not come to the exiled people of Israel from their own history, for life had indeed been painful and their hopes dashed. The prophecy is addressed directly to the "ruins of Jerusalem," to a glory that had been destroyed. So as you prepare this passage, keep that in mind alongside the fact that there are at least some in your assembly for whom this great holiday is not so easy a time. For many who have had a difficult or sorrowful year, holidays can accentuate the hardships. These people might be more attentive to Isaiah's address to the "ruins" than to the exuberance of the message. You,

like the messenger of the LORD described here, can bring comfort to the people.

The reading has two basic elements, the first the more exuberant part. As you prepare, think of the "good news" as the Christmas message itself in our time, for, though we remember the birth of Jesus at this feast, we also know that the Lord is fully present with us today as well.

The second element is the encouraging of the people after their time of strife. The reading encourages the people to join in

READING II Hebrews 1:1–6

A reading from the Letter to the Hebrews

Brothers and sisters:
In times past, God spoke in partial and various ways
    to our **ancestors** through the **prophets**;
    in these **last** days, he has spoken to us through the **Son**,
    whom he made **heir** of all things
    and **through** whom he created the **universe**,
    who is the **refulgence** of his **glory**,
    the very **imprint** of his **being**,
    and who **sustains** all things by his mighty **word**.

When he had accomplished **purification** from **sins**,
    he took his **seat** at the right hand of the **Majesty** on high,
    as far **superior** to the **angels**
    as the **name** he has inherited is more **excellent** than theirs.

For to **which** of the angels did God ever say:
    *You are my son; **this** day I have begotten you?*
Or again:
    *I will be a **father** to him, and **he** shall be a **son** to me?*
And again, when he leads the **firstborn** into the world, he says:
    *Let all the **angels** of God **worship** him.*

This is an overview of God's speaking to humanity in history, culminating in the "word" of the Son.

This theologically potent section is quite dense; do not rush through it.

This final part can be difficult because of the series of quotations. Be careful with this so that the liturgical assembly does not lose track.

singing because the LORD has rescued them. Announce this good news as if it is the first time. Be bold and capture the joy of this solemnity.

READING II The Letter to the Hebrews is complex, and its vocabulary is unique in the Bible. For this reason, this reading is not an easy one to proclaim. Before practicing it aloud, consider its meaning so that it will be familiar to you *before* you start practicing the physical and mechanical aspects of the proclamation.

The first part of the reading is a kind of theological overview, acknowledging that God has spoken in different ways and through different people over the centuries, but that these have all been fulfilled in the Son. (This theology is unique at Christmas because it sees Christ in God's speaking as well as in the manger at Bethlehem.)

The passage then moves on to a description of what has been accomplished in the Son, that is, who this Son is and what is accomplished in his very existence. This part is both potent in theology and difficult in rhetoric.

Finally, the passage shifts significantly in the last two verses, for the author is there asking questions, and in the questions he is citing passages. Notice that the questions are about the passages.

As ever, prepare the reading so that those who do not have the text and its punctuation marks in front of them can understand it. Your *tone* should make it clear when you are reading the cited passages in quotation marks. It might be helpful as you practice to highlight the three quotations, so

GOSPEL   John 1:1–18

A reading from the holy Gospel according to John

This opening prologue is dense, but good preparation will make it easy to proclaim with clarity and conviction.

In the **beginning** was the **Word**,
    and the Word was **with God**,
    and the Word **was** God.
He was in the **beginning** with God.
All things came to be **through** him,
    and **without** him **nothing** came to be.
What came to be through him was **life**,
    and this life was the **light** of the human **race**;
    the **light** shines in the **darkness**,
    and the **darkness** has not overcome it.

The metaphor of light begins a new section.

A man named **John** was sent from God.
He came for **testimony**, to testify to the **light**,
    so that **all** might **believe** through him.
He was **not** the light,
    but came to **testify** to the light.

The **true** light, which enlightens **everyone**,
        was coming into the world.
He was **in** the world,
    and the world came to be **through** him,
    but the world did not **know** him.
He came to what was his own,
    but his **own** people did **not** accept him.

that you can find a way of making your voice capture the difference between the words of the author of Hebrews and the words that the author cites.

GOSPEL   The Gospel of John, scripture scholars indicate, is the last Gospel written, likely near the end of the first century. By then, questions had begun to emerge about how Jesus was related to God the Father and about the existence of the Son in relation to God. These questions do not appear in the first three Gospels with the philosophical depth and insight seen in John, and there is no more philosophical part of the Gospel of John than the prologue, which is prescribed for the Mass of Christmas Day. In this prologue to the Gospel, the grammar is as light and easy as the theology is heavy and powerful.

This text may not seem as much of Christmas as do the infancy stories. The Gospel of John does not have a nativity narrative as do the Gospels of Matthew and Luke with their genealogies, magi and shepherds, Joseph and Mary, chorus of angels and manger. But it does have a poetic discourse of Christ's origins and of his becoming flesh that begins at the very start of this passage. Though this text may not be as engaging as the lovely infancy stories of

But to those who **did** accept him
   he gave **power** to become **children** of **God**,
   to those who believe in his name,
   who were born not by **natural** generation
   nor by **human** choice nor by a **man's** decision
   but of **God**.

And the Word became **flesh**
   and made his **dwelling** among us,
   and we saw his **glory**,
   the glory as of the Father's only **Son**,
   full of **grace** and **truth**.

John **testified** to him and cried out, saying,
   "**This** was he of whom I said,
   'The one who is coming **after** me ranks **ahead** of me
   because he existed **before** me.'"

From his **fullness** we have **all received**,
   grace in place of **grace**,
   because while the law was given through Moses,
   grace and **truth** came through Jesus **Christ**.
No one has ever seen **God**.
The only **Son**, God, who is at the Father's **side**,
   has **revealed** him.

[Shorter: John 1:1–5, 9–14]

Starting here, the prologue shifts to "we" and "us." Proclaimed well, this can be as engaging for the Church in our time as it was for the community for which it was written originally.

Matthew and Luke, it has contributed enormously to the Christian theological tradition. Be assertive with it, even with its philosophical vocabulary. The end of the opening section comes with the metaphor of light, which occupies the next section.

Recall that it is in the Gospel of John alone that one finds the saying of Jesus, "I am the light of the world." That comes later in the Gospel, but here already the Evangelist has introduced light and its opposite, darkness. Light and dark play key roles throughout the Gospel, and this begins in this prologue.

The next section is a summary of the Gospel, about Jesus' coming into the world and the world not receiving him. The use of the first person plural—"made his dwelling among us," "we saw his glory," "we have all received"—enables you, the proclaimer, to bring this ancient text up to the present. Proclaim it as if it were written for your community, for your proclamation to that community. Today is a solemnity, and the Gospel plays a major role in the Liturgy of the Word for Christmas.

HOLY FAMILY

Lectionary #17

READING I   Sirach 3:2–6, 12–14

Sirach = SEER-ak

The first part of the reading is delivered in the third person: "God," "a father" and "a mother," and "children."

A reading from the Book of Sirach

God sets a **father** in honor over his **children**;
a **mother's** authority he **confirms** over her **sons**.
Whoever honors his **father** atones for **sins**,
and **preserves** himself from them.
When he **prays**, he is **heard**;
he stores up **riches** who reveres his **mother**.
Whoever honors his **father** is **gladdened** by **children**,
and, when he prays, is **heard**.
Whoever reveres his **father** will live a long **life**;
he who **obeys** his father brings **comfort** to his **mother**.

The voice changes here to direct address, to "my son," using the first-person ("my") and second-person pronouns ("your," "you.")

My son, take **care** of your father when he is **old**;
grieve him **not** as long as he **lives**.
Even if his mind fail, be **considerate** of him;
revile him **not** all the days of his **life**;
kindness to a **father** will not be **forgotten**,
firmly **planted** against the debt of your **sins**
—a house raised in **justice** to you.

READING I In the Old Testament there are a number of stories of children who are remembered not for their obedience to their parents but for their deceit and cunning. Here, on this Sunday Feast of the Holy Family, the Old Testament balances it out by honoring and advising children who do not grieve their parents. Your good proclamation just might inspire the teens in your assembly to be extra nice to Mom and Dad, at least for a little while.

Sirach is one of the wisdom books, those inspired texts like Proverbs and Wisdom that offer age-old advice to the hearer or reader. The ancient wisdom in this passage is about respecting one's parents.

The reading itself is in two parts: The first speaks about relations between parents and children; the second speaks directly to the children about helping their parents as they grow old. The inspiring advice is as cogent for adult children as for the young. The passage ends by saying that kindness to parents will even help overcome sin.

The wisdom of the reading is clear. Even with the changes in life and culture that have taken place over the centuries between the writing of this text and today, the reading's advice holds strong. Proclaim it with respect for the wise words that it offered to children in antiquity and that it still offers to us today.

READING II   Colossians 3:12–21

A reading from the Letter of Saint Paul to the Colossians

Brothers and sisters:
Put **on**, as God's **chosen** ones, **holy** and **beloved**,
  heartfelt **compassion**, **kindness**, **humility**, **gentleness**,
    and **patience**,
  bearing with one another and **forgiving** one another,
  if one has a **grievance** against another;
  as the Lord has **forgiven** you, so must you **also** do.
And over **all** these put on **love**,
  that is, the bond of perfection.
And let the **peace** of Christ control your **hearts**,
  the peace into which you were **also** called in one body.
And be **thankful**.

Let the **word** of Christ dwell in you **richly**,
  as in all **wisdom** you **teach** and **admonish** one another,
  singing **psalms**, **hymns**, and spiritual **songs**
  with **gratitude** in your hearts to **God**.
And **whatever** you do, in **word** or in **deed**,
  do **everything** in the name of the Lord **Jesus**,
  giving **thanks** to God the Father through **him**.

Wives, be subordinate to your husbands,
  as is **proper** in the Lord.
Husbands, **love** your wives,
  and **avoid** any bitterness toward them.

Colossians = kuh-LOSH-unz

This first section is a lovely part of the sacred text; it stands as a good admonition about living in community and harmony: "let the peace of Christ control your hearts."

Pause before you begin the next section, "Let the word of Christ dwell in you richly." Proclaim this proudly, since you contribute to the construction of this dwelling.

READING II This passage has three parts. The first part is one of the most beautiful exhortations in the whole of the New Testament; the second is especially apt for yourself as a minister of the word, and the last part of the reading is among the most contentious exhortations in the Church today.

In the first part, notice the exhortation to "Put on . . . compassion." Lost in the translation from Greek to English is a very interesting link: The root of that verb is the

same word used to describe Jesus' own garments many times in the Gospels. Scripture scholars think that this text might have been an exhortation to the newly baptized; if so, then this imperative "put on" would have been a reminder of the white garment in which Christians are robed at Baptism, with the wearing of virtues likened to the wearing of the baptismal garment. In so living, Christians fashion themselves after their Savior.

The beginning of the next section can be a motto for you in your ministry of the word: "Let the word of Christ dwell in you richly." As a minister of the word, you witness to the community not just by what takes place in church. Those who commit themselves to the proclamation of the scriptures take responsibility for demonstrating with their lives and actions the values they proclaim with words in worship. This is no small undertaking. The ministry of Christ's word calls readers and believers to difficult tasks. This ministry is not simply one of

Children, obey your parents in everything,
    for this is pleasing to the Lord.
Fathers, do not provoke your children,
    so they may not become discouraged.

[Shorter: Colossians 3:12–17]

Find out if you are to read the longer version or shorter version of this passage.

GOSPEL   Matthew 2:13–15, 19–23

A reading from the holy Gospel according to Matthew

When the magi had departed, behold,
    the angel of the Lord appeared to Joseph in a dream and said,
      "Rise, take the child and his mother; flee to Egypt,
    and stay there until I tell you.
Herod is going to search for the child to destroy him."
Joseph rose and took the child and his mother by night
    and departed for Egypt.
He stayed there until the death of Herod,
    that what the Lord had said through the prophet
      might be fulfilled,
    Out of Egypt I called my son.

When Herod had died, behold,
    the angel of the Lord appeared in a dream
    to Joseph in Egypt and said,
      "Rise, take the child and his mother and
        go to the land of Israel,
    for those who sought the child's life are dead."
He rose, took the child and his mother,
    and went to the land of Israel.

The opening is important for setting the context by its mention of the magi. Be clear from the start of your proclamation.

The angel gives Joseph instructions twice in this passage. Here is the first.

Don't let the references to prophecies distract your proclamation from its main task of telling the story of the flight into Egypt.

Israel = IZ-ree-ul

---

speech, but of speech *and* action, or, as the letter says, "in word or in deed."

    The third part contains the exhortation "Wives, be subordinate to your husbands." The next verse balances this: "Husbands, love your wives, and avoid any bitterness toward them." The first is countercultural in our time and place. The reading reminds us just how challenging the Christian life can be.

GOSPEL This Gospel passage relates the flight of the holy family into Egypt, a story that is told by only one of the Evangelists, Matthew. Why is that? The Gospel of Matthew (the Gospel for this liturgical year A) is intent on establishing Jesus' Jewish roots. It is no surprise, then, that Matthew's narrative of the early years of Jesus contains a story of a flight into Egypt, for this Gospel writer was well aware that the nation of Israel had been in Egypt too. Matthew highlights many connections between the life of Jesus and the Hebrew Scriptures.

This reading has several quotations both direct words from the angel and some from other places in the Bible. There are two short citations of the prophecies that explain what is happening to Jesus and the family. These make the proclamation a little trickier. Don't lose the direction of the story.

    In the Gospel, this passage comes immediately after the familiar story of the magi bringing gold, frankincense, and myrrh. The calendar reverses the narrative sequence this year: today we hear that the

Archelaus = ar-keh-LAY-us
Judea = joo-DEE-uh

Nazorean = naz-oh-REE-un

But when he heard that **Archelaus** was ruling over **Judea**
in place of his father **Herod**,
he was **afraid** to go back there.
And because he had been **warned** in a **dream**,
he **departed** for the region of **Galilee**.
He went and dwelt in a town called **Nazareth**,
so that what had been spoken through the prophets
might be fulfilled,
*He shall be called a **Nazorean**.*

magi have left, and next week we hear
about the magi arriving.

In any case, Matthew tells us that the
magi learned *in a dream* that they were to
avoid Herod on their return trip. This dream
motif in revealing God's will comes up in a
number of places in Matthew's infancy narrative, first as a connection between the
patriarch Joseph (Genesis, chapters 38–50)
and Mary's husband Joseph, and then as
God's way of speaking to the magi.

MARY, MOTHER OF GOD

Lectionary #18

READING I   Numbers 6:22–27

A reading from the Book of Numbers

The LORD said to **Moses**:
"**Speak** to **Aaron** and his sons and **tell** them:
    This is how you shall **bless** the **Israelites**.

"Say to them:
    The LORD **bless** you and **keep** you!
    The LORD let his face **shine** upon you,
        and be **gracious** to you!
    The LORD look upon you **kindly**
        and give you **peace**!

"So shall they invoke my **name** upon the **Israelites**,
    and I will **bless** them."

The commentary below identifies the layers of this reading. Pause at each transition from one speaker to the next. Israelites = IZ-ree-uh-lits

Now Aaron and his sons speak to the Israelites. This blessing is the heart of the passage. Take your time with this beautiful blessing to allow the liturgical assembly to savor it.

This is a summary verse after the blessing.

READING I   The Book of Numbers is the fourth of the five books in the Pentateuch. At first glance, one might think that the Lectionary would draw often from this foundational text of the Hebrew tradition, which contains details of the Jewish Law and genealogies of Jewish families and tribes. Though these are very important in Jewish theology and therefore in Christian theology as well, the proclamation of legal codes and family trees does not make for engaging liturgical proclamation. Therefore, readings from the Book of Numbers do not appear frequently.

Nevertheless, there are parts of the book that are quite beautiful, and the passage you are preparing is one of these. It is not only beautiful in itself, it will sound familiar to the liturgical assembly because its blessing is often included in religious meditations.

There are a number of layers to this reading, and it will help your proclamation if you are aware of these layers. The innermost core is the blessing itself. This is what Aaron and his sons will say to the Israelites.

Moving outward, the next layer identifies Moses as the one who will instruct Aaron and his sons in what to say.

The next layer identifies the LORD as the one instructing Moses. This makes the reading a bit complex, for you are speaking to the assembly, and you tell them what the Lord told Moses to say to Aaron and his sons, and so on. Pause slightly between these layers so that there is less chance for confusion about who is speaking and to whom. It is a relatively short reading, but if hurried it will be lost in the proclamation.

Galatians = guh-LAY-shunz

This "born of a woman" is the kernel of this passage for today's solemnity. Proclaim it with deliberateness.

This verse it reveals that each of us is a child of God, and therefore like the Son.

READING II   Galatians 4:4–7

A reading from the Letter of Saint Paul to the Galatians

Brothers and sisters:
When the **fullness** of time had **come**, **God** sent his **Son**,
    born of a **woman**, born under the law,
    to **ransom** those under the law,
    so that **we** might receive **adoption** as **sons**.

As **proof** that you are sons,
    God sent the **Spirit** of his **Son** into our **hearts**,
    crying out, "**Abba**, **Father!**"
So you are no longer a **slave** but a **son**,
    and if a **son** then also an **heir**, through **God**.

At the end of the reading is a kind of summary, wrapping up the proclamation.

READING II This passage is assigned to this solemnity of Mary, Mother of God, because of these few words: "born of a woman."

It might be good in your proclamation to highlight the juxtaposition of "woman," referring to Mary, and "Abba, Father!," referring to God. This balance in the passage is lovely, for it both exalts the role of Mary, as the one chosen by God, and appreciates the

gift of life and faith through the generosity of God the Father.

The word *Abba!* is Aramaic, which Paul then repeats, translated into Greek, the language in which the apostle wrote his letters. For us, the Aramaic is maintained, while the Greek is translated again, into "Father." The Aramaic word carries notes of closeness and intimacy, and the translators likely kept it for this reason.

In your proclamation, therefore, take your time with what refers to the mother, because of the feast on which it is proclaimed, and in the verses about God the

Father, because the Aramaic word reveals God's special loving care for us.

GOSPEL This proclamation comes exactly one week after the solemnity of Christmas. The end of the passage reveals that the circumcision of Jesus took place "eight days" after his birth, and so the chronology of the liturgical year two millennia later is not far off from the chronology of the Evangelist Luke. For some time in the Christian tradition, this feast was called the Circumcision, based on the last verse of

As this reading reminds us, we are still in the Christmas season.
Bethlehem = BETH-luh-hem

Emphasize this verse, for here the Church, like the shepherds, is prompted to glorify and praise God for all we have heard and seen.

Pause before this final verse to mark the transition.

GOSPEL   Luke 2:16–21

A reading from the holy Gospel according to Luke

The **shepherds** went in **haste** to **Bethlehem**
    and found **Mary** and **Joseph**,
    and the **infant** lying in the **manger**.
When they saw this,
    they made **known** the message
    that had been **told** them about this child.
All who **heard** it were **amazed**
    by what had been **told** them by the **shepherds**.

And **Mary** kept all these things,
    reflecting on them in her **heart**.
Then the **shepherds** returned,
    glorifying and **praising** God
    for all they had **heard** and **seen**,
    just as it had been told to them.

When **eight** days were completed for his **circumcision**,
    he was named **Jesus**, the name given him by the **angel**
    before he was **conceived** in the womb.

this passage, in which the ritual circumcision of Jesus is recounted.

Now the solemnity focuses not on the event in the life of Jesus but on the maternity of Mary. In its origins, the feast arose from contentions about Mary's role in salvation history. In the fifth century in particular there was a debate between those who saw Mary's role as "Mother of Christ," *Christotokos,* and those who saw Mary's role as "Mother of God," *Theotokos.* The debate took place in the city of Ephesus, the same place to which the letter was written, in the year 431. Those who maintained that

Mary was the mother of God won, of course, and since that time there has been a feast celebrating this theological truth of Mary's maternity, celebrating her as the instrument of God's grace in the life of humanity.

In terms of your proclamation, this story has a few different narrative elements, characters, and places. Notice the changes, and pause slightly as the scenes shift; first there are angels and shepherds; next the holy family, then Mary herself; back to the shepherds, and finally on to the circumcision and naming.

On this solemnity, when we remember and celebrate the maternity of Mary—in the life of Jesus, in the life of the Church, and in the life of the world—proclaim the reading by highlighting the Mother of God.

EPIPHANY OF THE LORD

Lectionary #20

READING I   Isaiah 60:1–6

Isaiah = ī-ZAY-uh

Emphasize the elements of light and darkness in this first part.
Jerusalem = juh-ROO-suh-lem

A reading from the Book of the Prophet Isaiah

Rise up in **splendor**, **Jerusalem**! Your **light** has come,
    the **glory** of the LORD shines upon you.
See, **darkness** covers the earth,
    and **thick** clouds cover the **peoples**;
but upon you the LORD **shines**,
    and over **you** appears his **glory**.

Nations shall **walk** by your **light**,
    and **kings** by your **shining** radiance.
Raise your **eyes** and look **about**;
    they all **gather** and come to you:
your **sons** come from afar,
    and your **daughters** in the arms of their **nurses**.

Then you shall be **radiant** at what you see,
    your **heart** shall **throb** and **overflow**,
for the **riches** of the sea shall be emptied **out** before you,
    the **wealth** of nations shall be **brought** to you.
Caravans of **camels** shall **fill** you,
    dromedaries from Midian and Ephah;
all from Sheba shall come
    bearing **gold** and **frankincense**,
    and **proclaiming** the **praises** of the LORD.

This final section will delight those who have camels in their nativity sets at home!
Midian = MID-ee-un
Ephah = EE-fah
Sheba = SHEE-buh

READING I It is tempting to think that this prophecy from Isaiah was fulfilled in every detail in the life of Jesus. But scripture scholars such as Rev. Raymond Brown *(The Birth of the Messiah,* New York: Doubleday, 1979) have amply and convincingly demonstrated that the Evangelists shaped their infancy narratives from the Hebrew Scriptures. Even the responsorial psalm, Psalm 72, with its kings from faraway lands, contributed to the scene.

Artistic depictions of the magi in the Christian tradition usually show three kings, two white and one black, and many times the black king is in the back. (More recent artistic representations have varied the scene a bit.) None of the accounts in the Old or New Testaments number the magi, but the three gifts led artists to imagine three, each bearing a gift. Eventually the tradition gave them names: Caspar, Balthasar, and Melchior.

Notice that the reading has three parts: The first describes the coming of the light; the second has the nations coming to the light; the third expands on what the nations bring. In your proclamation, emphasize the imagery of light and dark, for the prayers for this day in the liturgy draw on these metaphors. If you are clear in proclaiming these opposite images of light and dawn and brightness, and darkness and thick darkness, the prayer texts will have the chance to sink into the liturgical experience of the assembly more deeply.

Be careful, as ever, with the place names. It is more important that you proclaim them with confidence than with exact accuracy.

READING II Since the Gospel has the magi and the first reading has gold and frankincense, their relation to

Ephesians = ee-FEE-zhunz

The author assumes that readers (and hearers) have heard someone addressing this topic already.

Pause slightly before "It was not. . . ."

There is a kind of list here describing what the Gentiles have become. That structure can help you proclaim the passage clearly and confidently.

READING II   Ephesians 3:2–3a, 5–6

A reading from the Letter of Saint Paul to the Ephesians

Brothers and sisters:
You have **heard** of the **stewardship** of God's **grace**
    that was given to me for your **benefit**,
        namely, that the **mystery** was made **known** to me
            by **revelation**.

It was not made known to people in **other** generations
    as it has **now** been revealed
    to his **holy** apostles and **prophets** by the **Spirit**:
    that the **Gentiles** are **coheirs**, **members** of the **same body**,
    and **copartners** in the **promise** in Christ **Jesus**
        through the **gospel**.

GOSPEL   Matthew 2:1–12

A reading from the holy Gospel according to Matthew

When **Jesus** was born in **Bethlehem** of Judea,
    in the days of King **Herod**,
        behold, **magi** from the **east** arrived in **Jerusalem**, saying,
        "**Where** is the newborn **king** of the Jews?
We saw his **star** at its **rising**
    and have **come** to do him **homage**."

The opening verse sets the stage for what is to happen.
Bethlehem = BETH-luh-hem
Judea = joo-DEE-uh
Herod = HAIR-ud
Jerusalem = juh-ROO-suh-lem

---

each other and to this day is clear. But the purpose in having this passage from the letter to the Ephesians on Epiphany is not as apparent.

The early tradition of the Church saw the magi as examples of strangers who find the faith attractive even though they are from faraway places with strange-sounding names. The feast of Epiphany is a celebration, among other things, of the universality of the Christian message. Look, the feast exclaims, even magi are on their way!

In the first century, the significant social challenge to the Church was not wise men on camels, but Gentiles (non-Jews) who wanted to join. There was a basic disagreement dividing the Church in the middle of the first century: How much of the Law was required of non-Jewish Christians? This passage is part of the early Church's discussion of this very issue.

The church in Ephesus was far from the birthplace of Christianity in Jerusalem, so the message about welcoming and receiving Gentiles would have been very important there. The apostle makes the point very clear. Gentiles are not to be excluded or discriminated against, the apostle commands his fellow Jews. This would have been hard to hear, because even those Jews who accepted Christ as the savior were not receptive to Gentiles as members.

Your proclamation can be vibrant if you think of this text as having a broader application than its historic setting. The message about receiving those unlike ourselves is fundamental to the Christian tradition through all generations. The reading is significant even if the link to the first-century contention is not known to all.

This large portion of the reading reveals the king's devious designs on the infant savior. The tone of your delivery can match the darkness and calculation of the king's scheming.

These are citations from the Hebrew Scriptures.
Judah = JOO-duh

Israel = IZ-ree-ul

When King **Herod** heard this,
   he was greatly **troubled**,
   and **all Jerusalem** with him.
Assembling all the chief priests and the scribes of the people,
   he inquired of them where the **Christ** was to be **born**.
They said to him, "In **Bethlehem** of Judea,
   for **thus** it has been **written** through the **prophet**:
   And **you**, *Bethlehem, land of Judah,*
   are by no means **least** *among the* **rulers** *of* **Judah***;*
   since from you shall **come** *a* **ruler***,*
   who is to **shepherd** *my people* **Israel***.*"

Then Herod **called** the **magi** secretly
   and ascertained from them the **time** of the star's **appearance**.
He sent them to **Bethlehem** and said,
   "**Go** and search **diligently** for the **child**.
When you have found him, **bring** me word,
   that I **too** may go and **do** him **homage**."

After their **audience** with the **king** they set **out**.
And **behold**, the **star** that they had **seen** at its **rising**
      preceded them,
   until it **came** and **stopped** over the place where the **child** was.
They were **overjoyed** at seeing the **star**,
   and on entering the house
   they saw the **child** with **Mary** his **mother**.

They **prostrated** themselves and did him **homage**.
Then they **opened** their **treasures**
   and **offered** him gifts of **gold**, **frankincense**, and **myrrh**.

And having been **warned** in a dream **not** to return to **Herod**,
   they **departed** for their **country** by another **way**.

Take your time in this familiar scene and with the names of the gifts.
myrrh = mer
The reading ends with this reminder of the king's plot to take the life of the infant.

GOSPEL **This is a long and familiar story from the Gospel of Matthew, among the best known of all the stories from the Gospels. Although artists have depicted the magi bearing their gifts to the infant Christ in romantic settings with rejoicing and good tidings, the larger point of the story is that King Herod is afraid of the newborn Messiah and wants him dead. In this aspect the story is a foreshadowing of the Passion and death at the other end of the Gospel.**

The narrative has a few different aspects to consider as you prepare. The first part introduces the magi. Immediately the plotting and fear of the king are brought into view. Do not read too hastily through these parts.

The next few verses are those most popular in art, when the child and his mother are visited by the magi, who open up their treasures for the newborn savior. The Evangelist does not close the story on that scene; rather, the magi will learn in a dream that they are to avoid Herod on their return trip.

The use of dreams for communicating messages from God is typical of Matthew's infancy narrative, first as a connection between the patriarch Joseph and Mary's husband Joseph, and then as God's medium to the magi, as here. It is a brilliant and engaging plot element, and one that you should highlight as you read this story to the assembly.

The challenge when reading a familiar passage of the scriptures is to keep a balance between knowing that the hearers already know what happens and proclaiming it anew so that the hearers have a fresh appreciation for the beloved story.

BAPTISM OF THE LORD

Lectionary #21

READING I   Isaiah 42:1–4, 6–7

Isaiah = ī-ZAY-uh

The opening line identifies the Lord as the speaker.

A reading from the Book of the Prophet Isaiah

Thus says the LORD:
Here is my **servant** whom I **uphold**,
    my **chosen** one with whom I am **pleased**,
upon whom I have put my **spirit**;
    he shall **bring** forth **justice** to the **nations**,
not crying out, **not** shouting,
    not making his **voice** heard in the street.
A **bruised** reed he shall not **break**,
    and a **smoldering** wick he shall not **quench**,
until he establishes **justice** on the **earth**;
    the **coastlands** will wait for his **teaching**.

These two metaphors, "a bruised reed" and "a smoldering wick," are lovely, but they are not easy to proclaim accessibly. Imagine them for yourself first, and then you will be better able to proclaim them.

I, the LORD, have called you for the victory of **justice**,
    I have **grasped** you by the **hand**;
I **formed** you, and **set** you
    as a **covenant** of the **people**,
    a **light** for the **nations**,
to **open** the eyes of the **blind**,
    to **bring** out prisoners from **confinement**,
    and from the **dungeon**, those who live in **darkness**.

These final lines might give hope to those for whom life has been hard. Deliver the ending in a tone of comfort and confidence.

READING I   Isaiah's most touching and consoling metaphors are not always the most accessible. Proclaim them so that their meaning is reinforced by your delivery. These poetic images of consolation are "a bruised weed he shall not break" and "a smoldering wick he shall not quench." The purpose of these images is to express the Lord's compassion on those who are hurting and in need.

Surrounding those two images are promises of justice. This fits in well with the images above, for the justice of the Lord will see to it that those who are beaten down will be restored and refreshed.

The reading reminds us that initiation into the Church will reverberate in the world, where the baptized will be as bold as the Lord himself was. This prophecy was written centuries before the incarnation of Jesus, but the theology of the passage is certainly compatible with the social teachings of Jesus.

The final paragraph is filled with hope that the Messiah will restore goodness and wholeness among the people of God. A strong proclamation of such a reading might give new hope and purpose to someone who has been beaten down by life.

READING II   The situation of Peter speaking to those assembled in Cornelius's house is not unlike your ministry in the Church today, speaking the word of God to those assembled to celebrate the Baptism of the Lord.

READING II   Acts 10:34–38

A reading from the Acts of the Apostles

Peter proceeded to speak to those gathered
    in the house of **Cornelius**, saying:

"In **truth**, I see that **God** shows **no partiality**.
Rather, in **every** nation **whoever** fears him and acts **uprightly**
    is **acceptable** to him.
You **know** the word that he sent to the **Israelites**
    as he proclaimed **peace** through Jesus **Christ**, who is Lord of **all**,
    what has happened all over **Judea**,
    beginning in **Galilee** after the baptism
    that **John** preached,
    how God anointed **Jesus** of Nazareth
    with the Holy **Spirit** and **power**.
He went about doing good
    and **healing** all those **oppressed** by the **devil**,
    for **God** was with him."

This verse sets the stage.
Cornelius = kor-NEEL-yus

Here begins Peter's speech, which continues to the end.

Israelites = IZ-ree-uh-lits

Judea = joo-DEE-uh
Galilee = GAL-ih-lee

Nazareth = NAZ-uh-reth

Peter summarizes the baptism and ministry of Jesus Christ.

This day is the bridge from the season of Christmas to Ordinary Time. This feast reminds us that our own baptism empowers us to minister to our community and to the world outside the Church.

This reading is from Acts. Here the apostle Peter is reflecting on Jesus' baptism and how it flowed into his ministry. As you prepare this text, keep in mind that your purpose in proclaiming this to the community before you is to deliver the word to the baptized so that they can take up the mission of Jesus.

Be exuberant particularly when talking about God's impartiality, for it captures how lavish is God's love for humanity. And this is a message that ever can be proclaimed with pride, truth, and joy.

GOSPEL As you prepare for this proclamation, it might not appear to be as perplexing as the early Church found it. John asks Jesus why he seeks baptism. Early detractors of the Church posed that very question. Christians claimed that Jesus, the Son of God, was equal to God the Father in all things. "If so," their interlocutors asked, "why did he need to be baptized?" The Church Fathers responded that Jesus was baptized to sanctify the waters for the Church, so that all future baptisms would be touched by the waters blessed by Jesus himself. (Some of the texts of the liturgy for this day and for the Easter Vigil still reflect that theology.)

The question is not as crucial for members of the Church today, for the restoration of the catechumenate and the RCIA enables us to witness first-hand how powerful is formation toward full initiation in the

Galilee = GAL-ih-lee

There are three direct quotations in this short passage, each from a different speaker. This first speech is from John the Baptist.

The second is Jesus' response to John.

Between the second and third quotations is the central action. Take your time in proclaiming this, for this passage ties our own baptism to that of Jesus by John the Baptist.

The third quotation is the voice from heaven, speaking of God's beloved Son.

GOSPEL   Matthew 3:13–17

A reading from the holy Gospel according to Matthew

Jesus came from **Galilee** to **John** at the **Jordan**
   to be **baptized** by him.
John tried to prevent him, saying,
   "**I** need to be baptized by **you**,
   and yet **you** are coming to **me**?"

Jesus said to him in reply,
   "**Allow** it now, for thus it is fitting for us
   to **fulfill** all **righteousness**."
Then he allowed him.

After **Jesus** was **baptized**,
   he came up from the **water** and **behold**,
   the **heavens** were **opened** for him,
   and he saw the **Spirit** of God **descending** like a dove
   and **coming** upon him.
And a **voice** came from the **heavens**, saying,
   "**This** is my **beloved Son**, with whom I am **well pleased**."

Christian faith. As the *General Instruction of Christian Initiation* says, "In the sacraments of Christian initiation . . . we receive the Spirit of filial adoption and are part of the entire people of God in the celebration of the memorial of the Lord's death and resurrection. Baptism . . . pardons all our sins, rescues us from the power of darkness, and brings us to the dignity of adopted children, a new creation through water and the Holy Spirit."

The Gospel reading is an interplay of narrative and direct discourse, a good rhetorical structure for engaging the assembly, but also a challenge because you need to proclaim the reading so that the members of the assembly who do not have the text (with its punctuation marks) before them can follow it clearly. When there is a direct quote, your voice should enable a hearer to know it is the words of someone. For some proclaimers, this comes easy; for others it is more difficult.

The quotations themselves break the narrative up into three parts. The Gospel passage is not long, and the final scene of the baptism itself and of the heavens opening for the Spirit's descent and for the voice is a strong finish. Make the most of the opportunity.

2ND SUNDAY IN ORDINARY TIME

Lectionary #64

READING I   Isaiah 49:3, 5–6

Israel = IZ-ree-ul

The passage begins and ends with direct quotations.

Imagine the closeness of a mother and her soon-to-be-born baby as you proclaim this passage. The prophet's image for the love of God for humanity is beautiful.

The last sentence has a fitting grandeur for the end of the passage. Capture this your delivery.

A reading from the Book of the Prophet Isaiah

The LORD said to me: **You** are my **servant**,
    Israel, through whom I **show** my **glory**.
Now the LORD has spoken
    who **formed** me as his **servant** from the **womb**,
    that **Jacob** may be brought back to him
    and **Israel** gathered to him;
    and **I** am made **glorious** in the **sight** of the LORD,
    and my **God** is now my **strength**!

It is **too little**, the LORD says, for **you** to be my **servant**,
    to **raise up** the tribes of **Jacob**,
    and **restore** the **survivors** of **Israel**;
I will make you a **light** to the **nations**,
    that my **salvation** may **reach** to the **ends** of the **earth**.

READING I | **This is a powerful passage to begin the scripture readings for the span of Ordinary Time between the Baptism of the Lord and Ash Wednesday.**

Isaiah's prophecy was originally addressed to members of his community who had suffered through very difficult times. It is no less important and consoling for the members of the Church to whom you address these words today. Your work is to proclaim the reading so that the members of the assembly recognize in themselves, in your time and place, those to whom this consolation is addressed.

The sanctity of the lives of the vulnerable is of supreme importance. Here is an image of the providence of God even in the womb. Take your time with this so that the assembly can appreciate the care God gives to the weak and vulnerable. No one in the assembly has been or will be exempt from difficulty and trial, and your clear and well-practiced proclamation will offer consolation and hope to those who, even as you minister, are in need.

The reading ends expansively, moving from "too little" to the "ends of the earth." Have the tone and projection of your voice capture that movement from smallness to expansiveness.

READING II | **This passage is the opening of the apostle Paul's First Letter to the Corinthians. This early letter is amazingly important to our understanding of early Christianity and its celebration of Baptism and the Lord's Supper. Because of the importance of the letter as a whole and because this short passage is key in setting**

READING II   1 Corinthians 1:1–3

A reading from the first Letter of Saint Paul to the Corinthians

Paul, called to be an apostle of Christ Jesus by the will of God,
    and Sosthenes our brother,
to the church of God that is in Corinth,
to you who have been sanctified in Christ Jesus,
    called to be holy,
with all those everywhere who call upon the name of our Lord
Jesus Christ, their Lord and ours.

Grace to you and peace from God our Father
    and the Lord Jesus Christ.

Most of the reading is taken up in practical matters, what we think of as the salutation of the letter. But in it Paul reveals important theological points (see below). Sosthenes = SOS-thuh-neez

The reading as a whole looks toward this offering of grace and peace. Pause before delivering it.

its context, take your time so that the assembly can appreciate and absorb the opening identification of the author.

Most of the reading simply identifies the authors (Paul and Sosthenes) and the recipients. This is more than biographical information, however, for when you the reader say, "to the church of God that is in Corinth," your hearers will identify that ancient, distant church with your own. Perhaps eye contact can help confirm this bridge between Paul and Sosthenes's ancient correspondence and our life in the Church today.

On the theological level, Paul calls the members of that ancient church "sanctified" and "called to be holy." If you read the whole First Letter to the Corinthians closely, you'll see that some of those members were far from what most churchgoers would think of as holy. Yet this is what they were in Paul's regard and address. Proclaim this so that the assembled parishioners realize that they too are holy.

Finally, be attentive to the proper names in this reading, particularly "Corinth" and the tongue-twisting "Sosthenes." Repeat the latter aloud during the week leading up to your proclamation so that it will roll off your tongue as easily as the most ordinary of names.

GOSPEL   When in the Gospel we hear words also used in liturgical texts, we might think that the liturgical use emerged because the passage existed first in the Bible. But in many instances, the opposite is probably true: Christian communities were worshiping before the Gospels themselves were written down in the form

GOSPEL   John 1:29–34

A reading from the holy Gospel according to John

John the **Baptist saw Jesus** coming toward him and said,
   "**Behold**, the **Lamb** of **God**, who **takes away** the **sin**
     of the world.
He is the one of **whom** I said,
   'A man is coming **after** me who ranks **ahead** of me
   because he existed **before** me.'
I did not know him,
   but the reason why **I** came **baptizing** with **water**
   was that **he** might be made **known** to **Israel**."

John testified further, saying,
   "**I saw** the **Spirit** come **down** like a **dove** from **heaven**
   and **remain** upon him.
I did not **know** him,
   but the one who **sent** me to **baptize** with **water** told me,
   'On **whomever** you see the **Spirit** come down and remain,
   he is the one who will **baptize** with the **Holy Spirit**.'
Now **I** have **seen** and **testified** that **he** is the **Son** of **God**."

Proclaim this so that the assembly can recognize the connection between the liturgical chant "Lamb of God" and the Gospel narrative.

Be careful with the quotation within a quotation.

Israel = IZ-ree-ul

Pause slightly at this midway point, before "John testified. . . ."

Here is another quotation within a quotation.

---

in which we know them. So phrases in the Gospels that sound like things we hear in our worship did not always precede their appearance in the liturgy; sometimes, perhaps many times, their use in the liturgy led to the Evangelists' inclusion of the phrases in the Gospels.

So when, in this reading, you proclaim the familiar liturgical text — "Behold, the Lamb of God, who takes away the sin of the world" — recognize that this was likely included in the Gospel because it was already part of the liturgical tradition where

John worshiped. Emphasize the words that the reading and the eucharistic liturgy have in common, so that the assembly might be alerted to the coincidence of these words appearing twice in the liturgy.

The closing sentence is attributed to the Baptist, who "saw" and "testified," but you can proclaim it with conviction from your own experience.

Be careful with the levels of quotation within the reading so that you can make them clear. Notice that in two places the

text begins with an attribution ("John . . . said" and "John testified"), moves to a quotation ('Behold . . .' and 'I saw the Spirit . . .'), and then progresses to another quotation within that quotation ("A man is coming . . ." and "On whomever . . ."). It will take some practice to have your proclamation alert the hearer to these levels within the story. You will have the advantage of the quotation marks on the printed page, but proclaim the Gospel so that the hearers know the levels of quotation even without the printed page.

3RD SUNDAY IN ORDINARY TIME

Lectionary #67

READING I Isaiah 8:23 — 9:3

A reading from the Book of the Prophet Isaiah

First the **Lord degraded** the land of **Zebulun**
    and the land of **Naphtali**;
    but in the end he has **glorified** the **seaward road**,
    the land west of the **Jordan**,
    the District of the **Gentiles**.

Anguish has taken wing, **dispelled** is **darkness**:
    for there is **no gloom** where but now there was **distress**.

The **people** who **walked** in **darkness**
    have **seen** a **great light**;
    upon those who **dwelt** in the **land** of **gloom** a **light** has **shone**.
You have brought them **abundant joy**
    and **great rejoicing**,
    as they **rejoice** before you as at the **harvest**,
    as **people** make **merry** when dividing **spoils**.

For the **yoke** that **burdened** them,
    the **pole** on their **shoulder**,
    and the **rod** of their **taskmaster**
    you have **smashed**, as on the day of **Midian**.

Be careful and confident with the place names.
Zebulun = ZEB-yoo-lun
Naphtali = NAF-tuh-lee

Gentiles = JEN-tils

The metaphors of darkness and light anticipate the balance of hardships and joys that comes next.

Midian = MID-ee-un

READING I Many parishioners will recognize that this reading is also proclaimed at the Midnight Mass on Christmas; it has been part of the scriptures of Christmas for centuries.

The different theological emphases of the liturgical year are reflected in the responsorial psalm, for then we sing "Today is born our Savior, Christ the Lord," while here in Ordinary Time we sing "The Lord is my light and my salvation." The psalm for Christmas emphasizes Jesus' nativity, while the psalm appointed for today emphasizes the light of salvation, a significant image to bear in mind and heart as you prepare and as you proclaim.

Meditative study of the Gospel will help you prepare for your proclamation. There you will find the Evangelist Matthew, who often quotes from the Hebrew Scriptures, quoting this very passage from Isaiah. Your effective proclamation will allow the assembly to retain the passage from Isaiah in their minds and hearts as it returns in the Gospel.

Our theology of Christmas is clear in prompting the Church to recognize how the birth of the Savior lifted the oppression of the people. Here, without the nativity context, your task is to highlight the shift from sorrow to joy; on the one hand, the gravity of the vocabulary describing life's hardships— "gloom," "anguish," "distress," "darkness," "yoke," "burden," "taskmaster"—and, on

READING II 1 Corinthians 1:10–13, 17

The first-person "I" here is the apostle Paul. Though you are not acting in a drama as the character Paul, you, as a minister of God's word, stand in his stead and deliver the word.

A reading from the first Letter of Saint Paul to the Corinthians

I **urge** you, **brothers and sisters**, in the **name** of our **Lord
    Jesus Christ**,
    that **all** of you **agree** in what you say,
    and that there be **no divisions** among you,
    but that you be **united** in the **same mind**
        and in the **same purpose**.

Chloe's = KLOH-eez

Be careful with the proper names "Apollos" and "Cephas."
Apollos = uh-POL-ohs
Cephas = SEE-fus

For it has been **reported** to me about you, my brothers and sisters,
    by Chloe's people, that there are **rivalries** among you.
I mean that each of you is saying,
    "I belong to **Paul**," or "I belong to **Apollos**,"
    or "I belong to **Cephas**," or "I belong to **Christ**."

These are important questions, so pause slightly before and after each.

Is **Christ** divided?
Was **Paul crucified** for you?
Or were you **baptized** in the name of **Paul**?

This is a strong ending. Let your voice reflect the strength of the apostle's words.

For **Christ** did not send me to **baptize** but to **preach** the gospel,
    and not with the wisdom of **human eloquence**,
    so that the **cross** of **Christ** might not be **emptied**
        of its **meaning**.

the other, the words of the hope of good things on the horizon—"glorified," "great light," "abundant joy," "great rejoicing," "make merry." Be mindful of those among your hearers whose lives have been burdened and weighed down. Address this prophecy of consolation to them as a sign of hope of good things to come.

READING II   The unifying effect of Baptism is the apostle's main point here, and he makes his point in four parts. The first section introduces Paul's purpose; the second describes what he has heard about the situation in the Corinthian church; part three speaks of Baptism and Paul's mission; and the final part is a theological conclusion to the passage. As you

prepare, consider each part for its theological content and for your best delivery; then put them together.

We can sometimes romanticize the early days of Christianity, imagining its communities as places of peace and blissful unity. This reading can be a consolation to the Church today, for it reflects a particular

GOSPEL Matthew 4:12–23

A reading from the holy Gospel according to Matthew

When **Jesus** heard that **John** had been **arrested**,
  he **withdrew** to **Galilee**.
He left **Nazareth** and went to live in **Capernaum** by the sea,
  in the region of **Zebulun** and **Naphtali**,
  that what had been **said** through **Isaiah** the **prophet**
  might be **fulfilled**:
  Land of Zebulun and land of Naphtali,
  the way to the sea, beyond the Jordan,
  Galilee of the Gentiles,
  the people who sit in darkness have seen a great light,
  on those dwelling in a land overshadowed by death
  light has arisen.
From that time on, **Jesus** began to **preach** and **say**,
  "**Repent**, for the **kingdom** of heaven is **at hand**."

As he was **walking** by the Sea of **Galilee**, he saw **two brothers**,
  Simon who is called Peter, and his brother **Andrew**,
  casting a **net** into the **sea**; they were **fishermen**.

Practice the pronunciation of these place names so that you can read them accurately. When you have mastered them, you will be able to proclaim them with confidence, which is more important.
Galilee = GAL-ih-lee
Nazareth = NAZ-uh-reth
Capernaum = kuh-PER-n*m
Isaiah = i-ZAY-uh
Zebulun = ZEB-yoo-lun
Naphtali = NAF-tuh-lee
Gentiles = JEN-tils

Pause slightly after the words of Isaiah so that the liturgical assembly can sense the switch from the quotation back to the Evangelist, Matthew.

community's difficulties only two decades or so after the death of Jesus. Already the Church was divided. This is not mentioned to disparage the church in Corinth, but to encourage Christians today who can be discouraged by the failings of church members and ministers. So though you proclaim a text from the middle of the first century, you stand in Paul's footsteps to deliver a message of hope.

The one thing that all members of the Church have in common is the sacrament of Baptism. The reading makes crystal clear that Baptism is a sacrament of unity, not of division. We can almost hear the disputes Paul is trying to quell; he trumps their claims by pointing to the One to whom we all belong.

The juxtaposition of Baptism and Christ's death is important, for the cross is the glory of Christ, and, as Paul says in another letter, we are baptized into Christ's death and Resurrection (Roman 6:3–4).

GOSPEL The reading has three parts. The first places Jesus in the geography of Israel, quoting from the prophet Isaiah, who names the same places. The second part is Jesus' calling of the disciples. The third part is a summary of Jesus' mission in Galilee.

This passage comes relatively early in Matthew's Gospel narrative. The first part sets a context with proper names, the names

Zebedee = ZEB-uh-dee

He said to them,
"**Come after me**, and I will make you **fishers** of **men**."
At **once** they **left** their nets and **followed** him.
He **walked** along from there and saw two **other brothers**,
James, the son of Zebedee, and his brother **John**.
They were in a **boat**, with their **father** Zebedee,
mending their nets.
He **called** them, and **immediately** they left their **boat**
and their **father**
and **followed** him.

He went around all of **Galilee**,
teaching in their synagogues, **proclaiming** the gospel
of the kingdom,
and **curing** every **disease** and **illness** among the **people**.

[Shorter: Matthew 4:12–17]

This final verse is a summary of Jesus' early ministry in Galilee.
synagogues = SIN-uh-gogz

of places. Some of the place names are familiar: "Galilee," "Jordan," and "Nazareth." Some do not appear so frequently and will take some attention: "Zebulun" and "Naphtali." As always, particularly when most in the assembly are not familiar with the names, more important than getting them correct according to the ancient languages of the Bible is to proclaim them with confidence. Stumbling only distracts hearers from the narrative.

The second part is a narrative of vocation, when Jesus is walking by the Sea of Galilee and calls the disciples from their work as fishermen. The four mentioned here are Peter, Andrew, James, and John, the most familiar of the disciples, featured in some of the main narratives of the Gospel of Matthew. As with place names, be confident with personal names.

The third part of the passage is a kind of summary of what Jesus was doing in the early part of his ministry in Galilee—teaching, proclaiming, and curing.

Although the three parts appear consecutively in the Gospel of Matthew, they are not tightly intertwined. For this reason you might pause slightly after each part as an indication that the story is shifting.

4TH SUNDAY IN ORDINARY TIME

Lectionary #70

READING I   Zephaniah 2:3; 3:12–13

A reading from the Book of the Prophet Zephaniah

These three appearances of the verb "seek" are imperatives, commands: Seek! Proclaim them in this way.

Seek the LORD, all you **humble** of the **earth**,
    who have **observed** his **law**;
seek justice, **seek humility**;
    perhaps you may be **sheltered**
    on the **day** of the LORD's **anger**.

Israel = IZ-ree-ul

But I will **leave** as a **remnant** in your midst
    a **people humble** and **lowly**,
who shall take **refuge** in the **name** of the LORD:
    the **remnant** of **Israel**.
They shall **do no** wrong
    and **speak no** lies;
nor shall there be **found** in their mouths
    a **deceitful** tongue;
they shall **pasture** and **couch** their **flocks**
    with **none** to disturb them.

The passage ends with a gentle, consoling tone.

READING I   Zephaniah is one of the minor prophets whose writings are grouped at the end of the Old Testament. The book of the prophet Zephaniah is short, and we do not hear from it often throughout the three-year Lectionary cycle of Sundays and feasts. For this reason, pronounce the opening identification line— "A reading from . . ."—clearly.

If you have ever done any sewing, you know what a remnant is. When you cut out the pieces of your project, there is fabric left behind in odd-shaped scraps that are too small to be used for anything. Those scraps are remnants. Think of that image when you come to the prophet's phrase, "the remnant of Israel."

After the many hardships of the nation of Israel, most notably their captivity in Babylon, those who survived to return to the precious land of Israel were called the "remnant" of Israel. Tattered and frayed, they made their way back. Now the prophet speaks to them, encouraging them to follow the ways of the Lord and to deal with one another justly and honestly. In spite of their sorrowful history and the devastated land around them, they will no longer live in fear.

Take your time in preparing this short but rich reading, making sure you understand its meaning. That is a prerequisite for conveying it to the assembly.

READING II   1 Corinthians 1:26–31

A reading from the first Letter of Saint Paul to the Corinthians

Consider your own calling, **brothers and sisters**.
Not **many** of you were **wise** by **human** standards,
    not **many** were **powerful**,
    not **many** were of noble **birth**.
Rather, God chose the **foolish** of the world to shame the **wise**,
    and God chose the **weak** of the world to shame the **strong**,
    and God chose the **lowly** and **despised** of the world,
    those who count for **nothing**,
    to **reduce** to **nothing** those who are **something**,
    so that **no human being** might **boast** before **God**.

It is due to **him** that **you** are in Christ **Jesus**,
    who became for us **wisdom** from **God**,
    as well as **righteousness**, **sanctification**, and **redemption**,
    so that, as it is written,
    "Whoever **boasts**, should **boast** in the **Lord**."

For emphasis, treat these three lines with equal gravity, for they have the same literary structure.

The juxtaposition of opposites strengthens Paul's argument.

Don't be distracted by the comma in the quotation at the end.

READING II Here Paul is talking to and about the assembly of those who prayed and believed together in Corinth's ancient Greek community of faith. Unlike much of Paul's writing, this passage is not in the first person—that is, it does not use the first-person pronouns "I," "me," and "my." But if you read closely you will see the prevalence of the second-person address—in phrases such as "your own calling," "not many of you," and "you are

Christ Jesus." This use of the second person presumes a speaker and a hearer; the speaker was Paul, and now, as the proclaimer of his words, the speaker is you.

You can capture the attention of the assembly well with such a reading as this, not by envisioning that ancient Greek church in Corinth, but by knowing that by baptism you, like Paul, have been called to do God's work among the people of God. When you have such a reading to proclaim, you speak to your brothers and sisters in Christ with the power of God's grace.

When you speak of the "foolish," "weak," "lowly and despised of the world," realize that there are people in front of you who may be deeply consoled by the apostle's words. Proclaim the passage as if you are speaking to those who have been beaten down, and minister to them with power and compassion, with strength and consolation.

GOSPEL   Matthew 5:1–12a

A reading from the holy Gospel according to Matthew

When Jesus saw the **crowds**, he went up the **mountain**,
　　and after he had sat down, his disciples **came** to him.
He began to **teach** them, saying:
"Blessed are the poor in **spirit**,
　　for **theirs** is the kingdom of **heaven**.
Blessed are they who **mourn**,
　　for they will be **comforted**.

"Blessed are the **meek**,
　　for they will **inherit** the **land**.
Blessed are they who **hunger** and **thirst** for **righteousness**,
　　for they will be **satisfied**.

"Blessed are the **merciful**,
　　for they will be **shown** mercy.
Blessed are the clean of **heart**,
　　for they will **see** God.

"Blessed are the **peacemakers**,
　　for they will be called **children** of God.
Blessed are they who are **persecuted**
　　for the sake of **righteousness**,
　　for **theirs** is the kingdom of **heaven**.

"Blessed are you when they **insult** you and **persecute** you
　　and utter every kind of **evil** against you falsely because of **me**.
Rejoice and be **glad**,
　　for your reward will be **great** in **heaven**."

After these opening lines, the remainder of the reading is in Jesus' words.

Because the passage is familiar and the literary form repetitive, take your time.

Pause here to make space for the shift of the ending.

This final verse is not a "beatitude" as the other verses are. Its imperatives, "rejoice" and "be glad," are important nonetheless.

GOSPEL   In the three-year Lectionary passages that are very well known come up fairly often, and this passage from the Gospel of Matthew is among them. The Beatitudes are known not only among Christians, but by many non-Christians as well, for they are one of the signature passages of religious literature. The Beatitudes are not only well-known but well-loved.

Beatitudes appear in both the Gospel of Matthew and the Gospel of Luke. In Luke they are balanced with "woes," that is, curses, and Luke has Jesus deliver them on a plain, level ground, not a mountain. Since one of Matthew's purposes in the Gospel is to demonstrate how Jesus fulfills all of what the Old Testament figures had been called to do, this scene echoes Moses' receiving the Ten Commandments on Mount Sinai. In the new Israel that is the Church, by Matthew's theology, the Beatitudes are the new commandments, the foundational guide for the community of faith.

One reason why these are known by so many people is because they have a memorable form, one with a repeating pattern. You can see the pattern of "Blessed are . . ." in the first half of the verse and "for they will . . ." in the second half. Beginning at 1:10, the message continues, but the pattern is left behind.

So how might you deliver these well-known sayings? Because they are such elemental guides for Christian living and are set in this patterned form, it would be best not to rush through them because they are already known. Rather, read through each Beatitude as if it were the only one; pause after each and give each one time to sink into the ears, minds, and hearts of your hearers.

5TH SUNDAY IN ORDINARY TIME

Lectionary #73

READING I   Isaiah 58:7–10

A reading from the Book of the Prophet Isaiah

Thus says the LORD:
Share your **bread** with the **hungry**,
    shelter the **oppressed** and the **homeless**;
clothe the **naked** when you see them,
    and do **not** turn your **back** on your **own**.

Then your **light** shall break **forth** like the **dawn**,
    and your **wound** shall quickly be **healed**;
your **vindication** shall go before you,
    and the **glory** of the LORD shall be your rear **guard**.
Then you shall **call**, and the LORD will **answer**;
    you shall **cry** for **help**, and he will say: **Here** I **am**!

If you **remove** from your midst **oppression**,
    false accusation and **malicious speech**;
if you bestow your **bread** on the **hungry**
    and **satisfy** the **afflicted**;
then **light** shall rise for you in the **darkness**,
    and the **gloom** shall become for you like **midday**.

Pause after "LORD" so that the assembly recognizes the change to direct quotation. The remainder of the reading is direct discourse.

Emphasize this section so that the assembly will appreciate the metaphor of "light" here in the first reading and recognize it again in the Gospel's "You are the light of the world."

Practice this quote within a quote so that the distinction is clear.

READING I   Your task as proclaimer of this reading is an important one, because the prophet Isaiah sets out the underpinnings for Israel's care for the most vulnerable in society. Millennia later the vulnerable are still in need of society's and the Church's care, so the passage you proclaim is as relevant to your community today as it was to those for whom Isaiah first prophesied centuries before the birth of Jesus.

Perhaps it will help you read this passage with conviction if you look around your own area, city, town, neighborhood, and parish for those whose cause the prophet Isaiah might take up if he were living where you are. Your ministry of the word is not simply one of thoughtful and clear proclamation, but one of recognizing the importance of the word in contemporary situations. Who, in your place, are the "hungry," "oppressed," "homeless," "naked"?

Your vocation in this proclamation includes an awareness of those in need, and such awareness will animate your ministry of the word. Your words spoken to the assembly can be effective in alleviating the sorrow of the poor.

As you prepare, recognize that this reading is paired with the Gospel reading because of the memorable imagery of the light breaking forth like the dawn.

On the practical level of confident proclamation, practice the pronunciation of some of the words that are not part of everyday speech. Consult a dictionary for pronunciations and definitions of those that are not familiar. These are key parts of the passage, and your proclamation will be better received if you do not hesitate over some of these uncommon elements.

Corinthians = kor-IN-thee-unz

Note the first-person ("I," "my") and second-person ("you," "your") pronouns. Consider how you will use voice and eye contact to proclaim these most effectively.

"Him crucified" is an uncommon turn of phrase, but important to the meaning. Understand its place in the reading so that you are at ease with the style.

The proclamation stops with a summary ending. Be clear and bold as you enunciate this closing line.

READING II   1 Corinthians 2:1–5

A reading from the first Letter of Saint Paul to the Corinthians

When I **came** to you, **brothers and sisters**,
    proclaiming the **mystery** of **God**,
    I did **not** come with **sublimity** of words or of **wisdom**.
For I resolved to know **nothing** while I was with you
    except **Jesus Christ**, and **him crucified**.

I **came** to you in **weakness** and **fear** and much **trembling**,
    and my **message** and my **proclamation**
    were **not** with persuasive words of **wisdom**,
    but with a demonstration of **Spirit** and **power**,
    so that your **faith** might rest **not** on human **wisdom**
    but on the **power** of **God**.

READING II   At the start of his First Letter to the Corinthians, Paul sets out a rhetorical device that he used often. He juxtaposes words and phrases of opposite meanings in order to highlight the strength of the Gospel. For example, in the first two sentences we find words of ignorance (like "know nothing") next to phrases of knowledge ("sublimity of words or of wisdom").

Though it will take some practice, a strong proclamation of this passage calls you to find a way of noting these opposites with your voice and your tone. Think of how we say "on the one hand" and "on the other hand." The apostle's rhetoric carries that sort of meaning and requires that intonation.

For those of us who are ministers of the word, Paul's words here can be an inspiration. For though we are all broken and sinful ministers, the Spirit works through us to a good end of building up the body of Christ. When, therefore, you hear Paul speak of coming to the Corinthians "in weakness and fear and much trembling," think of when you first came to the ministry and how nervous you were. Yet you have continued to work at the ministry, and have improved, by God's grace and your natural talent, so that your ministry can indeed be for the people of God "a demonstration of Spirit and power."

GOSPEL   In the Gospel of Matthew, Jesus speaks in the form of extended discourses. This passage is part of the first extended discourse, which occupies chapters 5 to 7 of Matthew. The Evangelist structured the Gospel in this way to empha-size the role of Jesus as teacher, following in the footsteps of the Israelite leaders who were as wise as they were strong.

GOSPEL Matthew 5:13–16

A reading from the holy Gospel according to Matthew

Jesus said to his **disciples**:
"**You** are the **salt** of the **earth**.
But if **salt** loses its **taste**, with **what** can it be **seasoned**?
It is no longer **good** for anything
 but to be **thrown out** and **trampled** underfoot.

"**You** are the **light** of the **world**.
A **city** set on a **mountain** cannot be **hidden**.
Nor do they light a **lamp** and then put it under a **bushel basket**;
 it is **set** on a **lampstand**,
 where it gives **light** to **all** in the **house**.
Just so, **your** light must shine before **others**,
 that they may **see** your good deeds
 and **glorify** your **heavenly Father**."

Pause here at the colon and change your tone so that the switch from narrative to direct discourse is clear.

With phrases as familiar as these "you are" phrases, you have an opportunity to make sustained eye contact with the assembly. Familiarize yourself with the sentences so that you can both look up and proclaim with conviction.

As usual, pause between the close of the passage and the closing "The Gospel of the Lord."

If you look at the context for this teaching in particular, you will see that Jesus speaks on a mountain. Matthew reminds us of another important figure in salvation history, Moses, who received the Law on Mount Sinai.

This long discourse contains some of the most well-known passages in the entire New Testament. In today's Gospel, the "you are" sentences are among these. Familiarize yourself with these beloved texts, for they enable you to sustain eye contact with the assembly listening to the words of Jesus through your proclamation.

The challenge with familiar passages is to proclaim them so that the members of the assembly don't mentally dismiss the words with, "Oh, yeah, I know this one," but rather pause to reconsider how their own vocations measure up to this challenge from Jesus' teaching. A strong proclamation might call some in the liturgical assembly to consider how much their own gifts "shine before others" or are hidden "under a bushel basket."

ASH WEDNESDAY

Lectionary #219

READING I   Joel 2:12–18

A reading from the Book of the Prophet Joel

Even **now**, says the LORD,
    return to me with your whole **heart**,
    with **fasting**, and **weeping**, and **mourning**;
Rend your **hearts**, not your **garments**,
    and **return** to the LORD, your **God**.
For **gracious** and **merciful** is he,
    slow to **anger**, **rich** in **kindness**,
    and **relenting** in punishment.
Perhaps he will again relent
    and leave behind him a **blessing**,
Offerings and **libations**
    for the LORD, your **God**.

Blow the **trumpet** in **Zion**!
    proclaim a **fast**,
    call an **assembly**;
Gather the **people**,
    notify the congregation;
Assemble the **elders**,
    gather the **children**
    and the **infants** at the **breast**;
Let the **bridegroom** quit his room,
    and the **bride** her **chamber**.

Joel = JOH-*l

Be clear with this "says the LORD," so that the assembly is able to distinguish between the words from the prophet and the words of the LORD.

Pause slightly at each of the breaks in the *Workbook* so that the assembly can let the words sink in as you proclaim.

Be bold as you read these commands. They rally the Church for the disciplines of Lent.

READING I   Ash Wednesday, though not a day of obligation, has always drawn crowds to church for the rite with ashes. The liturgy calls on the minor prophet Joel, who prophesied to the Jews in exile in Babylon. His inspired words capture some of the ritual traditions of the people, including this proclamation of a time of fasting. As then, so now, ritual traditions call a solemn assembly, the assembly in your own parish.

Consider yourself in the place of that prophet, as a prophet in a new place and at a new time, for with the reading of the text you proclaim the period of fasting and penitence.

Ash Wednesday has been the beginning of the period of preparation for Easter for many centuries. The *Missal of St. Pius V* (1570) petitions: "Grant us, O Lord, to begin our Christian warfare with holy fasts; that as we are about to do battle with spirits of evil we may be defended by the aid of self-denial." Lent is not supposed to be a period of merely individual penitence, but of communal observance and penitence. Easter Sunday is the day when we celebrate Christ's victory over death. It is also the day when the Church incorporates new members by the sacraments of initiation. So your proclamation—"Blow the trumpet!" and "Proclaim a fast!" and "Call an assembly!" and "Gather the people!"—might help the faithful recognize the importance of individually and corporately abstaining from excess in our lives in preparation for the celebration of the death and Resurrection of Christ.

Notice the many imperative phrases in the reading, how many times the prophet takes up the words of the Lord, who says

Between the porch and the altar
     let the **priests**, the **ministers** of the LORD, **weep**,
And say, "**Spare**, O LORD, your **people**,
     and make not your **heritage** a **reproach**,
     with the nations **ruling** over them!
Why should they say among the **peoples**,
     '**Where** is their **God**?'"

Then the Lord was stirred to concern for his land
     and took pity on his people.

Note that the last verse is not the words *of* the Lord, but words *about* the Lord. The passage comes to a gentle ending. Soften your voice, but still be clear as you read this final sentence.

READING II   2 Corinthians 5:20—6:2

A reading from the second Letter of Paul to the Corinthians

This short reading is very important to the Church's theology of Lent.

Brothers and sisters:
We are **ambassadors** for **Christ**,
     as if God were **appealing** through us.
We **implore** you on behalf of Christ,
     be **reconciled** to God.
For our sake he made him to **be** sin who did not **know** sin,
     so that we might become the **righteousness** of God in him.

Working **together**, then,
     we appeal to you **not** to receive the grace of God in **vain**.
For he says:
*In an **acceptable** time I **heard** you;*
     *and on a day of **salvation** I **helped** you.*
Behold, **now** is a very acceptable time;
     behold, **now** is the day of salvation.

The reading has a climax at the end. Emphasize the word "now" in its two places in the final verse.

to the people, "Return to me!" "Rend your hearts!" "Proclaim! Assemble! Gather!" Your proclamation here can be bold. Remember that you are a minister of the word of the Lord, like that prophet millennia ago. This awareness will prepare the way for the Gospel reading, which also focuses on fasting.

READING II Paul's Second Letter to the Corinthians does not come up in the Lectionary nearly as often as the

First Letter, but here is one of the strongest passages from this lesser-known missive. The concept of the assembly as "ambassadors for Christ" is an engaging one. Think of how a country's ambassadors go to foreign places to represent the leaders back home. So, too, then and now, are Christians called to give witness to their own experience of the crucified and risen Christ in the Church, and to be advocates for that risen Christ in the world. So make sure this phrase, "ambassadors for Christ," is proclaimed well.

Here at the beginning of Lent, this reading contributes two important theological notions. First, that "For our sake God made him to be sin who did not know sin," so that we might be saved. Second, the very end of the reading with its emphasis on *now* is important. None of us knows how long we will live. Though death is something we try not to think about, we must ever be prepared for the end. Lent is the season of the year when the Church rededicates itself to preparing for death, for meeting God face-to-face.

Except for these few opening words, the entire passage is made up of the words of Jesus. Pause slightly before and after this line so that the assembly hears this identification of who speaks and to whom he speaks.

synagogues = SIN-uh-gogz

GOSPEL   Matthew 6:1–6, 16–18

A reading from the holy Gospel according to Matthew

Jesus said to his **disciples**:
  "Take care **not** to perform righteous deeds
  in order that people may **see** them;
  otherwise, you will have **no** recompense
    from your heavenly **Father**.
When you give **alms**,
  do not blow a **trumpet** before you,
  as the **hypocrites** do in the **synagogues**
    and in the **streets**
  to win the praise of others.
Amen, I say to you,
  they have **received** their reward.
But when **you** give alms,
  do not let your **left** hand know what your **right** is doing,
  so that your almsgiving may be **secret**.
And your Father who **sees** in secret will **repay** you.

The progress of those who will be baptized, confirmed, and received into the full communion of the Church at the Easter Vigil provides us with a witness to the importance of faith in turning away from sin and toward the good news. A strong proclamation that "now is the acceptable time" and "now is the day of salvation" will help the assembly recognize that importance.

The passage is short, so take your time and be well prepared so that the assembly recognizes the gravity of this decisive time in the liturgical year.

GOSPEL   The exhortation of the Church prompts each member to recognize our tendency to sin and recognize the season of Lent as the opportunity to confess that sinfulness in thoughts and deeds and to make reparation for the ways our sinfulness drags down the Church and the society in which we live. Your ministry contributes to this recognition.

Ash Wednesday gives those who attend the liturgy a distinctive mark so that others recognize them as believers. The challenge

the ashes might offer, then, is to have our attitudes and actions so shaped by our faith that people will recognize Christians even when we do not have the black smudge on our foreheads.

Every year on Ash Wednesday, this reading from the Gospel of Matthew is proclaimed. This is because the passage mentions fasting explicitly and because it corrects our tendency to think that we earn God's attention by our good deeds. This reading reminds us that we do not do good

"When **you** pray,
    do not be like the **hypocrites**,
    who love to stand and pray in the **synagogues** and on
        street corners
    so that others may see them.
Amen, I say to you,
    they have **received** their reward.
But when **you** pray, go to your inner **room**,
    close the **door**, and pray to your Father in **secret**.
And your Father who **sees** in secret will **repay** you.

"When **you** fast,
    do not look **gloomy** like the **hypocrites**.
They neglect their **appearance**,
    so that they may **appear** to others to be fasting.
Amen, I say to you, they have **received** their reward.
But when **you** fast,
    anoint your **head** and wash your **face**,
    so that you may **not** appear to be fasting,
    except to your **Father** who is hidden.
And your Father who **sees** what is hidden will **repay** you."

In these last verses the text gets to the specific practice with which many associate Lent, fasting. To unite the words of Jesus with the practice, be clear with this imperative about fasting.

---

deeds—including fasting and almsgiving—so that God will love us; rather, God lavishes love on us, and our good deeds and penitential practices are our response to God's gifts of love and grace. We abstain to clear the path for the advent of God's life in us.

This is a moderately long passage, and almost all of it is a quotation of Jesus' words to the disciples after the Sermon on the Mount, which we heard proclaimed a few weeks ago.

This is one of the few times when what is described in the Gospel anticipates what members of the assembly themselves might do in the weeks to come. Here the challenges to almsgiving, prayer, and fasting will be taken up by members of the Church between this day and Holy Thursday, the end of Lent. For this reason, be measured and clear in your proclamation so that this link is made between Gospel and Church.

1ST SUNDAY OF LENT

Lectionary #22

READING I Genesis 2:7–9; 3:1–7

A reading from the Book of Genesis

The LORD **God formed** man out of the clay of the **ground**
    and blew into his **nostrils** the breath of **life**,
    and so man became a living **being**.
Then the LORD God planted a **garden** in **Eden**, in the east,
    and placed **there** the man whom he had **formed**.
Out of the **ground** the LORD God made various **trees** grow
    that were **delightful** to look at and **good** for food,
    with the tree of **life** in the **middle** of the garden
    and the tree of the knowledge of **good** and **evil**.

Now the **serpent** was the most **cunning** of all the animals
    that the LORD God had made.
The **serpent** asked the **woman**,
    "Did God **really** tell you not to eat
    from **any** of the trees in the garden?"
The woman answered the **serpent**:
    "We **may** eat of the fruit of the trees in the garden;
    it is **only** about the fruit of the tree
    in the **middle** of the garden that God said,
    'You shall **not** eat it or even **touch** it, lest you **die**.'"
But the serpent said to the **woman**:
    "You certainly will **not** die!
No, God knows well that the moment you **eat** of it
    your **eyes** will be **opened** and you will be like gods

These first three verses set the context for the dialogue to follow. Be clear in your proclamation; the details are engaging and familiar.

Pause to mark the transition whenever the speaker changes in this dialogue.

READING I Prepare for your proclamation by highlighting for yourself the key components of the story and of what the story reveals about God, about humanity, and about our tendency to sin. This is one of the most familiar stories in the whole of the Bible, both because it appears in the first few pages and also because what it reveals is so telling about human nature and about God's disposition toward humanity.

The advantage of the familiarity is that it marks the story as compelling. The disad-

vantage is that some might hear the beginning and dismiss it, thinking, "I know how this one goes." The challenge to you, the proclaimer of the familiar tale, is to proclaim it with a balance of the already familiar and the fresh. The freshness will come from your engagement with the story as you prepare.

Another challenge of the story is the use of direct discourse. The first takes place as the Lord addresses the man. But the more engaging dialogue is the exchange is between the serpent and the woman, a dialogue that has inspired a great deal of art over the millennia.

Keep in mind as you prepare and proclaim that you have the assistance of the quotation marks to distinguish the speakers from one another. You are not acting as if you are the LORD God, or Eve, or the serpent, but your voice can nevertheless reflect in tone the differences in the content of their words.

Practice and proclaim the story in this way. Pause slightly both before and after the direct quotations and also before the quotes within quotes. This will take some discernment on your part, and you might solicit help

who know what is **good** and what is **evil**."
The woman saw that the tree was good for food,
    pleasing to the **eyes**, and **desirable** for gaining **wisdom**.
So she **took** some of its fruit and **ate** it;
    and she **also** gave some to her **husband**, who was with her,
    and **he** ate it.

Then the **eyes** of both of them were **opened**,
    and they **realized** that they were **naked**;
    so they sewed **fig** leaves together
    and made **loincloths** for themselves.

This is the narrative resolution. Proclaim it so that the hearers picture the man and woman as their fate is sealed and their eyes are opened.

READING II   Romans 5:12–19

A reading from the Letter of Saint Paul to the Romans

Brothers and sisters:
Through one man **sin** entered the **world**,
    and through sin, **death**,
    and thus death came to **all** men, inasmuch as all sinned—
    for up to the time of the law, sin was in the world,
    though sin is **not** accounted when there is no law.

But **death** reigned from **Adam** to **Moses**,
    even over those who did not sin
    after the **pattern** of the trespass of **Adam**,
    who is the **type** of the one who was to come.

But the gift is **not** like the transgression.
For if by the **transgression** of the one, the many **died**,
    how much **more** did the **grace** of God

This is a historical summary of the origins of sin. Pause after "the one who was to come" to mark the transition to the next section.

In this section, Paul makes a comparison between "the one" who transgressed, and the "one man," Jesus Christ. See if you can carry in your tone this element of comparison between the first Adam and the new Adam.

to get the story correct and the characterizations in good shape for your proclamation.

    Though the reading is fairly long, the proclamation will not be helped by speeding through it. Take your time and let the narrative carry the assembly along in this arresting story from the rich tradition of the First Sunday of Lent.

READING II   Often in the Sunday Lectionary, there is a direct relationship between the first reading and the Gospel, and the second reading from a non-Gospel New Testament book is sometimes not easily related to the other two readings. Here this passage from Paul's Letter to the Romans is very fitting for the First Sunday of Lent, for the first reading describes Adam and Eve in the garden, and here Paul addresses the justification brought in Jesus Christ that countered the transgression of Adam. Many of the early bishops taught and preached about what was lost in the transgression of the first Adam and what was regained in the obedience of the new Adam, Jesus Christ. That theology was drawn from this key passage, which we find near the start of Lent.

    Though the theological rationale might be clear, the rhetoric of the passage is quite complex. Even before you start the oral practice of proclaiming this reading, the passage calls for some study and understanding. The assembly will not find the meaning accessible or profound unless you, the proclaimer of the reading, are clear about the argument as you deliver it. For this reading, your confidence must be built on your study of the text.

and the gracious **gift** of the one man Jesus **Christ**
overflow for the **many**.
And the **gift** is not like the **result** of the one who **sinned**.
For after one **sin** there was the judgment
that brought **condemnation**;
but the **gift**, after many transgressions, brought **acquittal**.

For **if**, by the transgression of the **one**,
death came to reign **through** that one,
how much **more** will those who receive the **abundance** of grace
and of the **gift** of justification
come to reign in **life** through the one Jesus **Christ**.

In **conclusion**, just as through one transgression
condemnation came upon **all**,
so, through one **righteous** act,
acquittal and **life** came to all.
For just as through the **disobedience** of the one man
the many were made **sinners**,
so, through the **obedience** of the one,
the many will be made **righteous**.

[Shorter: Romans 5:12, 17–19]

> **GOSPEL**   Matthew 4:1–11

A reading from the holy Gospel according to Matthew

At that time **Jesus** was led by the **Spirit** into the **desert**
to be **tempted** by the **devil**.
He fasted for **forty days** and **forty nights**,
and afterwards he was **hungry**.

From here on, the comparison of Adam and Jesus Christ continues, with each having a comparison in the same sequence, first Adam, then Christ.

Think of our common phrases, "on the one hand" and "on the other hand." Though the passage does not use those words exactly, see if your voice can communicate the sequence: first this one (Adam), then this one (Christ).

The first two and closing one verse establish a setting.

Emphasize the "forty days and forty nights" because the testimony of the temptation story contributed to the tradition of the duration of Lent, forty days.

A number of the words in this passage are abstract and polysyllabic. None is hard alone, but the repeated strings of abstractions in one reading might call for some concentrated attention as you prepare. If there are any particular tough spots for you, practice enunciating them clearly aloud until you become comfortable. Any stumbling on your part will distract the assembly from the beauty of Paul's message.

As you read, pause at the natural breaks supplied by the editors so that the assembly can digest this beautiful and weighty theology of grace in Jesus Christ.

In the shorter version, the comparison between Adam and Christ is put into bolder relief.

GOSPEL Each of the Synoptic Gospels (Matthew, Mark, and Luke) sets a temptation story at the beginning of Jesus' ministry. The version in Matthew is unique because the Evangelist supports it with references and quotations from the Old Testament, as Matthew so often does. Here there is a volley of quotations between Jesus and the devil in three parts. Each part has the devil start and Jesus answer back.

As you practice the reading, perhaps it would be helpful to mark up the text in this *Workbook* with three crayons or highlighters. With one color, mark anything that is not in quotation marks, for these create the context and advance the story.

With the second color, highlight the Old Testament quotations that both speakers offer; these are preceded by "it is written" in every case and appear in italics.

The dialogue begins here. See commentary for how to practice the dialogue for the best proclamation. After each temptation, pause to prepare for the next.

The **tempter** approached and said to him,
    "If you are the Son of **God**,
    command that these **stones** become loaves of **bread**."

He said in reply,
    "It is written:
    *One does not **live** on bread **alone**,*
    *but on every **word** that comes forth*
    *from the mouth of **God**.*"

The next temptation with its three parts.

Then the devil took him to the holy **city**,
    and made him stand on the parapet of the **temple**,
    and said to him, "If you are the Son of God,
        throw yourself **down**.
For it is written:
    *He will command his **angels** concerning you*
    *and with their hands they will **support** you,*
    *lest you dash your **foot** against a **stone**.*"
Jesus answered him,
    "**Again** it is written,
    *You shall not put the Lord, your **God**, to the **test**.*"

The third temptation with its three parts.

Then the devil took him up to a very high **mountain**,
    and showed him **all** the kingdoms of the world
        in their **magnificence**,
    and he said to him, "All these I shall **give** to you,
    if you will **prostrate** yourself and **worship** me."
At **this**, Jesus said to him,
    "Get **away**, **Satan**!
It is written:
    *The Lord, your **God**, shall you **worship***
    *and him **alone** shall you **serve**.*"

This final verse concludes the story after the contentious exchanges during the temptations.

Then the devil **left** him and, **behold**,
    angels came and **ministered** to him.

With the third color, highlight what is said by Jesus and the devil before and after the quotations from scripture.

With these elements clearly distinguished, you will be better equipped to imagine how the rhetoric of the reading progresses as you prepare. Since it is not good form to bring a cheat sheet with you to the ambo, practice these elements so that you know the setting, quotations, and speech well. This will enable you to approach your proclamation with confidence.

As ever, you need to find a tone for communicating the difference between what is a quotation and what is not. This is especially important with a reading like this, with its complexity of quotations being volleyed back and forth between Satan and Jesus.

2ND SUNDAY OF LENT

Lectionary #25

READING I   Genesis 12:1–4a

A reading from the Book of Genesis

The LORD said to **Abram**:
"Go **forth** from the land of your **kinsfolk**
   and from your father's **house** to a land that I will **show** you.

"I will make of you a great **nation**,
   and I will **bless** you;
I will make your name **great**,
   so that you will **be** a blessing.
I will **bless** those who **bless** you
   and **curse** those who **curse** you.
All the **communities** of the earth
   shall find **blessing** in you."

Abram **went** as the LORD **directed** him.

These few words identify the characters; pause between the identification of Genesis and the start of the passage so that the assembly hears who is speaking and to whom.

The family history of Israel is a fitting topic in the reading of Lent, for the next chapter of the Church's family history can be seen in the candidates for the sacraments of initiation.

A final verse of resolution.

READING I The readings from the Hebrew Scriptures in the first few Sundays of Lent mark some of the highlights of the history of the nation Israel. Recall the Eden story from the First Sunday of Lent; here we find the promise to Abraham; next Sunday we'll find Moses and the Israelites in the desert.

This is the shortest of those narratives, yet the most heartening because of God's promise to Abraham of a "great nation" of descendants. Consider the formation of the candidates for Baptism in your parish, and

imagine these words of the Lord addressed to the other ministers in your parish, to your fellow parishioners, and to the candidates themselves, for, as the Lord promises progeny to Abraham, so does Baptism provide the fulfillment of God's promise in the Church. The candidates are those in whom God's promise is fulfilled.

You might think of the LORD'S words to Abram on the order of a coach's words to athletes before the game. Just as there is a challenge in the game plan a coach gives to players, so there is a challenge in what the LORD asks of Abram: "Go forth from the land

of your kinsfolk and from your father's house to a land that I will show you." No small assignment. Abram is asked to leave his home on the strength of a promise. The catechumens and candidates are seeking the "land" God will show them as well.

READING II During the season of Lent, the Church takes up disciplines not as ends in themselves; their purpose is to help us get back to the state of grace, purity, sinlessness, and refreshment that we enjoyed at our Baptism, whether that

READING II   2 Timothy 1:8b–10

A reading from the second Letter of Saint Paul to Timothy

Beloved:
Bear your share of **hardship** for the **gospel**
  with the **strength** that comes from **God**.

He **saved** us and **called** us to a **holy** life,
  not according to our **works**
  but according to his own **design**
  and the **grace** bestowed on us in Christ **Jesus**
    before time began,
  but **now** made manifest
  through the **appearance** of our savior Christ **Jesus**,
  who destroyed **death** and brought **life** and **immortality**
  to light through the **gospel**.

GOSPEL   Matthew 17:1–9

A reading from the holy Gospel according to Matthew

Jesus took **Peter**, **James**, and **John** his brother,
  and led them up a high **mountain** by **themselves**.
And he was **transfigured** before them;
  his **face** shone like the **sun**
  and his **clothes** became white as **light**.
And **behold**, **Moses** and **Elijah** appeared to them,
  conversing with him.

The apostle speaks to Timothy directly. You can engage the assembly with this "you and I" relationship.

The meaning of the passage changes slightly at this point. Pause to let the first part of the reading sink in before you continue.

Elijah = ee-LĪ-juh

was decades ago or just last Easter. Lent is the season when the members of the Church support one another in realizing God's presence. The formation and disciplines of the candidates for Baptism are particularly revealing for those baptized long ago.

This reading from the Second Letter to Timothy helps reveal this purpose of Lent, for as Paul encouraged the letter's recipients— "Join with me in suffering for the Gospel"— so the Church encourages us to support one another in this communal preparation for Easter and its joys.

This is a relatively short reading, with two parts. The first part is an exhortation to "bear your share of hardship for the gospel" with the help of "the strength that comes from God." The second part narrows down to the gift wrought for humanity in the appearance of the Savior. Pause between the two sections so that the assembly can recognize the slight change of focus.

In this proclamation, your task as proclaimer is to stand in Paul's shoes. You are not imitating someone from the past like an actor on a stage; you share in the grace of God's life in the Church as the author of this

letter did centuries ago. So you can, with the confidence of faith, stand in the place of Paul and invite the assembly before you into the opportunities afforded by the season of Lent.

GOSPEL It is no coincidence that the narrative of the Lord's Transfiguration is proclaimed during Lent. In the great Forty Days of the Church year, both those preparing for Baptism and those already baptized are being formed into Christ's image. With the disciplines of Lent, prayer

There are three speakers and four speeches in this reading. Here Peter is speaking to Jesus. Note the direct discourse with your voice.

Then **Peter** said to Jesus in **reply**,
    "**Lord**, it is **good** that we are here.
If you **wish**, I will make three **tents** here,
    one for **you**, one for **Moses**, and one for **Elijah**."

While he was still speaking, **behold**,
    a bright **cloud** cast a shadow over them,
    then from the cloud came a **voice** that said,
    "**This** is my beloved **Son**, with whom I am well **pleased**;
    listen to him."

Here the voice from the cloud speaks, even before Peter is finished.

When the disciples **heard** this, they fell **prostrate**
    and were very much **afraid**.
But Jesus came and **touched** them, saying,
    "**Rise**, and do **not** be afraid."
And when the disciples raised their **eyes**,
    they saw **no one** else but Jesus **alone**.

The last two speeches are from Jesus to the disciples: a short one to calm the disciples and a longer one to tell them not to speak of what they have seen.

As they were coming **down** from the mountain,
    Jesus **charged** them,
    "Do not tell the vision to **anyone**
    until the Son of **Man** has been **raised** from the **dead**."

and abstinence, the people of God participate in the Transfiguration proclaimed today.

Notice that the clothes of Jesus are "white as light." In the Gospel of Matthew, one will not find a mention of white garments again until chapter 28, where the two angels at the tomb proclaim the Resurrection.

In the rite of Baptism for infants and for adults, the newly baptized are clothed with a white garment, not in imitation of these narratives from the Gospel, but as a participation in the life of Christ, who, in his

Transfiguration and Resurrection, is living in the Church and the world. For centuries, the vesture of the baptized was not often seen, for baptisms were generally celebrated with just the family, not the Sunday assembly. Since the reform of the liturgy and the promulgation of the RCIA, the Church at large witnesses baptisms. And so the white garments are more often seen.

The garments of the newly baptized at Easter are "white as light," as was your own baptismal garment when you were brought into the Church. (Whether you remember it or not, this vesture has been part of the rite

of Baptism for a very long time.) This connection between Christ's white clothes at the Transfiguration and the white robe of the newly baptized might not come to mind among many of your hearers as you proclaim the Gospel, but nevertheless be clear in this description so that they will remember it at Easter.

3RD SUNDAY OF LENT

Lectionary #28

READING I   Exodus 17:3–7

A reading from the Book of Exodus

In those days, in their thirst for **water**,
    the people **grumbled** against Moses,
    saying, "**Why** did you ever make us leave **Egypt**?
Was it just to have us **die** here of **thirst**
    with our **children** and our **livestock**?"
So Moses cried out to the LORD,
    "What shall I **do** with this people?
A little **more** and they will **stone** me!"

The LORD answered Moses,
    "Go over there in front of the **people**,
    along with some of the **elders** of Israel,
    holding in your hand, as you go,
    the **staff** with which you struck the **river**.
I will be standing there in **front** of you on the rock in Horeb.
Strike the rock, and the **water** will flow from it
    for the people to drink."
This Moses **did**, in the presence of the **elders** of Israel.

The place was called Massah and Meribah,
    because the Israelites **quarreled** there
    and **tested** the LORD, saying,
    "Is the LORD **in** our midst or **not**?"

Stress any references to water (or dryness or thirst) in anticipation of Easter's Baptisms!

This is a complaint. Don't whine, but make it sound like a complaint.

Israel = IZ-ree-ul

Horeb = HOH-reb

The Lord's instructions again emphasize water. This is a significant moment in the history of Israel, as the people are despairing and the Lord provides.

These etymologies of the Hebrew names are common in the Hebrew Scriptures.
Massah = MASS-ah

Meribah = MAIR-ih-bah

READING I   This reading anticipates the Gospel reading's image of water and the Church's use of water in the rites of Christian initiation. In the Gospel, Jesus will ask for a drink of water, and here the Israelites thirst for water. The consonance strengthens the symbol and the theology. These two readings have long been associated with Lent as the season of baptismal preparation. Keep that in mind as you practice.

This narrative is an episode in the long journey of the Israelites from slavery in Egypt to the Promised Land. From the Church's earliest days, that trek from Egypt to Israel was seen as a metaphor for the Paschal Mystery. The most engaging part of the journey of the Israelites is their walking on dry land through the Red Sea, and so the bishops of the early Church took up that trip through water as a metaphor for the catechumens' trip from unbelief to faith, and of the Christian's trip from sin to salvation gained in the death of Jesus.

Overall, the reading is laced with speeches, first the people complaint to Moses; then Moses' complaint to the Lord; then the Lord's instructions to Moses; and finally a quote from the people's complaining as an explanation of the names. As ever, make sure that by the tone of your voice the people can distinguish context from speech. Those who hear you should be able to recognize what is a quotation and what is not.

Paul's words are engaging; proclaim them so.

This is a profound theological truth.

A reading from the Letter of Saint Paul to the Romans

Brothers and sisters:
Since we have been justified by **faith**,
    we have **peace** with God through our Lord Jesus **Christ**,
    through whom we have gained **access** by faith
    to this **grace** in which we stand,
    and we **boast** in **hope** of the glory of **God**.

And **hope** does not **disappoint**,
    because the love of **God** has been poured **out** into our **hearts**
    through the Holy **Spirit** who has been **given** to us.
For **Christ**, while we were still **helpless**,
    died at the appointed **time** for the **ungodly**.
Indeed, only with difficulty does one die for a **just** person,
    though perhaps for a **good** person one **might** even
        find courage to **die**.
But God **proves** his love for us
    in that while we were still **sinners** Christ **died** for us.

READING II As he often does, Paul writes in an engaging literary form, employing first-person pronouns— "we," "our," "us." Sometimes he is speaking of his own life; other times, as here, he is identifying himself with the believers to whom he writes. Here he is speaking to the Church of Rome of the ways of God and human salvation.

With this in mind, then, you would do well not to think of your proclamation as an imitation of Paul, for your assembly is far from that church in Rome and our century far from the first. Yet, even with these distinctions, you and your assembly share a fundamental experience with Paul and the ancient Roman Christian assembly to which he wrote, and that experience is Baptism.

Baptism has made each member inextricably linked to all. While you and I and all our fellow believers, infants and adults, were still sinners (by original sin for the infants, original and personal sin for the adults), Christ saved us, just as he saved Paul and those ancient Christians whose letter you read. In this, we are connected to that ancient Christian assembly in Rome and to Paul himself. We, like they, "have gained access by faith to this grace in which we stand," the grace in which we all exist and have been set free by the unimaginable gift of God.

If you truly believe this gift to be yours from God's generosity, "because the love of God has been poured out into our hearts,"

GOSPEL   John 4:5–42

A reading from the holy Gospel according to John

Jesus came to a town of **Samaria** called **Sychar**,
    near the plot of land that **Jacob** had given to his son **Joseph**.
Jacob's **well** was there.
Jesus, tired from his **journey**, sat down there at the **well**.
It was about noon.

A woman of **Samaria** came to draw **water**.
Jesus said to her,
    "**Give** me a drink."
His disciples had gone into the town to buy food.

The Samaritan woman said to him,
    "How can **you**, a **Jew**, ask **me**, a **Samaritan** woman,
       for a **drink**?"
—For Jews use **nothing** in common with Samaritans.—
Jesus answered and said to her,
    "If you knew the **gift** of God
    and who is saying to you, '**Give** me a drink,'
    you would have asked him
    and he would have given you **living** water."

The woman said to him,
    "**Sir**, you do not even have a **bucket** and the cistern is **deep**;
    where then can you **get** this living water?
Are you greater than our father **Jacob**,
    who **gave** us this cistern and **drank** from it **himself**
    with his **children** and his **flocks**?"

The opening sets the stage by providing the details of place and time for the long narrative to follow.
Samaria = suh-MAIR-ih-uh
Sychar = SĪ-kar
Jacob = JAY-kub

This social transgression is foundational to the passage and to Jesus' ministry to Gentiles.

Pause slightly as you move from one speaker to the other so that the assembly can feel the shift.

---

then proclaim Paul's words as your own. Those before you will accept the words as true if you, from your faith and your experience, believe them to be so.

GOSPEL   This long reading from chapter 4 of the Gospel of John has been associated with the formation of catechumens for Baptism from ancient times. Indeed, it can be precisely placed in the liturgical calendar of the early Church, for then as now, its theology is

related to its place in the Church's conception of time and the Church.

One sees the Samaritan woman turn from unbelief to faith, and then we hear that she herself is testifying to Jesus. This progress in faith is similar to what happens each year when the faith of the newly baptized at the Vigil sparks an awakening of faith for the entire Church. It is similar too to the progress of faith in each Christian life from Baptism until death.

Whether or not the story is a reflection of baptismal formation in the Evangelist's own community, it is for the Church today a brilliant story of faith development offered by that Evangelist. By your clear proclamation the narrative can deepen the faith not only of those about to be baptized, but of all members of the assembly.

For you, the Gospel reader with such a long narrative to proclaim, there can be a temptation to think, "Hmm, I'd better keep up a good pace here so that the assembly does

Although the reading does not mention Baptism, imagine Baptism as celebrated in your parish. This metaphor of the water is deep in the Church's experience, particularly during the Lenten preparation for Baptism.

Jesus answered and said to her,
  "Everyone who drinks **this** water will be thirsty **again**;
  but whoever drinks the water **I** shall give will **never** thirst;
  the water I shall give will become in him
  a **spring** of water welling up to eternal **life**."

The woman said to him,
  "Sir, **give** me this water, so that **I** may not be thirsty
  or have to keep coming **here** to draw **water**."

Jesus said to her,
  "**Go** call your **husband** and come **back**."
The woman answered and said to him,
  "I do not **have** a husband."
Jesus answered her,
  "You are **right** in saying, 'I do not have a husband.'
For you have had **five** husbands,
  and the one you have now is **not** your husband.
What you have said is **true**."

Jesus speaks the truth about the complexity of her life, yet it does not drive her away.

The woman said to him,
  "Sir, I can see that you are a **prophet**.
Our **ancestors** worshiped on this **mountain**;
  but you people say that the place to worship is in **Jerusalem**."
Jesus said to her,
  "**Believe** me, woman, the hour is coming
  when you will worship the Father
  neither on this mountain **nor** in Jerusalem.

Jerusalem = juh-ROO-suh-lem

"**You** people worship what you do not understand;
  we worship what we understand,
  because **salvation** is from the **Jews**.

not get bored." Whether you proclaim the shorter form or the longer, it is better to give a strong proclamation that takes a little more time and engages the assembly than to give a speedy version with little of it clearly heard or well received.

As you prepare, notice the narrative breaks. The first part sets the context, and next is the opening exchange about water. This metaphor is, of course, very important as the catechumens and the Church look forward to Baptism at Easter.

The next part is where Jesus reveals his knowledge of the complexity of her life. It is important not to cast the woman as a sinner, for Jesus himself does not do this, but to demonstrate that this person with whom Jesus spent such a long time in conversation was someone of whom many would disapprove. Her faith clearly deepens during this exchange for she calls him first a prophet and then the Messiah.

In the next part, their conversation is broken by the return of the disciples, and by the exchange between them and Jesus about food.

The last section is a summary, in a way, but it reveals also a deep theology, for her word about Jesus brings many to faith, as the deepening faith of the catechumens enriches the faith of the Church into which they will be baptized. Your proclamation of this long narrative can make clear the link between the faith of the Samaritan woman, the faith of those being brought to the Church, and the faith of those who have been members for nearly their entire lives.

But the hour is **coming**, and is now **here**,
  when **true** worshipers will worship the Father
    in **Spirit** and **truth**;
  and indeed the Father seeks such people to worship him.
God is **Spirit**, and those who worship him
  must worship in **Spirit** and **truth**."

The woman said to him,
  "I know that the **Messiah** is coming, the one called the **Christ**;
  when he **comes**, he will tell us **everything**."
Jesus said to her,
  "**I** am he, the one **speaking** with you."

At that moment his disciples returned,
  and were **amazed** that he was talking with a **woman**,
  but still no one said, "What are you **looking** for?"
  or "Why are you talking with **her**?"
The woman **left** her water jar
  and went into the town and said to the people,
  "Come see a man who told me **everything** I have **done**.
Could he possibly be the **Christ**?"
They went out of the town and came to him.
Meanwhile, the disciples urged him, "Rabbi, **eat**."
But he said to them,
  "I have food to eat of which you do not know."
So the disciples said to one another,
  "Could someone have **brought** him something to eat?"

Jesus said to them,
  "**My** food is to do the will of the one who **sent** me
  and to finish his **work**.
Do you not say, 'In four months the harvest will be here'?
I tell you, look **up** and see the fields ripe for the **harvest**.

Messiah = meh-SĪ-uh

Jesus often scandalizes his followers, as here.

This section can be tricky to proclaim effectively, with the shift to a new set of images—food, sowing, harvesting, reaping.

The evangelism of the woman testifying to Jesus' word brings many to belief.

The **reaper** is already receiving **payment**
   and gathering **crops** for eternal **life**,
   so that the **sower** and **reaper** can rejoice **together**.
For here the saying is verified that '**One** sows and **another** reaps.'
I sent you to **reap** what you have not **worked** for;
   others have done the work,
   and **you** are sharing the **fruits** of their work."

Many of the Samaritans of that town began to **believe** in him
   because of the word of the woman who testified,
   "He told me **everything** I have done."
When the Samaritans **came** to him,
   they invited him to **stay** with them;
   and he stayed there two days.
Many **more** began to believe in him because of his **word**,
   and they said to the **woman**,
   "We no longer believe because of **your** word;
   for we have heard for **ourselves**,
   and we know that this is **truly** the savior of the **world**."

[Shorter: John 4:5–15, 19b–26, 39a, 40–42]

4TH SUNDAY OF LENT

Lectionary #31

READING I   1 Samuel 16:1b, 6–7, 10–13a

A reading from the first Book of Samuel

The LORD said to **Samuel**:
    "Fill your horn with **oil**, and be on your **way**.
I am sending you to **Jesse** of Bethlehem,
    for I have chosen my **king** from among his **sons**."

As Jesse and his sons came to the **sacrifice**,
    Samuel looked at **Eliab** and thought,
    "**Surely** the LORD's **anointed** is here before him."
But the LORD said to Samuel:
    "Do not judge from his **appearance** or from his lofty **stature**,
    because I have rejected him.
Not as **man** sees does **God** see,
    because **man** sees the **appearance**
    but the LORD looks into the **heart**."

In the same way Jesse presented **seven** sons before Samuel,
    but Samuel said to **Jesse**,
    "The LORD has not chosen **any** one of these."
Then Samuel asked Jesse,
    "Are these **all** the sons you **have**?"
Jesse replied,
    "There is still the **youngest**, who is tending the **sheep**."
Samuel said to Jesse,
    "**Send** for him;
    we will not begin the sacrificial **banquet** until he arrives **here**."

This reading alternates between narrative and direct discourse. Mark in your *Workbook* the words of the various speakers to help you follow the progress of this story of election.
Jesse = JES-ee
Bethlehem = BETH-luh-hem
Eliab = ee-LĪ-ub
Consider how you will proclaim *thoughts* differently than spoken words. Will this difference be understood by the assembly?

Can the assembly know from your voice that the LORD's words are different from those of Samuel?

Pause as speakers change so that the assembly can sense the change.

From this point, the text focuses on David. Be clear in reading the descriptions of him.

READING I   A Lenten reading about election—like the one you are preparing, in which David is chosen from among the sons of Jesse—cannot help but have layers of interpretations in the minds, hearts, and experiences of believers. One might think first of the life of Christ, the Savior for whom the Church and the world waits, the only-begotten son of the Father, the *chosen* one of God. Second, one might think of the *elect* preparing for Baptism, those in formation who will be brought into the Church at the Easter Vigil. Third, one might think of the community of faith in which you minister, for that community as a whole is the people of God the incarnate and risen Body of Christ, the Church. They, too, are the *chosen* of God. Fourth, one might think of all people, those who, by the gift of life which comes from God, were *chosen* to enjoy the company of family and friends and time and space. Finally, one can think of all living things, of all creation, which is also a gift of God.

As you prepare for proclaiming this reading from 1 Samuel and think about what will best bring it forth for the community, notice that David was at first overlooked by his family. His father has seven sons pass before Samuel without giving any

Jesse sent and had the young man brought to them.
He was **ruddy**, a youth **handsome** to behold
   and making a **splendid** appearance.
The LORD said,
   "There—anoint **him**, for **this** is the one!"

Then **Samuel**, with the horn of oil in **hand**,
   anointed **David** in the presence of his **brothers**;
   and from that day **on**, the spirit of the LORD
      rushed upon David.

This is a rite of election in which Jesse's
son David is marked with distinction.

READING II   Ephesians 5:8–14

Ephesians = ee-FEE-zhunz

A reading from the Letter of Saint Paul to the Ephesians

This opening is extremely important.

Brothers and sisters:
You were once **darkness**,
   but **now** you are **light** in the **Lord**.
Live as children of **light**,
   for **light** produces every kind of **goodness**
   and **righteousness** and **truth**.

The next few verses are encouragements
to the Church.

Try to learn what is **pleasing** to the Lord.
Take no part in the **fruitless** works of **darkness**;
   rather **expose** them, for it is **shameful** even to **mention**
   the things done by them in **secret**;
   but **everything** exposed by the **light** becomes **visible**,
   for **everything** that becomes visible is **light**.
Therefore, it says:

The final part, the quotation, is a rallying
cry. It is an imperative, a command.
Wake up!

   "**Awake**, O sleeper,
   and **arise** from the **dead**,
   and Christ will give you **light**."

thought to the possibility that the Lord would want David. He was the youngest, the keeper of the sheep. Who would want the little sheep-keeper?

Few of us are chosen for greatness in the eyes of the world, in the eyes of the Church, or even in the eyes of our parish. Yet we are magnificent in the eyes of God, because we belong to God, whatever our

state in life, whatever our abilities or disabilities. David was ignored by his family, yet, as Samuel met him, he was ruddy, handsome, and altogether splendid! What is not appreciated in the sight of the world is often appreciated in the sight of God, and what God appreciates is often never noticed in the world.

As you prepare and as you proclaim, keep this message in mind and heart, and deliver the reading to those in your assembly who are not appreciated in the world.

READING II   The meaning of this passage rests on the opposites of light and darkness. Your reflection on these images in the life of the Church during Lent will embolden your proclamation, so in the weeks leading up to this Sunday ponder the readings that include such images. Consider the various levels of the symbols to animate your delivery of the word to the Church.

GOSPEL   John 9:1–41

A reading from the holy Gospel according to John

As Jesus passed by he saw a man **blind** from **birth**.
His disciples asked him,
   "**Rabbi**, who **sinned**, this **man** or his **parents**,
   that he was born **blind**?"

Jesus answered,
   "**Neither** he **nor** his parents sinned;
   it is so that the works of **God** might be made **visible**
      through him.
We have to do the works of the one who sent me while it is **day**.
Night is coming when **no** one can work.
While I am in the **world**, I am the **light** of the world."
When he had said this, he **spat** on the ground
   and made **clay** with the **saliva**,
   and **smeared** the clay on his **eyes**, and said to him,
   "Go **wash** in the Pool of Siloam"—which means **Sent**.
So he **went** and **washed**, and came back able to **see**.

His **neighbors** and those who had seen him earlier
      as a **beggar** said,
   "Isn't **this** the one who used to sit and **beg**?"
Some said, "It **is**,"
   but **others** said, "**No**, he just **looks** like him."
He said, "I **am**."
So they said to him, "How were your eyes **opened**?"
He replied,
   "The man called Jesus made **clay** and **anointed** my eyes
   and told me, 'Go to Siloam and **wash**.'
So I **went** there and **washed** and was able to **see**."

The opening question, "who sinned?" is very important.

That Jesus Christ is himself the light is a key metaphor of the Gospel of John.

The tactile sign performed by Jesus is beautiful.

Siloam = sih-LOH-um

First, throughout the season of Lent, the ways of the Lord in opposition to the ways of sin are captured in the metaphors of illumination and light, on the one hand, and shadows and darkness, on the other. The work of Lent is the formation of the Church, as we are reshaped according to the Lord's light and revelation.

Second, think about the candidates for initiation at the Easter Vigil. The intense formation of the catechumens during Lent is another manifestation of the light vanquishing the darkness. They are living this experience, and for the rest of the Church praying for them and supporting them, they are a sign of the life and light of Christ in the world.

Third, think of the symbol of light as it will be manifest throughout the Fifty Days of the Easter season. At the Easter Vigil, as the people of God enter the darkened church in procession, the increase in the light as the Easter candle is brought forward is a sign of the birth of the Church in the salvation wrought in the Paschal Mystery of Jesus Christ. This reading anticipates and contributes to that depth of symbolism at Easter.

Proclaim this reading with power so that the reality and sign of light in darkness is awakened in the experience of the Church.

GOSPEL   As you prepare for the proclamation, understand that the healing of the man is the central physical change in the story, but the moral and theological issue of sin in human life is as

Pharisees = FAIR-uh-seez

And they said to him, "Where **is** he?"
He said, "I don't know."

They brought the one who was once blind to the **Pharisees**.
Now Jesus had made clay and opened his eyes on a **sabbath**.
So then the Pharisees **also** asked him how he was able to see.
He said to them,
    "He put **clay** on my eyes, and I **washed**, and now I can **see**."
So some of the Pharisees said,
    "This man is **not** from God,
    because he does not keep the **sabbath**."
But **others** said,
    "How can a **sinful** man do such signs?"
And there was a division among them.

The authorities are determined to get to the bottom of this.

So they said to the blind man **again**,
    "What do you have to say about him,
    since he opened your eyes?"
He said, "He is a **prophet**."

Now the Jews did not believe
    that he had been **blind** and gained his **sight**
    until they summoned the **parents** of the one
        who had gained his sight.
They asked them,
    "Is this your **son**, who you say was born **blind**?
How does he now **see**?"
His parents answered and said,
    "We **know** that this is our **son** and that he was born **blind**.
We do **not** know how he **sees** now,
    nor do we know who opened his eyes.
Ask **him**, he is of age;
    he can speak for **himself**."

important. At the start, the disciples' first question, "who sinned?" and Christ's answer are important for the Church's formation. Throughout the reading, this issue of the relationship of sickness and sin persists. People want to attribute the man's blindness to sin.

This is a perennial issue. Think of the many people in the Church whose lives have been touched by sickness and death. Think of those who have lost a child. Think of those who are widowed, who attended their spouses and family members through their last illnesses and then attended their funerals. Think of those whose own chronic illnesses make them wonder if God is somehow punishing them for some bad action or bad decision or bad attitude. Think even of those who attribute their minor illnesses to something they did wrong.

Jesus' answer, which you will proclaim to the Church, "Neither he nor his parents sinned," is no less important and no less good news for the people of God today than it was when written by the Evangelist John centuries ago. Your vocation is to proclaim it as good news.

Notice that this reading is filled with dialogue. As you practice, it might be helpful to highlight the words of each speaker in a distinct color so that you can be confident about the relationship of the actions and words in the story.

Do your best to engage the assembly's attention throughout, even though it is a long narrative without a sweeping finish.

His parents said this because they were afraid
of the Jews, for the Jews had already agreed
that if anyone **acknowledged** him as the **Christ**,
he would be **expelled** from the **synagogue**.
For this reason his parents said,
"**He** is of age; question **him**."

So a **second** time they called the man who had been **blind**
and said to him, "Give **God** the praise!
We know that this man is a **sinner**."
He replied,
"If he is a **sinner**, I do not **know**.
One thing I **do** know is that I was **blind** and now I **see**."
So they said to him,
"What did he **do** to you?
How did he open your eyes?"
He answered them,
"I told you **already** and you did not **listen**.
Why do you want to hear it **again**?
Do **you** want to become his disciples, too?"
They **ridiculed** him and said,
"**You** are that man's disciple;
we are disciples of **Moses**!
We know that God spoke to Moses,
but we do **not** know where this one is from."

The man answered and said to them,
"This is what is so **amazing**,
that you do not know where he is from,
yet he opened my eyes.
We **know** that God does not listen to **sinners**,
but if one is **devout** and does his **will**, he **listens** to him.

Isn't God's grace amazing? "I was blind
and now I see."

The obstinacy of the authorities is
growing.

The theological point about sickness and sin emerges again, this time with the authorities contradicting what Jesus said at the beginning of the reading.

It is **unheard** of that anyone ever opened the eyes
of a person **born** blind.
If this man were not from **God**,
he would not be able to do **anything**."
They answered and said to him,
"You were born **totally** in sin,
and are **you** trying to teach **us**?"
Then they threw him out.

When Jesus heard that they had thrown him out,
he found him and said, "Do you **believe** in the Son of **Man**?"
He answered and said,
"Who **is** he, sir, that I **may** believe in him?"
Jesus said to him,
"You have **seen** him,
the one speaking with you is he."
He said,
"I **do** believe, Lord," and he **worshiped** him.

During Lent, the catechumens and candidates are formed to follow the example of the man born blind. With him, they say, "I do believe, Lord."

Then Jesus said,
"I came into this world for **judgment**,
so that those who do **not** see **might** see,
and those who **do** see might become **blind**."
Some of the Pharisees who were with him heard this
and said to him, "Surely **we** are not also blind, **are** we?"
Jesus said to them,
"If you **were** blind, you would have no **sin**;
but now you are saying, 'We **see**,' so your sin **remains**."

[Shorter: John 9:1, 6–9, 13–17, 34–38]

5TH SUNDAY OF LENT

Lectionary #34

READING I   Ezekiel 37:12–14

Ezekiel = ee-ZEE-kee-ul

Pause briefly after the introductory identification of the Lord GOD as the speaker.

Israel = IZ-ree-ul

A reading from the Book of the prophet Ezekiel

Thus says the Lord GOD:
O my **people**, I will open your **graves**
    and have you **rise** from them,
    and bring you **back** to the land of **Israel**.
Then you shall know that **I** am the LORD,
    when I **open** your graves and have you **rise** from them,
    O my **people**!

I will put my **spirit** in you that you may **live**,
    and I will **settle** you upon your **land**;
    thus you shall know that **I** am the LORD.
I have **promised**, and I will **do** it, says the LORD.

These are dramatic words; proclaim them with conviction and authority.

READING I   This reading from the prophet Ezekiel was surely chosen for this Sunday because of today's Gospel reading, the raising of Lazarus. Your task is to get the assembly's ears and hearts prepared for that narrative by a strong proclamation of the excerpt from Ezekiel to which it is related.

    The passage from Ezekiel is short, but it is packed with a powerful message. Ezekiel's prophecy both indicts and consoles the people in their captivity in Babylon; this excerpt contains key components of the consolations and of God's dramatic promises to the people of Israel.

    As you proclaim, be mindful of expressing clearly the communal aspect of God's promises in this reading. Believers can sometimes think of Lent as time for individual preparation for Easter, rather than as a time for renewal, rebirth, and replenishment for the community of the Church together. Yet from its earliest days Lent has been clearly the season of renewal for the whole Church, not for individuals apart from the Church. The address in this reading, "O my people," captures this sense well, and as the proclaimer you should capture that sense for the Church in which and to which you minister.

    The prophecy is framed by an introductory identification of "the Lord GOD" as the speaker of the words delivered by the

| READING II | Romans 8:8–11 |

A reading from the Letter of Saint Paul to the Romans

Brothers and sisters:
Those who are in the **flesh** cannot **please** God.
But **you** are **not** in the **flesh**;
    on the **contrary, you** are in the **spirit,**
    if only the Spirit of **God dwells** in you.
Whoever does **not** have the Spirit of **Christ**
        does **not belong** to him.

But **if Christ** is in you,
    although the **body** is **dead** because of **sin,**
    the **spirit** is **alive** because of **righteousness.**

If the **Spirit** of the **one** who raised **Jesus** from the **dead**
        dwells in you,
    the **one** who raised **Christ** from the **dead**
    will give **life** to **your** mortal bodies **also,**
    through his **Spirit** dwelling in **you.**

The contrast set up by Paul is between the "spirit," on the one hand, and the "flesh" or "mortal bodies," on the other.

The "you" here is not simply referring to those in Rome who received the letter from Paul. Now it is addressed by you to your fellow believers, those assembled for worship on this day.

| GOSPEL | John 11:1–45 |

A reading from the holy Gospel according to John

Now a man was **ill, Lazarus** from **Bethany,**
    the village of **Mary** and her sister **Martha.**
Mary was the one who had **anointed** the Lord with perfumed **oil**
    and dried his **feet** with her **hair;**
    it was her **brother** Lazarus who was ill.

These opening verses introduce all the major characters in the long narrative. Start your proclamation so that the listening assembly knows who's who.
Lazarus = LAZ-uh-rus
Bethany = BETH-uh-nee

prophet and by a simple closing, "says the Lord." Use these as framing identifiers, but leave a little space between them and the words of the Lord. If you pause slightly, the assembly in front of you will be more alert and poised for listening to the dramatic prophesy for this key Sunday in the season of Lent and in the formation of the Church leading up to Easter.

READING II The theology of the body in the letters of Paul is complex. In 1 Corinthians we hear, "Do you not know that you are members of the body of Christ?" which is a positive use of the word "body," for being a member of Christ's Body means salvation. Yet here in the reading from Romans that you are preparing for your proclamation, the "body" seems to be associated with sin and death only. In the Corinthians text, the body is the community of faith at Corinth; here the body is the flesh, that which is inclined toward sin and death.

The important comparison in this passage from Romans is between life in the Spirit and life in the flesh. It is by the power of the Spirit that the mortal body, the body of flesh, can be given new life. As you prepare for your proclamation, highlight the contrast of Spirit and flesh, for the former does not

So the sisters sent word to Jesus saying,
  "**Master**, the one you **love** is ill."
When Jesus heard this he said,
  "This illness is **not** to end in **death**,
  but is for the glory of **God**,
  that the Son of God may be **glorified** through it."

Jesus' affection for the siblings is strong.

Now Jesus **loved** Martha and her **sister** and **Lazarus**.
So when he heard that he was **ill**,
  he remained for **two days** in the place where he was.
Then after this he said to his **disciples**,
  "Let us go back to **Judea**."
The disciples said to him,

Judea = joo-DEE-uh

  "**Rabbi**, the Jews were just trying to **stone** you,
  and you want to go **back** there?"
Jesus answered,
  "Are there not twelve hours in a **day**?
If one walks during the **day**, he does not **stumble**,
  because he sees the **light** of this world.
But if one walks at **night**, he **stumbles**,
  because the **light** is not **in** him."

Last Sunday's Gospel revealed that Jesus himself is the "light of the world," so here he is referring to himself. The juxtaposition of light and darkness is a Lenten theme.

Be careful and clear with the dialogue in this section.

He said this, and then told them,
  "Our friend Lazarus is **asleep**,
  but I am going to **awaken** him."
So the disciples said to him,
  "**Master**, if he is **asleep**, he will be **saved**."
But Jesus was talking about his **death**,
  while they thought that he meant ordinary **sleep**.
So then Jesus said to them **clearly**,
  "Lazarus has **died**.
And I am **glad** for you that I was not **there**,
  that you may **believe**.

annihilate the latter; we still live in the flesh even after we have received the Spirit. But the indwelling of the Spirit vivifies the mortal flesh so that it is not an impediment to grace, but an instrument of grace.

If your parish has catechumens and candidates for initiation into the Church at the Easter Vigil, you might bear in mind the changes and challenges that these people have encountered on account of accepting new life as members of the Church; they

have been transformed by grace and now move from initial faith formation into the community of faith, the Body of Christ. They might not compare life "in the flesh" (as the "before") to life "in the spirit" (as the "after"), but their sacrifices and preparations are examples of the kind of conversion about which the apostle Paul writes. On this scrutiny Sunday, consider the examples of faith in those who are preparing to join the Church, and the meaning of the reading will be more clear.

GOSPEL Since the restoration of the catechumenate and the promulgation of the RCIA (1972), the rites and the readings have been brought back together for the first time in many centuries. The Church is still learning what the catechumenate means for its growth and self-understanding and what it means as a ritual way of welcoming inquiring and new members. As proclaimer of this key Gospel of the raising of Lazarus, you are contributing to the

Let us go to him."
So **Thomas**, called Didymus, said to his fellow **disciples**,
    "Let us also go to **die** with him."

When Jesus **arrived**, he found that Lazarus
    had already been in the **tomb** for **four days**.
Now Bethany was near **Jerusalem**, only about two miles away.
And many of the Jews had come to Martha and Mary
    to **comfort** them about their **brother**.
When **Martha** heard that Jesus was coming,
    she went to **meet** him;
    but **Mary** sat at home.
Martha said to Jesus,
    "Lord, if you had **been** here,
    my brother would not have **died**.
But even now I **know** that **whatever** you ask of God,
    God will **give** you."
Jesus said to her,
    "Your brother will **rise**."

Martha said to him,
    "I **know** he will rise,
    in the **resurrection** on the last **day**."
Jesus told her,
    "**I** am the **resurrection** and the **life**;
    whoever believes in **me**, even if he **dies**, will **live**,
    and everyone who lives and believes in me will **never** die.
Do you **believe** this?"
She said to him, "**Yes**, Lord.
I have come to believe that you are the **Christ**, the Son of **God**,
    the one who is **coming** into the world."

The detail of "four days" is incredible, so make sure it is heard clearly.
Jerusalem = juh-<u>ROO</u>-suh-lem

Jesus' words about Lazarus' rising anticipate Christ's resurrection at Easter, just two weeks away.

Another of the theologically important "I AM" sayings of Jesus in the Gospel of John.

learning and experience of the Church in these rites of Lent and of the formation of the elect toward incorporation into the Church. You will need to be clear on the ritual and theological underpinnings so that the richness of this marvelous story can be brought out to the fullest.

This Gospel—as with the Gospels of the previous two Sundays—accompanies a scrutiny. The narrative lends meaning to the ritual action of the last of the three scrutinies of those being prepared for baptism. On the Third, Fourth, and Fifth Sundays of Lent, the scrutiny Gospels enable the Church to hear the story and note the changes in the characters of the stories: the woman at the well (John 4), the man born blind (John 9), and now Lazarus (John 11). These are not merely remembrances of things past, for the changes in the stories capture the changes in those being prepared for the sacraments. As you proclaim, be alert for the way the narrative reflects what they have been going through.

Of the many elements in this reading, you should emphasize those with a bearing on initiation and formation. These would be the theology of illness, death, and resurrection; the familial and communal relationships— brother, sisters, loved ones, fellow mourners; light and darkness; being awake and sleeping; the strips of cloth in which Lazarus is bound. From parish to parish, the rites may be done slightly differently, and you can emphasize those elements in the Gospel that

When she had said this,
    she went and called her sister Mary **secretly**, saying,
    "The **teacher** is here and is **asking** for you."
As soon as she **heard** this,
    she rose **quickly** and went to him.
For Jesus had not yet come into the **village**,
    but was still where Martha had **met** him.
So when the Jews who were with her in the house **comforting** her
    saw Mary get up quickly and go **out**,
    they **followed** her,
    presuming that she was going to the **tomb** to **weep** there.

When Mary came to where Jesus was and saw him,
    she **fell** at his feet and said to him,
    "Lord, if **you** had been here,
    my **brother** would not have **died**."
When Jesus saw her **weeping** and the Jews who had come
        with her weeping,
    he became **perturbed** and deeply **troubled**, and said,
    "Where have you **laid** him?"
They said to him, "Sir, come and **see**."
And Jesus **wept**.
So the Jews said, "See how he **loved** him."
But some of them said,
    "Could not the one who opened the eyes of the **blind** man
    have done something so that **this** man would not have **died**?"

So **Jesus**, perturbed **again**, came to the **tomb**.
It was a **cave**, and a **stone** lay across it.
Jesus said, "Take away the **stone**."
Martha, the dead man's **sister**, said to him,
    "Lord, by **now** there will be a **stench**;
    he has been **dead** for **four days**."

One of the shortest verses in the whole Bible, and one of the most moving.

Another arresting detail.

are most strongly reflected in your community's ritual of formation.

This Gospel is fascinating, both because of the inconceivable act performed by Jesus and because of the details that the Evangelist employed to relate the tale to his Church many years ago. The details are essential to the success of your ministry with the Gospel during this season of Lent. Make the story your own by being familiar with its course

and by relating it to your own experience of faith. The more intimately you can relate the Gospel to your own faith experience, the more engaging, convincing, and inspiring your proclamation will be.

Jesus said to her,
    "Did I not **tell** you that if you **believe**
    you will see the glory of **God**?"

So they took away the **stone**.
And Jesus raised his eyes and said,
    "**Father**, I **thank** you for **hearing** me.
I know that you **always** hear me;
    but because of the **crowd** here I have said this,
    that they may **believe** that you **sent** me."

And when he had said this,
    he cried **out** in a loud **voice**,
    "**Lazarus**, come **out**!"
The dead man came **out**,
    tied hand and foot with **burial** bands,
    and his **face** was wrapped in a **cloth**.
So Jesus said to them,
    "**Untie** him and let him **go**."

Now **many** of the Jews who had come to **Mary**
    and **seen** what he had done began to **believe** in him.

[Shorter: John 11:3–7, 17, 20–27, 33b–45]

Be bold as you proclaim this. Though you are not imitating Jesus' voice, you want to bring out the drama of his command, "Lazarus, come out!"

PALM SUNDAY OF THE LORD'S PASSION

Lectionary #37

GOSPEL AT THE PROCESSION   Matthew 21:1–11

Because it interrupts the usual order of the rite, this Gospel reading at the start of the liturgy may be disorienting. Confident proclamation is imperative.
Jerusalem = juh-ROO-suh-lem
Bethphage = BETH-fayj

A reading from the holy Gospel according to Matthew

When **Jesus** and the disciples drew near **Jerusalem**
    and came to **Bethphage** on the Mount of **Olives**,
    Jesus sent two **disciples**, saying to them,
    "Go into the **village** opposite you,
    and immediately you will find an **ass** tethered,
    and a **colt** with her.
Untie them and bring them **here** to me.
And if anyone should **say** anything to you, reply,
    'The **master** has need of them.'
Then he will send them at **once**."

This happened so that what had been spoken through the prophet
    might be **fulfilled**:
    Say to daughter **Zion**,
    *"***Behold***, your* **king** *comes to you,*
    meek *and riding on an* **ass**,
    and on a **colt**, *the* **foal** *of a beast of* **burden**."

Zion = ZĪ-ahn

foal = f ohl

PROCESSION GOSPEL **Passion Sunday is an extraordinary liturgical day for many reasons, not least because such a fullness of the word of God is proclaimed. Unlike Good Friday, which has the same Passion account proclaimed every year from the Gospel of John, Passion Sunday's Gospel readings follow a three-year cycle: the Passion narrative of Matthew in Year A, Mark in Year B, and Luke in Year C.**

The Gospel at the Procession, though shorter than the Gospel at the Liturgy of the Word, is as full a Gospel narrative as those the Church proclaims on Sundays in Ordinary Time. Here at the start of the liturgy, it accompanies the ritual action of the blessing of palm branches. This gesture, in the Gospel and in your community, is one of prophetic fulfillment and of the Lord's kingship.

The demonstration of a fulfillment of the prophecy is a common literary device in Matthew, which frequently looks to the Hebrew Scriptures for a warrant for what Jesus does. Here the prophecy of a king coming on a colt, on the foal of a donkey is introduced. Matthew highlights how Jesus' riding a donkey is a fulfillment of Zechariah 9:9, and how this very fulfillment is itself a foundation for the kingship of Jesus.

Another connection in the passage is with the assembly bearing palm branches and the people in the Gospel who "cut branches from the trees" and spread them on the road, another sign of the kingship of Christ.

As a liturgical link, you might be particularly clear with the crowd's "Hosanna," and so on, since it links the community of

The disciples went and did as Jesus had **ordered** them.
They brought the **ass** and the **colt** and laid their **cloaks** over them,
and he **sat** upon them.
The very large **crowd** spread their cloaks on the **road**,
while others cut **branches** from the **trees**
and **strewed** them on the **road**.
The crowds **preceding** him and those **following**
kept crying out and saying:
"**Hosanna** to the Son of **David**;
blessed is he who **comes** in the name of the **Lord**;
hosanna in the **highest**."

And when he entered **Jerusalem**
the whole **city** was **shaken** and asked, "Who **is** this?"
And the crowds **replied**,
"This is **Jesus** the **prophet**, from Nazareth in **Galilee**."

Lectionary #38

READING I   Isaiah 50:4–7

A reading from the Book of the Prophet Isaiah

The Lord **GOD** has given me
a well-trained **tongue**,
that I might **know** how to speak to the **weary**
a **word** that will **rouse** them.
Morning after **morning**
he opens my **ear** that I may **hear**;
and I have not **rebelled**,
have not turned **back**.

Matthew's Gospel with the liturgical tradition of the "Holy, Holy," which has been part of our worship for centuries and centuries.

READING I This passage from Isaiah is well suited for proclamation on the day of the Passion from the Gospel of Matthew, for its description of the servant who "gave my back to those who beat me" is realized in the way of the cross of Jesus.

You might be inclined to dispatch this reading from the prophet quickly. Resist that temptation. It has a beautiful message for ministers of the word as it declares, "The Lord GOD has given me a well-trained tongue, that I might know how to speak to the weary a word that will rouse them."

That theology of ministry can inspire and encourage you in your own ministry; the Liturgy of the Word does indeed provide guidance and consolation to many who listen. There may well be parishioners whose primary social activity for the week is their time at the liturgy. The word to the weary that your ministry offers can make a big difference.

It is the second half of the prophecy that makes the passage most fitting for this Passion Sunday. Many of the sufferings of the prophet as he spoke the Lord's unwelcome words to the people of Israel were visited on Jesus as he spoke words his hearers did not want to accept.

The history of the Church has witnessed many who gave up their lives for their faith and on behalf of others. In *Tertio Millennio Adveniente* Pope John Paul II wrote that "the Church of the first millennium was born of the blood of the martyrs." Still today there are many who give up or risk their lives as a

I gave my **back** to those who **beat** me,
my **cheeks** to those who plucked my **beard**;
my **face** I did not **shield**
from **buffets** and **spitting**.

The Lord **GOD** is my **help**,
therefore I am not **disgraced**;
I have set my face like **flint**,
knowing that I shall **not** be put to **shame**.

READING II   Philippians 2:6–11

Philippians = fil-LIP-ee-unz

A reading from the Letter of Saint Paul to the Philippians

Christ **Jesus**, though he was in the form of **God**,
did not regard **equality** with God
something to be **grasped**.
Rather, he **emptied** himself,
taking the form of a **slave**,
coming in **human** likeness;
and found **human** in appearance,
he **humbled** himself,
becoming **obedient** to the point of **death**,
even death on a **cross**.

Because of this, God greatly **exalted** him
and **bestowed** on him the **name**
which is above **every** name,

result of their baptismal call to serve the world. Many suffer for speaking the unwelcome truth, in line with Isaiah and with the Jesus of history. At this start of a millennium, we can say with the Pope that "the Church has become once again a Church of martyrs."

READING II The importance of this text in the tradition is not simply from its antiquity; its theology is deep and beautiful. Moreover, in the liturgy before the reform at the Second Vatican Council, this

text was a kind of stational hymn, a text that unfolded as the days of Holy Week passed. The first part of the text would have been sung on the first day; another part was added the following day, and so on. In this way the movement of the Church in time was paralleled by the movement of the faithful through the Latin text. This would have been complemented by physical movement, probably a procession. There are many ways that spiritual progress is marked by physical movement in the liturgy. The most familiar of these, practiced in many parishes during Lent, is the Stations of the Cross.

Although the Church does not punctuate the Holy Week liturgies with this text as it did decades ago, this passage is still central, with its theology of the Lord's Passion and in its theology of the communion between Jesus Christ and God the Father. For this reason your proclamation should not be rushed. Pause between the significant parts as catechesis on the Three Days for those celebrating them for the first time.

that at the name of **Jesus**
every knee should bend,
of those in **heaven** and on **earth** and **under** the earth,
and every tongue confess that
Jesus **Christ** is **Lord**,
to the **glory** of God the **Father**.

PASSION   Matthew 26:14—27:66

The Passion of our Lord Jesus Christ according to Matthew

(1) One of the **Twelve**, who was called Judas **Iscariot**,
    went to the chief priests and said,
    "What are you willing to give **me**
    if I hand him over to **you**?"
They paid him thirty pieces of **silver**,
    and from that time on he looked for an **opportunity**
        to hand him **over**.

(2) On the **first** day of the Feast of Unleavened **Bread**,
    the **disciples** approached Jesus and said,
    "Where do you want us to prepare
    for you to eat the **Passover**?"

Pause briefly after the introduction phrase identifying it as the Passion according to Matthew.
Judas = JOO-dus
Iscariot = is-KAIR-ee-ut

(4) The Passion reading moves through many of the scriptural events of Holy Week. The narrative of the Last Supper is important here, for on Holy Thursday, when the Mass of the Lord's Supper is celebrated, the Gospel is the footwashing of the Gospel of John.

PASSION   Every year, there are about 60 times when parishioners hear a Gospel passage proclaimed in the liturgy. The Gospel of Matthew, which is the Gospel for Year A, has a little more than a thousand verses. A little arithmetic leads one to suppose that these Gospel proclamations would be, on average, fifteen verses or so long. On Passion Sunday, however, we find a huge portion of the Gospel, about 13% of it, at one liturgy!

Proclaiming this long Passion narrative on this Sunday is an ancient tradition in the Church, going back to the fourth century and perhaps even earlier. From those ancient testimonies, we know what was read, but we learn nothing about how the Gospel was proclaimed. Perhaps in antiquity, believers were able to give their attention to one reader for longer periods of time. But no matter how it was proclaimed in the early Church, today it is clearly a challenge for ministers of God's word to bring that word to life for our assemblies.

DELIVERY. Over the years, various parishes have tried different approaches to the Passion narrative, including full-scale "dramatic interpretations." But the liturgy is not theater, and it diminishes the purpose of proclaiming the word of God in the community when that word is arranged to depict the actions of God in some past age as if God were not still present, living, and active in the world and the Church today. God is at work in our lives as vibrantly and actively as ever. In his apostolic letter on Sunday, *Dies Domini,* Pope John Paul II taught that what we experience of the risen Christ is not different from what the two followers of Christ found in their dialogue with him on the road to Emmaus (see Luke 24:13–35).

He said,
  "**Go** into the **city** to a certain **man** and tell him,
  'The **teacher** says, "My appointed **time** draws **near**;
  in your house I shall celebrate the **Passover**
    with my **disciples**." ' "
The disciples then **did** as Jesus had **ordered**,
  and prepared the **Passover**.

(3) When it was **evening**,
  he reclined at table with the Twelve.
And while they were **eating**, he said,
  "**Amen**, I say to you, **one** of you will **betray** me."
Deeply **distressed** at this,
  they began to say to him one after another,
  "**Surely** it is not **I**, Lord?"
He said in reply,
  "He who has dipped his hand into the dish with me
  is the one who will **betray** me.
The Son of Man indeed **goes**, as it is **written** of him,
  but **woe** to that man by whom the Son of Man is **betrayed**.
It would be **better** for that man if he had **never** been **born**."
Then Judas, his **betrayer**, said in reply,
  "Surely it is not **I**, Rabbi?"
He answered, "**You** have said so."

The Gospels are not a script for a play. If you look at the script of a play, you'll see that most of the text is the words to be spoken by the actors. Little attention is given to the context in which the spoken words are delivered. This is not what we find in the Gospels, where there is a balance of setting and dialogue, a balance of actions and words, and this is particularly so when we come to the Passion accounts. The characters in the Gospels do speak, but their speaking comes in the context of various settings, all of which carry meaning of their own.

Some parishes have thought that the members of the assembly might be more alert and attentive if they were able somehow to participate actively in the narration. This idea, which is not wholly bad, does have a downside. Their parts need to be printed and distributed, and the assembly's attention will be partly focused on coming in at the right time, taking away from attentive listening to the Gospel as it is proclaimed. It is not necessarily a bad practice, but it needs to be evaluated in light of the other demands of the liturgy.

INCULTURATION OF WORSHIP. The inculturation of the liturgy means that each community of faith conforms its values to the values given by the Church in the liturgy. Prayer, dialogue, discernment, and leadership all need to play a role in the process of strengthening our Christian lives through the liturgy. The work of liturgical renewal is not a once-and-for-all matter; it is the base for good liturgy at all times. For the Passion, this year or any year, a balance needs to be found between having the narrative seem interminably long and having the narrative turn into a kind of entertainment, which the

(4) While they were eating,
Jesus took **bread**, said the **blessing**,
broke it, and giving it to his **disciples** said,
"**Take** and **eat**; this is my **body**."
Then he took a **cup**, gave **thanks**, and gave it to them, saying,
"**Drink** from it, **all** of you,
for this is my **blood** of the **covenant**,
which will be **shed** on behalf of **many**
for the forgiveness of **sins**.
I tell you, from now on I shall not **drink** this fruit of the **vine**
until the **day** when I drink it with you **new**
in the kingdom of my **Father**."
Then, after singing a **hymn**,
they went out to the Mount of **Olives**.

(5) Then Jesus said to them,
"This night **all** of you will have your faith in me **shaken**,
for it is written:
*I will strike the **shepherd**,*
*and the **sheep** of the flock will be **dispersed***;
but after I have been raised up,
I shall go before you to **Galilee**."
Peter said to him in reply,
"Though **all** may have their faith in you **shaken**,
mine will **never** be."

Galilee = GAL-ih-lee

(5) Peter's promise of faithfulness and Jesus' prediction of Peter's denial are foreshadowing events to come.

liturgy should not be. Engaging and inspiring, yes; entertaining and amusing, no. What's important to remember is that by the narrative proclaimed in these words of the Gospel we are saved from sin and death and given new life in Christ.

THE HISTORICAL JESUS AND THE RISEN CHRIST. One note before we look to the text of the Passion reading itself. We know from the Church's scripture scholars that the Gospel of Matthew was written about the year 85, about a half-century after the historical events of Jesus' Passion and death narrated in the Gospel. Few, if any, of those in the community from which the Gospel of Matthew emerged would have been eyewitnesses to those events. The Evangelist Luke, who wrote at about the same time as Matthew, confesses in the introduction to his Gospel that these "events were handed on to us by those who were eyewitnesses," and that "I too have decided to write an orderly account for you" from what was handed down; see Luke 1:2–3. It is likely that Matthew, like Luke, was not an eyewitness since the two wrote in about the same period and share much of the same Gospel material.

If indeed the Evangelist Matthew was not an eyewitness but, like Luke, trusted the accounts of those who were, we share a great deal in common with these Evangelists and their communities. Matthew's experience of the Gospel came from his experience of the risen Christ, and that experience transformed his life so deeply that he was moved to write a Gospel himself, reflecting on the experiences of the community of faith to which he belonged. That is much the same as what we do; having been incorporated into the Church at Baptism, whether as infants or as adults, and having experienced

Jesus said to him,
  "**Amen**, I say to **you**,
  this very **night** before the **cock** crows,
  you will **deny** me **three** times."
Peter said to him,
  "Even though I should have to **die** with you,
  I will not **deny** you."
And **all** the disciples spoke **likewise**.

Then Jesus came with them to a place called **Gethsemane**,
  and he said to his disciples,
  "Sit **here** while I go over **there** and pray."
He took along **Peter** and the two sons of **Zebedee**,
  and began to feel **sorrow** and **distress**.

Then he said to them,
  "My soul is **sorrowful** even to **death**.
Remain here and **keep watch** with me."
He **advanced** a little and fell **prostrate** in prayer, saying,
  "My **Father**, if it is **possible**,
  let this cup pass from me;
  yet, not as **I** will, but as **you** will."
When he returned to his disciples he found them **asleep**.

Gethsemane = geth-SEM-uh-nee

Zebedee = ZEB-uh-dee

The link between the cup, the Eucharist, and suffering is important both in the narrative and in the lives of believers.

the life of faith in our community, we participate in the liturgy because there we meet the risen Christ. It is the experience of the Passion, death, and Resurrection of Jesus Christ in our community that brings us to the sacraments. Even in solemn liturgical moments like the proclamation of two long Passion readings in one week—Matthew on Passion Sunday and John on Good Friday—we come back because we know the story and we are part of that story, for we are indeed the body of Christ. The story of Christ is our story; it became our story at our

Baptism, and it becomes our story again and again with each year during Holy Week.

MATTHEW'S COMMUNITY. Matthew has an eye for detail. Sometimes the details make a particular part of the account more engaging. As you proclaim, imagine the details in your mind's eye so that the assembly will hear your proclamation as if you are describing what you have seen first-hand. Second, Matthew's community, much more than Mark's and Luke's communities, had a large number of Jewish Christians in it. One

result of this social fact is that Matthew frequently refers back to the Jewish Scriptures to ground his Gospel in the Hebrew Bible.

In the very first verse, his genealogy of Jesus describes him as "the son of David, the son of Abraham." This appeal to the Jewish patriarchs is a clue to his audience. Throughout the Passion narrative, you will find Matthew raising up texts of the Jewish Scriptures as the foundation for what is happening to Christ on the way of the cross. Discern for yourself as you prepare how much emphasis any one quote should have

He said to **Peter**,
 "So you could not keep **watch** with me for one **hour**?
Watch and pray that you may not undergo the test.
The **spirit** is willing, but the **flesh** is weak."
Withdrawing a **second** time, he prayed again,
 "My **Father**, if it is not **possible** that this cup pass
  without my **drinking** it, your will be done!"
Then he returned **once more** and found them **asleep**,
 for they could not keep their eyes open.
He **left** them and withdrew **again** and prayed a **third** time,
 saying the same thing again.
Then he **returned** to his disciples and said to them,
 "Are you still **sleeping** and taking your **rest**?
Behold, the hour is at **hand**
 when the Son of **Man** is to be handed over to **sinners**.
Get up, let us **go**.
Look, my **betrayer** is at **hand**."

(6) While he was still **speaking**,
 Judas, one of the Twelve, arrived,
  accompanied by a large **crowd**, with **swords** and **clubs**,
  who had come from the chief priests and the elders
   of the people.
His betrayer had arranged a **sign** with them, saying,
 "The man I shall **kiss** is the one; **arrest** him."
Immediately he went over to Jesus and said,
 "**Hail**, Rabbi!" and he **kissed** him.

(6) This gesture of intimacy as a sign of betrayal is so poignant.

---

for the assembly. Some can be read without much stress so as not to distract from the forward movement of Christ's walk toward Golgotha. You might find that other citations have more bearing for the assembly. No single approach to these texts can be universally applicable; use your judgment from experience.

The parenthetic numbers below and in the margin notes refer to sections of the Gospel text in the *Workbook.*

(1) "*Everything* has a price," you might think as you read and prepare for the opening scene of Matthew's Passion narrative,

as Judas approaches the chief priests for profit. Just before this, and not included in the Passion, a woman approaches Jesus in the house of Simon the leper and pours very costly ointment on Jesus' head. The disciples grumble about it; that expensive ointment could have been sold and the money given to the poor.

So, in the Gospel, Judas' selling out Jesus is contrasted with the woman's act of devotion and care. Here in the Passion Sunday Gospel pericope, the proclamation begins with the betrayal, a sign of things to come.

We can think of the disciples both as individuals with unique characteristics, qualities, and weaknesses, which is certainly true, and also as representatives of all Christians. We know that in our weaker moments the temptations of Judas are our temptations. By God's grace, we do not act toward such grave consequences, but we cannot so distance ourselves from Judas' weaknesses that we are ill-prepared for the temptation to sin when it is upon us. There but for the grace of God. . . . Since this betrayal begins the way toward the cross, proclaim it fully.

Jesus answered him,
　"**Friend**, do what you have **come** for."
Then stepping forward they laid hands on Jesus and **arrested** him.

And **behold**, one of those who accompanied Jesus
　　put his hand to his **sword**, drew it,
　　and **struck** the high priest's **servant**, cutting off his **ear**.
Then Jesus said to him,
　"Put your **sword** back into its **sheath**,
　　for all who **take** the sword will **perish** by the sword.
Do you think that I cannot call upon my **Father**
　　and he will not provide me at this **moment**
　　with more than twelve **legions** of **angels**?
But then how would the **Scriptures** be **fulfilled**
　　which say that it must come to pass in this way?"

At that hour Jesus said to the **crowds**,
　"Have you come out as against a **robber**,
　　with **swords** and **clubs** to seize me?
Day after day I sat **teaching** in the temple area,
　　yet you did not **arrest** me.
But all this has come to pass
　　that the writings of the **prophets** may be **fulfilled**."
Then all the disciples **left** him and **fled**.

(2) The coincidence of the Passover and Jesus' death is an integral part of the chronology of the first three Gospels, and here that chronology is put into the fore with the mention of the "first day of the Feast of Unleavened Bread." That detail would have carried great meaning to Matthew's community of Jewish Christians. For believers today the specificity of the detail adds a kind of ratification of the reality of the unfolding story, and for this it is important, but the chronology will not be particularly captivating to your hearers. This can be a kind of discernment for you as you meditate upon the Gospel you will proclaim and consider the elements that you will stress in your reading.

Also, in Jesus' instructions to the disciples about the man whom they would approach about preparing the meal, the Evangelist reveals Jesus' foreknowledge of what was to take place. This also hints at the inevitability of what happened.

(3) The specifics in the Gospel narratives can be both historic and symbolic. We interpret scripture conscious of God's Providence; God can see to it that literal events have symbolic dimensions, too. Here when the Evangelist reveals that "it was evening," it may have been a fact that it was dark, but this could also point to the dark events ahead. At other places and in other Gospels, the symbols of light and darkness have much weight independent of the time of the day when the events themselves took place.

The omniscience of Christ (seen in his instructions to the disciples about where to eat the Passover) is even weightier here. Jesus reveals that one of the twelve will betray him, the one who shares in the meal ritual of dipping his hand into the dish. With the context of ritual meal-sharing in both

Caiaphas = KĪ-uh-fuss

Sanhedrin = san-HEE-drun

(7) This section is filled with dialogue and quotations. Practice this well, and be clear about who is saying what and quoting what.

(7) Those who had **arrested** Jesus led him away
    to **Caiaphas** the high **priest**,
    where the scribes and the elders were **assembled**.

Peter was **following** him at a **distance**
    as far as the high priest's **courtyard**,
    and going inside he sat down with the servants
        to see the outcome.
The chief priests and the entire **Sanhedrin**
    kept trying to obtain false **testimony** against Jesus
    in order to put him to **death**,
    but they found **none**,
    though **many** false witnesses came forward.

Finally two came forward who stated,
    "This man said, 'I can **destroy** the temple of God
    and within **three** days **rebuild** it.'"
The high priest rose and addressed him,
    "Have you no **answer**?
What are these men **testifying** against you?"
But Jesus was silent.
Then the high priest said to him,
    "I **order** you to tell us under oath before the living God
    whether you are the **Christ**, the Son of **God**."

Judaism and early Christianity, this revelation about the betrayer's sharing in the dish with Jesus is poignant.

(4) The assembly hears this passage Sunday after Sunday during the Eucharistic Prayer. In your reading, to highlight the connection between the weekly sacred banquet and its scriptural basis, bracket this section with a pause at the start and at the finish. The eucharistic sacrifice is itself bracketed by the betrayal of Christ by Judas on the one side and the denial of Christ by Peter on the other. The pauses will accentuate this narrative context as well.

The ritual actions of the Eucharist are as ancient in the tradition as the words that accompany the actions: Jesus *took* bread, *blessed* it, *broke* it, and *gave* it to his followers; he *took* the cup, *gave thanks,* and *gave* it to them. The link between this sacrificial and ritual meal Jesus shared with his disciples and the Passion about to unfold contributes to Christian sacramental theology. As we participate in the Eucharist, our participation in the death of Christ is underlined in both the scriptural narrative and the ritual action.

(5) The portrait of the disciples is more positive in Matthew's Gospel than in the other two Synoptics. Peter, in particular, is favorably drawn in Matthew. His denial of Christ so close to the Passion must be grounded in inescapable history since, even in this Gospel that shows him in a good light, the denial is recounted in all its scandalous fullness. (Earlier in this Gospel, Jesus says to him, "You are Peter, and on this rock I will build my Church." That appears in no other Gospel.)

Peter's denial tells us that even for those closest to Christ, salvation is pure gift, not earned by any particular holiness of life. As you proclaim the acts of the disciples

Jesus said to him in reply,
"**You** have said so.
But I tell you:
From now on you will see 'the Son of Man
seated at the right hand of the **Power**'
and 'coming on the clouds of **heaven**'."
Then the high priest tore his **robes** and said,
"He has **blasphemed**!
What further **need** have we of **witnesses**?
You have now **heard** the blasphemy;
what is your opinion?"
They said in reply,
"He deserves to **die**!"
Then they **spat** in his face and **struck** him,
while some slapped him, saying,
"**Prophesy** for us, Christ: who is it that **struck** you?"

prophesy = PROF-uh-sī

(8) This section is a succession of dialogues between Peter and each of the three who accuse him of associating with Jesus the Galilean, the Nazarene.
Galilean = gal-ih-LEE-un

Nazorean = naz-oh-REE-un

(8) Now **Peter** was sitting outside in the courtyard.
One of the maids came over to him and said,
"**You** too were with Jesus the **Galilean**."
But he **denied** it in front of everyone, saying,
"I do not know what you are **talking** about!"
As he went out to the gate, **another** girl saw him
and said to those who were there,
"**This** man was with Jesus the **Nazorean**."

that send Jesus closer to Golgotha, know that such narratives capture truths of human life as true today as when the events were taking place. As Peter promises to Christ's face, "I will not deny you," but nevertheless does, so will believers today, however strong in our faith, doubt God's love when hard times come. God is more faithful than we are. Fortunately, our salvation is from God's love, not from our own effort.

There a poignant complement of Jesus' words about Peter and Peter's actions in this section. For Jesus asks that the disciples keep watch with him and he returns to find them asleep, fulfilling what the Lord had foretold. As with Peter's threefold denial, so is this a threefold falling asleep.

The connection between the Eucharist and the Passion is made more explicit here in Jesus' prayer to the Father, for his prayer, "let this cup pass from me," is symbolic of suffering. Three times does he pray in this way, yet the suffering will come; the cup of the Eucharist has come to represent the suffering that is an integral part of human life, for believers and non-believers alike.

This section ends with chilling words: The "betrayer is at hand."

(6) The action that began this Passion narrative, Judas' conspiring to betray Jesus, comes to its climax here, with the kiss as the sign of betrayal. In your proclamation, be clear with the bitter irony of a crowd with swords and clubs led by the man who betrays him with a kiss.

We can be inclined to assign both wonderfully good and horribly bad things to individuals, reluctant to admit that whole groups of people can contribute to most significant events, both good and bad. But our theology teaches that sin is both personal and corporate, with the two aspects inseparable in

Again he **denied** it with an oath,
"I do not **know** the man!"
A little later the bystanders came over and said to Peter,
"Surely **you** too are one of them;
even your speech gives you away."
At that he began to curse and to swear,
"I do not **know** the man."
And **immediately** a **cock** crowed.
Then Peter remembered the word that Jesus had spoken:
"Before the **cock** crows you will **deny** me **three** times."
He went out and began to weep **bitterly**.

When it was **morning**,
all the chief priests and the elders of the people
took counsel against Jesus to put him to **death**.
They **bound** him, led him **away**,
and handed him over to Pilate, the **governor**.

(9) Then Judas, his **betrayer**, seeing that Jesus had been
condemned,
deeply **regretted** what he had done.
He **returned** the thirty pieces of **silver**
to the chief priests and elders, saying,
"I have **sinned** in betraying **innocent** blood."
They said,
"What is that to **us**?
Look to it **yourself**."

This narrative of Judas' actions after the betrayal is more extensive in the Gospel of Matthew than in the other Gospels. Proclaim it clearly since it appears only once every three years (in Year A).

both the Fall and the Redemption. Here as you proclaim the betrayal, it is easy to cast Judas as the sole villain. But as you prepare, notice that there is a kind of inevitability in the narrative, that the betrayal had to be brought about by someone who loved Christ and whom Christ loved. Just a few verses after the betrayal, the other disciples flee.

(7) Matthew's storytelling skills are sharp. We have seen that he set up the scenario with Judas, then moved to another part of the story, and returned later to pick up what had been suspended in the hearer's mind. In this way the story keeps working

in the hearers even when the scene shifts for a bit. He does this with Peter's story as well; earlier, Peter told Jesus, "I will not deny you," and then the scene shifted. Now the Evangelist brings Peter to the fore here in the garden for a moment so that the hearers don't forget him.

The story continues. Caiaphas the high priest, as well as the scribes and elders, are searching for testimony against Jesus, even "false testimony," but (and the Gospel makes it perfectly clear) they find none. The Evangelist recognizes that Jesus, an innocent

man, was sent to his death without the testimony required for a fair trial.

Be careful as you prepare this section for proclamation, for there are some complex layers in the dialogue. There are the two who come forward and quote what Jesus said. A short span later, Jesus himself will quote the Hebrew Scriptures.

In addition to these scriptural citations, there is a lot of dialogue: speeches from the high priest, from Jesus, and from those who taunt Jesus to prophesy. As you prepare, know who the speakers are so that you will

Flinging the money into the **temple**,
  he **departed** and went off and **hanged** himself.
The chief priests gathered up the money, but said,
  "It is not **lawful** to deposit this in the temple treasury,
  for it is the price of **blood**."
After consultation, they used it to buy the **potter's** field
  as a burial place for **foreigners**.
That is why that field even today is called the Field of **Blood**.
Then was **fulfilled** what had been said through **Jeremiah**
    the **prophet**,
  *And they took the thirty pieces of **silver**,*
  *the value of a man with a **price** on his head,*
  a price set by some of the Israelites,
  *and they paid it out for the **potter's** field*
  *just as the Lord had **commanded** me.*

(10) Now Jesus stood before the **governor**, who questioned him,
  "Are you the **king** of the **Jews**?"
Jesus said, "**You** say so."
And when he was accused by the chief priests and elders,
  he made no answer.
Then **Pilate** said to him,
  "Do you not **hear** how many things they are **testifying**
    against you?"
But he did not answer him one word,
  so that the **governor** was greatly **amazed**.

Jeremiah = jair-uh-MĪ-uh

This is a long section with its own narrative units—Jesus' exchange with Pilate, Pilate's question to the crowd, the warning from Pilate's wife, and Pilate's hand-washing and declaration of his own innocence.

---

be confident with the narrative you will proclaim. The best preparation in sections of such complexity is simply to become familiar with the action and movement of the story; if you know the story well, you can proclaim it with assurance, even when the story is wrenching.

(8) The Evangelist now brings Peter to the front again. The assembly knows from Peter's explicit confessions to Christ how much he loves him and how dedicated his faith in Christ is, yet it knows too that he will not only deny knowing Jesus once, but he will do so again and again. The details of

the scene are important. Mark the details: the servant girls, a bystander, the cock crow, and, of course, be clear with the emotion. Peter weeps bitterly, a detail that makes this stalwart disciple's realization of his own contribution to his beloved Lord's Passion even more poignant.

As you prepare, pay attention to the snippets of dialogue from those who accuse Peter.

The final few verses of this section are broadening the scope again to the religious leaders, the priests and elders who lead Jesus away and hand him over to Pilate.

(9) The narrative device that the Evangelist used with Peter—three separate appearances before the dramatic scene of his ultimate denial—is used for Judas too. We have seen him twice: the opening scene and then the kiss of betrayal. Here he confesses that he compromised his convictions for money for "innocent blood." Wracked with remorse, he takes his own life.

As before, the Evangelist demonstrates that Jesus is completely innocent. Even the one who set Jesus up and handed him over declares Jesus' innocence as strongly as he can. Pause after proclaiming Judas' suicide,

Barabbas = buh-RAB-us

Now on the occasion of the **feast**
    the governor was accustomed to release to the crowd
    one **prisoner** whom they wished.
And at that time they had a **notorious** prisoner called **Barabbas**.
So when they had **assembled**, Pilate said to them,
    "**Which** one do you want me to **release** to you,
    Barabbas, or Jesus called **Christ**?"
For he knew that it was out of envy
    that they had handed him over.

While he was still seated on the bench,
    his **wife** sent him a **message**,
    "Have **nothing** to do with that **righteous** man.
I suffered **much** in a **dream** today because of him."

The chief priests and the elders persuaded the crowds
    to ask for **Barabbas** but to destroy **Jesus**.
The governor said to them in reply,
    "**Which** of the two do you want me to **release** to you?"
They answered, "**Barabbas**!"
Pilate said to them,
    "Then what shall I do with **Jesus** called **Christ**?"
They all said,
    "Let him be **crucified**!"
But he said,
    "**Why**? What **evil** has he done?"
They only shouted the **louder**,
    "Let him be **crucified**!"

and then move to the explanation of what happened with the money. Remember how important it is for the first Evangelist to base what happens in the Hebrew Scriptures, so he brings in the prophecy of Jeremiah.

(10) The irony in the exchange between Pilate and Jesus is deep. The innocent man without any power is talking with the governor about power. The exchange begins with the governor's question: "Are you the king of the Jews?" This dialogue with Pilate reveals that such the theology of the kingship of Christ has been part of the tradition from the start.

Pilate's power over Jesus' fate is emphasized by the custom of the governor's release of a prisoner on this feast. The decision for the "notorious prisoner" Barabbas over the innocent Jesus is yet another injustice, furthering Matthew's emphasis on the desperate situation in which Jesus is being judged.

Pilate will play a large role in the Passion of Good Friday, from the Gospel of John, and it is quite different from what is here in Matthew. His character has been interpreted in widely varying ways over the centuries. Here in the first Gospel Pilate is trying to get Jesus released; "What evil has he done?" he asks those accusing Jesus. The Evangelist adds that "Pilate saw that he was not succeeding at all," so, though Jesus' conviction and execution are due to his authority, the Gospel does not portray him as wholly evil. Indeed, the Evangelist has him say, "I am innocent of this man's blood."

As you proclaim this scene, be aware of Pilate's dual role as the governor who is responsible and who will hand Jesus over,

When Pilate saw that he was not succeeding at all,
    but that a **riot** was breaking out instead,
    he took **water** and washed his **hands** in the sight of the **crowd**,
    saying, "I am **innocent** of this man's **blood**.
Look to it **yourselves**."
And the whole people said in reply,
    "His blood be upon **us** and upon our **children**."
Then he released **Barabbas** to them,
    but after he had Jesus **scourged**,
    he handed him over to be **crucified**.

praetorium = prih-TOR-ee-um

(11) Then the **soldiers** of the governor took Jesus
    inside the **praetorium**
    and gathered the whole **cohort** around him.
They **stripped** off his **clothes**
    and threw a scarlet **military** cloak about him.
Weaving a **crown** out of **thorns**, they placed it on his **head**,
    and a **reed** in his right hand.
And kneeling before him, they mocked him, saying,
    "**Hail**, King of the **Jews**!"

As Jesus approaches his death, the taunting and deriding increase, sharpening the indignity of what happened.

Be attentive to the descriptive details.

They **spat** upon him and took the reed
    and kept **striking** him on the head.
And when they had **mocked** him,
    they **stripped** him of the **cloak**,
    dressed him in his own **clothes**,
    and **led** him off to **crucify** him.

Cyrenian = sī-REE-nee-un
Simon of Cyrene's part in the Passion developed into a Station of the Cross. His name will be familiar from that devotion.

(12) As they were going out, they met a **Cyrenian** named **Simon**;
    this man they pressed into **service**
    to carry his **cross**.

but also makes an effort to realize justice in having Jesus set free. Make this section particularly accessible. The issues of authority and power and kingship have a deep place not only in the Passion narrative but in the theology of the Church through the ages.

(11) The descriptions of the soldiers' actions toward Jesus are saddening; they are even more painful in light of the story's revelation that their leaders knew that Jesus was indeed an innocent man. This part of the reading has the group of soldiers dressing Jesus in a kind of regal "costume" so that they can mock him.

Such mockery is often evidence of insecurity, which makes it no less despicable. Here the Evangelist uses it to reveal the precarious social and political scene. If Jesus had been a man of no importance, there would have been no need for such displays of prejudice.

The vulnerability of the stripping and then the symbolism of the "royal" costume the soldiers put on him—a scarlet military cloak, a crown of thorns, a reed in his right hand—give physical details that, while they might not have the resonance for us that they did for the original assembly for which

they were written, still convey the sense of humiliation and grief. Do not rush through these details on the way of the cross.

(12) Jesus' disciples fled earlier in the reading, but we find unexpected characters coming to Jesus' aid between here and the end of the Gospel. This contains a theological truth: God is often present and active in unexpected places.

The first character whom we meet in this role is introduced only briefly: Simon from Cyrene. (Catholics are familiar with him from the Stations of the Cross.) The Evangelist not only gives us the information

Golgotha = GOL-guh-thuh

And when they came to a place called **Golgotha**
   —which means Place of the **Skull**—
  they gave Jesus **wine** to drink mixed with **gall**.
But when he had **tasted** it, he **refused** to drink.

(13) After they had **crucified** him,
  they divided his **garments** by casting **lots**;
  then they sat down and kept watch over him there.

And they placed over his head the written **charge** against him:
  This is **Jesus**, the King of the **Jews**.
Two **revolutionaries** were crucified **with** him,
  one on his **right** and the other on his **left**.

This charge is abbreviated as INRI (from the Latin translation) on many crucifixes.

Those passing by **reviled** him, shaking their **heads** and saying,
  "You who would **destroy** the temple and **rebuild** it
    in **three** days,
  save **yourself**, if you are the Son of **God**,
  and come down from the **cross**!"

Likewise the chief **priests** with the scribes and **elders**
    mocked him and said,
  "He saved **others**; he cannot save **himself**.
So he is the **king** of Israel!
Let him come down from the cross **now**,
  and we will **believe** in him.
He trusted in **God**;
  let him deliver him **now** if he wants him.
For he said, 'I am the Son of **God**.'"
The **revolutionaries** who were **crucified** with him
  also kept abusing him in the same way.

Israel = IZ-ree-ul

(14) From noon onward, **darkness** came over the whole land
  until **three** in the afternoon.

---

that someone was pressed into service to help Jesus, but makes a point of his being from far away.

    The name "Golgotha" is defined here as "Place of the Skull." Artistic tradition for centuries and centuries has seen that skull as the skull of Adam. In Paul's theology, as in the Letter to the Romans, Christ is the new Adam. As death came from one man, so has new life come from one man. In paintings and sculptures of the crucifixion, Adam is often symbolized by a skull at the foot of the cross, furthering the suggestion in this passage.

(13) Over Jesus' head the charge against him is posted for all passersby to read. Matthew and Luke tell us the sign read, "This is Jesus, the King of the Jews." Mark gives us a shorter version, "The King of the Jews."

    Most crucifixes display an abbreviation of the inscription described in the Gospel of John: "Jesus of Nazareth, the King of the Jews." In Latin, which was the language of the Church for centuries, that is "Jesus Nazarenus Rex Judaeorum." Since in Latin inscriptions, the letter I is used for the letter J, the initial letters of the inscription from John are INRI. Once the artistic tradition

was set, many believers came to learn about the faith from seeing visual renderings of scenes that otherwise would have been incomprehensible for many.

    Here the taunting continues, not only from those passing by but from the two crucified with him. Your proclamation through these scenes should be grave, reflecting the sadness of the story you are telling.

    (14) Jesus' cry from the cross is not in English or the Evangelist's ordinary Greek; it is a transliteration of Aramaic, the spoken language of Jesus and his followers. While proclaiming the exclamation accurately is

(14) The Passion of Matthew nears its end as Jesus speaks his final words, the words of the beginning of Psalm 22. Eli, Eli, lema sabachthani = ay-LEE, ay-LEE, luh-MAH sah-bahk-TAH-nee

Elijah = ee-LĪ-juh

And about three o'clock Jesus **cried out** in a loud voice,
 "Eli, Eli, lema sabachthani?"
 which means, "My **God**, my **God**, why have you **forsaken** me?"
Some of the bystanders who heard it said,
 "This one is calling for **Elijah**."
Immediately one of them ran to get a **sponge**;
 he soaked it in **wine**, and putting it on a **reed**,
 gave it to him to **drink**.
But the rest said,
 "**Wait**, let us see if **Elijah** comes to **save** him."
But Jesus cried out **again** in a loud voice,
 and gave up his **spirit**.

[Here all kneel and pause for a short time.]

These details of the earthquake and the dead being raised confirm the cosmic gravity of his death.

And **behold**, the veil of the **sanctuary**
 was **torn** in two from top to **bottom**.
The earth quaked, **rocks** were split, **tombs** were opened,
 and the **bodies** of many saints who had fallen asleep
 were **raised**.
And coming forth from their **tombs** after his **resurrection**,
 they entered the holy **city** and appeared to **many**.

This proclamation from the centurion is a confession of faith from one of Jesus' opponents at the time of death. The narrative changes its tone after the centurion's words. Pause slightly to catch your breath and to mark the shift.

As in all the Gospels, the women are faithful to the end. Their devoted presence marks the beginning and end of this section, with Joseph of Arimathea's care for the body of Jesus in the middle.

The **centurion** and the men with him who were
 keeping **watch** over Jesus
feared **greatly** when they saw the earthquake
and all that was happening, and they said,
"Truly, **this** was the Son of **God**!"

Magdalene = MAG-duh-lun

(15) There were many **women** there, looking on from a **distance**,
 who had **followed** Jesus from **Galilee**, ministering to him.
Among them were Mary **Magdalene** and Mary
 the mother of **James** and **Joseph**,
 and the mother of the sons of **Zebedee**.

important, far more important is that you proclaim it with confidence and without stumbling. A confidently mispronounced foreign word is far less distracting than a nervous, stumbling, but technically accurate rendition of the word.

Matthew gives us the time when the darkness came over the land and the time when Jesus cried out. This is the source of the tradition that Jesus suffered for three hours, noon until three o'clock. At three, Jesus breathed his last. (Here we acknowledge that last breath by kneeling in silence for a time.)

As proclaimer, you are the one to discern the length of this important period of silence: long enough to deepen into prayer, not so long that people's focus begins to wander. It might be worthwhile to consult with others about the appropriate length of time.

In Matthew, the death of Jesus is accompanied by cosmological occurrences that do not appear in Mark. The earth quakes, rocks split, tombs open and the dead are raised, as Christ's death opens up a way that had not been open before. The dead enter into the holy city, referring to the

designation of heaven as the new and eternal Jerusalem.

(15) Although the disciples were not faithful to the very end, there were those who were. The Gospel points out the women, present and watching from a distance. The first named of these is Mary Magdalene.

There is also Joseph of Arimathea, who, according to the Evangelist, asked Pilate for the body of Jesus. He wrapped the body in clean linen and put it in his own new tomb. (There is a tradition that this cloth was a baptismal cloth. Matthew uses the Greek word *sindon* for this cloth, and

Arimathea = air-ih-muh-THEE-uh

Pharisees = FAIR-uh-seez

These final details about the security of the tomb reflect the concern of the Evangelist; in the liturgy they anticipate Easter's narrative of the empty tomb.

When it was **evening**,
  there came a **rich** man from **Arimathea** named **Joseph**,
  who was himself a **disciple** of Jesus.
He went to **Pilate** and asked for the **body** of **Jesus**;
  then Pilate ordered it to be handed over.
Taking the body, Joseph **wrapped** it in clean **linen**
  and laid it in his new **tomb** that he had hewn in the **rock**.
Then he rolled a huge **stone** across the entrance to the tomb
    and **departed**.
But Mary **Magdalene** and the other **Mary**
  remained sitting there, **facing** the tomb.

(16) The next day, the one following the day of **preparation**,
  the chief priests and the Pharisees
  gathered before Pilate and said,
  "Sir, we remember that this **impostor** while still **alive** said,
  'After **three days** I will be **raised** up.'
Give orders, then, that the grave be **secured** until the third day,
  lest his **disciples** come and **steal** him and say to the people,
  'He has been **raised** from the **dead**.'
This **last** imposture would be worse than the **first**."
Pilate said to them,
  "The guard is **yours**;
  go, secure it as best you **can**."
So they went and **secured** the tomb
  by fixing a **seal** to the stone and setting the **guard**.

[Shorter: Matthew 27:11–54]

this is the only place he uses it. That is the same Greek word that Mark used for the cloth left behind by the young man who runs off naked at the end of chapter 14.) As ever, the link between the body of Jesus and the assembly of the Church is to be emphasized in your reading whenever possible.

(16) This last section reveals that sometime between the writing of the Gospel of Mark and the writing of Matthew, there emerged a rumor that the disciples had stolen the body of Jesus to strengthen their claim that he had been raised. So Matthew's Gospel includes an episode that makes clear that the tomb was sealed and guarded. The Gospel ends with two sets of sentries, insiders and outsiders: Mary Magdalene and the other Mary who sit facing the tomb, and a guard of Roman soldiers. By comparison one can see that the Christian message has spread more widely between the writing of Mark and Matthew, for in Matthew, the sense of opposition to the Gospel and to the followers of Jesus is significant.

At this point, at the end of the Gospel proclamation on Passion Sunday, there are six and a half days until the Easter Vigil, when the Gospel proclamation will conclude the narrative of Matthew that was begun here on Passion Sunday.

The sealing and securing of the tomb is a fitting scene on which to end the proclamation, for the reading comes to a close as the tomb itself is closed.

HOLY THURSDAY: MASS OF THE LORD'S SUPPER

Lectionary #39

READING I   Exodus 12:1–8, 11–14

A reading from the Book of Exodus

The LORD said to **Moses** and **Aaron** in the land of **Egypt**,
"**This** month shall stand at the **head** of your **calendar**;
     you shall reckon it the **first** month of the year.
Tell the whole community of **Israel**:
     On the **tenth** of this month every one of your families
          must procure for itself a **lamb**, one **apiece** for each **household**.
If a family is too **small** for a **whole** lamb,
     it shall join the nearest **household** in procuring one
     and shall **share** in the lamb
          in proportion to the number of **persons** who **partake** of it.

"The lamb must be a **year-old male** and without **blemish**.
You may **take** it from either the **sheep** or the **goats**.
You shall **keep** it until the **fourteenth** day of this month,
     and **then**, with the whole assembly of **Israel** present,
          it shall be **slaughtered** during the evening **twilight**.
They shall take some of its **blood**
          and apply it to the two **doorposts** and the **lintel**
     of every house in which they **partake** of the lamb.
That same night they shall **eat** its roasted **flesh**
     with unleavened **bread** and bitter **herbs**.

Your tone and delivery at the start can reflect what the reading is, a prescription for how to celebrate the annual Passover remembrance.
Aaron = AIR-un
Israel = IZ-ree-ul

The literary content has the appearance of a historical account of what *was* done at the event of the slaughtering of the lamb when the nation was in flight, but the instructions themselves are more likely describing what *is to be* done in the Jewish ritual at which the remembrance of the past is unifying.

READING I   In the earliest centuries of Christian worship, this reading was the primary reading from the Old Testament at the Easter Vigil in most communities. The Gospel at the Easter Vigil in the earliest days was the story of the death of Jesus, the Passion narrative, rather than the Resurrection narrative that came to find its place at the Vigil in the late fourth and early fifth centuries. The Old Testament reading that accompanied the Passion was the Passover lamb, since Christian theology was coming to associate Christ with the metaphor of the lamb, as we still proclaim him: "Lamb of God, who takes away the sin of the world."

In those earliest centuries there was no Easter Three Days from Holy Thursday to Easter Sunday; there was only the Easter Vigil. Once the Three Days emerged, the Gospel for the Easter Vigil became the Resurrection, for Good Friday the Passion, and for Holy Thursday the Last Supper. As the arrangement of the Gospels shifted, so did the Old Testament readings. The crossing of the Red Sea was matched to the Resurrection, the suffering-servant prophecy of Isaiah matched to the Passion, and eventually the Passover lamb matched to the Mass of the Lord's Supper. This tradition has been in place for a millennium and a half, and you will continue the tradition by proclaiming this reading from Exodus on Holy Thursday evening.

"**This** is how you are to **eat** it:
with your **loins** girt, **sandals** on your **feet** and your **staff**
in **hand**,
you shall eat like those who are in **flight**.
It is the **Passover** of the LORD.

"For on this **same** night I will go through **Egypt**,
striking **down** every **firstborn** of the land, both **man** and **beast**,
and executing **judgment** on all the gods of Egypt—**I**, the LORD!

"But the **blood** will mark the **houses** where **you** are.
Seeing the **blood**, I will **pass over** you;
thus, when I strike the land of **Egypt**,
no destructive blow will come upon **you**.

"**This** day shall be a memorial **feast** for you,
which all your **generations** shall **celebrate**
with **pilgrimage** to the LORD, as a perpetual **institution**."

The final verse holds up the commemoration as the significant Jewish memorial feast that it has been for millennia.

READING II   1 Corinthians 11:23–26

A reading from the first Letter of Saint Paul to the Corinthians

Brothers and sisters:
I **received** from the Lord what I also **handed on** to you,
that the Lord **Jesus**, on the **night** he was handed **over**,
took **bread**, and, after he had given **thanks**,
broke it and said, "**This** is my **body** that is for **you**.
Do this in **remembrance** of me."

In the **same** way also the **cup**, after **supper**, saying,
"This **cup** is the new **covenant** in my **blood**.

Be measured and clear with the identifying "A reading from the first Letter of Saint Paul to the Corinthians."

This reading tells the Lord's Supper narrative for the feast, since the Gospel reading is the footwashing from the Gospel of John.

The reading is long, and it will not be easy to sustain the attention of the assembly throughout the whole of the law's prescription for how the Passover lamb is to be chosen, slaughtered, and prepared for the meal. Therefore, emphasize those parts of the readings that are most important for the Holy Thursday rite; these would be the prescription for sharing the meal—"If a family is too small for a whole lamb, it shall join the nearest household"—since the Eucharist is similarly a meal to be shared. Also to be

emphasized is the clear statement that "It is the Passover of the Lord." Finally, take your time in completing the reading, for the final verse, from "This day shall be a memorial feast for you" to "a perpetual institution," is significant for what it gives to the theology of the annual Christian observance.

READING II Many Christians think of the Last Supper narratives of the four Gospels as the oldest recorded evidence of the Eucharist, but the passage here from the First Letter to the Corinthians is

older than those. The earliest Gospel narrative (Mark) was written around AD 70, but the first letter Paul wrote to Corinth is more than fifteen years earlier. You can see that the Last Supper account he records is even older than that, for he begins this section by revealing that "I received from the Lord what I also handed on to you." These two bits of information, that Paul wrote in AD 53 or 54, and that this had been handed down to him, make clear that this account of the Last Supper is one of the very earliest narratives in the whole New Testament.

Pause briefly before proclaiming the last line about proclaiming the death of Christ.

Do this, as often as you **drink** it, in **remembrance** of me."
For as often as you **eat** this **bread** and **drink** the **cup**,
      you **proclaim** the **death** of the Lord until he **comes**.

GOSPEL   John 13:1–15

A reading from the holy Gospel according to John

This reading not only narrates a unique moment in the ministry of Jesus, it has an exchange between Peter and Jesus that is very important for the meaning of the action.

Judas = JOO-dus
Iscariot = is-KAIR-ee-ut

Before the feast of **Passover**, Jesus **knew** that his hour had **come**
      to pass from **this** world to the **Father**.
He **loved** his own in the world and he **loved** them to the **end**.

The **devil** had already induced **Judas**, son of Simon the **Iscariot**,
            to hand him **over**.
So, during **supper**,
      fully aware that the Father had put everything into his **power**
      and that he had come **from** God and was returning **to** God,
      he **rose** from supper and took off his outer **garments**.
He took a **towel** and tied it around his **waist**.
Then he poured **water** into a **basin**
      and began to **wash** the disciples' **feet**
      and **dry** them with the **towel** around his **waist**.

Take the time to appreciate each of their positions and what the exchange itself leads to, both in the historical time when the Gospel was written and for churches proclaiming and ritualizing the action in our day.

He came to Simon **Peter**, who said to him,
      "**Master**, are you going to wash **my** feet?"
Jesus answered and said to him,
      "What I am **doing**, you do not understand **now**,
      but you **will** understand **later**."
Peter said to him, "You will **never** wash my **feet**."
Jesus answered him,
      "Unless I **wash** you, you will have no **inheritance** with me."

      Because tonight's is the "Mass of the Lord's Supper" and the Gospel passage is the footwashing, your proclamation of the Last Supper from First Corinthians is very important. Because the passage is relatively short, you can take your time and assure a clear and powerful reading for those assembled. Pause after the opening address, "Beloved," as well as before and after each of the quotations, "This is my body. . . ." and "This cup is. . . ."

      Finally, note that the final verse of the reading is also used as one of the memorial acclamations of the Eucharistic Prayers. Proclaim it slowly and deliberately so that it can be recognized as it is proclaimed from its source in First Corinthians.

GOSPEL   The awkward intimacy of bending down to wash another's feet is outdone only by the awkward intimacy of allowing another member of the community to bend down to wash

one's own feet. Feet are not beautiful, and it is a gesture of humility both to bathe them and have them bathed. Your proclamation of the narrative in which Jesus performed this action for his followers will lend a context with which those participating in the rite can anticipate this unique annual tradition.

      The opening part sets up the context. Beginning at the point where Jesus pours water into a basin, proclaim more emphatically, so that the members of your church

A new section teaching about service begins here.

Simon Peter said to him,
      "**Master**, then not **only** my feet, but my **hands**
            and **head** as well."
Jesus said to him,
      "Whoever has **bathed** has no need
            except to have his **feet** washed,
      for he is clean all **over**;
            so **you** are clean, but not **all**."
For he knew who would **betray** him;
      for this reason, he said, "Not **all** of you are clean."

So when he had washed their **feet**
      and put his **garments** back on and reclined at **table** again,
      he said to them, "Do you **realize** what I have **done** for you?
You call me '**teacher**' and '**master**,' and rightly so, for indeed I **am**.
If **I**, therefore, the **master** and **teacher**, have washed **your** feet,
      you ought to wash one **another's** feet.
I have given you a **model** to follow,
      so that as **I** have done for **you**, **you** should **also** do."

will understand the ancient roots of the ritual that will be carried out in their midst.

The dialogue between Jesus and Peter is important for its bearing on the ritual act and its theological significance, so be careful to distinguish the narrative set-up ("Jesus answered," "Peter said to him," and so on) from the direct discourse. Those who participate in the Holy Thursday liturgy are usually dedicated parishioners, so don't be overly concerned about time. Your clear, accessible Gospel proclamation will reward their dedication.

GOOD FRIDAY: CELEBRATION OF THE LORD'S PASSION

Lectionary #40

READING I   Isaiah 52:13—53:12

A reading from the Book of the Prophet Isaiah

The reading begins with an imperative: See! It is a command to attend to this.

See, my **servant** shall **prosper**,
   he shall be raised **high** and greatly **exalted**.
Even as many were **amazed** at him—
   so **marred** was his **look** beyond human **semblance**
   and his **appearance** beyond that of the sons of **man**—
so shall he **startle** many **nations**,
   because of him **kings** shall stand **speechless**;
for those who have **not** been told shall **see**,
   those who have **not** heard shall **ponder** it.

These next few sections take up the humiliations and rejections of the Lord's servant. Without being maudlin, you want to carry in your voice the gravity and significance of the suffering of the Lord's servant, as described in detail by the prophet.

Who would **believe** what we have **heard**?
   To whom has the **arm** of the LORD been **revealed**?
He grew up like a **sapling** before him,
   like a **shoot** from the parched **earth**;
there was in him no **stately** bearing to make us **look** at him,
   nor **appearance** that would **attract** us to him.
He was **spurned** and **avoided** by people,
   a man of **suffering**, accustomed to **infirmity**,
one of those from whom people **hide** their **faces**,
   spurned, and we held him in no **esteem**.

Pause after the question and before the metaphor of the "sapling" to mark the literary change.

Yet it was our **infirmities** that he **bore**,
   our **sufferings** that he **endured**,
while we thought of him as **stricken**,
   as one **smitten** by God and **afflicted**.

These next two sections have been part of the Liturgy of the Word for Good Friday for centuries, and they have widely and deeply shaped our understanding of the life of Christ.

READING I   This reading as a whole is long and very rich with arresting images. These many beautiful, poignant images will capture the meditative attention of some members of the assembly here and there, so, though your reading should be clear from beginning to end, you might be aware of the most moving parts of the reading so that you can recapture their attention with the tone of your voice.

For this Good Friday, the most touching element of the proclamation is this: "He was spurned and avoided by people, / a man of suffering, accustomed to infirmity, / one of those from whom people hide their faces / spurned, and we held him in no esteem." Those in your community to whom this might offer the greatest consolation might not be the front-pew participants; those who are most vulnerable are often those who are least noticed. Address them as you proclaim these words, for they, who may seem to be held "in no esteem," are close to the Lord.

The final section tells of the servant's vindication. As you prepare for the Good Friday proclamation, try to commit a part of this section to memory, so that you might make eye contact with the assembly at this point. Those whose lives have been marked by anguish and infirmity between the last Three Days and this might feel a closer bond with the Lord's servant whose sufferings are proclaimed from your lips.

The metaphor of the lamb is central to Christian theology and to the Eucharist, with its "Lamb of God, who takes away the sin of the world."

But he was **pierced** for our **offenses**,
    crushed for our **sins**;
upon **him** was the chastisement that makes us **whole**,
    by **his** stripes we were **healed**.

We had all gone astray like **sheep**,
    each following his own way;
but the LORD laid upon **him**
    the guilt of us **all**.

Though he was harshly **treated**, he submitted
    and opened not his **mouth**;
like a **lamb** led to the **slaughter**
    or a **sheep** before the **shearers**,
    he was **silent** and opened not his **mouth**.

Oppressed and **condemned**, he was taken **away**,
    and who would have thought any **more** of his **destiny**?
When he was cut **off** from the land of the **living**,
    and **smitten** for the **sin** of his **people**,
a **grave** was assigned him among the **wicked**
    and a burial place with **evildoers**,
though he had done no **wrong**
    nor spoken any **falsehood**.
But the LORD was pleased
    to crush him in **infirmity**.

If he gives his **life** as an offering for **sin**,
    he shall see his **descendants** in a long **life**,
    and the will of the LORD shall be **accomplished** through **him**.

Because of his **affliction**
    he shall see the **light**
    in **fullness** of days;

Here begins the light after darkness.

Because the reading is long, take advantage of the breaks that the Lectionary pages supply. These breaks are placed where a break in your proclamation is fitting. When the breaks fall at places that you consider significant in the passage, use them as opportunities to make eye contact with the people for whom you are the minister of the word in this very important liturgy of the Lord's Passion.

READING II The theology of the Letter to the Hebrews is hard work to understand; the letter is not as accessible as other books of the New Testament. Your task, as proclaimer of God's word on this Good Friday, is to make the letter's portrait of Jesus, the Son of God, ring in the hearts and minds and souls of your assembly. It is a beautiful theology of what Jesus accomplished for humanity by his suffering.

This reading is an integral part of the theology of the Three Days and of Good Friday in particular because the suffering in our own lives is not separate from the suffering of the Son, who sympathizes. As you prepare for this proclamation, think of your own life and the lives of some of those you know in your church, and consider the ways the suffering of the people of God contributes to making the world a better place. We do not seek out suffering, but we accept

through his **suffering**, my servant shall justify **many**,
   and their **guilt** he shall **bear**.

Therefore **I** will give him his **portion** among the **great**,
   and **he** shall divide the **spoils** with the **mighty**,
because he **surrendered** himself to **death**
   and was **counted** among the **wicked**;
and he shall take **away** the sins of **many**,
   and win **pardon** for their **offenses**.

READING II   Hebrews 4:14–16; 5:7–9

A reading from the Letter to the Hebrews

Brothers and sisters:
Since we have a great **high priest** who has passed
   through the **heavens**,
   Jesus, the Son of **God**,
   let us hold **fast** to our **confession**.
For we do **not** have a high priest
   who is unable to **sympathize** with our **weaknesses**,
   but one who has **similarly** been tested in **every** way,
   yet without **sin**.
So let us **confidently** approach the throne of **grace**
   to receive **mercy** and to find **grace** for timely **help**.

In the days when **Christ** was in the **flesh**,
   he offered **prayers** and **supplications** with loud **cries** and **tears**
   to the one who was able to **save** him from **death**,
   and he was **heard** because of his **reverence**.

The theology of this reading is deep, and the Letter to the Hebrews is not an easy book. See the commentary for helpful information.

Like us, Jesus learned from his suffering. Like him, we do not seek out suffering, but endurance when it comes will help us "find grace for timely help."

---

the inevitability of suffering, and, like the Son, we offer up our prayers and supplications as in our suffering we participate in the Paschal Mystery.

PASSION   Scripture scholars tell us that the Gospel of John was written near the end of the first century, more than a half-century after the events that are told in this Passion. Few, if any, of those in the community from which the Gospel of John emerged would have been eyewitnesses to those events. They knew Jesus from their life of faith in the community. That is the same as our experience: Having been incorporated into the Church by Baptism, whether as infants or as adults, and having experienced the life of faith in our community, we participate in the liturgy because there we meet the risen Christ. Even in solemn liturgical moments like the proclamation of two long Passion readings in one week—Matthew on Passion Sunday and John on Good Friday—we come back because we know the story and we are part of that story, for we are indeed the body of Christ. The story of Christ is our story;

Son though he **was**, he learned **obedience** from what he **suffered**;
and when he was made **perfect**,
he became the source of eternal **salvation** for **all** who
obey him.

PASSION   John 18:1—19:42

The Passion of our Lord Jesus Christ according to John

(1) **Jesus** went out with his **disciples** across the Kidron **valley**
to where there was a **garden**,
into which he and his disciples **entered**.
Judas his **betrayer** also knew the place,
because Jesus had often met there with his disciples.
So **Judas** got a band of **soldiers** and **guards**
from the chief **priests** and the **Pharisees**
and went there with **lanterns**, **torches**, and **weapons**.

Jesus, knowing **everything** that was going to **happen** to him,
went out and said to them, "Whom are you **looking** for?"
They answered him, "Jesus the **Nazorean**."
He said to them, "**I AM**."
Judas his betrayer was also with them.
When he said to them, "**I AM**,"
they turned **away** and fell to the **ground**.
So he **again** asked them,
"Whom are you **looking** for?"
They said, "Jesus the **Nazorean**."
Jesus answered,
"I told you that **I AM**.

(1) Ease into the Passion narrative. The narrative itself carries intensity; the proclaimer doesn't need to add any.
Kidron = KID-run
Judas = JOO-dus

Pharisees = FAIR-uh-seez

Throughout the proclamation, take advantage of these breaks even more than in a typical Sunday Gospel proclamation. Here they will be helpful to you to maintain your voice and to the assembly that listens to it.

The Passion has a number of typically Johannine "I AM" sayings, and here are three.

Notice the irony, that those who seek to arrest him fall to the ground in worship.

Nazorean = naz-oh-REE-un

it became your story at Baptism, and it becomes our story again and again with each Holy Week.

Below are five general *theological* characteristics of the Passion in the Gospel of John that make its portrait of Christ unique; appreciating these as background for your proclamation will help you with your ministry of proclaiming this account to the Church assembled on Good Friday.

CHRISTOLOGY. The portrait of Jesus in the Gospel of John is moving, striking, and beautiful. In the last of the canonical Gospels to be written, Jesus is depicted with details that reveal his divinity beyond doubt. One of many examples of this high Christology of the Gospel of John is the indication of Jesus' knowledge of all things. At the start of the Passion, the Evangelist describes Jesus as "knowing everthing that was going to happen to him," an incredible claim about a human being, and then, nearer the end of the Passion, that Jesus was "aware that everything was now finished." By faith, two millennia later, we have no qualms about such a theology of omniscience, but for the early Church this was taking the divinity of Jesus to a level that had not been claimed by the Synoptics, Mark, Matthew, and Luke. Be aware of this high Christology as you prepare for the proclamation of the Johannine Passion.

So if you are looking for **me**, let **these** men go."
This was to **fulfill** what he had said,
　"I have not lost **any** of those you **gave** me."

(2) Only this Gospel adds the detail of the
high priest's slave whose ear Peter cuts off.

Malchus = MAL-kus

(2) Then Simon **Peter**, who had a **sword**, drew it,
　struck the high priest's **slave**, and cut off his right **ear**.
The slave's **name** was **Malchus**.
Jesus said to Peter,
　"Put your **sword** into its **scabbard**.
Shall I not drink the **cup** that the Father **gave** me?"

So the band of **soldiers**, the **tribune**, and the Jewish **guards**
　　seized Jesus,
　bound him, and brought him to **Annas** first.
He was the father-in-law of **Caiaphas**,
　who was high priest that year.
It was **Caiaphas** who had counseled the Jews
　that it was better that **one** man should die
　　rather than the **people**.

Caiaphas = KĪ-uh-fus

(3) This unnamed disciple is the one
sometimes called the "beloved disciple"
because of the anonymity. He did
not appear in the Gospel until well into
the second half, but he plays a major
role in the Passion, death, empty tomb,
and appearance accounts in this
Fourth Gospel.

(3) Simon Peter and **another** disciple **followed** Jesus.
Now the **other** disciple was **known** to the high **priest**,
　and he entered the **courtyard** of the high priest with **Jesus**.
But **Peter** stood at the gate **outside**.
So the **other** disciple, the **acquaintance** of the high priest,
　went out and spoke to the **gatekeeper** and brought Peter **in**.
Then the **maid** who was the gatekeeper said to **Peter**,
　"You are not one of this man's disciples, **are** you?"
He said, "I am **not**."
Now the slaves and the guards were standing
　　around a charcoal **fire**
　that they had made, because it was **cold**,
　and were **warming** themselves.
Peter was **also** standing there keeping warm.

Peter's "I am not" is the reverse of the
statement of Jesus, "I AM," that prompted
the soldiers and guards to fall to the
ground. Each is a short statement, but their
effect in the story is very different.

I AM STATEMENTS. In a number of places, John has Jesus use simple statements that reveal theologically deep ideas and experiences. Many of these are the most well-known things Jesus ever said, and they start with the simple first-person statement, "I AM."

You will readily recognize sayings unique to John's portrait of Jesus, such as, "I AM the bread of life," "I AM the light of the world," "I AM the gate for the sheep," "I AM the good shepherd," "I AM the resurrection and the life," "I AM the way, the truth, and the life," and "I AM the vine, you are the branches." In the Passion narrative, you will find that this construction, "I AM," is revelatory even in his arrest. The soldiers approach Jesus, and he asks them, "Whom are you looking for?" They answered him, "Jesus the Nazarene." He said to them, "I AM." Then, "When he said to them, 'I AM,'" they turned away and fell to the ground. So he again asked them, 'Whom are you looking for?' And they said, 'Jesus the Nazarene.' Jesus answered, 'I told you that I AM.'" So, as you prepare for proclaiming this Passion, find a way of subtly emphasizing this unique theological element of John.

PETER. The role of Peter in the Passion generally is contrasted with the role of the "beloved disciple" in this Gospel, who appears at the table, the cross, and the empty

(4) This questioning by the high priest is an interruption in the story of Peter's threefold denial of Jesus. Pause after the questioning so that assembly recognizes the shift when the narrative turns back to Simon Peter.
synagogue = SIN-uh-gog

(4) The high priest **questioned** Jesus
    about his **disciples** and about his **doctrine**.
Jesus answered him,
    "I have spoken **publicly** to the world.
I have always taught in a **synagogue**
    or in the **temple** area where all the Jews **gather**,
    and in **secret** I have said **nothing**. Why ask **me**?
Ask those who **heard** me what I said to them.
They know what I said."

When he had said this,
    one of the temple guards standing there **struck** Jesus and said,
    "Is this the way you answer the high **priest**?"
Jesus answered him,
    "If I have spoken **wrongly**, **testify** to the wrong;
    but if I have spoken **rightly**, why do you **strike** me?"
Then **Annas** sent him bound to **Caiaphas** the high priest.

Now Simon **Peter** was standing there keeping warm.
And they said to him,
    "You are not one of his disciples, **are** you?"
He denied it and said,
    "I am **not**."
One of the **slaves** of the high priest,
    a **relative** of the one whose **ear** Peter had cut **off**, said,
    "Didn't I see you in the **garden** with him?"
Again Peter denied it.
And **immediately** the **cock crowed**.

The cock crowing is a consequential detail; read this clearly and allow a pause for its gravity to be felt.
praetorium = prih-TOR-ee-um

(5) Then they brought Jesus from **Caiaphas** to the **praetorium**.
It was **morning**.
And they **themselves** did not enter the **praetorium**,
    in order not to be **defiled** so that they could eat the **Passover**.

tomb. Since this disciple is not named, proclaim this character as one in whom members of the Church might find their own faith experience, both as believers who find difficulties in their first-hand experience and as believers whose faith brings them to new realizations that deepen their lives and give them meaning.

MARY. Although many believers turn to the Gospel of Luke for a Marian theology, it is in John that Mary appears at the foot of the cross. Most depictions of the crucifixion throughout Christian history, in fact, have been drawn from the Gospel of John, and we know this because of the presence of the "beloved disciple." In the other Gospels, there are no male followers at the cross. The scene with Mary and the beloved disciple is very brief, yet its theology and meaning are very significant for the tradition, so proclaim the scene with care. As he anticipates his own death, Jesus commends his mother to the care of the beloved disciple, and vice versa. For those in the church today who care for aging relatives, the tender crucifixion scene with Mary is very important; proclaim it well.

WORSHIP IN JOHN'S GOSPEL. An important yet enigmatic detail of the Passion according to John is the description of the piercing of Jesus' side with a spear, and from his side flowed "blood and water."

So **Pilate** came out to them and said,
   "What **charge** do you bring against this man?"
They answered and said to him,
   "If he were not a **criminal**,
   we would **not** have handed him over to you."
At **this**, Pilate said to them,
   "Take him **yourselves**, and judge him according to **your** law."
The Jews answered him,
   "We do not have the **right** to execute **anyone**, "
   in order that the word of Jesus might be **fulfilled**
   that he said indicating the kind of **death** he would die.

So **Pilate** went back into the **praetorium**
   and summoned **Jesus** and said to him,
   "Are **you** the King of the **Jews**?"
Jesus answered,
   "Do you say this on your **own**
   or have **others** told you **about** me?"
Pilate answered,
   "**I** am not a Jew, **am** I?
Your own **nation** and the chief **priests** handed you over to me.
What have you **done**?"
Jesus answered,
   "My **kingdom** does not belong to **this** world.
If my kingdom **did** belong to this world,
   my **attendants** would be **fighting**
   to keep me from being handed **over** to the **Jews**.
But as it **is**, my **kingdom** is not **here**."
So Pilate said to him,
   "Then you **are** a king?"
Jesus answered,
   "You **say** I am a king.

(5) As before, we find more irony in this Passion, with Jesus, the innocent man accused of a crime, in conversation with Pilate, the governor, about the meaning of "kingdom" and "truth."

There have been many debates about the ritual life of the community from which this Gospel emerged, but regardless of its witness for the late first and early second centuries, this detail should be highlighted in your proclamation.

   The evening before the proclamation of the Passion of John, the Church celebrates the Mass of the Lord's Supper, at which the blood of Christ is central. The evening after the proclamation of the Passion of John is the Easter Vigil, with its initiation with water. Therefore, as you prepare for proclaiming the Gospel of John on Good Friday, be pointed in highlighting this detail of the "blood and water" flowing from the side of Jesus because of its place between the *blood* and the *water* of Holy Thursday and the Easter Vigil.

(1) As a proclaimer of the Gospel, you probably know already that John has some of the longest Gospel stories. The Passion narrative is a carefully constructed account, built to make significant theological points. Here in this first section, you see the Evangelist's emphasis on Jesus' I AM statements. This high Christology needs to be proclaimed clearly because it sums up the Gospel to this point. It also resonates in the

For **this** I was born and for **this** I came into the world,
    to testify to the **truth**.
Everyone who **belongs** to the truth **listens** to my voice."
Pilate said to him, "What is **truth**?"

(6) When he had said this,
    he **again** went out to the **Jews** and said to them,
    "I find no **guilt** in him.
But you have a **custom** that I release one **prisoner**
      to you at **Passover**.
Do you want me to release to you the King of the **Jews**?"
They cried out again,
    "Not **this** one but **Barabbas**!"
Now **Barabbas** was a **revolutionary**.

(7) Then Pilate took Jesus and had him **scourged**.
And the **soldiers** wove a **crown** out of **thorns**
      and placed it on his **head**,
    and **clothed** him in a purple **cloak**,
    and they came to him and said,
    "**Hail**, King of the **Jews**!"
And they **struck** him repeatedly.

Once **more** Pilate went out and said to them,
    "**Look**, I am bringing him **out** to you,
    so that you may **know** that I find no **guilt** in him."
So Jesus came **out**,
    wearing the crown of **thorns** and the purple **cloak**.
And he said to them, "**Behold**, the man!"

When the chief **priests** and the **guards** saw him they cried out,
    "**Crucify** him, **crucify** him!"
Pilate said to them,
    "Take him **yourselves** and crucify him.

Barabbas = buh-RAB-us

The Gospel of John gives more detail about what Jesus wore during the Passion and about the garments found in the empty tomb.

The Latin of this statement of Pilate, "Behold the man!" *Ecce homo,* has been used as the title for many paintings of the Passion.

Church through the Easter mysteries and the Fifty Days, when the Gospel of John is proclaimed frequently. Throughout the Fifty Days the risen Savior will be manifest to the Church as the face of God in the worshiping assembly, and this opening scene of the Passion of John for Good Friday brings this up close.

(2) Take your time here in order to appreciate the symbol of the *cup,* a sign of the suffering that Jesus will undergo. His followers want to spare him the suffering to come, yet his question shows that he sees the will of God in what lies ahead.

Good Friday is the only day of the liturgical year when the Church does not celebrate the Eucharistic sacrifice of the Mass, but only a communion service. The Church, following an ancient custom, fasts from the Eucharist until the Easter Vigil. This question of Jesus about the cup appears at the right time, for this is an apt day for a Eucharistic reminder of the inevitability of suffering and the uniqueness of Good Friday in the Church's year.

(3) The Gospel of John is the only Gospel in which Peter's threefold denial of Christ is rehabilitated later with a threefold profession of love. The denial is not far different in the other three Gospel accounts, but John's Gospel allows Peter to make amends. Take your time in describing the setting as you narrate this scene, for the details—those who question, the fire, the cold weather—add immediacy. Again, it is not a drama, but it is meant to invite the participation of the assembly's imagination.

I find no **guilt** in him."
The Jews answered,
   "We have a **law**, and according to that law he ought to **die**,
   because he made himself the Son of **God**."

Now when **Pilate** heard this **statement**,
   he became even **more** afraid,
      and went back into the **praetorium** and said to Jesus,
   "**Where** are you **from**?"
Jesus did not answer him.

So Pilate said to him,
   "Do you not **speak** to me?
Do you not know that I have power to **release** you
   and I have power to **crucify** you?"
Jesus answered him,
   "You would have **no** power over me
   if it had not been **given** to you from **above**.
For this reason the one who handed me **over** to you
   has the **greater** sin."
Consequently, Pilate **tried** to release him; but the Jews cried **out**,
   "If you **release** him, you are **not** a Friend of **Caesar**.
Everyone who makes himself a king **opposes** Caesar."

When Pilate heard **these** words he brought Jesus out
      and **seated** him on the **judge's** bench
      in the place called **Stone Pavement**, in Hebrew, **Gabbatha**.
It was **preparation** day for **Passover**, and it was about **noon**.
And he said to the Jews,
   "**Behold**, your **king**!"
They cried out,
   "Take him **away**, take him **away**! **Crucify** him!"

Pilate and Jesus' discussion of weighty matters continues.

Gabbatha = GAB-uh-thuh

(4) One complexity of this Passion is the deceptiveness of appearances. This episode with the high priest and Jesus would almost be comical in its irony, if it were not leading to so tragic an end. Jesus, who has no power or authority, is cross-examining Annas, in whose hands his fate rests. The exchange between Jesus and the high priest is inserted into the story of Peter's denial, and so this ends with the crowing of the cock.

There are several authority figures in the Passion, so as you prepare for your proclamation, be clear for yourself about who's who, so that in your own mind you have Pilate, Annas, and Caiaphas clearly established. This will illuminate your proclamation and make the story more accessible to those who hear your proclamation.

(5) Again, the roles are reversed, and Jesus, the one under arrest, is interrogating the one with ultimate power, Pilate. Yet their exchange is on kingship, ending with the final enigmatic question from Pilate to Jesus, "What is truth?" That's not the kind of question you expect a powerful person to ask a person under arrest.

(6) There is some ambiguity here in the Hebrew name "Barabbas."

Think of the word Jesus used for the heavenly Father, "Abba," a term of endearment and intimacy addressed to one's father. The prefix "bar" means "son of," as we see in Scripture in names like Simon bar Jonah,

Pilate said to them,
   "Shall I crucify your **king**?"
The chief priests answered,
   "We **have** no king but **Caesar**."

Then he handed him **over** to them to be **crucified**.

(8) So they **took** Jesus, and, carrying the cross **himself**,
   he went out to what is called the Place of the **Skull**,
   in Hebrew, **Golgotha**.
There they **crucified** him, and with him two **others**,
   one on either **side**, with Jesus in the **middle**.

Pilate **also** had an **inscription** written and put on the cross.
It read,
   "**Jesus** the **Nazorean**, the **King** of the **Jews**."
Now many of the Jews **read** this inscription,
   because the place where Jesus was crucified was near the city;
   and it was written in **Hebrew**, **Latin**, and **Greek**.

So the chief priests of the Jews said to Pilate,
   "Do not write 'The **King** of the **Jews**,'
   but that he said, 'I am the King of the **Jews**'."
Pilate answered,
   "What I have **written**, I have **written**."

When the soldiers had **crucified** Jesus,
   they took his **clothes** and **divided** them into four **shares**,
   a share for each **soldier**.
They also took his tunic, but the tunic was **seamless**,
   woven in **one** piece from the top down.
So they said to one another,
   "Let's not **tear** it, but cast **lots** for it to see whose it will be,"

Golgotha = GOL-guh-thuh

The inscription on the cross—in three languages—emphasizes the universality of Jesus' salvation, achieved in his life and Passion.

meaning Simon, son of Jonah. "Barabbas," "bar" and "abba," means "son of the father." The Evangelist may have been deliberately ironic here. A criminal "son of the father," or a "criminal" Son of the Father?

(7) When Saint Jerome translated the New Testament into Latin, Pilate's announcement of Jesus coming out with the crown of thorns and red cloak, "Behold the man!" was rendered as *"Ecce homo!"* That noun *homo* means an individual man, so

"Behold the man" is an absolutely correct rendering. In this instance, it also carries a note of irony. The Roman governor pointing to this suffering innocent man thinks that he is only a man like any other. Pilate has no idea that he is showing the crowds the Son of Man.

(8) As mentioned above, the Gospel of John was likely the last of the Gospels in the New Testament to be written, and the

Good News had already spread significantly. Here, the inscription on the cross is stated to be in Hebrew, Latin, and Greek, revealing that the message has already grown by the end of the first century, when this is written. So, in our own time, the Gospel continues to spread in every language, carrying on what the Evangelist acknowledges here.

in order that the passage of **Scripture** might be **fulfilled**
 that says:
 *They divided my **garments** among them,*
 *and for my **vesture** they cast **lots**.*
This is what the soldiers did.

Standing by the **cross** of Jesus were his **mother**
 and his mother's sister, **Mary** the wife of **Clopas**,
 and Mary of **Magdala**.

When Jesus saw his **mother** and the **disciple** there whom he **loved**
 he said to his mother, "**Woman**, behold, your **son**."
Then he said to the **disciple**,
 "Behold, your **mother**."
And from that hour the disciple took her into his **home**.

After **this**, aware that **everything** was now **finished**,
 in order that the **Scripture** might be **fulfilled**,
 Jesus said, "I **thirst**."
There was a **vessel** filled with common **wine**.
So they put a **sponge** soaked in wine on a sprig of **hyssop**
 and put it up to his **mouth**.
When Jesus had **taken** the wine, he said,
 "It is **finished**."
And bowing his **head**, he handed over the **spirit**.

[Here all kneel and pause for a short time.]

Now since it was **preparation** day,
 in order that the **bodies** might not remain
 on the cross on the **sabbath**,
 for the sabbath day of **that** week was a **solemn** one,
 the Jews asked Pilate that their **legs** be **broken**
 and that they be taken **down**.

Since this is the only Gospel that mentions the mother of Jesus at the cross, proclaim well who is present at the cross. Also unique to this Gospel is the entrusting of Mary to the Beloved Disciple.

sabbath = SAB-uth

The chief priests complain to Pilate that he wrote "The King of the Jews" instead of "he said, 'I am the King of the Jews'," the difference between an objective description and a delusion. The acknowledgment of Pilate's authority over Jesus is captured in his reply to the chief priests: "What I have written, I have written." That is a significant moment in the Passion, poignant as we near Jesus' death. Take your time so that this scene is received well.

The scene with Jesus' mother and the beloved disciple is as significant as it is brief. The anonymity of the beloved disciple in the Gospel of John makes him a figure who might represent any believer in relation to the mother of God. So take your time in preparing and proclaiming this vignette at the end of the Johannine Passion.

So the **soldiers** came and broke the legs of the **first**
and then of the **other** one who was crucified with Jesus.
But when they came to **Jesus** and saw that he was already **dead**,
they did not break **his** legs,
but **one** soldier thrust his **lance** into his **side**,
and **immediately blood** and **water** flowed out.

An **eyewitness** has testified, and his testimony is **true**;
he **knows** that he is speaking the **truth**,
so that you **also** may come to **believe**.

For this **happened** so that the Scripture passage might be **fulfilled**:
*Not a **bone** of it will be **broken**.*
And again **another** passage says:
*They will **look** upon him whom they have **pierced**.*

Arimathea = air-ih-muh-THEE-uh

After **this**, Joseph of **Arimathea**,
secretly a **disciple** of Jesus for fear of the Jews,
asked **Pilate** if he could remove the **body** of Jesus.
And Pilate **permitted** it.
So he came and **took** his body.

The final details about the burial and the cloths in which the body is wrapped are important.
Nicodemus = nik-uh-DEE-mus

Nicodemus, the one who had **first** come to him at **night**,
also came bringing a mixture of **myrrh** and **aloes**
weighing about one hundred **pounds**.
They took the **body** of Jesus
and **bound** it with **burial** cloths along with the **spices**,
according to the Jewish **burial** custom.
Now in the place where he had been **crucified** there was a **garden**,
and in the garden a new **tomb**, in which no one
had yet been **buried**.
So they laid Jesus **there** because of the Jewish **preparation** day;
for the **tomb** was close **by**.

End solemnly as you narrate how Jesus' body was laid in the new tomb.

Lectionary #41

READING I   Genesis 1:1—2:2

Genesis = JEN-uh-sis

Take each day as a mini-reading with its own unique elements. Pause significantly after each day so that the new world you are proclaiming can flourish in the imaginations of those to whom you read.

Our cosmology is quite different from that of the author of this passage, but imagine the world just as it is described so that your words will themselves draw a picture of this world and a theology of God's loving care.

Significant pause after the second day. The text is portraying God's providence and generosity.

A reading from the Book of Genesis

In the **beginning**, when God created the **heavens** and the **earth**,
   the earth was a formless **wasteland**, and **darkness**
     covered the **abyss**,
   while a mighty **wind** swept over the **waters**.

Then God said,
   "Let there be **light**," and there **was** light.
God saw how **good** the light was.
God then **separated** the light from the **darkness**.
God called the light "**day**" and the darkness he called "**night**."
Thus **evening** came, and **morning** followed—the **first** day.

Then God said,
   "Let there be a **dome** in the middle of the waters,
   to separate **one** body of water from the **other**."
And so it **happened**:
   God made the dome,
   and it separated the water **above** the dome
     from the water **below** it.
God called the dome "the **sky**."
Evening came, and **morning** followed—the **second** day.

Then God said,
   "Let the water under the sky be **gathered** into a single **basin**,
   so that the **dry land** may appear."

READING I | In most communities, the Church's symbols have been used more generously in the years since Vatican II. One rich symbol that can always bear a little more emphasis is the Easter fire, a significant fire for a significant moment in the life of the community. This fire, lit and blessed outside the church building, signifies the destruction of what had gone before; it is a sign that the old world is passing away, that the rebirth of the Church is fierce and even a little frightening, that it is also exciting and refreshing.

The first reading of the Easter Vigil is the first Creation account of the Hebrew Scriptures, the narrative of God's creation of the world in six days. A significant fire at the start of the Vigil is a wonderful complement to the reading you will proclaim. The fire is a symbol of the old world destroyed and succeeded by a new Creation.

The reading before you is a patterned proclamation, with repeated elements that have been read in assemblies for centuries, for millennia even. You join the long stream of witnesses to God's providence, and your proclamation announces God's oversight and loving care of the world. Because of

And so it **happened**:
> the water **under** the sky was gathered into its **basin**,
> and the **dry land** appeared.

God called the **dry land** "the **earth**,"
> and the **basin** of the water he called "the **sea**."

God saw how **good** it was.

Then God said,
> "Let the earth bring forth **vegetation**:
> every kind of **plant** that bears **seed**
> and every kind of **fruit** tree on earth
> that bears **fruit** with its **seed** in it."

And so it **happened**:
> the earth brought forth **every** kind of plant that bears **seed**
> and **every** kind of fruit tree on **earth**
> that bears **fruit** with its **seed** in it.

God saw how **good** it was.

Evening came, and **morning** followed—the **third** day.

Then God said:
> "Let there be **lights** in the dome of the **sky**,
> to separate **day** from **night**.

Let them mark the fixed **times**, the **days** and the **years**,
> and serve as **luminaries** in the dome of the **sky**,
> to shed **light** upon the **earth**."

And so it **happened**:
> God made the two great **lights**,
> the **greater** one to govern the **day**,
> and the **lesser** one to govern the **night**;
> and he made the **stars**.

God set them in the dome of the sky,
> to shed light upon the earth,
> to govern the **day** and the **night**,
> and to separate the **light** from the **darkness**.

Significant pause after the third day. Have you seen some of the photographs of the earth from space? Call those to mind as you proclaim this text. Capture some of the wonder that comes with knowing how beautiful and bountiful this world God made is.

the length and the repetitious style of the text, you should make a significant pause between each day of creation. (As ever, the inclination with a long reading is to rush; but take your time. The assembly will be more engaged by a strong reading than by a quick reading.)

As you prepare this text, perhaps you can underline or highlight the similar elements in the *Workbook,* using a different color for each. This can help you with the patterned nature of your proclamation: "Then God said"; "God called"; "And so it happened"; "God saw that it was good"; "Evening came, and morning followed." The parts of the reading that are not part of the pattern contain poetic details about the world, so these can include your own appreciation of the created world. Proclaim the reading as if you are seeing the world anew, and share that newness with the gathered parishioners.

READING II This second reading of the Easter Vigil is not as long as the first, but it is still quite a long passage if compared to the the readings from other Sundays in the liturgical year. Because of the length of the reading, because it is one of many readings, and because tonight is the climax of the liturgical year, you will need your best proclamation skills to maintain the assembly's interest and engagement.

Significant pause after the fourth day.
There are sea monsters ahead—they'll
catch people's interest!

God saw how **good** it was.
Evening came, and **morning** followed—the **fourth** day.

Then God said,
"Let the water **teem** with an abundance of living **creatures**,
and on the earth let **birds** fly beneath the dome of the **sky**."
And so it **happened**:
God created the great **sea monsters**
and all **kinds** of swimming creatures with which
the water **teems**,
and all **kinds** of winged birds.
God saw how **good** it was, and God **blessed** them, saying,
"Be **fertile**, **multiply**, and **fill** the water of the **seas**;
and let the **birds** multiply on the **earth**."
Evening came, and **morning** followed—the **fifth** day.

Then God said,
"Let the earth bring forth all **kinds** of living **creatures**:
cattle, **creeping** things, and wild **animals** of all **kinds**."
And so it **happened**:
God made all **kinds** of wild **animals**, all **kinds** of **cattle**,
and all kinds of **creeping** things of the earth.
God saw how **good** it was.

Then God said:
"Let us make **man** in our **image**, after our **likeness**.
Let them have **dominion** over the **fish** of the sea,
the **birds** of the air, and the **cattle**,
and over **all** the wild **animals**
and **all** the creatures that **crawl** on the **ground**."
God **created** man in his **image**;
in the image of **God** he created him;
male and **female** he created them.

Significant pause after the fifth day.
Think of this day as the critical point,
for by this time the assembly has heard
of the five days, and they are starting
to recognize the pattern here. Just as they
might start to get impatient, you come
to the creation of human beings. So be
prepared to animate the reading here, for
you are nearing the end and you want to
sustain their listening.

Although this story is suspenseful, most believers know that the story has a happy ending. Given that all know the story, the sacrifice of Isaac can be seen with the theological meaning of the inevitable difficulties of human living, of the crossroads all of us, even the most saintly, come to in our days.

Our faith is mediated through God's word and sacrament, through ministrations of the priesthood, and by the prayerful solidarity of the faith community. The will of God is discerned by believers in the context of the Church's faith.

As you prepare to proclaim this reading, be mindful of the times when, in your own life or the lives of those you love, the will of God has called you to difficult decisions. Even those called to Baptism tonight have had to make difficult decisions on their way to faith. Keep all those people and situations in mind as you prepare to proclaim this narrative of Abraham, who was called to such a difficult act in his journey of faith.

READING III There are not many times when the scripture readings do not end with one of the dialogues—with "The word of the Lord" and "Thanks be to God," or "The Gospel of the Lord" and "Praise to you, Lord Jesus Christ." This reading that you are preparing for the Easter Vigil is one of these, a ritual action that alerts the people of God that something new is at hand. The newness during the Easter

God **blessed** them, saying:
  "Be **fertile** and **multiply**;
  fill the earth and **subdue** it.
Have **dominion** over the **fish** of the sea, the **birds** of the air,
  and **all** the living things that **move** on the **earth**."

God also said:
  "**See**, I give you every seed-bearing **plant** all over the **earth**
  and every **tree** that has seed-bearing **fruit** on it to be your **food**;
  and to all the **animals** of the land, all the **birds** of the air,
  and **all** the living creatures that crawl on the **ground**,
  I give all the green **plants** for **food**."
And so it **happened**.

God looked at **everything** he had made, and he found it
    very good.
Evening came, and **morning** followed—the **sixth** day.

Thus the **heavens** and the **earth** and all their array
    were **completed**.
Since on the **seventh** day God was **finished**
    with the work he had been **doing**,
    he **rested** on the **seventh** day from all the work
    he had **undertaken**.

[Shorter: Genesis 1:1, 26–31a]

READING II Genesis 22:1–18

A reading from the Book of Genesis

God put **Abraham** to the **test**.
He called to him, "**Abraham**!"
"Here I **am**," he replied.

As you approach this wrap-up, pause and take a breath. The summary calls for a warm, satisfied tone; after all, it is very good.

Genesis = JEN-uh-sis

The length of this narrative from Genesis is eased by the dialogue throughout the passage.
Abraham = AY-bruh-ham

Vigil is the celebration of the Resurrection; the celebration of initiation; the singing of "Alleluia" after weeks of omitting it; and in general, the complete renewal of the Church.

This rare ritual moment also calls for some coordination. Consult with the pastor or liturgy director and music director so that you are clear about the transition from the scripture reading to the canticle that follows it immediately.

Like most of the readings of the Easter Vigil, this story is familiar to most in the assembly, so your ministry as lector is not so much to hold the assembly in suspense as to emphasize the elements of the reading that are most important to the Easter Vigil. The unique ritual at the heart of the Vigil is the rites of initiation, which begin with the rite of Baptism. This reading could not be more appropriate as an anticipation of the baptismal rite of the Vigil. For this reason, therefore, as you prepare, highlight the elements in the story that are related to water: Moses stretching his hand out over the sea, the Israelites proceeding across the dry sea bed, the death-dealing waters for the Egyptians, and the celebration on the seashore.

Isaac = Ī-zik

Moriah = moh-RĪ-uh

holocaust = HOL-uh-kawst

This part, the action, provides some contextual details.

The dialogue continues with Abraham's instructions to the servants.

The action follows logically from the exchange that preceded.

This fourfold exchange between father and son is unnerving, because, unlike Isaac, the assembly knows what Abraham has promised to do. The exchange is followed by the details of the action.

Then God said:
  "Take your son **Isaac**, your only **one**, whom you **love**,
  and go to the land of **Moriah**.
There you shall offer him up as a **holocaust**
  on a **height** that I will point out to you."

Early the next **morning** Abraham saddled his **donkey**,
  took with him his son **Isaac** and two of his servants as well,
  and with the **wood** that he had cut for the **holocaust**,
  set out for the **place** of which **God** had told him.

On the **third** day **Abraham** got sight of the **place** from afar.
Then he said to his **servants**:
  "Both of you stay **here** with the donkey,
  while the boy and I go on over **yonder**.
We will **worship** and then come **back** to you."
Thereupon Abraham took the **wood** for the **holocaust**
  and **laid** it on his son Isaac's **shoulders**,
  while he himself carried the **fire** and the **knife**.

As the two **walked** on **together**, Isaac spoke
    to his father Abraham:
  "**Father**!" Isaac said.
"Yes, son," he replied.
Isaac continued, "Here are the **fire** and the **wood**,
  but **where** is the **sheep** for the **holocaust**?"
"**Son**," Abraham answered,
  "God himself will provide the **sheep** for the **holocaust**."
Then the two continued going forward.

When they came to the **place** of which God had **told** him,
  Abraham built an **altar** there and arranged the **wood** on it.
Next he tied up his son **Isaac**,
  and put him on **top** of the wood on the **altar**.

This moment in the life of ancient Israel is important in its own way, but the life of God continues in communities of faith. The occasion of the Easter Vigil and the relationship of this reading to what is happening in your parish and around the world is more important than the historical moment behind the story itself. Inspire the gathered Christians and those to be baptized as you proclaim this wonderful reading of Israel's rescue by the Lord.

READING IV The fourth reading has three basic parts. Part 1 describes a marriage and its history; part 2 is a comparison of the spouses' reconciliation to the LORD's oath to Noah after the flood; and part 3 is a promise to the wife of prosperity and security to come.

After the various texts the assembly has already heard at this point in the Liturgy of the Word, this passage represents still another kind of text, a theology in which the Creator's relationship to Israel, in the Jewish tradition, and to the Church, in the Christian tradition, is compared to that of husband and wife. This relationship is not one of uninterrupted loving bliss. No, the wife described by the prophet was cast off, and now the husband is turning back to the wife who had been forsaken. The passage then looks to the destruction of the earth in the flood of Noah and to the LORD's promise that it would never happen again.

The next speech comes from the angel who interrupts (to our relief) the action of Abraham.

Then more details of the scene, this time with the ram caught in the thicket.

Yahweh-yireh = YAH-way-YEER-ay

The final four verses are not from the Lord directly but from the angel of the Lord who had just stopped Abraham. The angel delivers God's promise to Abraham and his descendents, a promise that will be referred to many times in scripture.

Then he reached out and took the knife to **slaughter** his son.
But the LORD's **messenger** called to him from **heaven**,
　"**Abraham**, **Abraham**!"
"Here I **am**," he answered.
"Do **not** lay your **hand** on the **boy**," said the **messenger**.
"Do **not** do the **least** thing to him.
I **know** now how **devoted** you are to God,
　since you did not **withhold** from me your own beloved **son**."
As Abraham looked about,
　he spied a **ram** caught by its **horns** in the **thicket**.
So he went and took the ram
　and offered it up as a **holocaust** in place of his **son**.
Abraham **named** the site **Yahweh-yireh**;
　hence people now say, "On the mountain the LORD will **see**."

Again the LORD's messenger called to Abraham from heaven
　　and said:
　"I swear by myself, declares the **LORD**,
　that because you acted as you did
　in not **withholding** from me your beloved **son**,
　I will **bless** you **abundantly**
　and make your descendants as **countless**
　as the **stars** of the **sky** and the **sands** of the **seashore**;
　your **descendants** shall take possession
　of the gates of their **enemies**,
　and in your descendants all the **nations** of the earth
　　shall find **blessing**—
　all this because you **obeyed** my **command**."

[Shorter: Genesis 22:1–2, 9a, 10–13, 15–18]

The theological reason for the passage at the Easter Vigil is as consolation in the steadfastness of God. The Easter Vigil is a liturgy of rebirth, both for those who will be initiated and also for the whole community of faith who have belonged to the Church for decades. The consolation offered by this reading will speak to those who have felt that God has been far away at times in the past, and for those to be initiated the consolation is that God will support them and stand by them, as in a marriage.

The third part of the reading begins with the direct address, "O afflicted one." Pause before you move into this part, for it is an important change in address and in content. There are some difficult words in that section, with the names of the stones, but the particulars open up in the final two verses to an overarching promise of prosperity and of keeping oppression, fear, and terror at a distance. The Church can help in times of need, and the consolation of the passage will speak to those who have looked to the Church in times of difficulty.

READING V Because most members of the Church did not receive their first Eucharist at their baptism, the Eucharist is not often seen as the sacrament of initiation that it is. At the Easter Vigil, the Eucharist is celebrated with Baptism and Confirmation, and this order and cohesion is a restoration of the awe-inspiring rites of initiation of the early Church.

READING III   Exodus 14:15—15:1

A reading from the Book of Exodus

The LORD said to Moses, "Why are you crying out to me?
Tell the Israelites to go forward.
And you, lift up your staff and, with hand outstretched
    over the sea,
    split the sea in two,
    that the Israelites may pass through it on dry land.
But I will make the Egyptians so obstinate
    that they will go in after them.
Then I will receive glory through Pharaoh and all his army,
    his chariots and charioteers.
The Egyptians shall know that I am the LORD,
    when I receive glory through Pharaoh
    and his chariots and charioteers."

The angel of God, who had been leading Israel's camp,
    now moved and went around behind them.
The column of cloud also, leaving the front,
    took up its place behind them,
    so that it came between the camp of the Egyptians
    and that of Israel.
But the cloud now became dark, and thus the night passed
    without the rival camps coming any closer together
        all night long.

Then Moses stretched out his hand over the sea,
    and the LORD swept the sea
    with a strong east wind throughout the night
    and so turned it into dry land.

The readings at the Vigil highlight the important moments and people in the history of Israel. We heard about Abraham in the second reading, and here we hear about Moses, to whom the Lord speaks directly in the first four verses of the reading.
Israelites = IZ-ree-uh-lits

Pharaoh = FAIR-oh

Israel = IZ-ree-ul

The details of Moses' and the Egyptians' actions in the unfolding of the miracle are important. Imagine yourself seeing such an event so that you can inspire those in the assembly to imagine it for themselves.

The reading that you are preparing to proclaim at the Easter Vigil is significant to the celebration of the sacraments of initiation because it mentions the elements of Baptism (prayer, water, white snow [like the white garment], word of God) and the Eucharist together (prayer, bread, wine, water) even though the prophet would not have written the passage for this sacramental association.

It is clear that the water of the opening invitation, "come to the water," is not water for washing, as it would be for the full metaphorical link to baptism. The water here is part of a feasting metaphor, as it is addressed to "all you who are thirsty" rather than to "all you who need a bath" or "all you who are dirty"! But the proclamation can

bear the invitation in both directions, as an invitation by the LORD to those who are thirsty and hungry and as an invitation to the waters of Baptism.

The middle part of your proclamation takes up the ruler David, and moves to calling the people to the LORD and calling the wicked and the unrighteous to change their lives. The passage alternates between

When the **water** was thus **divided**,
　the Israelites **marched** into the **midst** of the sea on dry **land**,
　with the water like a **wall** to their **right** and to their **left**.

The **Egyptians** followed in **pursuit**;
　all Pharaoh's **horses** and **chariots** and **charioteers**
　　went after them
　right into the **midst** of the **sea**.
In the night watch just before dawn
　the LORD cast through the column of the fiery **cloud**
　upon the Egyptian force a **glance** that threw it into a **panic**;
　and he so **clogged** their chariot wheels
　that they could hardly **drive**.
With **that** the Egyptians sounded the retreat before Israel,
　because the LORD was fighting for them **against** the Egyptians.

Then the LORD told **Moses**, "Stretch out your **hand** over the **sea**,
　that the **water** may flow **back** upon the **Egyptians**,
　upon their **chariots** and their **charioteers**."
So Moses **stretched** out his hand over the **sea**,
　and at dawn the sea flowed **back** to its normal depth.
The Egyptians were fleeing **head on** toward the **sea**,
　when the LORD **hurled** them into its **midst**.
As the water flowed **back**,
　it covered the **chariots** and the **charioteers**
　　of Pharaoh's whole **army**
　which had **followed** the Israelites into the **sea**.
Not a single **one** of them **escaped**.

But the **Israelites** had marched on dry **land**
　through the midst of the **sea**,
　with the water like a **wall** to their **right** and to their **left**.
Thus the LORD **saved Israel** on that day
　from the power of the **Egyptians**.

The LORD delivers the instructions and Moses carries them out.

direct commands—such as "come," "listen," "seek"—and more descriptive sentences—such as "I made him a witness," and "my thoughts are not your thoughts." Perhaps as you prepare you can note which parts are commands and which more descriptive. That will help you recognize the tone to use for each.

READING VI The sixth reading is different from the other readings from the Old Testament because it comes from a book that rarely appears in the Lectionary for Mass. It finds its place at the Easter Vigil because it captures a significant moment in the history of Israel, the Babylonian captivity, in a concise summary and with hope for the future in which the people will live by the law of God and live in happiness.

The Babylonian captivity was a period of over a half-century (587–521 BC) when Israel was conquered, Jerusalem destroyed, and the people of Israel captured and carried off as prisoners to a foreign land, Babylon. Because the holy land was and still is itself so precious and sacred to the Jews, this displacement of the nation to a foreign country occasioned a huge crisis in their theology and in their identity. "If we were the people of God," they would

When Israel saw the **Egyptians** lying **dead** on the **seashore**
    and beheld the great **power** that the LORD
    had shown against the Egyptians,
    they **feared** the LORD and **believed** in him
        and in his servant **Moses**.

Then Moses and the Israelites sang this **song** to the LORD:
    I will sing to the **LORD**, for he is gloriously **triumphant**;
    horse and chariot he has **cast** into the **sea**.

The end of the reading leads up to the canticle.

Isaiah = ī-ZAY-uh

The first section speaks of the LORD in the third person, at a distance. This changes in the next section, so prepare your proclamation aware of this shift in point of view.

READING IV   Isaiah 54:5–14

A reading from the Book of the Prophet Isaiah

The One who has become your **husband** is your **Maker**;
    his **name** is the LORD of **hosts**;
your **redeemer** is the **Holy** One of **Israel**,
    called **God** of all the **earth**.
The LORD calls you **back**,
    like a **wife** forsaken and grieved in spirit,
    a **wife** married in **youth** and then cast **off**,
        says your God.

For a brief moment I **abandoned** you,
    but with great **tenderness** I will take you **back**.
In an outburst of **wrath**, for a **moment**
    I hid my face from you;
but with enduring **love** I take **pity** on you,
    says the LORD, your **redeemer**.

have asked themselves, "how could this tragedy have befallen us? How could we have lost the most important gift from God?" The reading from Baruch is from this time of questioning.

The reading is about the conversion of the people, and in this regard its placement at the Easter Vigil is fitting. Though we tend to think of conversion as a change in the life of an individual, conversion also happens to

groups, to communities, and Baruch's word to Israel can be held up at the Vigil as an encouragement to your community for its own conversion.

It would be good for you to emphasize the symbol of light in the last few verses of the passage, for the Easter candle is there burning in the darkened church for all to see. Though the reading does not concentrate on the light until the end, it is still good for you to focus on this symbol in the reading for attentive listeners who might grasp the link.

READING VII There is some complexity in this reading. There are some sentences in the first person ("me," "my," "I"), some in the second person (with "your," "you"), and some in the third person ("their," "they," "them"). Before you start practicing your reading aloud, it would be good to sort out to whom each of these refers. Otherwise it might be confusing.

This reference to the flood is appropriate as the community will soon be celebrating Baptism, welcoming new members or being reminded of their own baptism by sprinkling.

This is for **me** like the days of **Noah**,
   when I swore that the **waters** of Noah
   should **never** again **deluge** the earth;
so I have sworn **not** to be angry with you,
   or to **rebuke** you.
Though the **mountains** leave their **place**
   and the **hills** be **shaken**,
my love shall **never** leave you
   nor my covenant of **peace** be shaken,
   says the LORD, who has mercy on you.

Pause before you start this section. There are some difficult phrases and uncommon words, so practice this section so that your proclamation is not impeded by unfamiliarity.
carnelians = kar-NEEL-yuns
carbuncles = KAR-bung-k*lz

O **afflicted** one, **storm-battered** and **unconsoled**,
   I lay your **pavements** in **carnelians**,
   and your **foundations** in **sapphires**;
I will make your **battlements** of **rubies**,
   your **gates** of **carbuncles**,
   and all your **walls** of precious **stones**.

The closing promise brings the passage to a close on a positive note.

All your children shall be taught by the LORD,
   and great shall be the **peace** of your **children**.
In **justice** shall you be **established**,
   far from the fear of **oppression**,
   where destruction cannot **come** near you.

READING V   Isaiah 55:1–11

Isaiah = ī-ZAY-uh

This invitation to the table is lovely. Proclaim it as an invitation to God's feast.

A reading from the Book of the prophet Isaiah

Thus says the LORD:
All you who are **thirsty**,
   come to the **water**!

Throughout the entire passage, the first-person voice consistently refers to the LORD. With "I poured out my fury," for example, it is the Lord who did the pouring out.

The phrase "Son of man," at the beginning of the second line, is a direct address. The LORD is speaking directly to a human being, the prophet, and through the prophet, and you, to us. The first half of the reading speaks about the Israelites, so the third person refers to Israel. When the LORD says, "I scattered *them* among the nations," "them" refers to the Israelites.

Further down, "Therefore say to the house of Israel, / Thus says the Lord GOD" marks a shift. Now the LORD is addressing Israel, not speaking about Israel. For the rest of the reading, "you" means Israel.

Do not be afraid of this rhetorical complexity; reading it is not as difficult as reading about it. Moreover, the passage is striking in its theology, so taking the time to understand those voices will make your proclamation very effective. Because of the shift, it might be good in your first practice to read only up to that point. Then, once you have become comfortable with that, turn to the second half. Then, having been oriented to

The tone is even more persuasive here.

You who have no money,
   come, receive grain and **eat**;
come, without **paying** and without **cost**,
   drink wine and **milk**!
Why spend your **money** for what is not **bread**,
   your **wages** for what fails to **satisfy**?
Heed me, and you shall eat **well**,
   you shall **delight** in rich **fare**.
Come to me **heedfully**,
   listen, that you may have **life**.
I will **renew** with you the **everlasting** covenant,
   the **benefits** assured to **David**.

As I made him a **witness** to the **peoples**,
   a **leader** and commander of **nations**,
so shall you summon a **nation** you knew **not**,
   and nations that knew you **not** shall **run** to you,
because of the LORD, your **God**,
   the **Holy** One of **Israel**, who has **glorified** you.

Now back to invitation, this time to seek and forsake rather than to eat and drink.

Seek the LORD while he may be found,
   call him while he is near.
Let the **scoundrel** forsake his **way**,
   and the **wicked** man his **thoughts**;
let him turn to the LORD for **mercy**;
   to our **God**, who is **generous** in **forgiving**.

For **my** thoughts are not **your** thoughts,
   nor are **your** ways **my** ways, says the LORD.
As high as the **heavens** are above the **earth**,
   so high are **my** ways above **your** ways
   and **my** thoughts above **your** thoughts.

---

the two halves individually, put them together with confidence, appreciating the passage as a whole.

The end of the reading is beautiful first because of the image of cleansing water, which is very important in the rituals of the Easter Vigil. But the beauty is also in the poetic imagery of the "stony hearts" and the "natural hearts."

EPISTLE **Paul's Letter to the Romans** was written almost two thousand years ago, yet its foundational theology of Baptism can be heard as if it had been written today.

There are a number of challenges to you as the proclaimer of this significant passage about Baptism. The *first* challenge is the liturgical occasion at which you are to

read this passage, the Easter Vigil. For centuries, the Easter Vigil was not celebrated by the whole parish. The Vigil still held onto vestiges of its past as the time for initiation, and there were were few parishioners, if any, besides ordained priests, who heard or experienced that. Since Vatican II and particularly since the restoration of the catechumenate and the RCIA, the primary reason for the Vigil was restored, that of initiating

These metaphors from nature emphasize God's generosity. The final gift mentioned in the excerpt is God's word, which you yourself share with the assembly at the Vigil.

For just as from the heavens
　　the **rain** and **snow** come **down**
and do not **return** there
　　till they have **watered** the **earth**,
　　making it **fertile** and **fruitful**,
giving **seed** to the one who **sows**
　　and **bread** to the one who **eats**,
so shall my **word** be
　　that goes forth from my **mouth**;
my **word** shall not return to me **void**,
　　but shall do my **will**,
　　achieving the **end** for which I **sent** it.

READING VI　　Baruch 3:9–15, 32 — 4:4

Baruch = buh-ROOK

The reading begins with a command: "Hear!" Your voice should carry that imperative tone at the start.
Israel = IZ-ree-ul

A reading from the Book of the Prophet Baruch

Hear, O Israel, the **commandments** of **life**:
　　listen, and know **prudence**!
How **is** it, Israel,
　　that you are in the land of your foes,
　　grown **old** in a foreign **land**,
defiled with the **dead**,
　　accounted with those destined for the **netherworld**?
You have **forsaken** the fountain of **wisdom**!
　　Had you **walked** in the way of **God**,
　　you would have **dwelt** in enduring **peace**.

---

new members into the community for the renewal of the life of the Church. This reading about Baptism marks a significant moment in the life of the parish, and the challenge to you is to let Paul's theology be heard clearly.

The *second* challenge of the passage is in the second-person ("you") and first-person ("we" and "our") voices of the Letter to the Romans. The challenge for you is to proclaim

the reading not as a recital of the theology of first-century Rome, but as the theology of your own community in your time and your place. There is nothing in the passage to distance your community from the theology Paul sets out in it.

The *third* challenge is the excitement and vulnerabilities of those waiting to be initiated. The elect and the candidates for reception have been formed over a long period, and this is the night for which they

have been waiting. The passage you proclaim will touch their hearts not only because it is a rich theology of Baptism but because they likely pondered this text deeply during their formation.

Take your time with this lovely passage; be clear with its theology; engage the assembly and the elect in its midst at this moment just before their initiation.

The first three "where" phrases are dependent grammatically on the "learn," and the next two "where" phrases depend on "know."

Learn where **prudence** is,
 where **strength**, where **understanding**;
that you may know **also**
 where are length of **days**, and **life**,
 where light of the **eyes**, and **peace**.
Who has found the place of **wisdom**,
 who has entered into her **treasuries**?

The One who knows **all** things knows **her**;
 he has **probed** her by his **knowledge**—
the One who established the earth for all **time**,
 and filled it with four-footed **beasts**;
 he who dismisses the **light**, and it **departs**,
 calls it, and it **obeys** him **trembling**;
before whom the **stars** at their posts
 shine and **rejoice**;
when he **calls** them, they answer, "**Here** we are!"
 shining with **joy** for their Maker.

Such is our **God**;
 no **other** is to be **compared** to him:
he has traced out the whole way of **understanding**,
 and has given her to **Jacob**, his **servant**,
 to **Israel**, his beloved **son**.

Since then she has appeared on **earth**,
 and moved among **people**.
She is the **book** of the precepts of **God**,
 the **law** that endures **forever**;
all who **cling** to her will **live**,
 but those will **die** who **forsake** her.

Turn, O Jacob, and **receive** her:
 walk by her **light** toward **splendor**.

Jacob = JAY-kub

GOSPEL   Although the narrative of the Resurrection is extraordinary, after these many readings it might seem like just another episode in the life of Jesus Christ as told in the Gospels. But remember that the assembly will have just heard from Paul's Letter to the Romans. There the proclaimer read the words of the apostle, "We will certainly be united with him in a resurrection like his." The narratives of the death and Resurrection of Christ are powerful because, by God's gift and by Jesus' life, the community of faith participates in these in different ways than in other narratives.

As a story, the passage is broken up by the words of the women to one another, the words of the angel, and the words of Jesus. Take your time with these quotations, for they reveal much about the experience of the disciples then and about our theology of Resurrection today.

Among the other details of the Gospel proclamation, you probably know which ones to emphasize for the community in which you minister. But two in particular are significant at the Easter Vigil. First, that the Resurrection takes place at dawn on "the first day of the week" is important, for the Christian assembly on Sunday is the sustenance of the Church's liturgical life. The

Pause here, as you are about to start the final section. The "alien race" are the captors, who held the Israelites against their will. Pause also before a strong proclamation of the benediction, which begins with, "Blessed are we. . . ."

Give not your **glory** to another,
    your **privileges** to an alien **race**.
Blessed are we, O **Israel**;
    for what pleases God is **known** to us!

READING VII   Ezekiel 36:16–17a, 18–28

Ezekiel = ee-ZEE-kee-ul

The passage has two basic directions. Here the LORD is chastising Israel for its disobedience and misconduct.
Israel = IZ-ree-ul

A reading from the Book of the Prophet Ezekiel

The word of the LORD came to me, saying:
    Son of **man**, when the house of **Israel** lived in their **land**,
    they **defiled** it by their **conduct** and **deeds**.
Therefore I poured out my **fury** upon them
    because of the **blood** that they poured out on the **ground**,
    and because they **defiled** it with **idols**.
I **scattered** them among the **nations**,
    dispersing them over foreign **lands**;
    according to their **conduct** and **deeds** I **judged** them.

But when they **came** among the nations **wherever** they came,
    they served to **profane** my holy **name**,
    because it was said of them: "**These** are the people of the **LORD**,
    yet they had to leave their **land**."

The second direction starts here, with the LORD speaking directly to Israel, telling them that this is an opportunity for a new relationship.

So I have **relented** because of my holy **name**
    which the house of Israel **profaned**
    among the nations where they **came**.
Therefore say to the house of **Israel**: **Thus** says the Lord **GOD**:
    Not for **your** sakes do I act, house of **Israel**,
    but for the sake of my holy **name**,
    which you **profaned** among the nations to which you **came**.

Easter Vigil is held after dark on Saturday night because of the tradition, drawn from the Gospels, of meeting on Sunday, the "first day of the week." And of all the Sundays of the year, Easter Sunday is fundamental.

    The second detail might depend on whether there will be baptisms at the Vigil and whether these newly baptized will be dressed in albs (or "white garments"). If so, then your proclamation should take advantage of a particular detail: the angel's clothing was "white as snow." As with Paul's theology of the Resurrection, so too in this Gospel narrative of the Resurrection: Our ritual actions and symbols are drawn from the canonical texts that we proclaim.

I will prove the **holiness** of my great name,
    profaned among the **nations**,
  in whose midst you have **profaned** it.
Thus the nations shall **know** that **I** am the LORD,
    says the Lord GOD,
  when in their sight I **prove** my holiness through **you**.

For I will take you **away** from among the nations,
    gather you from all the foreign **lands**,
  and bring you **back** to your **own** land.

I will sprinkle clean **water** upon you
    to **cleanse** you from all your **impurities**,
  and from all your **idols** I will **cleanse** you.

I will give you a new **heart** and place a new **spirit** within you,
    taking from your **bodies** your **stony** hearts
  and giving you **natural** hearts.
I will put my **spirit** within you and make you live by my **statutes**,
    careful to observe my **decrees**.
You shall **live** in the land I gave your **fathers**;
  you shall be my **people**, and **I** will be your **God**.

From here to the end is a beautiful theology, with poetic images. Practice this last section so that you can proclaim it with confidence and hope.

Romans = ROH-munz

The reading starts right in with direct address, "Are you unaware . . ." Paul is speaking directly to the assembly before you.

The Vigil stands between Good Friday's remembrance of the death of Jesus and the Easter season's celebration of the Resurrection. The theology of death and resurrection you proclaim is essential to this moment in the liturgical year, and essential to our faith.

The union between Christ's death and our death, between Christ's Resurrection and our resurrection could not be clearer. Proclaim this with confidence.

EPISTLE   Romans 6:3–11

A reading from the Letter of Saint Paul to the Romans

Brothers and sisters:
Are you **unaware** that we who were **baptized** into Christ **Jesus**
    were **baptized** into his **death**?
We were indeed **buried** with him through baptism into **death**,
    so that, just as Christ was **raised** from the dead
    by the **glory** of the Father,
    we **too** might **live** in newness of **life**.

For if we have grown into **union** with him
    through a **death** like his,
    we shall also be **united** with him in the **resurrection**.
We know that our **old** self was **crucified** with him,
    so that our **sinful** body might be done **away** with,
    that we might no longer be in **slavery** to sin.
For a **dead** person has been **absolved** from sin.
If, then, we have **died** with Christ,
    we believe that we shall also **live** with him.

We know that **Christ**, raised from the **dead**, dies no **more**;
    death no longer has power over him.
As to his **death**, he died to sin **once** and for **all**;
    as to his **life**, he lives for **God**.
Consequently, you **too** must think of **yourselves**
    as being **dead** to sin
    and **living** for God in Christ **Jesus**.

GOSPEL Matthew 28:1–10

A reading from the holy Gospel according to Matthew

After the **sabbath**, as the **first** day of the week was **dawning**,
　Mary **Magdalene** and the other **Mary** came to see the **tomb**.
And **behold**, there was a great **earthquake**;
　for an angel of the **Lord** descended from **heaven**,
　approached, **rolled** back the stone, and **sat** upon it.
His **appearance** was like **lightning**
　and his **clothing** was white as **snow**.
The guards were **shaken** with **fear** of him
　and became like **dead** men.

Then the **angel** said to the women in **reply**,
　"Do **not** be afraid!
I **know** that you are seeking **Jesus** the **crucified**.
He is not **here**, for he has been **raised** just as he **said**.
Come and see the place where he **lay**.
Then go **quickly** and tell his **disciples**,
　'He has been **raised** from the **dead**,
　and he is going **before** you to **Galilee**;
　there you will **see** him.'
　Behold, I have **told** you."

Then they went away **quickly** from the tomb,
　fearful yet **overjoyed**,
　and ran to **announce** this to his **disciples**.

And **behold**, Jesus **met** them on their way and **greeted** them.
They **approached**, embraced his **feet**, and did him **homage**.
Then Jesus said to them, "Do not be **afraid**.
Go tell my brothers to go to **Galilee**,
　and **there** they will **see** me."

The "first day of the week" is Sunday, the day of Easter.
sabbath = SAB-uth
Magdalene = MAG-duh-lun

These dramatic details are recorded by Matthew only; imagine the scene so that your proclamation will be as fresh and new as that morning in the garden.

The clothing of the angel was white, like the baptismal garments that the neophytes receive tonight.

Galilee = GAL-ih-lee

The women's proclamation of the Resurrection, like your proclamation of the Easter Gospel to the assembly, carries a message that needs to be spread.

The risen Christ is with them as they, like you at the Easter Vigil, tell the good news of the Resurrection.

EASTER SUNDAY

Lectionary #42/46

READING I   Acts 10:34a, 37–43

A reading from the Acts of the Apostles

Peter proceeded to speak and said:
"You **know** what has happened all over **Judea**,
    beginning in Galilee after the baptism
    that John **preached**,
    how God anointed **Jesus** of **Nazareth**
    with the Holy **Spirit** and **power**.
He went about doing **good**
    and **healing** all those **oppressed** by the **devil**,
    for God was with him.

"**We** are **witnesses** of all that he **did**
    both in the country of the Jews and in Jerusalem.
They put him to **death** by hanging him on a **tree**.
This man God **raised** on the third **day** and granted
        that he be **visible**,
    not to **all** the people, but to **us**,
    the **witnesses** chosen by God in advance,
    who **ate** and **drank** with him after he rose from the **dead**.

"He **commissioned** us to preach to the **people**
    and **testify** that he is the one appointed by God
    as **judge** of the **living** and the **dead**.
To him all the **prophets** bear **witness**,
    that **everyone** who **believes** in him
    will receive **forgiveness** of sins through his **name**."

Pause briefly after each of the two identifications: the book of the Bible, the Acts of the Apostles; and the speaker, Peter (addressing those in the house of Cornelius). See below for the explanation of proclaiming this as a letter rather than as a narrative.
Judea = joo-DEE-uh
Galilee = GAL-ih-lee
Nazareth = NAZ-uh-reth

Jerusalem = juh-ROO-suh-lem

From this verse forward, the reading nearly transcends time.

READING I   Often liturgical readings are *either* a narrative *or* an apostolic letter. With a *letter* the context comes when the lector says, for example, "A reading from the Letter of Saint Paul to the Galatians." With a *narrative* there is a progress of action. Moreover, the author of a letter has an audience in mind and addresses them directly: "Brothers and sisters," or "Saints of God," for example. Both types of liturgical reading are mentioned here for your preparation because this reading is a narrative of action by one of the

apostles, Peter; but that action is his speaking to a gathering in the home of a fellow believer. His speech could be cast as a letter. We find the speaker in first-person plural pronouns—"We are witnesses"—and those spoken to in second-person plural pronouns—"You know what has happened."

As you prepare for the proclamation, therefore, approach this *narrative* reading as if it were a *letter*. It will not take too much imagination to deliver the words of Peter to those in Cornelius' house as if they are indeed your own words to those in your own community, for the theology of Easter in this

part of the Acts of the Apostles transcends the centuries.

This passage is Peter's description of the activity of the Christian faith from the baptism John announced up to the moment when Peter speaks. The details of this account are engaging, and you can animate them in your ministry to the assembly. Be clear and colorful in the descriptive elements: "all . . . oppressed by the devil," "by hanging him on a tree," "us . . . who ate and drank with him after he rose," which ends the second part and brings the reading up to the Church on

Colossians = kuh-LOSH-unz

As the author was writing to his brothers and sisters, so do you proclaim to yours.

The Church, the assembly of the baptized, celebrates and lives not only its participation in the glorification of Christ, but its participation in the death of Christ as well. The author is clear: "you have died."

READING II   Colossians 3:1–4

A reading from the Letter of Saint Paul to the Colossians

Brothers and sisters:
If then you were **raised** with **Christ**, seek what is **above**,
    where Christ is **seated** at the right hand of **God**.
Think of what is **above**, not of what is on **earth**.
For you have **died**, and your life is **hidden** with Christ in **God**.
When Christ your life **appears**,
    then you **too** will appear with him in **glory**.

Or:

Corinthians = kor-IN-thee-unz

Highlight the transformation captured in the metaphor of the yeast and the dough, for this is the central image of the reading.

The first manifestation is the transformation from the "old yeast" to the "fresh batch."

The second manifestation expands the metaphor, adding how these are seen in the life of the community, whether in ancient Corinth or today.

READING II   1 Corinthians 5:6b–8

A reading from the first Letter of Saint Paul to the Corinthians

Brothers and sisters:
Do you not know that a little **yeast** leavens all the **dough**?
Clear **out** the **old** yeast,
    so that you may become a **fresh** batch of dough,
    inasmuch as you are **unleavened**.
For our paschal **lamb**, **Christ**, has been **sacrificed**.
Therefore, let us **celebrate** the feast,
    not with the **old** yeast, the yeast of **malice** and **wickedness**,
    but with the **unleavened** bread of **sincerity** and **truth**.

this very Easter Sunday on which you proclaim. Address the assembly with paschal power on this Easter celebration.

There is a choice of second readings today. Speak with the liturgy coordinator or the homilist to find out which reading will be used.

READING II **COLOSSIANS.** Although some believers think of the Christ-event as something that existed only in the past and that we merely remember now, this reading for Easter Sunday clearly

weds the life of Jesus Christ with the life of those in the Church right now. The Paschal Mystery, so the reading proclaims, is this wedding of Jesus Christ and the community of faith, and this is so whether it is that ancient Greek Church at Colossae, to which this passage was originally addressed, or the Church to which you belong and in which you minister the word of God.

The reading is placed here on Easter itself because this is the feast when the efficacy of the Paschal Mystery in Jesus Christ hits closest to home for the Church. A reading like this, proclaimed with conviction, can

bring the efficacy of the Paschal Mystery up close in the minds and hearts of the assembly. Before you get to the specifics of proclamation, take some time to appreciate the theology and meaning of the short passage, and then, with that accomplished, consider how you will best minister this word to your Church.

Notice that the entire reading is completely in the second person, as are many of the readings in the Lectionary from New Testament letters. In proclaiming such texts, the best approach is to stand as if in the person and power and conviction of the original

The "first day of the week" is Sunday.

Magdala = MAG-duh-luh

This "other disciple whom Jesus loved" is not named anywhere in the Gospels where he appears. Therefore, you need to be clear with the identification. It might be useful to consider the description as a name: "The-other-disciple-whom-Jesus-loved."

John describes these cloths in the tomb in more detail than the other Gospels. Take your time in describing what the two disciples found.

The sight of the burial cloths in the empty tomb brings "the-other-disciple" to belief. Emphasize this as well.

GOSPEL   John 20:1–9

A reading from the holy Gospel according to John

On the first day of the **week**,
　　Mary of **Magdala** came to the **tomb** early in the **morning**,
　　while it was still **dark**,
　　and saw the **stone** removed from the **tomb**.
So she **ran** and went to Simon **Peter**
　　and to the **other** disciple whom Jesus **loved**, and told them,
　　"They have taken the **Lord** from the **tomb**,
　　and we don't know where they **put** him."

So **Peter** and the **other** disciple went out and came to the **tomb**.
They **both** ran, but the **other** disciple ran **faster** than Peter
　　and arrived at the tomb **first**;
　　he bent **down** and saw the **burial** cloths there, but did
　　　　not go in.

When Simon Peter arrived **after** him,
　　he went **into** the tomb and saw the **burial** cloths there,
　　and the cloth that had covered his **head**,
　　not with the **burial** cloths but rolled **up** in a separate **place**.
Then the **other** disciple **also** went in,
　　the one who had arrived at the tomb **first**,
　　and he **saw** and **believed**.
For they did not yet **understand** the Scripture
　　that he had to **rise** from the **dead**.

author, not imitating that author, but claiming the power of your baptism and ministry as they did.

　　So, just as the author of this short reading addressed these words with power to the church in Colossae in the first century, you can address it with power to the people to whom you minister the word of God on Easter Sunday. This reading is a kind of kick-off into the Easter season, for Easter Sunday is itself the beginning of the Fifty Days (which lasts until Pentecost).

　　The Paschal Mystery has not diminished or waned in the intervening centuries.

The risen Christ is present to the Church today in the sacraments. As a minister of the word, you have an important part in this presence. Therfore, proclaim with conviction on this Easter Sunday.

READING II　CORINTHIANS. It might be surprising that this reading from First Corinthians, a relatively minor part of our theologies of Easter today, was among the most important scriptural passages in the earliest theology of Easter. The single Greek word *pascha* (here translated

as "paschal lamb") simply meant "Passover," or "paschal," or, later, "Easter." In English we do not have a noun equivalent for *pascha*, and "paschal" is an adjective that modifies something else—sometimes "lamb," sometimes "mystery," sometimes "feast." This slightly expanded translation has the advantage of connecting the depth of the mystery celebrated on this day, the death and Resurrection of Christ, with the liturgical anthem sung at every Eucharist, "Lamb of God." In the Sequence today we sing: "Christians! to the Paschal Victim offer your thankful praises. The Lamb the sheep

Lectionary #46

AFTERNOON GOSPEL   Luke 24:13–35

A reading from the holy Gospel according to Luke

That very day, the **first** day of the week,
  two of Jesus' disciples were going
  to a village seven miles from Jerusalem called **Emmaus**,
  and they were **conversing** about all the things
    that had **occurred**.
And it **happened** that while they were conversing and debating,
  Jesus **himself** drew near and **walked** with them,
  but their eyes were **prevented** from recognizing him.

He **asked** them,
  "What are you **discussing** as you walk along?"
They **stopped**, looking downcast.
One of them, named **Cleopas**, said to him in reply,
  "Are you the **only** visitor to Jerusalem
  who does not **know** of the **things**
  that have taken place there in these days?"

And he **replied** to them, "What **sort** of things?"
They said to him,
  "The **things** that happened to **Jesus** the **Nazarene**,
  who was a **prophet** mighty in **deed** and **word**
  before **God** and **all** the people,
  how our chief **priests** and **rulers both** handed him over
  to a sentence of **death** and **crucified** him.
But we were **hoping** that **he** would be the **one** to **redeem** Israel;
  and **besides** all this,
  it is **now** the **third day** since **this** took place.

A number of elements in this Gospel reading are concrete, making it easy to connect the story with your assembly. This opening, placing the events of the narrative on Sunday, is a primary link.
Jerusalem = juh-ROO-suh-lem
Emmaus = eh-MAY-us

Another common element is that we often do not recognize fellow believers as revealing the presence of Christ to us.

Cleopas = KLEE-oh-pus

This is a summary of the Paschal Mystery for the "only visitor to Jerusalem" who apparently does not know of it.
Nazarene = naz-uh-REEN

Israel = IZ-ree-ul

redeems: Christ, who only is sinless, reconciles sinners to the Father. Death and life contended in that conflict stupendous: the Prince of Life, who died, deathless reigns."

This reading has had another influence on the liturgy in that specific description of "unleavened bread." The Roman Catholic prescription for Eucharistic bread calls for unleavened bread in faithfulness to that description.

Even with all these vital matters packed into this passage from Paul's letter, the reading is short, only two and a half verses. The main issue to highlight in your proclamation

is the change from "old yeast" to the "new batch" of dough, from the bread of "malice and wickedness" to the unleavened bread of "sincerity and truth." The Church has been reborn in its celebration of the Easter Vigil, and the movement from the Forty Days of Lent to the Fifty Days of the season of Easter (now until Pentecost) is captured in this metaphor.

GOSPEL   The Evangelists wrote their Gospels for the churches to which they belonged, where they worshiped. Like your own community of faith, their communities were filled with unique individuals

who together made up a church unlike any other. The variations in the Gospels are a result of each Evangelist's effort to shape the text so that it would be well heard and readily received by their own community, which was unlike any other.

In the narratives of the discovery of the empty tomb, the uniqueness of each Evangelist's effort is apparent. Each Evangelist emphasized different elements of the Paschal Mystery based on their church's experience of the death and Resurrection of Christ. For this reason, you will find that the Evangelist John included elements not

Another common element is the proclamation and interpretation of the scriptures
that Jesus did for the two disciples on
the road, and that you, in proclaiming and
preaching the Gospel, also do.

The final and perhaps most poignantly
continuous element is that meal of bread
taken, blessed, broken, and shared, in
which the risen Christ is recognized.

In the season of Easter, the risen Christ
reveals himself again and again to
different people in different places, as
Christ has done ever since, whenever
people come together for worship and
the sacraments.

Some **women** from our group, however, have **astounded** us:
   they were at the tomb **early** in the **morning**
   and did **not** find his **body**;
   they came **back** and reported
   that they had **indeed** seen a vision of **angels**
   who **announced** that he was **alive**.

"Then some of those **with** us went to the tomb
   and found things **just** as the women had **described**,
   but **him** they did not **see**."

And he said to them, "Oh, how **foolish** you are!
How **slow** of **heart** to **believe** all that the prophets **spoke**!
Was it not **necessary** that the Christ should suffer **these things**
   and **enter** into his **glory**?"

Then beginning with **Moses** and all the **prophets**,
   he **interpreted** to them what referred to him
   in **all** the **Scriptures**.
As they **approached** the village to which they were **going**,
   he gave the impression that he was going on **farther**.
But they **urged** him, "**Stay** with us,
   for it is nearly **evening** and the day is almost **over**."
So he went in to **stay** with them.

And it **happened** that, while he was with them at **table**,
   he **took bread**, **said** the **blessing**,
   broke it, and **gave** it to them.
With **that** their **eyes** were **opened** and they **recognized** him,
   but he **vanished** from their **sight**.

found in the story of the discovery of the
empty tomb in Matthew, Mark, or Luke.
    Part of your task in proclaiming the
Gospel on this Easter Sunday is letting the
uniqueness of John's narrative come through.
For example, you will not find the foot race
between Peter and the disciple Jesus loved
in the empty tomb stories in the other three
Gospels. In John it is a major element in the
story, reflecting a theology and characters
that were important. (Who wins the race?
The beloved disciple is identified elsewhere
in the Gospel of John as the youngest of the
disciples. He reaches the tomb before Peter

does, but in respectful recognition of Peter's
authority, he lets Peter go in first.)
    Why emphasize the uniqueness of this
particular Gospel narrative? Like that ancient
community of faith to which John belonged,
your own parish community also has a unique
experience of the Paschal Mystery. Each
parish community worldwide, from the earliest to now and on into the future, is unique,
a result of the unique assembly of individuals gathered in the power of the Holy Spirit,
but we are all gathered together in unity in
one, holy, catholic, and apostolic Church.

AFTERNOON GOSPEL | This passage
from the end
of the Gospel of Luke has made an immeasurable contribution to our sacramental theology and to the celebration of the Eucharist.
It is also a fairly long Gospel reading, so you
will need to use your best and most engaging story-telling and proclamation abilities
to keep the assembly attentive to what
unfolds. There are a couple of characteristics of the reading that will help.
    First, the reading has a strong narrative
progression, a clear beginning, middle, and
end. There are no extended exhortations in

Then they said to each other,
"**Were** not our **hearts burning** within us
while he **spoke** to us on the way and **opened** the **Scriptures**
to us?"

So they set out at **once** and **returned** to Jerusalem
where they found gathered together
the **eleven** and those **with them** who were saying,
"The **Lord** has **truly** been **raised** and has **appeared** to **Simon**!"

Then the two **recounted**
what had taken place on the **way**
and how he was made **known** to them in the **breaking** of **bread**.

the middle of the story, but some simple exchanges that advance the action.

Second, the proclaimer and the listeners have more information than the two disciples on the way to Emmaus have. The Evangelist reveals that "Jesus himself drew near and walked with them, but their eyes were prevented from recognizing him." The assembly knows a secret that two of the main characters do not! You can use this dramatic irony to hold the assembly's attention.

Third, the assembly before you shares a number of things with the two disciples. Like them, the Church is together on "the first day of the week," Sunday. Moreover, the two have the scriptures opened and explained to them, just as in your Sunday liturgy, the scriptures are proclaimed and preached. Next, the risen Christ is with the two on the way to Emmaus just as the risen Christ is with the Church gathered for Sunday Mass. Finally, the sign in which the risen Christ is recognized is the bread broken and shared. The Eucharistic and sacrificial meal is an enduring reality in the Church in which the risen Christ is recognized, adored, celebrated, and consumed.

As you prepare and as you proclaim, deliver these ritual elements so that those in the assembly recognize them for what they are. It is important that—as time moves on, as the Church proclaims the Good News in new places—there are some ritual commonalities uniting the people of God. And in this unity we experience the presence of the risen Christ.

Lectionary #43

READING I   Acts 2:42–47

A reading from the Acts of the Apostles

They **devoted** themselves
    to the **teaching** of the apostles and to the **communal** life,
    to the breaking of **bread** and to the **prayers**.

Awe came upon **everyone**,
    and many **wonders** and **signs** were done through the **apostles**.

All who **believed** were **together** and had all things in **common**;
    they would sell their **property** and **possessions**
    and divide them among **all** according to each one's **need**.
Every day they **devoted** themselves
    to meeting **together** in the **temple** area
    and to breaking **bread** in their **homes**.
They ate their meals with **exultation** and sincerity of **heart**,
    praising **God** and enjoying **favor** with all the **people**.
And every day the Lord **added** to their number
        those who were being **saved**.

These basic works of the Church continue to this day: teaching, fellowship, breaking bread, and praying.

In the Church today we share goods still. The Church's advocacy for economic justice has been especially strong since Vatican II.

The early communities did not have daily Mass. People took portions of the Eucharistic bread home from the Sunday gathering for physical and spiritual nourishment.

READING I For you, as proclaimer of the first reading, the Acts of the Apostles has a particular bearing on your ministry during this season. During all the other times of the liturgical year, the first of the three readings for the Sunday liturgy is from the Old Testament, but during the Fifty Days the first reading comes from Acts, the second part of the two-part work by the Evangelist Luke.

If you page through this *Workbook* and look at all the first readings on the Sundays of Easter in Year A, you will notice that they are ordered in sequence as they fall in the Bible. Today, the first Sunday after the Easter celebration, the reading comes from the earlier part of Acts, 2:42–47. It describes how the community of faith was built up after the death, Resurrection, and Ascension of Christ. Acts is where we learn of the progress of the Church in narrative form. You will proclaim the building up of the Church by the baptism of many and by the Church's building up of those less fortunate.

Archaeologists have found Eucharistic vessels that people used to bring home pieces of the consecrated bread. The custom of celebrating Mass during the week (between Sundays) did not emerge until the fourth century or so. When people left Mass on Sunday, they brought Eucharistic bread home to receive the Lord during the week, to stay linked to the Church's praise of God, and to be strengthened physically and spiritually until the gathering again on the following Sunday. Though this custom is no

READING II · 1 Peter 1:3–9

A reading from the first Letter of Saint Peter

Blessed be the **God** and **Father** of our Lord Jesus **Christ**,
   who in his great **mercy** gave us a **new** birth to a living **hope**
   through the **resurrection** of Jesus **Christ** from the **dead**,
   to an **inheritance** that is **imperishable**, **undefiled**,
      and **unfading**,
   kept in **heaven** for you
   who by the power of **God** are **safeguarded** through **faith**,
   to a **salvation** that is ready to be **revealed** in the final **time**.

In this you **rejoice**, although now for a little while
   you may have to **suffer** through various **trials**,
   so that the **genuineness** of your faith,
   more precious than **gold** that is perishable even though
      tested by **fire**,
   may prove to be for **praise**, **glory**, and **honor**
   at the **revelation** of Jesus **Christ**.

Although you have not **seen** him you **love** him;
   even though you do not **see** him now yet **believe** in him,
   you **rejoice** with an indescribable and glorious **joy**,
   as you attain the **goal** of your faith, the **salvation** of your **souls**.

The blessings of Easter and its season are wonderful, and God is to be praised for the gifts of Easter. This reading proclaims such Easter praise.
Be careful with these two lines; practice them until they are familiar.

As you proclaim this part about suffering, be mindful of those in your community who even during the Easter season bear many heavy burdens.

The "gold . . . tested by fire" is a vivid image. Practice it so that even though it is split by the phrase "that is perishable," it can be appreciated.

These words about rejoicing bring the reading to a satisfying close. Match the "glorious joy" and hope of Peter's words with your proclamation.

---

longer part of our practice, the remembrance of it in the reading is important.
   Proclaim the reading having practiced well and with Easter joy in your ministry.

READING II This reading is theologically weighty, and well placed on the Sunday after Easter.
   Christians think of Baptism as "new birth," in the sacrament that the Church administers to a person. Yet that "new birth" is as much the new birth of the community

as it is the new birth of the person being baptized. The Church should feel itself reborn whenever it adds a new member to its worshiping community, whether the person is being baptized a few days after birth or a few days before death. So be bold in declaring that God "gave *us* a new birth," for the Church receives the gift whenever the Rite of Baptism is celebrated.
   Another weighty theological point in the Letter of Peter is suffering. We night think that Lent is the forty-day season for

suffering and Easter the fifty-day season for rejoicing. But, for better or worse, the ups and downs of human life are not so neat, and human lives, even of the baptized, are not always played out in "seasons" of sorrow and joy according to the liturgical calendar. The metaphor used by Peter, gold tested by fire, is fitting. As the baptized, we have already gotten the "gold," but our baptism does not exempt us from the difficulties of human life.

Proclaim this time element clearly, for Easter is celebrated for Fifty Days. Post-resurrection appearances are important to the season.

The phrase "Peace be with you" is repeated throughout the passage, a fruit of the liturgy of the community of John's Gospel. (Read below for more.)

This is "doubting Thomas," familiar to the tradition from this passage before you. Take your time with this important narrative.

GOSPEL   John 20:19–31

A reading from the holy Gospel according to John

On the **evening** of that **first** day of the **week**,
    when the **doors** were **locked**, where the disciples were,
    for fear of the Jews,
    Jesus **came** and stood in their **midst**
    and said to them, "**Peace** be with you."
When he had said this, he showed them his **hands** and his **side**.
The disciples **rejoiced** when they saw the Lord.

Jesus said to them **again**, "**Peace** be with you.
As the Father has sent **me**, so I **send** you."

And when he had said this, he **breathed** on them
        and said to them,
    "**Receive** the Holy **Spirit**.
Whose sins you **forgive** are **forgiven** them,
    and whose sins you **retain** are **retained**."

Thomas, called Didymus, one of the **Twelve**,
    was not **with** them when Jesus came.
So the **other** disciples said to him, "We have **seen** the **Lord**."
But he said to them,
    "Unless I see the mark of the **nails** in his **hands**
    and put my **finger** into the **nailmarks**
    and put my **hand** into his **side**, I will **not** believe."

This final section of the passage looks toward the revelation of Jesus Christ to come. It anticipates that time when we will see him and rejoice in the fullness of the experience. In the Easter season here and now, before that glorious time to come, our experience of Christ is not one of absence, for Christ is always present in the Church, in the particular community to which you minister. Claim that experience as your own, and proclaim it boldly to the assembly before you. The salvation of our souls is not only yet to come in the future. Christ is among us in the community of faith and in the Eucharist.

GOSPEL   The Gospel readings during the seasons of Lent and Easter are taken from the Gospel of John. Today's Gospel is from chapter 20 of the Fourth Gospel. The Lectionary cycle is of *three* years, not *four,* so that the Fourth Gospel, with its unique theology, meets the spiritual meanings of Lent and the Easter season.

In the chronology of the text and of the Church year 2005, this passage comes just a little after the Resurrection. The reading starts with a time reference, "On the evening of *that first day* of the week," that is, the day Jesus rose from the dead.

In the same way, the Church gathered at Easter a week ago, and here, on the Second Sunday of Easter, we continue to celebrate the Resurrection as told in the Gospel and as experienced and celebrated in the Church still today.

Another time element, one that captures the weekly gathering, just as the Church continues to this day.

Now a week **later** his disciples were **again** inside
and Thomas was **with** them.
Jesus came, although the **doors** were **locked**,
and stood in their **midst** and said, "**Peace** be with you."
Then he said to **Thomas**, "Put your finger **here** and see my **hands**,
and bring your **hand** and put it into my **side**,
and do not be **unbelieving**, but **believe**."
Thomas answered and said to him, "My **Lord** and my **God**!"

Jesus said to him, "Have you come to **believe**
because you have **seen** me?
Blessed are those who have **not** seen and have **believed**."

Now, Jesus did many **other** signs in the presence of his disciples
that are not **written** in this book.
But **these** are written that you may come to **believe**
that Jesus is the **Christ**, the Son of **God**,
and that **through** this belief you may have **life** in his **name**.

Notice that throughout this Gospel we find the phrase "Peace be with you," which is still part of the liturgical tradition. Many think that the phrase found its way into the liturgy because it was part of the Gospel, but it is historically more likely the other way around: The community of John's Gospel was probably using the phrase "Peace be with you" in its liturgy before the Gospel was written. So the Gospel phrase as you proclaim it is a fruit of the liturgy. Your proclamation can emphasize these words on the lips of the risen Christ so that some in the assembly will pick up on the consonance of Bible and worship.

In the same way, the tactile experience of Thomas—touching the wounds of Christ—is also part of our liturgical experience. All the sacraments call for some physical exchange (except, perhaps, Reconciliation when celebrated in a closed confessional). As with the liturgical phrase, so with the physical experience of the liturgy: Emphasize these elements in your proclamation.

The final paragraph closes grandly. Proclaim it so.

3RD SUNDAY OF EASTER

Lectionary #46

READING I   Acts 2:14, 22–33

A reading from the Acts of the Apostles

Then **Peter** stood up with the **Eleven**,
  raised his **voice**, and **proclaimed**:
"You who are **Jews**, indeed **all** of you staying in **Jerusalem**.
Let this be **known** to you, and **listen** to my words.
You who are **Israelites**, **hear** these words.
Jesus the **Nazarene** was a man commended to you by **God**
  with **mighty deeds**, **wonders**, and **signs**,
    which God worked **through** him in your **midst**,
      as you yourselves **know**.
This **man**, delivered up by the set **plan** and **foreknowledge**
    of God,
  you **killed**, using lawless men to **crucify** him.

"But God raised him **up**, releasing him from the throes of **death**,
  because it was **impossible** for him to be held by it.
For David says of him:
  *I saw the Lord **ever** before me,*
  *with him at my **right hand** I shall not be **disturbed**.*
  *Therefore my **heart** has been **glad** and my **tongue** has **exulted**;*
  *my flesh, **too**, will dwell in **hope**,*
  *because you will not **abandon** my soul to the **netherworld**,*
  *nor will you suffer your **holy** one to see **corruption**.*
  *You have made **known** to me the paths of **life***
  *you will **fill** me with joy in your **presence**.'*

These opening lines set the scene. Pause before beginning so that the assembly is poised to hear you describe the setting. Jerusalem = juh-ROO-suh-lem

Israelites = IZ-ree-uh-līts

Nazarene = naz-uh-REEN

This sentence is complex. Although what seems to be the subject comes at the start, "Jesus of Nazareth," what happened to him ("you killed") is not given for a bit. Mark off what is modifying what so that you are clear before you begin what the meaning should be.

READING I The Baptism of new members today and the power of the Spirit after the death and Resurrection of Jesus are not as far apart in the life of God as they are in the span of human history, for the Spirit moves the Church forward in times of difficulty and times of renewal. As a community of faith, you and your parish need to be reminded of the story of salvation history from the early days, and your vocation in this gathering is to proclaim this reading from Acts about the life of the Church long ago.

The Acts of the Apostles is the second part of the two-part work by the Evangelist Luke. This first reading from Acts and the Gospel reading are from the same hand of Luke, but in the proclamation in the liturgy the readings are transposed in time. The first reading is from the beginning of Acts, that is, the beginning of part two; the Gospel reading is from the end of Luke, that is, the end of part one.

Acts is about the building up of the Church in its early days. The first half of the book, more or less, is taken up with the ministry and work of Peter and the second

half is occupied with the ministry and Mediterranean travels of Paul. Here, early in the Easter season, we are still in the beginning of Acts (chapter 2), so Peter is the focus of the story. He is preaching to the Jewish crowd about Jesus of Nazareth, and he is explaining Jesus' life in the context of history and the Jewish tradition. Peter looks to the patriarch David for words to support the Paschal Mystery and revelation in Jesus.

Be careful with the text, for there are some tricky spots in it. Notice that the first few lines are setting the context, and then

Pause here where the Lectionary gives a slight space.

"My brothers, one can **confidently** say to you
about the patriarch **David** that he **died** and was **buried**,
and his **tomb** is in our midst to this **day**.
But since he was a **prophet** and knew that God had sworn
an **oath** to him
that he would set one of his **descendants** upon his **throne**,
he **foresaw** and **spoke** of the resurrection of the **Christ**,
that neither was he **abandoned** to the **netherworld**
nor did his **flesh** see **corruption**.

The last two lines are consoling and filled with hope. Proclaim them with a tone that bears this meaning.

"God **raised** this Jesus;
of this we are all **witnesses**.
Exalted at the right hand of God,
he received the promise of the Holy **Spirit** from the Father
and poured him **forth**, as you **see** and **hear**."

READING II   1 Peter 1:17–21

A reading from the first Letter of Saint Peter

Beloved:
If you invoke as **Father** him who judges **impartially**
according to each one's **works**,
conduct yourselves with **reverence** during the time
of your **sojourning**,
realizing that you were **ransomed** from your futile conduct,
handed on by your **ancestors**,
not with **perishable** things like **silver** or **gold**
but with the precious **blood** of Christ
as of a **spotless** unblemished **lamb**.

This short reading is theologically weighty. Take your time; study the rhetoric of the passage so that you are clear with what it means.

This middle part is poetic and beautiful. It is a long sentence with a few nested prepositional phrases. Determine what modifies what to clarify your proclamation before you minister.

comes Peter's speech that goes to the end. Within that speech, Peter quotes David. Practice the reading so that your hearers will recognize and appreciate these nuances.

READING II This reading is beautiful but complex, and some of the complexities make it important for you to take your time to prepare this proclamation well. Notice, for example, that the second sentence is a long one. Sustaining the

attention of the assembly with such an extended and theologically dense idea will not be easy.

The poetic imagery in that long middle sentence is potent. The author was thinking of perishable things with which to compare the imperishable, and chose gold and silver. These were good choices, not only because they were familiar and valuable in the first century, but because they are still familiar

and valuable. But "the precious blood of Christ" surely outweighs the precious metals.

The writing was much closer in time to the death of Jesus than we are, but even so, it was still a long time after that death. It is likely that the blood the author had in mind was both the blood of the suffering Christ and the Eucharistic wine. In this sense, the reading has a deep meaning for your assembly that shares the cup in this liturgy.

He was **known** before the foundation of the **world**
  but **revealed** in the **final** time for you,
  who **through** him believe in **God**
  who **raised** him from the **dead** and gave him **glory**,
  so that your **faith** and **hope** are in **God**.

GOSPEL   Luke 24:13–35

A reading from the holy Gospel according to Luke

That very **day**, the **first** day of the week,
  two of Jesus' **disciples** were going
  to a village seven miles from Jerusalem called **Emmaus**,
  and they were **conversing** about all the things
    that had **occurred**.
And it **happened** that while they were **conversing** and **debating**,
  Jesus **himself** drew near and **walked** with them,
  but their **eyes** were prevented from **recognizing** him.

He asked them,
  "What are you **discussing** as you walk along?"
They **stopped**, looking **downcast**.
One of them, named **Cleopas**, said to him in **reply**,
  "Are you the **only** visitor to **Jerusalem**
  who does **not** know of the things
  that have taken **place** there in these days?"

A number of elements in this Gospel reading will make the text immediate to your assembly. The opening time identification ("the first day of the week," that is, Sunday) is one of these.
Jerusalem = juh-ROO-suh-lem
Emmaus = eh-MAY-us

Another common element is that we often do not recognize the presence of Christ in our fellow Christians.

Cleopas = KLEE-oh-pus

This is a summary of the Paschal Mystery delivered to the "only visitor to Jerusalem" who does not know of it.

GOSPEL   This reading from the end of the Gospel of Luke has made an immeasurable contribution to our sacramental theology and to the celebration of the Eucharist. It is also a fairly long Gospel passage, so you should use your most engaging story-telling and proclamation abilities to keep the assembly attentive to what unfolds. There are a couple of characteristics of the reading that will help.

First, the reading has a strong narrative progression, a clear beginning, middle, and end. There are no extended exhortations in the middle of the story, merely some exchanges that advance the action.

Second, the proclaimer and the listeners have more information in the story than do the two disciples going along the way to Emmaus. The Evangelist reveals to the hearers that "Jesus himself drew near and walked with them, but their eyes were prevented from recognizing him." The assembly before you knows a secret that two of the main characters do not. You can use this to hold the assembly's attention.

Third, the assembly before you shares a number of things with the two disciples. Like them, the Church comes together on "the first day of the week," Sunday. Moreover, the stranger explained the scriptures to the two, just as in the Sunday Eucharist the scriptures are proclaimed and interpreted.

Nazarene = naz-uh-REEN

Israel = IZ-ree-ul

And he replied to them, "What **sort** of things?"
They said to him,
    "The things that happened to **Jesus** the **Nazarene**,
    who was a **prophet** mighty in **deed** and **word**
    before **God** and all the **people**,
    how our chief **priests** and **rulers** both handed him **over**
    to a sentence of **death** and **crucified** him.
But we were **hoping** that he would be the one to redeem **Israel**;
    and besides all **this**,
    it is now the third **day** since this took **place**.
Some **women** from our group, however, have **astounded** us:
    they were at the **tomb** early in the **morning**
    and did not find his **body**;
    they came **back** and reported
    that they had **indeed** seen a vision of **angels**
    who announced that he was **alive**.

"Then some of those **with** us went to the tomb
    and found things **just** as the women had **described**,
    but him they did **not** see."

And he said to them, "Oh, how **foolish** you are!
How slow of **heart** to believe all that the **prophets** spoke!
Was it not **necessary** that the Christ should **suffer** these things
    and enter into his **glory**?"

Another common element is the proclamation and interpretation of the scriptures, which Christ did for the two disciples, and which you, in proclaiming and preaching today, will also do.

Then beginning with **Moses** and all the **prophets**,
    he **interpreted** to them what **referred** to him
    in all the **Scriptures**.
As they approached the **village** to which they were **going**,
    he gave the **impression** that he was going on **farther**.
But they urged him, "**Stay** with us,
    for it is nearly **evening** and the day is almost **over**."
So he went in to **stay** with them.

Next, the risen Christ is with the two on the way to Emmaus just as the risen Christ is present in the Church gathered for Sunday Mass. Finally, the sign in which the risen Christ is recognized in the Church is the bread broken and shared.

As you prepare and as you proclaim, deliver these ritual common elements in such a way that they are recognizable to those in the assembly. It is important that—as time moves on, as the Church proclaims the Good News in new places—there are some rituals that unite the people of God over the centuries. And in this unity they experience the presence of the risen Christ, and recognize that their experience is indeed that of God's gift in the Son.

The final continuous element is the sacred meal of bread taken, blessed, broken, and shared, in which the risen Christ is recognized.

And it **happened** that, while he was **with** them at **table**,
he took **bread**, said the **blessing**,
broke it, and **gave** it to them.
With that their **eyes** were **opened** and they **recognized** him,
but he **vanished** from their **sight**.

Then they said to each other,
"Were not our hearts **burning** within us
while he **spoke** to us on the **way** and opened the **Scriptures**
to us?"

So they set out at **once** and returned to **Jerusalem**
where they found gathered together
the **eleven** and those **with** them who were saying,
"The Lord has truly been **raised** and has appeared to **Simon**!"

Then the two recounted
what had taken place on the **way**
and how he was made **known** to them in the **breaking** of **bread**.

In the season of Easter, the risen Christ reveals himself again and again to different people, in different places, as he has done ever since, whenever people come together for worship and the sacraments.

4TH SUNDAY OF EASTER

Lectionary #49

READING I   Acts 2:14a, 36–41

A reading from the Acts of the Apostles

Then **Peter** stood up with the **Eleven**,
  raised his voice, and **proclaimed**:
"Let the whole house of **Israel** know for certain
  that **God** has made both **Lord** and **Christ**,
  this **Jesus** whom you **crucified**."

Now when they heard **this**, they were cut to the **heart**,
  and they **asked** Peter and the other **apostles**,
  "What are we to **do**, my brothers?"
Peter said to them,
  "**Repent** and be **baptized**, every **one** of you,
  in the name of Jesus **Christ** for the **forgiveness** of your **sins**;
  and you will **receive** the **gift** of the Holy **Spirit**.
For the promise is made to **you** and to your **children**
  and to **all** those far **off**,
  whomever the Lord our God will **call**."

He testified with many **other** arguments,
    and was **exhorting** them,
  "**Save** yourselves from this **corrupt** generation."
Those who accepted his message were **baptized**,
    and about three **thousand** persons were **added** that day.

READING I   When the Evangelist reports that Peter "raised his voice, and proclaimed," he could not give a better example to you in your ministry of the word: Raise your voice! Make eye contact! Address the believers before you!

The Easter season is the season of celebrating and remembering Baptism. The fruit of welcoming those who were baptized and confirmed at the Easter Vigil and of the sprinkling rites of the Easter season is that the members of the Church recall their own saving baptism and the coming of the Holy Spirit. This reading will help the assembly in recalling Baptism since this is mentioned explicitly in this early part of Acts.

The rite of Baptism is no less efficacious for those who were baptized as infants, that is, before we could know what was happening. So as you prepare, be mindful that this passage has importance for the strengthening of our fellow believers. This reading does not make the result of Baptism any deeper, but it does provide an opportunity to appreciate our salvation in the gift of the Holy Spirit and to appreciate how the rite of Baptism has endured in the two millennia of Christian history, from that first Pentecost until this very Easter season in which you exercise your ministry.

READING II   You will notice as you prepare this reading that there is a verse in italics in the middle of the passage. The author is quoting from the prophet Isaiah, but the quote is not identified as such. Because the quote fits in seamlessly with the rest of the passage, it is better

READING II   1 Peter 2:20b–25

A reading from the first Letter of Saint Peter

Beloved:

If you are **patient** when you **suffer** for doing what is **good**,
     this is a **grace** before **God**.
For to **this** you have been **called**,
     because Christ **also** suffered for **you**,
     leaving you an **example** that you should **follow** in his **footsteps**.
*He committed **no** sin, and no **deceit** was found in his **mouth**.*

When he was **insul**ted, he returned **no** insult;
     when he **suffered**, he did not **threaten**;
     instead, he handed himself over to the one who judges **justly**.

He **himself** bore our **sins** in his **body** upon the **cross**,
     so that, **free** from **sin**, we might **live** for **righteousness**.
By his **wounds** you have been **healed**.

For you had gone astray like **sheep**,
     but you have now returned to the **shepherd** and **guardian**
          of your **souls**.

On how to handle this quote, read the commentary below. Basically, proclaim it as if the italics were not there.

This verse is theologically very important. Pause slightly before you proclaim it.

The final metaphor of "shepherd and guardian of your souls" is beautiful.

not to proclaim the quoted verse in a different tone or with any particular emphasis. In most instances, it *is* important to distinguish such a quote from its context, but here, that would be disorienting for the hearers.

The reading has three fundamental parts. The first and third parts address the hearers directly, "you" and "your." Practice the reading so that it becomes familiar enough that you can look up from the Lectionary during the proclamation. Then, as you proclaim these parts of direct address, engage the assembly with eye contact. The word of God is indeed living and active, and

it is as powerful proclaimed by you in the assembly today as it was in the early days of the Church about which we hear.

The second part of the reading is theologically very important. Some of its profundity is in its reflections on suffering. In the celebration of the Resurrection during the Easter season, the rising of Christ is not separable from Christ's death. These are embraced in the Paschal Mystery, and the community of faith into which the baptized are inducted both experiences and celebrates the death and the Resurrection, as the reading you proclaim will remind the Church.

The reading assures the Church that in his own body Christ bore the sins of those of us who live today. As the reading says, we are freed from sin because he bore our sins in his body. As the reading itself proclaims, "By his wounds you have been healed." Believe this and proclaim it with conviction.

GOSPEL   In all three years (A, B, and C) this Fourth Sunday of Easter is Good Shepherd Sunday. Here we find this Gospel passage from John expanding on this metaphor, with Jesus as the gate

GOSPEL   John 10:1–10

A reading from the holy Gospel according to John

Pause slightly between the identification of the Gospel and the first line so that it is heard clearly.

Jesus said:
"**Amen**, **amen**, I say to you,
    whoever does not enter a **sheepfold** through the **gate**
    but climbs over **elsewhere** is a **thief** and a **robber**.
But whoever enters through the **gate** is the **shepherd** of the sheep.
The gatekeeper **opens** it for him, and the sheep hear his **voice**,
    as the shepherd **calls** his own sheep by **name**
        and leads them **out**.
When he has driven out all his own,
    he walks **ahead** of them, and the sheep **follow** him,
    because they **recognize** his **voice**.
But they will **not** follow a **stranger**;
    they will run **away** from him,
    because they do **not** recognize the voice of **strangers**."
Although Jesus used this figure of **speech**,
    the Pharisees did **not** realize what he was trying to **tell** them.

Pharisees = FAIR-uh-seez

The first of the I AM sentences characteristic of the Gospel of John. (See below.)

So Jesus said **again**, "**Amen**, **amen**, I say to you,
    I am the **gate** for the **sheep**.
All who came **before** me are **thieves** and **robbers**,
    but the sheep did not **listen** to them.
I am the gate.

The second I AM statement.

Whoever enters through **me** will be **saved**,
    and will come **in** and go **out** and find **pasture**.
A thief comes only to **steal** and **slaughter** and **destroy**;
    I came so that they might have **life**
        and have it more **abundantly**."

The final line is a touching description of Jesus' mission; its positive meaning is a good ending for the passage, so take your time with it for clarity.

for the sheep. The metaphors of shepherd and sheep are not unique to the Gospel of John, of course; the other Gospels have narratives and parables in which sheep and shepherds are essential. But the theology of the Gospel of John takes up the metaphor in a unique way.

One of the many unique aspects of the Fourth Gospel is the emphasis of such metaphors by a very simple grammatical structure. More familiar than today's "I am the gate" are the other I AM passages of this Gospel, such as "I am the bread of life," "I am the vine," "I am the resurrection and the life," and so on. This Gospel reading has two such passages; the first is preceded by a characteristic literary introduction of John, "Amen, amen, I say to you," a signal that what follows is important, and then "I am the gate for the sheep." We Christians believe that all salvation is mediated by God's Son, Jesus Christ, so the simplicity of the second "I AM" statement is matched by its theological depth: "I am the gate."

Most of the reading for this Good Shepherd Sunday is made up of words from Jesus, with an introductory line at the start and another few lines in the middle that reveal the Pharisees' lack of understanding. This misunderstanding or lack of understanding is a characteristic literary device in this Gospel, whether it is the disciples who misunderstand or Jesus' opponents.

5TH SUNDAY OF EASTER

Lectionary #52

READING I   Acts 6:1–7

A reading from the Acts of the Apostles

As the **number** of **disciples** continued to **grow**,
    the **Hellenists** complained against the **Hebrews**
    because their **widows**
    were being **neglected** in the daily **distribution**.
So the **Twelve** called together the **community** of the disciples
        and said,
    "It is not **right** for us to **neglect** the word of **God**
        to serve at **table**.
Brothers, **select** from among you **seven reputable** men,
    filled with the **Spirit** and **wisdom**,
    whom we shall **appoint** to this task,
    whereas **we** shall devote ourselves to **prayer**
    and to the ministry of the **word**."

The proposal was **acceptable** to the whole **community**,
    so they chose **Stephen**, a man filled with **faith**
        and the Holy **Spirit**,
    also **Philip**, **Prochorus**, **Nicanor**, **Timon**, **Parmenas**,
    and **Nicholas** of **Antioch**, a convert to **Judaism**.
They **presented** these men to the **apostles**
    who **prayed** and laid **hands** on them.

This neglect of the widows can be a indirect consolation to us. We often romanticize the early Church, thinking that all was wonderful then and has deteriorated ever since, but this makes clear that our forebears in the Church were as imperfect as we are.

This list of the seven deacons has a few unfamiliar names. More important than accuracy is confidence. Pronounce them as easily as the more familiar names and the assembly will follow the story, not be distracted by the strange names.
Prochorus = PROCK-uh-rus
Nicanor = nī-KAY-ner
Timon = TĪ-mun
Parmenas = PAR-muh-nus
Antioch = AN-tee-ahk

READING I   The Easter season began with a reading from Acts that told us of the baptism of three thousand people on one occasion. That revealed the enthusiasm and fervor of those earliest days. The reading from Acts for this Fifth Sunday of Easter is also revelatory about the building up of the Church in those early years, but here, in chapter 6 of Acts, the increase is not so huge. Those added were to serve in the community, and there was a process of discernment in choosing the "seven reputable men."

It might be appropriate to think of these two types of Church increase as a balance of charism and office, both under the guidance of the Holy Spirit, with the former a spontaneous gift in the service of the Church at a particular time and the latter more like what we today think of as ordination. Complementing this "office" is the ritual gesture of the laying on of hands, which has long been a traditional rite for the completion of formation for orders and the

beginning of ministry. The Church thrives because of the energy stirred up by both those who are enthusiastic in their Church work and those who are committed for the long haul.

Tradition has come to designate Stephen and his six fellow ministers as the first deacons. The etymology of the word "deacon" reveals that it means to "serve at table." In the passage we do not find the word "deacon," but we find the original meaning.

Jerusalem = juh-ROO-suh-lem
The last line tells us of the increase in the Church as a result of the ministers chosen. Proclaim with an optimistic tone in this Easter season; the Spirit is still at work.

The word of God continued to **spread**,
 and the **number** of the disciples in Jerusalem increased **greatly**;
 even a large group of **priests** were becoming **obedient**
  to the **faith**.

READING II   1 Peter 2:4–9

A reading from the first Letter of Saint Peter

Beloved:
Come to him, a living **stone**, rejected by human beings
 but **chosen** and **precious** in the sight of God,
 and, like **living** stones,
 let **yourselves** be built into a spiritual **house**
 to be a holy **priesthood** to offer spiritual **sacrifices**
 acceptable to God through Jesus **Christ**.

Recall the "stone that the builders rejected," which follows below.

For it says in **Scripture**:
 *Behold, I am laying a **stone** in Zion,*
 *a **cornerstone**, chosen and **precious**,*
 and whoever believes in it shall not be put to shame.
Therefore, its **value** is for you who have **faith**,
  but for those **without** faith:
*The stone that the builders **rejected***
*has become the **cornerstone**,*
*and a **stone** that will make people **stumble**,*
*and a **rock** that will make them **fall**.*
They **stumble** by disobeying the **word**, as is their **destiny**.

Zion is the promised land, a holy place.
Zion = ZĪ-ahn

The writer drew from other sources in sacred Scripture in which the metaphors of building and stones were used. Proclaim these as quotations.

Not to be missed is the neglect of the widows that prompted the complaint. This might be a consolation to those in the Church who sometimes think that things were terrific in the early Church and have gone downhill ever since. This neglect of the widows tells us that this was not so, that even soon after the death of Jesus, the Church was not always attentive to those in need.

READING II One of the most beautiful rites of the Church is one that most people never experience, the Rite of Dedication of a Church. In this rite, the bishop comes to the new building. It is mentioned here because this passage from the First Letter of Peter is not only one of the readings in the Lectionary for the Rite of Dedication, but the metaphors in this passage that you will proclaim punctuate the prayers in the Rite of Dedication from start to finish.

Important in the theology of the dedication of a church and on this Sunday of Easter when you minister to your assembly is the application of the metaphor of the living stone to both the Lord and to the Church, the people of God.

The letter is written to a particular recipient, and that reader is addressed in the second person, "you." In this beautiful passage, Peter writes, "let yourselves be built into a spiritual house," and "for you

The images of darkness and light were central to the readings of Lent and they persist into the Easter season. This is important since the Easter candle, a symbol of Christ, burns throughout the season of Fifty Days.

You are *a **chosen** race, a royal **priesthood**,*
*a holy **nation**, a people of his **own**,*
*so that you may announce the **praises** of him*
who called you **out** of **darkness into** his wonderful **light**.

GOSPEL John 14:1–12

A reading from the holy Gospel according to John

Jesus said to his **disciples**:
"Do not let your **hearts** be **troubled**.
You have faith in **God**; have faith also in **me**.
In my Father's **house** there are **many** dwelling places.
If there were **not**,
would I have **told** you that I am going to prepare
a **place** for you?
And if I go and prepare a **place** for you,
I will come **back** again and take you to **myself**,
so that where **I** am you **also** may be.
Where **I** am going **you** know the **way**."

Thomas said to him,
"**Master**, we do not know **where** you are going;
how can we know the way?"

The images of houses and dwelling places connect this reading to the second reading.

Thomas is usually remembered for his moment of doubt. Here he asks for clarification.

---

who have faith," and "you are a chosen race, a royal priesthood." Whenever such direct address appears in the text you are to proclaim, you are not imitating the author as you proclaim his words. But, like that author, you are ministering the word of God to the one, holy, catholic, and apostolic assembly, to the Body of Christ, or, to pick from the language of this reading, to a "holy nation," those with whom you worship. As in the early Church, so now: These are the people of God, the living stones built up by the sacraments and by the ministry of the word, which you proclaim.

GOSPEL Throughout most of the Lectionary, there is a consonance between the first reading (from the Hebrew Scriptures) and the third reading (from the Gospel). Today, the link is more clearly between the second reading (from the First Letter of Peter) and the third reading (from the Gospel of John). The images that the readings share are those of buildings.

The second reading, which you might read as preparation for your own proclamation, has images of "stones," a "cornerstone," and a "rock." The Gospel reading has the "dwelling places" and the places which Jesus promises to prepare for his followers. Be mindful of these metaphorical connections so that your proclamation can facilitate the assembly's appreciation of the Lectionary's structure.

Here is the "I AM" sentence so characteristic of the theology of this Gospel.

Jesus said to him, "I am the **way** and the **truth** and the **life**.
No one comes to the **Father** except through **me**.
If you know **me**, then you will **also** know my **Father**.
From now **on** you **do** know him and have **seen** him."

Like Thomas, Philip is not often mentioned among the disciples.

Philip said to him,
    "**Master**, **show** us the Father, and that will be **enough** for us."

Jesus said to him, "Have I been with you for so long a time
    and you **still** do not know me, Philip?
Whoever has seen **me** has seen the **Father**.
How can you say, 'Show us the **Father**'?
Do you not believe that **I** am in the **Father**
        and the **Father** is in **me**?
The words that **I** speak to you I do not speak on my **own**.
The Father who **dwells** in me is doing his **works**.
Believe me that **I** am in the **Father** and the **Father** is in **me**,
    or else, believe because of the works **themselves**.
Amen, **amen**, I say to you,
    whoever believes in **me** will do the works that I do,
    and will do **greater** ones than these,
    because **I** am going to the **Father**."

Pause before the final verse, and address the assembly with conviction and encouragement as you proclaim these words of Jesus.

In this Gospel we also find the characteristically Johannine "I AM" phrase. This is not used in the synoptic Gospels as in John, yet most Christians are familiar with these sayings: "I am the good shepherd"; "I am the bread of life"; "I am the light of the world"; "I am the resurrection and the life"; "I am the true vine." Even approaching the cross, Jesus tells the guards looking for him, "I AM," after which the guards fall prostrate. The Gospel you prepare has another of these sayings: "I am the way and the truth and the life."

These images of the life and ministry and true identity of Jesus Christ are foundational to Christian thought and theology. For many of the sayings mentioned above, the context is familiar to those who hear it, but in the Gospel you prepare, the "I AM" saying is not as reflective of the context as some of the others. Your work is to proclaim the passage clearly so that, when the "I AM" sentence comes, the assembly recognizes its gravity.

The disciples mentioned by name in the passage, Thomas and Philip, are not mentioned in scripture as often as some of their fellow disciples. So be clear in reading their names so that this, one of the few narratives with their words, will be well received.

6TH SUNDAY OF EASTER

Lectionary #55

READING I   Acts 8:5–8, 14–17

A reading from the Acts of the Apostles

Samaria = suh-MAIR-ee-uh
This first half of the reading tells us of the extraordinary ministry of the apostles, Philip in particular.

Philip went down to the city of **Samaria**
    and proclaimed the **Christ** to them.
With one **accord**, the crowds paid **attention**
      to what was said by Philip
    when they **heard** it and saw the **signs** he was doing.
For unclean **spirits**, crying out in a loud **voice**,
    came out of many possessed **people**,
    and many **paralyzed** or **crippled** people were **cured**.
There was great **joy** in that city.

Jerusalem = juh-ROO-suh-lem

The second half has the ritual and sacramental elements that are still part of our Church life. Take your time here and proclaim clearly so that your hearers can appreciate the connection between the experience of the early Church and their own experience.

Now when the apostles in **Jerusalem**
    heard that **Samaria** had accepted the word of **God**,
    they sent them **Peter** and **John**,
    who went down and **prayed** for them,
    that they might **receive** the Holy **Spirit**,
    for it had not yet **fallen** upon **any** of them;
    they had **only** been baptized in the **name** of the Lord **Jesus**.
Then they **laid** hands on them
    and they **received** the Holy **Spirit**.

READING I   A few months ago, during Lent, as the Church was getting itself (and its candidates for initiation) ready for Easter, we heard a long Gospel reading from John in which Jesus asked an anonymous woman at the well for something to drink. In that reading, the Evangelist mentions that "Jews use nothing in common with Samaritans." Yet Jesus was violating the custom and law by conversing with the Samaritan woman who had been married five times. Here we find ourselves again reading and hearing about Samaritans, this time not from the Evangelist John, but from the Evangelist Luke, who wrote the Acts of the Apostles as the second part of his theological chronicle.

As you prepare the reading, notice in the second half of the passage the ritual actions that are still part of our life in the Church today. Philip proclaimed the Messiah and the Samaritans accepted the word of God. There is also the prayer for the reception of the Holy Spirit and the laying on of hands for the Holy Spirit. These are part of the tradition that the Church maintains, and they are especially important to your proclamation during the Fifty Days of this Church season.

In the first half of the reading, we find the extraordinary deeds of the apostles. "Unclean spirits, crying out in a loud voice, came out of many possessed people; and many paralyzed or crippled people were cured." These are not completely unheard of among Christians today, but they are not as familiar as the prayers for the Holy Spirit and the proclamation of the word that are also mentioned. As you proclaim the reading, be confident in these actions of God and

READING II   1 Peter 3:15–18

A reading from the first Letter of Saint Peter

Beloved:

Sanctify Christ as **Lord** in your **hearts**.
Always be **ready** to give an explanation
    to **anyone** who asks you for a reason for your **hope**,
      but do it with **gentleness** and **reverence**,
      keeping your conscience **clear**,
      so **that**, when you are **maligned**,
      those who defame your good conduct in **Christ**
      may **themselves** be put to **shame**.
For it is **better** to suffer for doing **good**,
    if **that** be the will of **God**, than for doing **evil**.

For Christ **also** suffered for sins once,
    the **righteous** for the sake of the **unrighteous**,
    that he might lead you to **God**.
Put to **death** in the **flesh**,
    he was brought to **life** in the **Spirit**.

Address the assembly as if this letter had been written by you to them. You are not pretending that these are your words, but by your strong reading you are encouraging and teaching the assembly about living the Christian life.

This theological point is important for the Easter season. We know that, though Jesus had died, he is alive in the Spirit.

in the power of the Spirit so that your confidence will bring conviction to the assembly to which you minister.

In places where the Ascension of the Lord is celebrated next Sunday, May 8, the second reading and the Gospel of the Seventh Sunday of Easter (lectionary #59) may be read today. Check with the liturgy coordinator or homilist to find out which readings will be used today.

READING II Scholars have discovered some Christian books and letters that are as old as or even older than those included in the New Testament but were excluded from scripture because they did not provide such a measure of help for the Christian life. The second readings at Sunday Mass, letters from early Church leaders giving advice to Church members, are often written as direct address, from "me" to "you." Readings in this literary style are not merely a perspective on antiquity, on the age in which the apostles and Jesus' followers lived. They often give a theology that is as timely today as it was then. For this reason, as a proclaimer of the word, you stand in the place of the writer of the letter, and you animate the word of God for your community; you bring the word of God to life in a new time and new place.

The reading you are preparing for this Sunday has many important theological and moral points: "do it with gentleness and reverence"; "keeping your conscience clear"; "Christ also suffered for sins once," he was "put to death in the flesh," and "brought to life in the Spirit." The letter of Peter is proclaimed in this joyful season of Easter, but it

GOSPEL   John 14:15–21

A reading from the holy Gospel according to John

Jesus said to his **disciples**:
"If you **love** me, you will keep my **commandments**.
And I will ask the **Father**,
　　and he will give you another **Advocate** to be with you **always**,
　　the Spirit of **truth**, whom the world cannot **accept**,
　　because it neither **sees** nor **knows** him.
But **you** know him, because he **remains** with you,
　　and will be **in** you.

"I will not leave you **orphans**; I will come to you.
In a **little** while the **world** will no longer **see** me,
　　but **you** will see me, because **I** live and **you** will live.
On **that** day you will realize that **I** am in my **Father**
　　and **you** are in **me** and **I** in **you**.

"Whoever **has** my commandments and **observes** them
　　is the one who **loves** me.
And whoever loves **me** will be loved by my **Father**,
　　and **I** will love him and **reveal** myself to him."

This opening line of the Gospel is the only part not spoken from the lips of Jesus. Pause between the identification of the reading and this opening so that the assembly will hear these five words of context.

Pause here, for this begins a new topic.

Pause here as well.

takes up painful issues. The Paschal Mystery embraces death and resurrection, suffering and new life, and this letter reflects that mystery in its theology of suffering and death during the Fifty Days.

　　The timelessness of such a reading makes your ministry even clearer. Be confident in your proclamation by taking the words to heart according to your own experience of faith and the Church.

GOSPEL   **We are still two weeks away from the Solemnity of Pentecost, the close of the Fifty Days of the**

Easter season, yet already the readings are hinting at the animating presence of the Spirit in the Church. When this Gospel was written, the Church had already experienced the presence of this Advocate. The things written here of the Spirit's activity in the world and the community of John's Gospel were not foretelling the future but describing what that particular community knew of the Spirit's life. For this reason this Gospel about the Holy Spirit's presence in the world and Church and about observing the commandments of Christ is as relevant and

essential for the Church today as it was when the Evangelist wrote them down.

　　As you prepare for this proclamation, notice that many of the key words and ideas appear more than once. This should not incline you to proclaim it quickly, but to discern its meaning carefully and deliver the text in a measured way so that its theology of Easter and of the presence of the Spirit will come through clearly in the Liturgy of the Word. Your proclamation will be more convincing as you are convinced of the power of the Spirit of truth and of the love of God the Father.

ASCENSION OF THE LORD

Lectionary #58

READING I   Acts 1:1–11

A reading from the beginning of the Acts of the Apostles

Theophilus = thee-OFF-uh-lus

The "I" here is the author of Acts, the Evangelist Luke. These opening three verses are the introduction to the whole book of Acts.

In the **first** book, **Theophilus**,
   I dealt with all that Jesus **did** and **taught**
   until the day he was taken **up**,
   after giving **instructions** through the Holy **Spirit**
   to the **apostles** whom he had **chosen**.
He presented himself **alive** to them
   by many **proofs** after he had **suffered**,
   appearing to them during **forty** days
   and **speaking** about the kingdom of **God**.

Jerusalem = juh-ROO-suh-lem

While **meeting** with them,
   he **enjoined** them not to depart from **Jerusalem**,
   but to wait for "the **promise** of the Father
   about which you have heard me **speak**;
   for **John** baptized with **water**,
   but in a few **days** you will be baptized with the Holy **Spirit**."

Pause before beginning this section, for here the text picks up the topic of the Holy Spirit.

When they had gathered together they **asked** him,
   "**Lord**, are you at this time going to restore
   the kingdom to **Israel**?"

Israel = IZ-ree-ul

If the Ascension of the Lord is celebrated next Sunday, May 8, today's readings are used then in place of those for the Seventh Sunday of Easter.

READING I   At the start of Acts, the Evangelist Luke names the person to whom he is writing, as he did at the start of the Gospel. The name Theophilus means "one who loves *[-philus]* God *[theo-]*." Luke's two books might be written for a single particular person of the first century, or they might be addressed more generally to anyone who loves God. If so, the Gospel and Acts were and are addressed to all who love God.

This is a long first reading, so it will require some skill to keep the assembly engaged by your proclamation. The reading has three basic parts: an introduction to the book of Acts, an anticipation of the coming of the Holy Spirit, and the narrative of the Ascension.

Luke is the only Evangelist to mention "forty days" between the Resurrection and the Ascension. For the first few centuries of the Church's worship, the Ascension was proclaimed in the Easter season but not forty days after Easter. Only at the end of the fourth century did the Ascension find its place on the fortieth day of the season on Ascension Thursday, as it came to be known. Even today there is no consensus in the Church about when the Ascension is to be celebrated. In some dioceses, it is on Ascension Thursday, while in others it is on the Sunday after that. Such variety is to be expected in the inculturation of the liturgy.

Because the reading has three distinct topics, pause after each so that the assembly can absorb it. Be most clear and

Judea = joo-DEE-uh
Samaria = suh-MAIR-ee-uh

These final three verses are the narrative
of the Ascension. Take your time and be
clear with it, for this is the only scriptural
Ascension story proclaimed today. The
Gospel does not include the Ascension.

The "white garments" are symbols of the
Paschal Mystery, also reflected in the
white vestments worn throughout the
Easter season.

Galilee = GAL-ih-lee

He answered them, "It is not for you to know the **times**
  or **seasons**
    that the **Father** has established by his own **authority**.
But you will receive **power** when the Holy **Spirit** comes upon you,
  and you will be my **witnesses** in **Jerusalem**,
    throughout Judea and Samaria,
    and to the ends of the **earth**."

When he had **said** this, as they were looking **on**,
  he was lifted **up**, and a cloud **took** him from their **sight**.
While they were looking intently at the **sky** as he was **going**,
  suddenly **two** men dressed in white **garments**
    stood beside them.

They said, "Men of **Galilee**,
  why are you **standing** there looking at the **sky**?
This **Jesus** who has been taken **up** from you into **heaven**
  will **return** in the same way as you have **seen** him
    going into **heaven**."

engaging in the third part, since it bears the
christological element at the heart of the
liturgical celebration of the Ascension.

READING II This is a reading of cosmic
scope. Since Christianity is
now a world religion, phrases like "far
above every principality, authority, power,
and dominion" may not sound surprising.
But when we consider how small the Church
was when this prayer of Ephesians was
written, we can see how grand the hope of
the early communities really was.

As you prepare for this proclamation, it
might be useful to think about this increase
in the Church over the years. It is important
to bear in mind that the mission of the
Church is to lead the pilgrim people to God.
The Church has faced many difficulties over
the years (listen to Pope John Paul II on sin
and forgiveness in the Church), but recall
the many contributions that the Church has
made to culture, to education, to the poor
and downtrodden, and to so many areas of
life. On its best days, it truly is a reflection of
God's "surpassing greatness" and the "exercise of his great might."

You can see from the first word of the
reading that the author was offering this
community his own prayer for it. Even though
the passage moves quickly into the universe
in its scope, it starts with the author's prayer
for the community of faith. Your proclamation can also be offered to the gathered
faithful with the same vigorous prayer and
hope, as the text itself says, with the "eyes
of your hearts . . . enlightened."

This reading is proclaimed on the
Ascension because it captures the exaltation of Christ as he takes his place at the

Ephesians = ee-FEE-zhunz

READING II   Ephesians 1:17–23

A reading from the Letter of Saint Paul to the Ephesians

Brothers and sisters:
May the **God** of our Lord Jesus **Christ**, the Father of **glory**,
  give you a Spirit of **wisdom** and **revelation**
  resulting in **knowledge** of him.
May the **eyes** of your **hearts** be **enlightened**,
  that you may **know** what is the **hope** that belongs to his **call**,
  what are the riches of **glory**
  in his **inheritance** among the **holy** ones,
  and what is the surpassing **greatness** of his **power**
  for us who **believe**,
  in accord with the **exercise** of his great **might**,
  which he worked in **Christ**,
  raising him from the **dead**
  and **seating** him at his **right** hand in the **heavens**,
  far above every **principality**, **authority**, **power**, and **dominion**,
  and **every** name that is **named**
  not only in **this** age but also in the one to **come**.

And he put **all** things beneath his **feet**
  and gave him as **head** over **all** things to the **church**,
  which is his **body**,
  the **fullness** of the one who fills **all** things in every **way**.

Notice the first-person identification, "us who believe." Since the word is living and active, this first-person speaker in your assembly is yourself. Proclaim the passage with spirited conviction. Address the assembly directly as the "you" of Paul's letter.

From this point to the end, the reading talks about the manifestation of God's power in the Resurrection. The exaltation of Christ described in this part is lofty; consider how you would imagine the scene described in the letter, and let your proclamation be strengthened by the visual images.

right hand of the Father. The Ascension is not described explicitly in the text, but it speaks of God raising Christ from the dead for all ages to come.

GOSPEL   Christ's charge to the disciples in this Gospel is often called the Great Commission. Here the risen Christ gives the command and the authority to his disciples, minus Judas, to go out, spread the word, baptize, and teach. Only the Gospel of Matthew has such a formal, authoritative charge.

This part of Matthew's narrative is brief. Moreover, it appears in the Lectionary only once in the three-year cycle. So, aware of its brevity, its theological importance, and its infrequent appearance in the liturgy, proclaim it well.

A few things to think about as you prepare for the proclamation. First, the Gospel has two basic parts, one setting up the context in narrative form and the other giving us the words that Jesus delivered there on the mountain. Like the liturgy itself, always with

a balance of action and words in the sacraments and scriptures, the Gospel has balance. Second, the mission to which Jesus directs the disciples has that same balance of word ("teaching") and action ("baptizing them in the name of the Father and of the Son and of the Holy Spirit").

In the Gospel of Matthew, in particular, where the Evangelist seeks to show the fulfillment of the Hebrew Scriptures in the life of Jesus, scenes on mountains have a unique gravity. The Evangelist has plotted out the life of Jesus as the fulfillment of the life of

This Gospel reading is relatively short, so don't rush through it. This first part sets the scene for the risen Jesus' address to the eleven disciples (the twelve minus Judas). Galilee = GAL-ih-lee

Here begins the proclamation from Jesus, in which he directs the disciples to go out into the world and make disciples by baptism. They did, and the Church is still doing what he said!

The finale is a message of comfort and consolation.

GOSPEL   Matthew 28:16–20

A reading from the holy Gospel according to Matthew

The eleven **disciples** went to **Galilee**,
    to the **mountain** to which Jesus had **ordered** them.
When they saw him, they **worshiped**, but they **doubted**.

Then Jesus **approached** and said to them,
    "All power in **heaven** and on **earth** has been **given** to me.
Go, therefore, and make **disciples** of all **nations**,
    baptizing them in the name of the **Father**,
    and of the **Son**, and of the Holy **Spirit**,
    teaching them to **observe** all that I have **commanded** you.

"And **behold**, I am with you **always**, until the end of the **age**."

Moses. So Matthew places events on mountains that are elsewhere in other Gospels (as, for example, Matthew has Jesus deliver the Beatitudes on a mountain—the Sermon on the Mount—but Luke places the Beatitudes on a plain). This scene at the end of the first Gospel was important for the community then, and continues its importance in the Easter season, when the Church discerns its work in the world.

    Although this is not the only place in the Bible where the Father, the Son, and the Holy Spirit are mentioned together, it is the only place in the Bible where the liturgical phrase "in the name of the Father, and of the Son, and of the Holy Spirit" is used. Even though this is an ancient and resonant part of the prayer tradition of the Church, it appears only in this one place in scripture, and that one place does not come up every year in the Lectionary. So let the familiar prayer text resonate in the proclamation of the Gospel phrase.

7TH SUNDAY OF EASTER

Lectionary #59

READING I   Acts 1:12–14

A reading from the Acts of the Apostles

After **Jesus** had been taken up to **heaven** the **apostles**
  returned to **Jerusalem**
  from the mount called **Olivet**, which is near **Jerusalem**,
  a sabbath day's journey away.

When they entered the **city**
  they went to the upper **room** where they were **staying**,
  Peter and **John** and **James** and **Andrew**,
  Philip and **Thomas**, **Bartholomew** and **Matthew**,
  James son of **Alphaeus**, **Simon** the **Zealot**,
  and **Judas** son of **James**.

All these **devoted** themselves with one accord to **prayer**,
  together with some **women**,
  and **Mary** the mother of **Jesus**, and his **brothers**.

READING II   1 Peter 4:13–16

A reading from the first Letter of Saint Peter

Beloved:
Rejoice to the extent that you **share** in the sufferings of **Christ**,
  so that when his glory is **revealed**
  you may also rejoice **exultantly**.

This opening sentence provides the setting for the narrative to come. Pause between the identification of the reading and the start of the reading so that the assembly is ready to listen. That opening phrase reveals that this happened after the Ascension, a key piece of information.
Jerusalem = juh-ROO-suh-lem
Olivet = OL-ih-vet
sabbath = SAB-uth

Most of these names are familiar, but practice those are less common so that you will proclaim them with confidence.
Bartholomew = bar-THOL-uh-myoo
Alphaeus = AL-fee-us
Zealot = ZEL-ut

This is the last appearance of Mary in Acts' chronology of the early Church. Take your time so that the assembly can appreciate her inclusion among the apostles.

Make eye contact when you address the assembly directly with the opening "Beloved."

If the Ascension of the Lord is celebrated today, see pages 165–168 for the appropriate readings.

READING I Artistic depictions of Pentecost in the Roman Catholic tradition often have Mary the mother of Jesus in the midst of the apostles. In the Gospels, she does not often appear in the life and ministry of the adult Jesus. Here we find her with the apostles at this important moment in the life of the Church.

It is not a great surprise that Luke is the one who includes Mary in such a post-Resurrection account, for he has Mary as the protagonist of his infancy narrative at the beginning of his Gospel. In fact most of our scriptural knowledge of Mary is from Luke. Luke wrote both the Gospel and Acts decades after the events, and he saw Mary as a cardinal figure in the birth of Jesus and in the birth of the Church. Vatican II ratifies her prominent place in its teaching on the Church, holding her up as a model for the Church.

This reading is relatively short, and a big chunk of it is occupied with the list of apostles. Most of the names are familiar, but there are a few that might trip you up if you do not consult the pronunciation guide and rehearse them a few times.

READING II For most of this Easter season, our readings have come from the First Letter of Peter. This letter, addressed to a particular community of Christians, is about the life of the Church founded by Christ and sustained by the Holy Spirit. Readings like this are very appropriate for proclamation in the Easter season,

If you are **insulted** for the name of **Christ**, **blessed** are you,
for the Spirit of **glory** and of **God** rests **upon** you.

But let **no one** among you be made to suffer
as a **murderer**, a **thief**, an **evildoer**, or as an **intriguer**.
But **whoever** is made to suffer as a **Christian**
should not be **ashamed**
but glorify **God** because of the **name**.

The final exhortation is uplifting. Proclaim it as such.

GOSPEL   John 17:1–11a

A reading from the holy Gospel according to John

Jesus raised his eyes to heaven and **said**,
"**Father**, the hour has **come**.
Give **glory** to your son, so that your **son** may glorify **you**,
just as you gave him **authority** over all **people**,
so that your son may give eternal **life** to all you gave him.
Now **this** is eternal **life**,
that they should know **you**, the only true **God**,
and the one whom you **sent**, Jesus **Christ**.

"I **glorified** you on **earth**
by accomplishing the **work** that you gave me to **do**.
Now glorify **me**, Father, with **you**,
with the glory that **I** had with you before the world **began**.

Because almost the entire Gospel reading is from the lips of Jesus, it is important that the assembly hear clearly that Jesus is looking up to heaven as he speaks.

---

for we, like those long-ago believers, still face some of the same situations.

Since Jesus, who bore the sin and suffering of all, had ascended to his Father, the Church by the time of this letter would have been at a point where it was finding suffering in the lives of individual members, and in the life of the community, perhaps. And they were likely perplexed at this, for if Christ had borne these things for them, why was life so hard? Why was the Church itself prone to division and sinfulness? Why were members of the community finding themselves reviled because of their faith?

These are indeed hard questions, not only for the early community to which the letter was originally addressed, but for us today, who ask ourselves many of these same questions. These issues could take up much space, but your proclamation for this Sunday is short. Do not rush into it, or during it, or out of it.

Take your place, pause for a moment, and after announcing "A reading from the First Letter of Saint Peter," look up from the page so that you are making eye contact with the assembly as you deliver the opening word, "Beloved." These were written to

Christians long since gone to their reward, but as part of our scriptures, they are meant to be brought to life in your proclamation and in your parish community. (As you make eye contact, it might be best not to look too pointedly at anyone who is "a murderer, a thief, an evil-doer, or as an intriguer.") Deliver the word with the conviction of its author.

GOSPEL   You will notice that in the Lectionary much of the passage, indeed all but the first line, is in quotation marks, directly from the mouth of Jesus.

This is a kind of philosophical summary of Jesus' mission of glorifying the Father. It does not speak of the particulars of healings or teachings, but rather of the people Jesus loved, those to whom he ministered.

These people are indeed the Church, both universal and particular, that is, the people in your community. Imagine Jesus' words as if the Evangelist had written it for the very assembly before you as you proclaim.

"I revealed your **name** to those whom you **gave** me
    out of the world.
They belonged to **you**, and you gave them to **me**,
    and they have kept your **word**.
Now they **know** that everything you gave **me** is from **you**,
    because the words you gave to **me** I have given to **them**,
    and they **accepted** them and truly **understood**
        that I came from you,
    and they have **believed** that you **sent** me.

"I pray for **them**.
I do not pray for the **world** but for the ones you have **given** me,
    because **they** are **yours**, and everything of **mine** is **yours**
    and everything of **yours** is **mine**,
    and I have been **glorified** in them.
And now **I** will no longer be in the world,
    but **they** are in the world, while **I** am coming to **you**."

Because there is so little context supplied before the protracted quotation, you need to consider how to deliver the words of Jesus so that they are well heard by the Church.

As you proclaim the Gospel, you speak on behalf of the assembly, the community of faith, the Body of Christ, that body risen in the Paschal Mystery celebrated in the season of Fifty Days as it nears its end. So as you prepare and as you proclaim this unique passage, think of your ministry as offering up to God the reflections of Jesus on behalf of the collection of individuals before you, some whom you know well, some whom you do not know at all. The words of Jesus are a good model for anyone who ministers in the Church: "They belonged to you, and you gave them to me, and they have kept your word. . . . I pray for them . . . for the ones you have given me." This was the prayer of Jesus and is the prayer of the Body of Christ today, whose spokesperson you are in the Liturgy of the Word.

Jesus' compassion for his people is deep, and this passage, if delivered well, will engage the assembly. By this point in the Gospel, Jesus has been betrayed and likely disappointed to an unimaginable degree, and his Passion will begin soon. He is near the cross, yet he speaks of glorification. The cross and the Resurrection are so close in the theology of the Gospel of John that Jesus' prayer just before his Passion is about glorification. The Paschal Mystery is not a theology of death displaced by resurrection, but of death *and* resurrection. Today's reading reflects this mystery of faith and the compassion of Jesus. Proclaim it well.

PENTECOST VIGIL

Lectionary #62

READING I   Genesis 11:1–9

A reading from the Book of Genesis

The story of the tower of Babel gives the hearers the facts, that is, what happened. There are four basic parts to the story's unfolding. The first part provides two verses of introductory setting; pause briefly after them.
Shinar = SHĪ-nar

bitumen = bih-T**OO**-m*n

The next section presents the plans the people have for making a name for themselves.

The next has the LORD's thoughts and plans after descending to see the city and its tower.

The final section wraps up the story and tells what happened to the people after the LORD intervened.

The whole **world** spoke the same **language**, using the
    same **words**.
While the people were **migrating** in the east,
   they came upon a **valley** in the land of **Shinar** and **settled** there.
They said to one another,
   "**Come**, let us mold **bricks** and harden them with **fire**."
They used bricks for **stone**, and bitumen for **mortar**.

Then they said, "**Come**, let us build ourselves a **city**
   and a **tower** with its **top** in the **sky**,
   and so make a **name** for ourselves;
   otherwise we shall be **scattered** all over the **earth**."

The LORD came down to **see** the city and the tower
   that the people had built.
Then the LORD said: "If now, while they are **one** people,
   all speaking the same **language**,
   they have started to do **this**,
   nothing will **later** stop them from doing
     whatever they presume to do.
Let us then go **down** there and **confuse** their language,
   so that one will not **understand** what another says."

Thus the LORD **scattered** them from there all over the **earth**,
   and they stopped building the city.

There is a choice of first readings today. Speak with the liturgy coordinator or homilist to find out which reading will be used.

READING I **GENESIS.** The narrative of the tower of Babel appears early in the first book of the Bible, and as a metaphor of language and competition the story is familiar to many. Yet some of the details are not as familiar. As you prepare for this proclamation for the Vigil of Pentecost, read the passage slowly and

carefully, gleaning from it the core theological elements as they relate to this time at the end of the Fifty Days of the Easter season, that is, Pentecost.

Note that the story has a few shifts; it might help you to think of it in its four parts before you assemble them.

As a whole, the story is a description of what happened with little theological exegesis of these events.

The first part gives us the setting in place and in language.

In the second part we discover the plans of the people who came to the land of

Shinar. They sought to build not something practical, but simply to make a name for themselves so that they would not be scattered abroad over the earth.

In the third part, the LORD comes down to see the city and the tower, and there we find the LORD's response. The story does not reveal why the LORD responds that way.

The final part describes the LORD's scattering of the people.

The role of the Holy Spirit is the building up of the Church in charity, growth, healing, virtue—special graces called charisms. And for this reason, the placement of the tower

That is why it was called **Babel**,
    because **there** the LORD confused the **speech** of all the **world**.
It was from that place that he **scattered** them all over the **earth**.

Or:

READING I   Exodus 19:3–8a, 16–20b

A reading from the Book of Exodus

Moses went up the mountain to **God**.
Then the LORD **called** to him and said,
"**Thus** shall you say to the house of **Jacob**;
    tell the Israelites:
        You have seen for **yourselves** how I treated the **Egyptians**
        and how I **bore** you up on eagle **wings**
        and **brought** you here to **myself**.

"**Therefore**, if you hearken to my **voice** and keep my **covenant**,
    you shall be my special **possession**,
    dearer to me than all **other** people,
    though **all** the earth is **mine**.
You shall **be** to me a kingdom of **priests**, a **holy** nation.
That is what you must tell the **Israelites**."

So Moses **went** and summoned the **elders** of the people.
When he set before them
    all that the LORD had **ordered** him to tell them,
    the people all answered **together**,
    "Everything the LORD has **said**, we will **do**."

Jacob = JAY-kub

Israelites = IZ-ree-uh-līts

The expression "on eagle wings" is
beautiful and beloved by many; proclaim it
clearly.

Emphasize "special possession," again
another beautiful phrase from the Hebrew
Scriptures.

of Babel story here is fitting, if not readily
apparent. Your proclamation can reawaken
the story for those in your community, and
perhaps the associations of this narrative in
the minds and hearts of those ministering
and in the assembly will be sparked. The
Spirit is not mentioned in the story, but the
scattering of the people leaves the opportunity for the Holy Spirit's work in knitting
the scattered back into a community united
in faith.

    EXODUS. It is an ancient tradition—
part of the Jewish calendar long before
Christianity appeared in the Mediterranean

world—that Pentecost was a time for celebrating the covenant, the pact between God
and Israel. This theology of covenant was
taken up in some early Christian communities, and the theological issue of covenant
characterized the Christian Pentecost as
well, at least in some places in those first
few centuries.

    This reading from the Book of Exodus
suggests that this issue of Pentecost and
the covenant was taken up again in early
Christianity. For early Christians the Easter
season was an integral span of Fifty Days,
at the end of which a reading about the

Sinai covenant was proclaimed, most likely.
That the Church has placed this Exodus narrative as one of the choices for the Vigil of
Pentecost reveals that in the reform of the
liturgical year after Vatican II this covenan-
tal issue is making a claim again for the
Church's theology at Pentecost.

    As the proclaimer of this reading, you
cannot single-handedly reveal the millenia-
long tradition of the covenant attached to
Pentecost, but you can deliver the reading
with well-prepared deliberation to have it
come alive for those who are present to
celebrate as you minister.

Here we find a vivid description of an amazing event. Storms! Lightning! Trumpet blasts! Smoke! Earthquakes! God descending in fire and speaking in thunder! Proclaim this with might.

On the morning of the **third** day
    there were peals of **thunder** and **lightning**,
    and a heavy **cloud** over the **mountain**,
    and a very loud **trumpet** blast,
    so that all the people in the camp **trembled**.
But Moses led the people **out** of the camp to meet **God**,
    and they **stationed** themselves at the **foot** of the mountain.
Mount **Sinai** was all wrapped in **smoke**,
    for the LORD came down upon it in **fire**.
The smoke **rose** from it as though from a **furnace**,
    and the whole **mountain** trembled **violently**.
The **trumpet** blast grew **louder** and **louder**,
      while Moses was speaking,
    and God **answering** him with **thunder**.

When the LORD came **down** to the top of Mount **Sinai**,
    he summoned **Moses** to the top of the mountain.

Or:

READING I   Ezekiel 37:1–14

A reading from the Book of the Prophet Ezekiel

The **hand** of the LORD came **upon** me,
    and he led me **out** in the **spirit** of the LORD
    and **set** me in the center of the **plain**,
    which was now filled with **bones**.
He made me **walk** among the bones in **every** direction
    so that I **saw** how many they were on the **surface** of the plain.

Ezekiel = ee-ZEE-kee-ul

This is a wonderful passage; proclaim it with animation. There is direct address (the LORD speaking to the prophet, the prophet speaking to the LORD, and so on) and narrative. You can discern how best to use your voice and eye contact for the most effective proclamation of the passage.

There are some more familiar stories of Moses and God in the Hebrew Scriptures, but this one is compelling and poetic. There is that exciting scene up on that mountain, with the trumpet blasts and the thunder claps. Take your time and be clear with such descriptions, for all in the assembly know these sounds, musical and natural, and the imagery will capture their attention. Moreover, the reading includes the familiar image of being borne up "on eagle wings" and keeping the covenant as the LORD's "special possession."

EZEKIEL. In the Gospel of Luke we learn that the Holy Spirit overshadowed Mary so that she would conceive and bear a son in the flesh. We see in many of these readings for the Vigil of Pentecost that the role of the Holy Spirit here too is incarnation, the divine putting on flesh for the salvation of humanity.

The passage from the prophet Ezekiel for this Vigil of Pentecost is a beautiful and poetic incarnational part of the Hebrew Scriptures, perhaps the most well known of the prophecies of this major prophet. For Christians, the power of the Spirit makes the life of God incarnate in Christ and in the Church, so this reading from Ezekiel is very fitting for this Vigil.

Pentecost is when the Church is set on its course to sustain the word of God in the life of Christ. The image of the living human bodies being raised up from the "dry bones" is a wonderful image for this time of the liturgical year. As the proclaimer of this passage, you will need to be both measured and animated.

There are two particular pairs of words to be attentive to here: Distinguish the verb "prophesy" (PROF-uh-sī, in the reading) from the noun "prophecy" (PROF-uh-see, not in the

prophesy = PROF-uh-sī

sinews = SIN-yooz

prophesied = PROF-uh-sīd

prophesying = PROF-uh-sī-ing

As the bones begin to live again, you might find a spot in the sanctuary or in the gathering place where you can visualize the coming together of the bones, of the sinews, of the body.

Israel = IZ-ree-ul

How **dry** they were!
He asked me:
　Son of **man**, can these **bones** come to **life**?
I answered, "Lord **GOD**, you **alone** know that."

Then he said to me:
　Prophesy over these bones, and **say** to them:
　Dry **bones**, hear the **word** of the **LORD**!
Thus says the Lord **GOD** to these **bones**:
　See! I will bring **spirit** into you, that you may come to **life**.
I will put **sinews** upon you, make **flesh** grow over you,
　cover you with **skin**, and put **spirit** in you
　so that you may come to **life** and know that **I** am the **LORD**.

I, Ezekiel, prophesied as I had been **told**,
　and even as I was **prophesying** I heard a **noise**;
　it was a **rattling** as the bones came **together**, **bone** joining **bone**.
I saw the **sinews** and the **flesh** come upon them,
　and the skin **cover** them, but there was no **spirit** in them.

Then the **LORD** said to me:
　Prophesy to the **spirit**, **prophesy**, son of **man**,
　and **say** to the spirit: Thus says the Lord **GOD**:
　From the four winds **come**, O spirit,
　and **breathe** into these **slain** that they may come to **life**.
I prophesied as he **told** me, and the **spirit** came into them;
　they came **alive** and stood **upright**, a vast **army**.

Then he said to me:
　Son of **man**, these **bones** are the whole house of **Israel**.
They have been saying,
　"Our **bones** are dried **up**,
　our **hope** is **lost**, and we are cut **off**."

reading). Also, distinguish the verb "breathe" (breeth, in the reading once) from the noun "breath" (breth, in the reading five times). Take your time in preparing, and be confident about how to say these words. Your confidence is dependent on your understanding.

To make the proclamation vivid, visualize the scene that the prophet is describing here, and your proclamation will paint a picture in the imaginations of those in the assembly.

JOEL. At the start of the Acts of the Apostles, the apostle Peter stands up at Pentecost and explicitly admits that the prophecy he is proclaiming comes from the prophet Joel. The prophecy that he delivers to that assembly is this very text. You can be consoled, then, that as Peter proclaimed the words of the prophet Joel for the inspiration and conversion of the assembly at that first Pentecost nearly two millennia ago, you too are called to proclaim to a new assembly of God's people at this Pentecost in 2005.

There are four major and twelve minor prophets in the Old Testament, inspired texts of the biblical canon for Jews and Christians. The major prophets are the four that most believers know—Isaiah, Jeremiah, Ezekiel, and Daniel—but remembering all twelve minor ones can be tough even for the most dedicated Bible readers.

The book of Joel is only three chapters long, just a few pages in most editions of the Old Testament. This passage for Pentecost captures an important aspect of the role of the Holy Spirit in the life of faith, the animation of flesh by the spirit. The prophet could not say it more clearly: "Thus says the Lord: I will pour out my spirit upon all flesh," a beautiful and direct theology of the spirit's work that cannot be repeated too often.

Here at the end of the Easter season, this theology of the rising from the grave is important. Be bold in proclaiming and portraying this prophecy of rising from the grave.

Therefore, **prophesy** and say to them: **Thus** says the Lord **GOD**:
   O my **people**, I will **open** your graves
   and have you **rise** from them,
   and bring you **back** to the land of **Israel**.

Then you shall **know** that **I** am the **LORD**,
   when I **open** your graves and have you **rise** from them,
   O my **people**!
I will put my **spirit** in you that you may **live**,
   and I will **settle** you upon your **land**;
   thus you shall **know** that **I** am the **LORD**.
I have **promised**, and I will **do** it, says the **LORD**.

Or:

<hr>

READING I   Joel 3:1–5

<hr>

Pause slightly before announcing the book. We do not hear from the prophet Joel very often in the liturgy.

prophesy = PROF-uh-sī
This prophecy is vivid. As you proclaim "your sons and daughters," and "your old men," and "your young men," address your own assembly.

A reading from the Book of the Prophet Joel

Thus says the **Lord**:
I will pour out my **spirit** upon all **flesh**.
Your **sons** and **daughters** shall **prophesy**,
   your **old** men shall dream **dreams**,
   your **young** men shall see **visions**;
even upon the **servants** and the **handmaids**,
   in those days, I will **pour** out my **spirit**.
And I will work **wonders** in the **heavens** and on the **earth**,
   blood, **fire**, and columns of **smoke**;
the **sun** will be turned to **darkness**,
   and the **moon** to **blood**,

These cosmological images are fascinating. Imagine them through the prophet's eyes, and proclaim the prophecy as if you yourself have seen this.

In our commercial culture, we are often told that our flesh is a failure, a disappointment, not strong enough, not beautiful enough, not tall enough, not thin enough (so, say the ads, go buy something!). The role of the Spirit in animating and sanctifying the human body in the celebration of the sacraments is an important sign of contradiction.

Take your time with the rather short prophecy, and make the imagery come alive for those who hear you proclaim it at this Vigil of Pentecost, for this is the time for the Church to be awakened to the role of the Spirit in our human lives of faith and in the communal life of the assembly in which you worship and minister.

READING II   The Letter to the Romans came near the end of Paul's writing life, as far as we know, about the year 58 or 59. It was centuries before the theology of the Holy Spirit was developed and the relationship between the Father and the Son and the Holy Spirit discerned (as in the Creed recited in Church each Sunday). We find here one of the earliest Christian teachings about the role of the Spirit in the Church. This is fitting for Pentecost, and it also reveals that the experience of the Holy Spirit in the life of the Church preceded the theologizing.

Paul reveals here that the Holy Spirit "helps us in our weakness," so—against the culture that says that every accomplishment and every success depend on our own efforts as individuals—we know that in the end God will supply what we need. God's will for us is wiser than we are. That is why the celebration of Pentecost is

Zion = ZĪ-ahn

Jerusalem = juh-ROO-suh-lem

at the coming of the day of the LORD,
the **great** and **terrible day**.

Then everyone shall be **rescued**
who calls on the name of the LORD;
for on Mount **Zion** there shall be a **remnant**,
as the LORD has said,
and in Jerusalem **survivors**
whom the LORD shall **call**.

READING II   Romans 8:22–27

A reading from the Letter of Saint Paul to the Romans

The reading is short yet very important in its theology of the Holy Spirit; take your time with the proclamation.

Brothers and sisters:
We know that all **creation** is **groaning** in **labor** pains
even until **now**;
and not only **that**, but we **ourselves**,
who have the **firstfruits** of the Spirit,
we **also** groan within ourselves
as we wait for **adoption**, the redemption of our **bodies**.

Attend to the significance of the meaning and sound of the words repeated in this part—"hope," "hopes," "saved," "sees," "see."

For in **hope** we were **saved**.
Now **hope** that **sees** is **not** hope.
For who **hopes** for what one **sees**?
But if we hope for what we do **not** see, we wait with **endurance**.

In the **same** way, the Spirit **too** comes to the **aid** of our **weakness**;
for we do not know **how** to pray as we **ought**,
but the Spirit **himself** intercedes with inexpressible **groanings**.

---

imperative, so that we know that we individuals are not the final measure of goodness and strength. This is the experience of God's presence in the Church and the sacraments; we do not ignore our personal experience, but, as the baptized, we hold this experience in tandem with the communal experience of the liturgy. It will help the members of your Church appreciate the Spirit's role if your proclamation is made with conviction.

Almost invisible in the reading is the reference to the "holy ones." Do your best to have the assembly recognize that when in

the first century Paul wrote about "holy ones," often translated "saints," he was not thinking of what we think of with that word. The process of canonization of saints did not start until 1588, after the Council of Trent. When Paul wrote of the "holy ones," he was thinking of the believers who worshiped in Rome, the church to whom he was writing.

We attend to the Church's teaching about the saints of the calendar, but in line with the reading, envision the people with whom we celebrate the liturgy week after week as saints, holy men and women, chosen of God. The heroes of the tradition are

recognized on the calendar and celebrated in the liturgy, but the number of saints has never been limited to only those who have been officially canonized.

GOSPEL   Although the Evangelist did not write these words in anticipation of the liturgical year as we know it today, the opening of your proclamation is fitting for its place at Pentecost. It is an identification of time for the ancient community of the Gospel of John, and the Evangelist specified the time of this as "the

Pause briefly before beginning the final section, for it carries the significant theology of the Holy Spirit that makes the reading so fitting for this celebration.

And the one who searches **hearts**
     knows what is the **intention** of the **Spirit**,
because he **intercedes** for the **holy** ones
according to God's **will**.

GOSPEL   John 7:37–39

A reading from the holy Gospel according to John

This time indication is not pointing to Pentecost, but in this place it is fitting for this "last day" of the Easter season. (See below.)

On the **last** and **greatest** day of the feast,
     Jesus stood up and **exclaimed**,
     "Let anyone who **thirsts** come to me and **drink**.
As Scripture says:
     *Rivers of living **water** will flow from **within** him*
          who **believes** *in me.*"

The Holy Spirit's role is essential in attracting inquirers and potential members to the Church, and the means of their membership is Baptism, the "rivers of living water."

He said this in reference to the **Spirit**
     that those who came to **believe** in him were to **receive**.
There **was**, of course, no Spirit **yet**,
     because **Jesus** had not yet been **glorified**.

---

last and greatest day of the feast." Pentecost is not only a one-day celebration, but the closing of the season of Easter. The third-century north African theologian Tertullian called the Easter season the *laetissimum spatium,* that "most joyful span" of time, which closed at Pentecost, the feast for which you prepare this reading. In the words of the Gospel itself, Pentecost is "the last and greatest day of the feast" of the Easter season.

This is one of the shortest Gospel readings in the Lectionary. For this reason, pace yourself during the proclamation. Use significant pauses so that the assembly is ready to hear you proclaim the words of the Evangelist.

Since Pentecost is the close of the Easter season, during which the Church celebrates and remembers Baptism—*celebrating* at the Easter Vigil or during the Easter season itself, and *remembering* those of the members of the Church—the text's mention of "living water" is a good echo of the "living water" that constitutes the Church. Pentecost is the celebration of the birth of the Church in the power of the Holy Spirit.

The Church whose birth and rebirth are celebrated at Pentecost is not some abstract Church, but the very community gathered for the liturgy as you proclaim. It is the advent of the Holy Spirit that brings the Church together Eucharist after Eucharist, and in faith we trust that the Holy Spirit gathered this particular community that hears your proclamation. Proclaim the reading clearly as a testimony to the Spirit's power to realize Christ's presence in the people brought together.

PENTECOST

Lectionary #63

READING I   Acts 2:1–11

A reading from the Acts of the Apostles

When the time for **Pentecost** was fulfilled,
    they were all in one place **together**.
And **suddenly** there came from the sky
    a **noise** like a strong driving **wind**,
    and it filled the entire house in which they were.
Then there appeared to them **tongues** as of **fire**,
    which **parted** and came to rest on **each** one of them.
And they were all **filled** with the Holy **Spirit**
    and began to **speak** in different **tongues**,
    as the **Spirit** enabled them to **proclaim**.

Now there were devout **Jews** from every nation under heaven
    staying in Jerusalem.
At this **sound**, they gathered in a large **crowd**,
    but they were **confused**
    because **each** one heard them **speaking** in his own **language**.
They were **astounded**, and in **amazement** they asked,
    "Are **not** all these people who are speaking **Galileans**?
Then how does **each** of us hear them in his native **language**?
We are Parthians, Medes, and Elamites,
    inhabitants of Mesopotamia, Judea and Cappadocia,

Be clear in this description, for the "tongues" of fire are a well-known element in artistic depictions of Pentecost.

Jerusalem = juh-ROO-suh-lem

Galileans = gal-ih-LEE-unz

Parthians = PAR-thee-unz
Medes = meedz
Elamites = EE-luh-mīts
Mesopotamia = mes-uh-poh-TAY-mee-uh
Judea = joo-DEE-uh
Cappadocia = kap-uh-DOH-shuh

READING I You bear a bigger responsibility than usual for your ministry as your prepare for this reading. Most of the feasts in the liturgical year are reflected in a narrative in the *Gospel* reading—on Christmas or Easter or the Transfiguration, and so on. But the *first* reading on this feast narrates the central event, the descent of the Holy Spirit. Your proclamation, therefore, needs to be excellent.

Potentially tricky in this proclamation is the chain of proper names near the end. You will need to prepare well enough that none of these place names trips you up. Worse than mispronouncing one of the cities would be drawing too much attention to any one of them by stumbling over it. Proclaiming them accurately is important but secondary to proclaiming them with confidence. The point that the assembly should take from the chain of strange place names is simply that there was a great variety of nations and peoples and cultures represented in this extraordinary event. Take your time with these verses, but do not draw unnecessary attention to them.

In addition to the difficulties with the vocabulary, the narrative is fairly long, but that does not call for rushing through the reading. Rather, enunciate clearly, pause between sections, and bring the assembly with you by your own engagement with what you proclaim.

Phrygia = FRIJ-ee-uh
Pamphilia = pam-FIL-ee-uh
Cyrene = si-REE-nee

Cretans = KREE-tuns
Arabs = AIR-ubs

Corinthians = kor-IN-thee-unz

Notice the parallels created here by Paul,
each balancing the word "different" on
the one side and "the same" on the other.
Pause slightly after each of the pairs
so that the hearers can recognize the
structure.

The theology of the body of Christ, usually
considered in relation to the Eucharist,
is here applied to the members of the
Church. Proclaim this so that your hearers
can appreciate the link between the
Eucharistic elements and the assembly
of which they are a part.

Pontus and Asia, Phrygia and Pamphylia,
Egypt and the districts of Libya near Cyrene,
as well as travelers from Rome,
both Jews and converts to Judaism, Cretans and Arabs,
yet we hear them speaking in our own **tongues**
of the mighty acts of **God**."

READING II   1 Corinthians 12:3b–7, 12–13

A reading from the first Letter of Saint Paul to the Corinthians

Brothers and sisters:
No one can say, "Jesus is Lord," **except** by the Holy **Spirit**.
There are different **kinds** of spiritual **gifts** but the same **Spirit**;
    there are different **forms** of **service** but the same **Lord**;
    there are different **workings** but the same **God**
    who produces **all** of them in **everyone**.
To each **individual** the manifestation of the Spirit
    is given for some **benefit**.

As a **body** is one though it has many **parts**,
    and all the **parts** of the body, though **many**, are one **body**,
    so also **Christ**.
For in one **Spirit** we were all **baptized** into one **body**,
    whether **Jews** or **Greeks**, **slaves** or **free** persons,
    and we were **all** given to drink of one **Spirit**.

READING II   The letters of Saint Paul constitute the earliest extant Christian literature, for, though the letters appear in the Bible after the Gospels, many were written earlier than the Gospels by a few decades. Each of the readings for this Sunday gives some theology of the Holy Spirit, but this reading that you are preparing tells us how the Holy Spirit was revealed to the apostle Paul at the earliest stage of Christian theology that has survived for us.

With this chronology in mind, consider this passage in relation to your own ministry as a proclaimer of the word of God. The reading should fortify your contribution, for this passage from First Corinthians sees the activity of gifts in the Church as manifestations of the Spirit in the Church. Though you may not have been conscious of this when you first began your ministry of the word, your contribution to the Church as a lector is indeed a manifestation of the Spirit at work in your community of faith.

This particular reading contributes a theology that can be a corrective in our culture, where an extremely high priority is given to the rights of the individual. Yet the value of the Church as a *body*, a community of faith made up of many individuals, stands in contrast to the value of the individual as we know it outside the context of faith. The healing that Jesus wrought in his ministry is not given to any of us as an individual, but as a member of a community of faith. As the body of Christ, we are able to minister to those in need of healing and support and companionship.

GOSPEL John 20:19–23

A reading from the holy Gospel according to John

On the **evening** of that **first** day of the **week**,
    when the **doors** were **locked**, where the disciples were,
    for fear of the **Jews**,
    Jesus came and stood in their **midst**
    and said to them, "**Peace** be with you."
When he had said this, he showed them his **hands** and his **side**.
The disciples **rejoiced** when they saw the Lord.

Jesus said to them **again**, "**Peace** be with you.
As the **Father** has sent me, so **I** send **you**."

And when he had said this, he **breathed** on them
        and said to them,
    "**Receive** the Holy **Spirit**.
Whose sins you **forgive** are **forgiven** them,
and whose sins you **retain** are **retained**."

The time element bears an important clue to the liturgical and theological meaning of the day. (See below.)

The consonance of this phrase with our liturgy should be emphasized.

This phrase is also important; it is still used in the liturgy.

The gift of the Spirit for the building up of the Church is a theological foundation of this feast, yet the Spirit is mentioned only this one time.

GOSPEL It would be understandable to think that the liturgical phrase "Peace be with you" is a fruit of passages such as this one, in which Jesus himself speaks the phrase. But once we realize that the Gospels were written decades after the death of Jesus and that their authors incorporated into them remembrances of the life of Jesus as well as the experiences of their own churches, we can guess that phrases like this "Peace be with you" were not only words of the historical Jesus but

that they were also liturgical phrases that were transcribed into the Gospels. So in your proclamation of this passage, consider highlighting the phrase.

It is the gift of the Spirit that brings the assembly together week after week. So the liturgical exchanges and ritual gestures of the early church that may be reflected in this reading, as above, are very fitting in the proclamation for Pentecost.

The time indication of the reading, on the evening of "that first day of the week," is important here. It demonstrates that the

Resurrection (which was proclaimed at the start of the Fifty Days, that is, on Easter Sunday) and the reception of the Holy Spirit happened on the same day. This helps us appreciate how the third-century theologian Tertullian could call the Fifty Days one "great Sunday." It also helps the Church appreciate the endurance of the first day of the week, Sunday, as the day of the liturgy from the earliest period until today. The Sunday assembly is the original gift of the Holy Spirit's work in the life of the Church.

HOLY TRINITY

Lectionary #164

READING I   Exodus 34:4b–6, 8–9

A reading from the Book of Exodus

Early in the **morning** Moses went up Mount **Sinai**
  as the LORD had **commanded** him,
  taking along the two stone **tablets**.

Having come down in a **cloud**, the LORD stood with Moses there
  and proclaimed his **name**, "LORD."
Thus the LORD **passed** before him and cried **out**,
  "The **LORD**, the **LORD**, a **merciful** and **gracious** God,
  slow to anger and **rich** in **kindness** and **fidelity**."

Moses at **once** bowed down to the **ground** in **worship**.
Then he said, "If I find **favor** with you, O Lord,
  do come along in our **company**.
This is indeed a **stiff-necked** people; yet **pardon** our wickedness
    and **sins**,
  and **receive** us as your **own**."

Sinai = SĪ-nī

The assembly will appreciate this reading's significance if you proclaim the name "LORD" so that it is clearly a *new* revelation to the people of Israel.

Pause slightly to mark the shift from narrative to quotation.

Again pause to mark the reverse, from quotation back to narrative.

READING I This first reading of Trinity Sunday alternates between the progress of the relationship between the LORD and the Israelites and the three phrases in quotation marks. The first quote designates the name, "LORD." The revelation is shown to be greatly significant by its setting, that is, on Mount Sinai as the Lord descends in a cloud.

The second speech calls for some practice. It is not quite a sentence, but rather a description from the mouth of the LORD of the divine character, a kind of explanation of the name. Though it is as long as a sentence might be, it is not a sentence with subject, verb, and object. It is an expansion of the name, and the assembly will understand it only if you are well aware of its form.

The third speech is from Moses, in which he shows his trust in what the LORD has just announced—"merciful and gracious, slow to anger"—and asks that the LORD "pardon our wickedness and sins."

Notice that each of the three sections of the reading ends with a speech. With the first, do not pause much before the name "LORD" so that the assembly will recognize it as that name. For the second and third, however, a slight pause between the narrative and the speech will help the assembly recognize that the voice has changed from third-person narration ("Early in the morning Moses went up . . ." "Thus the LORD passed . . ." "Moses at once bowed . . ."), to the speech of one of the characters in the narrative.

Be most deliberate in proclaiming the LORD's self-description as "slow to anger and rich in kindness and fidelity," and in describing the people with Moses as "a stiff-necked people." The description of the LORD is not only familiar, it is a consolation

READING II 2 Corinthians 13:11–13

A reading from second Letter of Saint Paul to the Corinthians

Brothers and sisters, **rejoice**. **Mend** your ways,
    encourage one another,
  agree with one another, live in **peace**,
  and the God of **love** and **peace** will be **with** you.
Greet one another with a holy **kiss**.
All the **holy** ones greet you.

The **grace** of the Lord Jesus **Christ**
  and the love of **God**
  and the **fellowship** of the Holy **Spirit** be with **all** of you.

The verbs in the first two sentences—"mend your ways," "encourage," "agree," "live," and "greet"—are all in the imperative mood. These are instructions for the community in the form of direct commands.

Those whom Paul calls "holy ones" are living people of the Church.

This final verse, invoking God, Jesus Christ, and the Spirit, is the reason for the passage's placement on Trinity Sunday.

and revelation to the ancient Israelites then and to believers ever since.

READING II All three of the readings for this Trinity Sunday are fairly short, and this is the shortest. Its significance for the building up of the Church, however, is not to be abbreviated.

Paul's Second Letter to the Corinthians was written in about the year 55 to follow up on the more familiar First Letter, written a short while before. In our three-year Lectionary cycle, the Second Letter does not appear too often. You might be a little more deliberate as you open with "A reading from the *second* Letter of Saint Paul to the Corinthians," simply because this New Testament book does not get a lot of attention compared to its epistolary partner.

Notice that this was written nearly two thousand years ago, but the exhortations of Paul to the church at Corinth are as important and necessary to us today as they were for the community to which he wrote. The issues of agreement in the Church, of peace, and of God's love are ever imperative in Christian communities. For the liturgy, what we know as the "sign of peace" was a "kiss of peace" in the earliest communities, so the exhortation to "Greet one another with a holy kiss" is relevant to Church life today.

The final verse is why this reading finds its home here on Trinity Sunday. Here, just twenty-five years after the death of Jesus, long before the discussions of the persons of the Trinity—Father, Son, and Holy Spirit—the apostle names the three in one sentence.

This is a key verse; proclaim it with confidence.

GOSPEL   John 3:16–18

A reading from the holy Gospel according to John

God so **loved** the world that he gave his only **Son**,
    so that everyone who **believes** in him might not **perish**
    but might have eternal **life**.

For God did **not** send his Son into the world
        to **condemn** the world,
    but that the world might be **saved** through him.
Whoever **believes** in him will **not** be condemned,
    but whoever does **not** believe has **already** been condemned,
    because he has **not** believed in the **name** of the only
        Son of **God**.

GOSPEL   The opening verse of the passage from the Gospel of John from the lips of Jesus, "God so loved the world that he gave his only Son," is very well-known. (Who hasn't seen "John 3:16" on bumper stickers, t-shirts, and placards at sporting events?) It is important that you proclaim this verse with confidence. All Christians share this faith. Proclaim it with conviction.

The Gospel passage plays a key role in our theology of the Trinity because it reveals the unique relationship of the Father and the Son, a relationship in which God's love for the world is manifest.

The readings for this Trinity Sunday are, as a set of three, perhaps the shortest in the Lectionary. Because of the brevity of the passages, take your time so that the few words are heard and appreciated in their fullness.

The entire reading is a direct quotation of the words of Jesus to Nicodemus, yet because in these words Jesus speaks of himself in the third person, "God did not send his Son . . . to condemn the world," rather than in the first person, "God did not send me . . . to condemn the world," you, the proclaimer of the Gospel, can proclaim them as if they are your own testimony to the love of God for the salvation of the world. You offer this proclamation from the Gospel of John to your fellow believers.

BODY AND BLOOD OF CHRIST

Lectionary #167

READING I   Deuteronomy 8:2–3, 14b–16a

Deuteronomy = doo-ter-AH-nuh-mee

The name of Moses, who is the speaker, is mentioned only this one time. Do your best to let the assembly hear this identification for this reason; a deliberate start would help. (See below.)

Hunger and feeding are important in the imagery of this feast.

Your voice can suggest the fearsomeness of these things in the reading: the terrible desert, saraph serpents, scorpions.

saraph = SAIR-uf

A reading from the Book of Deuteronomy

Moses said to the **people**:
"**Remember** how for forty **years** now the LORD, your **GOD**,
has directed **all** your journeying in the **desert**,
so as to **test** you by affliction
and find out whether or not it was your intention
to keep his **commandments**.

He therefore let you be afflicted with **hunger**,
and then **fed** you with **manna**,
a food **unknown** to you and your **fathers**,
in order to show you that not by bread **alone** does one live,
but by every **word** that comes forth
from the mouth of the LORD.

"Do not **forget** the LORD, your **God**,
who brought you out of the land of **Egypt**,
that place of **slavery**;
who guided you through the vast and terrible **desert**
with its saraph **serpents** and **scorpions**,
its **parched** and waterless **ground**;
who brought forth **water** for you from the flinty **rock**
and **fed** you in the desert with **manna**,
a food **unknown** to your **fathers**."

READING I In the reading there is a strong link between the sign of bread as nourishment and the word of God, which you proclaim, as nourishment, where it says that "not by bread alone does one live, but by every word that comes forth from the mouth of the LORD." Since you are proclaiming that word of the LORD, do your best to emphasize this support from and for your own ministry.

There are two other details in the passage for which you can prepare. First, the "saraph serpents and scorpions" will capture anyone's imagination (particularly any children in the assembly attending to what you proclaim). As ever, take advantage of such images and their poetic strength.

Second, at the Easter Vigil, we heard the reading of Israel crossing the Red Sea as a central narrative, and here are references to water that will remind the church of that. So emphasize the "LORD, your God, who brought you out of the land of Egypt," as well as the water flowing "for you from the flinty rock."

READING II This particular passage has long caused discussion among biblical scholars and liturgical scholars, for the two basic elements of the Eucharist, the bread and the cup, are mentioned here in reverse order from what we read in the Gospels (except Luke) and from what we do in the liturgy now, centuries later. First Corinthians has the cup blessed first, then the bread broken. While this might be interesting to academics, their speculation about the order of the elements in Corinth need not bear much on how you would proclaim this short passage.

The main task falling on you, the minister of the word on the Solemnity of the Body

Because the reading is short, only three sentences, pause after each of the opening questions.

The symbolic ambiguity of bread as the "body of Christ" and of "we, though many" as "one body" can be captured in your voice in this proclamation. Enunciate clearly and slowly.

One of the familiar "I AM" sayings of the Gospel of John.

READING II 1 Corinthians 10:16–17

A reading from the first Letter of Saint Paul to the Corinthians

Brothers and sisters:
The **cup** of blessing that we **bless**,
　is it not a participation in the **blood** of **Christ**?
The **bread** that we **break**,
　is it not a participation in the **body** of **Christ**?

Because the loaf of **bread** is **one**,
　we, though **many**, are **one body**,
　for we **all** partake of the **one loaf**.

GOSPEL John 6:51–58

A reading from the holy Gospel according to John

Jesus said to the Jewish crowds:
　"**I** am the living **bread** that came down from **heaven**;
　whoever **eats** this bread will live **forever**;
　and the bread that **I** will give
　is my **flesh** for the life of the **world**."

The Jews **quarreled** among themselves, saying,
　"How can this man give us his **flesh** to eat?"

Jesus said to them,
　"**Amen**, **amen**, I say to you,
　unless you **eat** the **flesh** of the Son of Man and **drink** his **blood**,
　you do not have **life** within you.

and Blood of Christ, is to be clear in capturing the reading's link of two presences of Christ as described by Paul, in the "bread we break" and in the "we, though many."

The Constitution on the Sacred Liturgy of Vatican II spoke of the fourfold presence of Christ in the celebration of the Eucharist: in the person of the priest, especially in the Eucharistic species, in the word, and in the assembly. In reading this particular passage, your ministerial proclamation of the scriptures in the liturgy is a manifestation of the third of these presences, and the

passage itself addresses the second and fourth presences.

The brevity of the proclamation affords you the opportunity to be clear and to take your time with its significant verses.

GOSPEL The sixth chapter of the Gospel of John has first a multiplication of loaves and fishes, then a storm at sea, and then a discourse on the bread of life. The Gospel reading on this Solemnity of the Body and Blood of Christ is taken from the very end of that Eucharistic

discourse. Countless theological debates over the course of Christian history have taken up the meaning of this Eucharistic theology of the Gospel of John; it is the basis of the theology of real presence and sacramental realism. So the Fourth Gospel is unique for the absence of a Last Supper and the presence of a weighty Eucharistic theology.

To help the assembly catch the connection between the first reading from Deuteronomy and the Gospel, the penultimate verse of the latter is key ("This is the bread that came down from heaven. . . .").

The Eucharistic theology of the Gospel of John is high and solemn. Capture some of its solemnity in the tone of your proclamation.

"Whoever **eats** my flesh and **drinks** my blood
    has eternal **life**,
    and I will **raise** him on the last **day**.
For my **flesh** is true **food**,
    and my **blood** is true **drink**.
Whoever **eats** my flesh and **drinks** my blood
    remains in me and I in **him**.

"Just as the living Father sent **me**
    and I have life **because** of the Father,
    so also the one who **feeds** on me
    will have life **because** of me.
This is the bread that came down from **heaven**.
Unlike your **ancestors** who ate and still **died**,
    whoever eats **this** bread will live **forever**."

These verses link this reading to the first reading from Deuteronomy.

Proclaim this part of the reading with clarity and appropriate emphasis.

Notice as you prepare that three short parts of the reading provide context: "Jesus said to the Jewish crowds," "The Jews quarreled among themselves, saying," and "Jesus said to them." Except for the one question from the people, "How can this man give us his flesh to eat?" the remainder of the reading is from the mouth of Jesus. As you prepare for your proclamation, take note of the differences in how you establish the setting and how you speak the words of Jesus and the people.

Some early Christians were misunderstood by outsiders who heard words like those in this Gospel: Eat my flesh, drink my blood. You can imagine how they might have been heard outside their sacred context. These words should still be startling as a sign of Jesus' sacrifice and the Father's gift then and today.

10TH SUNDAY IN ORDINARY TIME

Lectionary #88

READING I   Hosea 6:3–6

Hosea = hoh-ZAY-uh

A reading from the Book of the Prophet Hosea

In their **affliction**, people will say:
"Let us **know**, let us **strive** to know the **Lord**;
    as certain as the **dawn** is his **coming**,
    and his **judgment** shines forth like the light of **day**!
He will **come** to us like the **rain**,
    like spring **rain** that waters the **earth**."

This comparison of the Lord's appearance to dawn and the spring rain is beautiful.

Ephraim = EF-rum
Judah = JOO-duh

What can I do with **you**, Ephraim?
    What can I do with **you**, Judah?
Your **piety** is like a morning **cloud**,
    like the **dew** that early passes **away**.
For this reason I **smote** them through the **prophets**,
    I **slew** them by the words of my **mouth**;
for it is **love** that I desire, not **sacrifice**,
    and **knowledge** of God rather than **holocausts**.

holocausts = HOL-oh-cawsts

READING I   We do not hear from the short book of the prophet Hosea much in our liturgical year, indeed, only three times in the three-year cycle. This reading found its place on this Tenth Sunday in Ordinary Time mostly likely because of Hosea's "It is love that I desire, not sacrifice," which harmonizes with the Gospel's words on Jesus' lips, "I desire mercy, not sacrifice." The passage from Hosea also includes some strikingly beautiful poetic elements.

This reading is filled with lovely images from the natural world, demonstrating how the Lord's love and goodness animates life.

What listener in the assembly would not be delighted by the images of "spring rain that waters the earth" or the "dew that early passes away"? The gardeners in your assembly will surely be struck by Hosea's images for they know how transformative water from the skies is as it reaches the earth. This image is likened by the prophet to the knowledge of the Lord. If you yourself love growing things, be mindful of your garden as you proclaim the reading; if not, think of friends who do, and proclaim with passion that will reach their ears.

There are a few proper names in the reading, Hosea, Ephraim, and Judah. As ever, pronouncing the names with confidence is as important as proclaiming them correctly.

READING II   The layers of theological traditions in this passage make it difficult to proclaim fruitfully, but if you take some time to appreciate what the apostle Paul is trying to communicate to the Romans, that will make the proclamation stronger.

READING II   Romans 4:18–25

A reading from the Letter of Saint Paul to the Romans

Brothers and sisters:
Abraham **believed**, **hoping** against **hope**,
    that he would become the *father* of many *nations*,
    according to what was said, *Thus shall your* **descendants** *be*.
He did not **weaken** in faith when he considered his own **body**
    as already **dead**—for he was almost a **hundred** years old—
    and the dead womb of **Sarah**.
He did not **doubt** God's promise in **unbelief**;
    rather, he was **strengthened** by faith and gave **glory** to God
    and was **fully** convinced that what he had **promised**
    he was **also** able to **do**.

That is why it was *credited* to him as *righteousness*.
But it was not for him **alone** that it was written
    that *it was credited to him*;
    it was also for **us**, to whom it will be **credited**,
    who believe in the **one** who raised Jesus our **Lord** from the **dead**,
    who was **handed** over for our **transgressions**
    and was **raised** for our **justification**.

Paul is capturing the character of Abraham with these descriptions of his faith and mention of Sarah. Study the rhetoric of the apostle carefully. This is not an easy passage to understand or proclaim.
Abraham = AY-bruh-ham

These quotations from scripture (in italics) contribute to the complexity of Paul's rhetoric. As before, study Paul's argument. Once you understand its purpose within the reading, you will be able to proclaim it well.

Consider the context of the quotations. In the first sentence, there are two quotations from the Old Testament, printed in italics. The first describes Abraham as "the father of many nations," and you can proclaim this without any particular emphasis. The second quotation is identified explicitly as a quotation, for Paul precedes it with "according to what was said." Because of this, have your voice reflect that it is a quotation.

In the next section, Paul uses some elements in the life of Abraham to demonstrate his strong faith as an example to the Romans. This is as vital to your community

today as it was to the community in Rome to which Paul wrote two thousand years ago, though perhaps that vitality is not as apparent to people in our day as it was then.

Paul's purpose was to link the time of Abraham to the time when Paul was writing to the church in Rome, the middle of the first century. Your proclamation will make the link between the first century and the twenty-first century. You can be confident in your proclamation of the details of Abraham's faith—"almost a hundred years old" and the "dead womb of Sarah," in particular—so that the church before you will see the

importance of faith in God even in the face of seemingly impossible odds.

By your strong proclamation the assembly is reminded of the foundation of our faith: that God raised Jesus from the dead for our justification, which is the main point of the passage.

GOSPEL   In the three-year cycle of the Lectionary, Year A is dedicated to the proclamation of the Gospel of Matthew. But during the long Lent-Easter span that we have just completed, the

The opening section is a story of calling, and the name of "Matthew" in the introduction of the reading is important. The one Jesus calls in this passage is "Matthew" as well.

Pharisees = FAIR-uh-seez
It is Jesus' open table fellowship that really irks the Pharisees.

GOSPEL   Matthew 9:9–13

A reading from the holy Gospel according to Matthew

As Jesus passed on from there,
    he saw a man named **Matthew** sitting at the **customs** post.
He said to him, "**Follow** me."
And he got up and **followed** him.
While he was at table in his **house**,
    many **tax** collectors and **sinners** came
    and sat with **Jesus** and his **disciples**.
The Pharisees **saw** this and said to his disciples,
    "**Why** does your teacher eat with **tax** collectors and **sinners**?"

He heard this and said,
    "Those who are **well** do not **need** a physician, but the **sick** do.
Go and learn the **meaning** of the words,
    'I desire **mercy**, not **sacrifice**.'
I did **not** come to call the **righteous** but **sinners**."

Lectionary took a long detour into the Gospel of John, which does not have its own year as the other three do. Each year there are many passages from John in Lent and the Easter season.

Because it has been so long since our course of reading through Matthew was suspended, you might put a little more emphasis on the opening "A reading from the holy Gospel according to Matthew," so that the assembly, consciously or unconsciously, registers that we have returned to the guiding text of the year. The Gospel of

Matthew will be proclaimed until the start of Advent on November 28, 2005, and a clear enunciation of the Evangelist's name on the first few Sundays of the return to the first Gospel will help with catechesis and preaching on and about this Gospel.

Another reason to emphasize the Evangelist's name is that today's reading is the story of the call of a character named Matthew. Although these two Matthews were probably not the same person (the Matthew in the story lived at the start of the century and the Evangelist lived in the second generation of Christians), in the end the

tradition has united them. Today's proclamation has both present, the Evangelist in the opening, "A reading from . . ." and the tax collector in the narrative.

The narrative of the Gospel is straightforward, and its key theological point is in the final sentence, "I did not come to call the righteous but sinners," a message of consolation to all believers. Be attentive to the compassion of Jesus as you finish the proclamation with this important point.

11TH SUNDAY IN ORDINARY TIME

Lectionary #91

READING I   Exodus 19:2–6a

A reading from the Book of Exodus

In those days, the **Israelites** came to the desert of **Sinai**
> and pitched **camp**.
While Israel was **encamped** here in front of the **mountain**,
> **Moses** went up the mountain to **God**.
Then the LORD **called** to him and said,
> "Thus shall you say to the house of **Jacob**;
> **tell** the Israelites:
> You have seen for **yourselves** how I treated the **Egyptians**
> and how I **bore** you up on **eagle** wings
> and **brought** you here to **myself**.
Therefore, if you **hearken** to my voice and **keep** my covenant,
> you shall be my special **possession**,
> **dearer** to me than all other **people**,
> though all the earth is mine.
You shall be to me a kingdom of **priests**, a **holy** nation."

Israelites = IZ-ree-uh-līts
Sinai = SĪ-nī

Here there is a switch from the narrative to a direct quote from the LORD. Mark the change in your proclamation.
Jacob = JAY-kub

Here is a quote within a quote. The punctuation on the page makes the changes clear to you, and your voice should communicate these shifts for those who are not looking at the text.

READING I The first few lines of this reading set up the context for the quotation from the LORD, which takes up the majority of the passage. This opening is descriptive.

That description is followed by a direct quotation of what the LORD says to Moses, and in this the hearer discovers what the LORD is going to have Moses say to the house of Jacob.

Within that part, however, is another layer. The LORD is telling Moses what to tell the house of Jacob, and here the house of Jacob is instructed about what to tell the Israelites. Because of these layers of instruction, not only is there complexity for your proclamation, nearly half the passage is setting up the theological element, which is the passage's key. The burden is on you to practice your proclamation so that these three levels are understandable.

Most significant to the proclamation is the revelation about the relationship between the people and God. While the opening sets the time and place, the second part is timeless in its characterization of that relationship. Try to commit this to memory so that you can maintain eye contact during this last part: that "you shall be my special possession," that "all the earth is mine," and that "You shall be for me a kingdom of priests, a holy nation."

"Kingdom of priests" is another way of naming the "holy nation," which is to say, the primary duty of this kingdom is to pray and offer worship before God and then serve the people.

READING II When as a lector you are assigned a reading from one of Paul's letters, the passage often gives you the opportunity to speak as a person of

The use of the first-person plural pronoun, "we," embraces the entire people of God to whom you proclaim, yourself included. Address the assembly directly with the reading.

As ever, the theology of Romans is rich.

Pause at the midway point to give yourself and the assembly a chance to absorb the preceding theological points.

READING II   Romans 5:6–11

A reading from the Letter of Saint Paul to the Romans

Brothers and sisters:
Christ, while we were still **helpless**,
    yet **died** at the appointed **time** for the **ungodly**.
Indeed, only with **difficulty** does one **die** for a **just** person,
    though **perhaps** for a **good** person
    one **might** even find courage to **die**.
But God **proves** his love for **us**
    in that while we were still **sinners** Christ **died** for us.
How much **more** then, since we are now **justified** by his **blood**,
    will we be **saved** through him from the **wrath**.

Indeed, if, while we were **enemies**,
    we were **reconciled** to God through the **death** of his **Son**,
    how much **more**, once **reconciled**,
    will we be **saved** by his life.
Not only **that**,
    but we also **boast** of God through our Lord Jesus **Christ**,
    through whom we have now received **reconciliation**.

faith witnessing to a community of faith as Paul did. Paul's frequent use of "I" and "we" makes this easy. While the singular pronoun is more personal, the plural "we" embraces the communal dimension of Christian life.

In antiquity the communal dimension would have been the "we" of Paul and the members of the church at Rome, and today the communal dimension is the "we" of you and the members of your community of faith, united with Christians around the world. You are not imitating Paul when you proclaim the words he wrote, but like him you are proclaiming the living word of God.

As you prepare, consider how the reading characterizes the change that was brought about by the saving death of Christ. On the "before" side, we hear "helpless," "ungodly," "sinners," "the wrath," and "enemies." On the "after" side, we hear "just person," "love," "justified," "reconciled," "saved," and "reconciliation." Paul was seeking to emphasize the total gift that the coming of Christ was and is for the world. He came not because we had deserved or earned this gift, but out of the supreme generosity of a loving God.

Do your best to highlight this aspect of the passage so that those in your community can appreciate that they are loved by God and by Christ not because they are good people, but that they are able to be good people because they are so loved.

GOSPEL   This Gospel passage has three clear sections, and their literary forms are as varied as their content. The three are related loosely to the issue of vocation or calling, but within this, they vary. As you practice in preparation, consider each section as a distinct part first, and then

GOSPEL   Matthew 9:36—10:8

A reading from the holy Gospel according to Matthew

At the **sight** of the **crowds**, Jesus' **heart** was moved
    with pity for them
  because they were **troubled** and **abandoned**,
  like **sheep** without a **shepherd**.
Then he said to his disciples,
  "The harvest is **abundant** but the laborers are **few**;
  so ask the **master** of the harvest
  to send out **laborers** for his harvest."

Then he **summoned** his twelve disciples
  and gave them **authority** over unclean **spirits**
  to drive them **out** and to cure **every** disease and **every** illness.
The **names** of the twelve apostles are **these**:
  first, **Simon** called **Peter**, and his brother **Andrew**;
  James, the son of **Zebedee**, and his brother **John**;
  Philip and **Bartholomew**, **Thomas** and **Matthew**
    the **tax** collector;
  James, the son of **Alphaeus**, and **Thaddeus**;
  Simon from **Cana**, and **Judas Iscariot** who **betrayed** him.

Jesus sent **out** these twelve after **instructing** them thus,
  "Do **not** go into **pagan** territory or **enter** a Samaritan **town**.
Go **rather** to the **lost** sheep of the house of **Israel**.
As you go, make **this** proclamation:
    'The **kingdom** of **heaven** is at **hand**.'
Cure the sick, **raise** the dead, **cleanse** lepers, **drive** out demons.
Without **cost** you have **received**; without **cost** you are to **give**."

As always with proper names, practice them until you are familiar with them. But more important than accuracy is facility, that they be pronounced without stumbling as much as possible.

Zebedee = ZEB-uh-dee
Bartholomew = bar-THAHL-uh-my<u>oo</u>
Alphaeus = AL-fee-us
Thaddaeus = THAD-ee-us
Cana = KAY-nuh
Judas = J<u>OO</u>-dus
Iscariot = is-KAIR-ee-ut

Samaritan = suh-MAIR-uh-tun
Israel = IZ-ree-ul

A string of imperatives from Jesus' lips: "Go! Cure! Raise! Cleanse! Drive out!" Proclaim them as commands, which is what they are.

---

bring them together while maintaining a slight pause between them as you proclaim.

In the first section Jesus addresses the crowd and afterward offers a reflection to the disciples employing an agricultural image: too few workers for the harvest.

The second section is a solemn conveyance of authority to the *twelve* apostles, and a solemn naming of them. Since Matthew's Gospel, more than the other three, was written for a community that included many believers of Jewish background, this naming of the apostles is a constitution of the new Israel, echoing the twelve tribes of ancient

Israel. Not all of these twelve have a fully drawn portrait in the New Testament, but the list of the twelve, including the betrayer, is the solemn element.

The third section is Jesus' first instructions to the twelve. Jesus commands them to exercise his gifts in the world to gather the lost sheep of Israel. As mentioned above, the community of Matthew's Gospel included many Jews, so this limit of the mission of the disciples in this passage is no surprise.

The final line is true of God's gracious gift to each of us, a gift from God completely undeserved and to be shared with others as

a gift. Augustine of Hippo, the doctor of the Church who wrote in the late fourth and early fifth centuries, described grace as *prorsus indebitum*, "completely undeserved." Since grace and life are themselves utter gifts of a generous God, we ourselves imitate God's generosity by giving as a gift what we have received. The reading ends on this poignant theological note after Jesus has instructed the disciples.

12TH SUNDAY IN ORDINARY TIME

Lectionary #94

READING I   Jeremiah 20:10–13

Jeremiah = jair-uh-MĪ-uh

After the identification of the reading, pause before these first two words, for from them alone will the hearers know that all of what follows is from the voice of the prophet. Jeremiah's exasperation does not call for you to imitate it, but it can subtly shape the style and tone of your proclamation.

Note here that the prophet is quoting those who have talked around him and about him.

This verse is addressed to the LORD, who is Jeremiah's "you," as in "you who test," "you take," "to you I have entrusted."

This final verse is addressed to assembly as an exhortation: "Sing!" "Praise the LORD!" Capture the imperative of the prophet's exhortation in your tone.

A reading from the Book of the Prophet Jeremiah

Jeremiah said:
"I hear the **whisperings** of many:
    '**Terror** on every side!
    Denounce! let us **denounce** him!'
All those who were my **friends**
    are on the watch for any **misstep** of mine.
'Perhaps he will be **trapped**; then we can prevail,
    and take our **vengeance** on him.'

"But the LORD is with me, like a mighty **champion**:
    my persecutors will **stumble**, they will not triumph.
In their **failure** they will be put to utter **shame**,
    to **lasting**, **unforgettable confusion**.

"O LORD of **hosts**, you who test the **just**,
    who probe **mind** and **heart**,
let me witness the **vengeance** you take on them,
    for to **you** I have entrusted my cause.

"**Sing** to the LORD,
    praise the LORD,
for he has **rescued** the life of the **poor**
    from the **power** of the **wicked**!"

READING I   This passage is a bit tricky because the one (or ones) to whom the prophet is speaking changes in the course of the passage. In preparation for your proclamation, it might be helpful to mark out the parts that are addressed to different hearers.

The first part tells us Jeremiah's situation; the next part is addressed to the LORD, and in it he quotes the whisperers and friends; after that, the speaker does not speak *to* the LORD but *about* the LORD; and where the quotation marks appear in the last two verses, the prophet is addressing first the LORD, and then the assembly listening to the prophet.

The theology of the reading is unique, for the rhetoric changes; by the end the prophet is praising the LORD. It will be a help to you to study the shifts in tone, for having your reading reflect the content is important here. It would be an impediment to the assembly's understanding if the reader were to maintain a tone of indictment when the words are of praise, for example.

For your part, as you are reading to the Church, be aware of the different persons whom Jeremiah exhorts so that you can help the assembly appreciate the nuances of the prophecy.

Consider how—with eye contact, perhaps, or a variety of vocal indications—the assembly will pick up from your proclamation the different persons to whom the prophet speaks. As you practice, might solicit the help of a friend or family member for suggestions about how to make these different "audiences" of the prophecy distinguishable in the reading.

A reading from the Letter of Saint Paul to the Romans

Brothers and sisters:
Through **one** man **sin** entered the world,
    and through sin, **death**,
    and thus **death** came to **all** men, inasmuch as all **sinned**—
    for up to the time of the **law**, sin was **in** the world,
    though sin is **not** accounted when there **is** no law.

But **death** reigned from **Adam** to **Moses**,
    even over those who did not **sin**
    after the pattern of the trespass of **Adam**,
    who is the **type** of the one who was to **come**.

But the **gift** is **not** like the **transgression**.
For if by the **transgression** of the **one** the **many** died,
    how much **more** did the grace of **God**
    and the gracious **gift** of the **one** man Jesus **Christ**
    overflow for the **many**.

Romans = ROH-munz

This is not a gradual beginning. The words of the apostle are strong from the start.

Here the theology changes from the darkness of humanity before Christ's coming to the salvation brought as a "free gift" in Jesus.

The final sentence is complex in both theology and grammar. Read below to parse out its meaning for a clear proclamation.

READING II   This reading from the Letter to the Romans starts off strong, so you will want to be measured, paced, and poised in your approach to the ambo, in your announcement of the source, and in your start.

Most of the reading bears a dark theology. Its main thrust and vocabulary are about humanity's dark side, with the "sin," "death," and "trespass." As the proclaimer of the passage, you might be consoled to realize that the last third is as bright with

hope as the first two-thirds are gloomy. The gift of salvation by God's grace will be appreciated as even more undeserved by humanity if that grim first part is proclaimed clearly and with strength and conviction.

The Letter to the Romans is foundational for what it has brought to Christian tradition, yet it can sometimes seem impenetrably complex. The challenge to you, as you prepare to proclaim such a reading, is to have your voice, style, and tone reflect that theology as a complement to the meaning of the words themselves.

The most hopeful aspect of the passage is the last sentence, but its construction is as complex as its meaning is hopeful. Consider the sentence's "bare bones," its simplest elements: "For [even] if the many died, the grace and the gift overflow." This is good news! But the sentence must be delivered with the dependent phrases: "through the transgression of the one," "how much more," "of the one man Jesus Christ," and "for the many." These make the sentence complex, even though its theology is important. Study the sentence in the context of

---

GOSPEL Matthew 10:26–33

A reading from the holy Gospel according to Matthew

Jesus said to the **Twelve**:
"Fear **no** one.
Nothing is **concealed** that will not be **revealed**,
    nor **secret** that will not be **known**.
What I **say** to you in the **darkness**, **speak** in the **light**;
    what you hear **whispered**, proclaim on the **housetops**.

"And do **not** be afraid of those who kill the **body**
        but cannot kill the **soul**;
    rather, be afraid of the one who can destroy
        both soul **and** body in Gehenna.
Are not two **sparrows** sold for a small **coin**?
Yet not one of them falls to the **ground**
        without your Father's **knowledge**.
Even all the hairs of your **head** are **counted**.
So do not be **afraid**; you are worth **more** than **many** sparrows.

"Everyone who **acknowledges** me before **others**
    I will acknowledge before my heavenly **Father**.
But whoever **denies** me before **others**,
    I will deny before my heavenly **Father**."

The speaker here is Jesus and the hearers are the twelve. But the second-person address of the imperatives and exhortations can be addressed to the members of your community as they were to the twelve.

Gehenna = geh-HEN-ah
In the midst of the exhortations and imperatives comes this question. Mark the tone by the tone of your voice.

These last two verses are neither exhortations or questions, but statements. Jesus promises to acknowledge or deny to the Father whoever acknowledges or denies him.

---

the whole passage, and make its meaning your own.

GOSPEL Matthew addressed a predominantly Jewish community, and for that reason he portrays Jesus as the fulfillment of some of the significant Old Testament patriarchs. This reading is part of the second of the five long discourses by Jesus in the Gospel of Matthew. Some scripture scholars have posited that the five discourses of Jesus are the fulfillment of the Pentateuch's five books of the Law: Genesis, Exodus, Deuteronomy, Numbers, and Leviticus.

Notice that after the introductory setting in the first verse, the remainder of the reading is from the lips of Jesus, yet the purpose of the words from Jesus changes throughout the text; there is story, command, question, and description.

As you practice the reading, you might mark in different colors what is narrative (the first two lines), imperatives in the second person ("speak in the light," "proclaim on the housetops," "do not fear those who kill the body," "rather, be afraid"), the question ("Are not two sparrows . . . ?"), and its answer ("Yet not one . . . many sparrows."). If you can distinguish the different purposes of the various parts of the reading and be familiar with them, you will be better equipped to deliver a clear proclamation.

13TH SUNDAY IN ORDINARY TIME

Lectionary #97

READING I   2 Kings 4:8–11, 14–16a

A reading from the second Book of Kings

One day **Elisha** came to Shunem,
  where there was a woman of **influence**, who urged him
    to **dine** with her.
Afterward, **whenever** he passed by, he used to **stop** there to **dine**.
So she said to her **husband**, "I know that **Elisha** is
  a **holy** man of **God**.
Since he visits us **often**, let us arrange a little room on the **roof**
  and **furnish** it for him with a **bed**, **table**, **chair**, and **lamp**,
    so that when he **comes** to us he can **stay** there."
Sometime **later** Elisha **arrived** and **stayed** in the room overnight.

Later Elisha asked, "Can something be **done** for her?"
His servant Gehazi answered, "**Yes**!
  She has no **son**, and her **husband** is getting **on** in years."
Elisha said, "**Call** her."
When the **woman** had been **called** and stood at the **door**,
  Elisha promised, "**This** time **next** year
  you will be fondling a baby **son**."

Elisha = ee-LĪ-shuh
Shunem = SH<u>OO</u>-nem

Be careful with the proper names in the opening line, particularly that of the prophet Elisha.

This paragraph sets up the narrative. The plan the wealthy woman reveals to her husband manifests the hospitality that is so strong in the tradition.

Pause after the woman's words to her husband. Time passes. The woman's plan is carried out.

Gehazi = geh-HAY-zī

Take your time with the exchange between Elisha and Gehazi, for it sets up what comes next. Pause after "Call her," because there is a transition to the final exchange, between the prophet and the woman.

This last verse is the resolution. Read it with care and clarity.

READING I   This is a narrative, a story with a beginning, a middle, and an ending. Your proclamation should animate the progress from barrenness to birth. The first and last verses hold together the story of the prophet's answer to the wealthy woman's hospitality.

Between these two narrative pieces are three dialogues. It will help the assembly appreciate the movement through the story if you pause slightly after each of the dialogues as a way of indicating that the scene is changing.

The first dialogue is between the wealthy woman and her husband. In it, only the woman speaks, letting us know that the prophet regularly passes their way and that the couple is hospitable to him. (This part of the story is that on which the Gospel will be built.)

The second dialogue has fewer words than the first, but two characters have speaking parts: the prophet and his servant Gehazi. The servant somehow knows the woman's situation and offers that insight to the prophet. This dialogue ends with the prophet ordering the servant to summon the woman. Pause slightly between this part and the next.

The third dialogue is the revelation of the prophecy, which indicates the Lord's regard for her childlessness. Be clear in proclaiming the prophet's word to her.

Take your time with that prophecy; if possible, commit it to memory so that you can make eye contact and be confident as you reveal the prophet's words.

READING II   Romans 6:3–4, 8–11

A reading from the Letter of Saint Paul to the Romans

For this opening salutation, look up from the Lectionary and make eye contact with your "brothers and sisters." Pause before you move into the grave question to follow, and then proclaim it with solemnity.

The comma between "that" and "just" indicates that the long phrase between the commas is to be proclaimed as a unit. The intervening phrase is a description of what happened to Christ as a model of what happens to us.

Note the parallel structure in these two lines, with "death" in the first and "life" in the second. Proclaim them so that the parallel is heard.

Pause before the concluding verse and proclaim it by animating the imperative.

Brothers and sisters:

Are you **unaware** that we who were **baptized** into Christ **Jesus**
    were **baptized** into his **death**?
We were indeed **buried** with him through **baptism** into **death**,
    so that, just as Christ was **raised** from the dead
    by the glory of the **Father**,
    we **too** might live in **newness** of **life**.

If, then, we have **died** with Christ,
    we believe that we shall also **live** with him.
We know that **Christ**, **raised** from the dead, dies no **more**;
    death no longer has **power** over him.
As to his **death**, he died to sin **once** and for **all**;
    as to his **life**, he lives for **God**.
Consequently, you **too** must think of yourselves as **dead** to **sin**
    and **living** for God in Christ **Jesus**.

READING II   No passage from Paul is as consequential to a theology of Baptism as this reading. It has had a deep place in the tradition for the many centuries of its presence in Christian lectionaries.

You might notice that this is the only reading from Paul at the Easter Vigil, preceding the proclamation of the Resurrection at the tomb. Many in the assembly to which you proclaim were baptized as infants, and they might not think much about the salvific consequences of a rite they do not remember. Yet a strong proclamation of texts like

this will contribute to a new appreciation of Baptism's power in the lives of individuals and in the life of the Church as a whole.

As you read, address the opening question to the Church as real inquiry. Be confident in the closing exhortation: "Consequently, you too must think of yourselves as dead to sin and living for God in Christ Jesus."

GOSPEL   Here we find another excerpt from one of Jesus' long discourses in the Gospel of Matthew, continuing what was proclaimed last week.

The first line of the proclamation for this Sunday is taken from earlier in the Gospel to set the context for Jesus' words. Therefore, after the identifying "A reading from the holy Gospel according to Matthew," pause so that the assembly will be poised to hear the opening.

The Gospels contain a number of passages in which the families of believers are impediments to the faith, as in today's passage. Since many people were brought to Baptism by their families and belong to families of practicing Christians, these texts

GOSPEL   Matthew 10:37–42

A reading from the holy Gospel according to Matthew

Jesus said to his **apostles**:
"Whoever loves **father** or **mother** more than **me** is not **worthy**
   of me,
      and whoever loves **son** or **daughter** more than **me** is not
         worthy of me;
      and whoever does not take up his **cross**
      and **follow** after me is not **worthy** of me.
Whoever **finds** his life will **lose** it,
   and whoever **loses** his life for my sake will **find** it.

"Whoever receives **you** receives **me**,
   and whoever receives **me** receives the one who **sent** me.
Whoever receives a **prophet** because he **is** a prophet
      will receive a prophet's **reward**,
      and whoever receives a **righteous** man
      because he **is** a righteous man
      will receive a **righteous** man's **reward**.
And whoever gives only a cup of cold **water**
      to one of these **little** ones to drink
      because the little one is a **disciple**—
      amen, I say to you, he will surely **not** lose his **reward**."

Most of the Gospel reading is direct discourse. The first line sets the context for Jesus' discourse. Proclaim it clearly.

Each "whoever" begins a new clause or sentence and a new element in the discourse. Take advantage of the repetition.

sometimes strike us as strange. But as you prepare for proclaiming this reading, perhaps it would be helpful to imagine some of the people who have gone through the catechumenate and the RCIA over the past few years. Many adult inquirers and catechumens were not raised in religious or Christian families. Indeed, for some, their decision to join the Church might have cut them off from their families. For them, choosing faith when that choice was so consequential is a brave act and a striking witness to those who witnessed their conversion and initiation. Imagine some of these brave people as you proclaim this part of the reading.

The second half of the proclamation is a more easily heard part of the Gospel of Matthew, in which the Evangelist identifies welcoming those in need with welcoming Christ himself.

The most poignant and, perhaps, poetically engaging of the exhortations from Jesus here is the final one. Both because it is so and because it is the final line of the Gospel reading, be bold in proclaiming this verse.

14TH SUNDAY IN ORDINARY TIME

Lectionary #100

READING I   Zechariah 9:9–10

A reading from the Book of the prophet Zechariah

Thus says the LORD:
Rejoice **heartily**, O daughter **Zion**,
    shout for **joy**, O daughter **Jerusalem**!
See, your king shall **come** to you;
    a just **savior** is he,
meek, and riding on an **ass**,
    on a **colt**, the **foal** of an ass.

He shall **banish** the **chariot** from **Ephraim**,
    and the **horse** from **Jerusalem**;
the warrior's **bow** shall be **banished**,
    and he shall proclaim **peace** to the **nations**.
His **dominion** shall be from **sea** to **sea**,
    and from the **River** to the ends of the **earth**.

Capture the prophet's command:
"Rejoice!" and "Shout!"

Zion = ZĪ-ahn

Jerusalem = juh-ROO-suh-lem

The first half of the reading is in the second person, addressed to the assembly directly as "you."

This is irony, with the most august ruler entering the city on a humble little donkey.
foal = fohl

Be careful with the geographic names.
Ephraim = EF-rum

The second half describes what the king will do.
bow = boh

READING I   Zechariah is one of the twelve minor prophets of the Hebrew Scriptures, and not well known in the tradition. Readings from this prophet appear only twice in the three-year Lectionary cycle. So be clear in pronouncing the prophet's name when you step up to announce the book from which the passage comes; be confident in your pronunciation.

Zechariah prophesied after the Israelites had returned from exile to a city and temple destroyed by the conquerors, so one of the themes in the prophet's work is the rebuilding of the temple.

Your reading for this Sunday is poetic and ironic. Its message is as important today as it was when the prophet preached. There are two basic points in the passage. First, we find the triumphant king riding not just a donkey, but a little donkey colt. The king is humble in victory. This image is taken up by the Evangelists Matthew and John in their description of Jesus' entrance into Jerusalem. (See Matthew 21:5 and John 12:15, which integrate this image from Zechariah into the Gospel narratives.)

Second, the king described by Zechariah is intent on doing away with the weapons of war—and here Zechariah calls to mind the fierce war chariots that any survivor of the conquest of Israel would remember with a shudder—for, as the reading declares, "he shall proclaim peace." Such a declaration of peace by a ruler is ever welcome in the tradition, so practice the proclamation and be sure of what its images represent. Your own appreciation of the poetic images is a sure foundation for the assembly's understanding and appreciation of your proclamation.

READING II Romans 8:9, 11–13

A reading from the Letter of Saint Paul to the Romans

Brothers and sisters:
You are **not** in the **flesh**;
   on the **contrary**, you are in the **spirit**,
   if only the Spirit of God **dwells** in you.
Whoever does **not** have the Spirit of Christ
   does not **belong** to him.

If the **Spirit** of the one who raised **Jesus** from the dead
   dwells in you,
   the one who raised Christ from the dead
   will give life to your mortal bodies **also**,
   through his **Spirit** that dwells in **you**.

Consequently, brothers and sisters,
   we are not **debtors** to the **flesh**,
   to live according to the flesh.
For if you live according to the flesh, you will **die**,
   but if by the **Spirit** you put to **death** the deeds of the **body**,
   you will **live**.

Proclaim the reading as a person of faith exhorting those to whom you are united by Baptism. Those before you as you proclaim are indeed your "brothers and sisters."

Be careful with this long verse. The structure here is if-then, although the "then" is understood. "If the Spirit . . . dwells in you, [then he] . . . will give life to your mortal bodies also." Your voice can carry that tone.

The same "if-then" structure is present in the final verse, starting with "if . . . you put to death, [then] you will live."

READING II Notice that throughout this reading the speaker addresses the faithful directly as "you." For this reason it will help your proclamation if you can make good eye contact with the assembly as you deliver the words of the apostle Paul. The opening and closing verses use this second-person address, so perhaps you can commit them to memory enough to sustain eye contact with the assembly as you proclaim them. The apostle's message is as vital to your church today as it was for the ancient church in Rome.

When taken out of the context of all of Paul's letters, this passage is difficult. The first part is not so hard, for in it the apostle is making a distinction between the "flesh" and the "Spirit." But further on there is a nuance to be understood: There is a difference between the "flesh" and the "body," and this is a little more complex.

Generally, in the theology of the apostle Paul, the "flesh" (in Greek, *sarx*) is inherently inclined toward sin, while the "body" (in Greek, *soma*) is used as an image for the Church, that is, the Church as the "body of Christ." (See 1 Corinthians 6:20, where Paul commands, "Glorify God in your body.") In that letter Paul equated the body of Christ with the "temple of the Holy Spirit," but here we find, on the one hand, the positive—"the Spirit of the one who raised Jesus . . . will give life to your mortal bodies"—yet, on the other, the negative—"if . . . you put to death the deeds of the body."

A confident proclamation will be based on our faith that without God's help our bodies are indeed inclined toward sin, but with God's grace they can mediate new life and the sacraments. Keep this in mind as you prepare for your ministry with this reading.

The reading has three basic parts; this first part is Jesus addressing his Father.

This image of us as "little ones" resonates with God as Father, as our provider.

In this second part, Jesus addresses the disciples about the relationship of the Father and the Son. The vocabulary is repetitious, but do not emphasize the repetitions too much. Keep the proclamation animated.

This third part is among the most consoling and well-known messages of Jesus in the Gospels, and it cannot be repeated often enough. Many will welcome a strong, deliberate delivery of these inspired and inspiring words.

GOSPEL   Matthew 11:25–30

A reading from the holy Gospel according to Matthew

At that time Jesus exclaimed:
"I give **praise** to you, Father, **Lord** of heaven and **earth**,
    for although you have **hidden** these things
    from the **wise** and the **learned**
    you have **revealed** them to **little** ones.
Yes, Father, such has been your gracious **will**.

"**All** things have been handed **over** to me by my **Father**.
No one knows the **Son** except the **Father**,
    and no one knows the **Father** except the **Son**
    and anyone to whom the Son wishes to reveal him.

"**Come** to me, all you who **labor** and are **burdened**,
    and I will give you **rest**.
Take my yoke upon you and **learn** from me,
    for I am **meek** and humble of **heart**;
    and you will find **rest** for yourselves.
For my yoke is **easy**, and my burden **light**."

GOSPEL   In front of the main building on the campus of the University of Notre Dame, the "Golden Dome," is a late nineteenth-century statue of the Sacred Heart of Jesus. The inscription on the base of the statue is *Venite ad me omnes*, "Come to me, all," the first part of the verse in the middle of this Gospel reading. It begins one of the most beloved statements of Jesus in the whole of the New Testament. The traditional image of the Sacred Heart shows Jesus' heart encircled by a crown of thorns, an image that for centuries has prompted Christians to recognize the unity of their own sufferings and the Passion of Christ.

This Gospel is also used for the Sacred Heart of Jesus, in the Gospel antiphon, and is one of the choices for All Souls, when the community of faith remembers its dead. The Gospel's presence on those days reveals the consolation this scriptural passage provides to people of faith in difficult times.

Your proclamation should highlight the importance of this text for those in your assembly who have borne suffering and difficulty, and they are many. In many of our Gospel proclamations, the Lord is imploring his followers to live holier lives. Here the consolation is that the Lord shares our burdens and recognizes that life is often hard. As the spokesperson for the community of faith, proclaim this with all the compassion and support you can offer to the assembly.

Pause just before you start into the most familiar part, "Come to me . . ." to recapture the attention of the assembly. You might pause in the same way before the last line, "For my yoke is easy, and my burden light," another beloved Christian text.

15TH SUNDAY IN ORDINARY TIME

Lectionary #103

READING I Isaiah 55:10–11

Isaiah = ī-ZAY-uh

The first lines set up a comparison between how things come from heaven in nature, and how the word goes forth from the mouth of God.

A reading from the Book of the Prophet Isaiah

Thus says the LORD:
Just as from the heavens
   the **rain** and **snow** come **down**
and do not return there
   till they have **watered** the earth,
   making it **fertile** and **fruitful**,
giving **seed** to the one who **sows**
   and **bread** to the one who **eats**,
so shall my **word** be
   that goes forth from my **mouth**;
my word shall **not** return to me **void**,
   but shall do my will,
   achieving the end for which I sent it.

The entire reading is actually one sentence. For your hearers' comprehension, though, the semicolon can be read as if it were a period, ending the sentence, and "my word shall not return . . ." as the beginning of another.

READING I As the proclaimer of such a beautiful nature image, of the rain and snow coming down from heaven to bring forth new life, you can appreciate the uniqueness of the passage before the assembly hears it. As you prepare, consider the proclamation as painting an image for the congregation who has not yet heard the passage. Your enthusiasm and engagement in describing God's providence over the natural world will animate the reading for the people and thereby animate their appreciation of God's generosity.

References to snow are not frequent in the scriptures. This beautiful image will not be immediately related to the weather as you prepare this passage, here in midsummer. It might be raining as you proclaim this passage, but that will help the assembly resonate with the text, damp though they may be.

The passage is only two verses long, so take your time and deliver the prophecy with a deliberate pace for maximum appreciation of the beautiful image of God's word bearing fruit in the world. You do not want the assembly to be still settling down for the Liturgy of the Word as you finish.

Notice that the opening identifies the speaker as the LORD. Then the remainder of the reading is the voice of the LORD mediated by you. Proclaim it with confidence.

READING II This is a theologically potent text. Its rhetoric is complex and deep, so your proclamation must aim at delivering it in the most accessible way for those in the assembly.

Romans = ROH-munz

The first two sentences are complex. Study them and ascertain their meaning in order to facilitate your proclamation. The clearer the meaning is to you, the clearer will be its delivery by you.

Take a slight pause here for the assembly to absorb that long sentence and heavy theology.

The more familiar images of labor pains and adoption balance out the gravity of the earlier theology and cosmology.

Setting the scene at the start.

READING II . Romans 8:18–23

A reading from the Letter of Saint Paul to the Romans

Brothers and sisters:
I consider that the **sufferings** of this **present** time are as **nothing**
　compared with the glory to be **revealed** for us.
For **creation** awaits with eager **expectation**
　the **revelation** of the children of **God**;
　for **creation** was made subject to **futility**,
　not of its **own** accord but because of the one who **subjected** it,
　in hope that creation **itself**
　would be set **free** from slavery to **corruption**
　and share in the glorious **freedom** of the children of **God**.

We know that **all** creation is groaning in **labor** pains
　even until **now**;
　and not only **that**, but we **ourselves**,
　who have the **firstfruits** of the Spirit,
　we **also** groan within ourselves
　as we wait for **adoption**, the **redemption** of our **bodies**.

GOSPEL   Matthew 13:1–23

A reading from the holy Gospel according to Matthew

On that day, Jesus went **out** of the house and sat down by the **sea**.
Such large **crowds** gathered around him
　that he got into a **boat** and sat **down**,
　and the whole **crowd** stood along the **shore**.

First, notice that this is a letter from one person, Paul, addressing a community of believers in the middle of the first century. Each section begins with a first-person pronoun. In the first (and longer) part, the pronoun is singular, "I," and quickly shifts to the plural, with "the glory to be revealed for *us.*" Proclaim the line identifying the text clearly, so that the assembly knows that the speaker is indeed Paul when you start the reading.

The second part of the reading starts with the plural number, "We know . . . ," and sustains this to the end, "we . . . groan,"

"we wait." The theologically deep part of the reading comes between these sections. This theology might be apparent to those who have studied scripture, but phrases like "creation made subject to futility," or "because of the one who subjected it," or creation's "slavery to corruption" are so opaque at first hearing that you might opt not to emphasize them too much in the proclamation. Rather, opt for emphasizing the opening verse and closing two verses, trusting that most of the assembly can receive these with facility and that those who know the

passage already will understand the theology that is difficult to take in on first hearing.

GOSPEL　Your preparation for proclaiming this long reading of the parable of the sower can be divided up fairly easily, for the Evangelist Matthew made such a division when he wrote it down. The first part sets the stage and then Jesus describes what the sower did and what happened after that, with birds, seedlings, thorns, good soil.

The parable itself, with the four different places on which the seed was scattered.

And he spoke to them at length in **parables**, saying:
  "A **sower** went out to **sow**.
And **as** he sowed, **some** seed fell on the **path**,
  and **birds** came and ate it **up**.
Some fell on **rocky** ground, where it had little **soil**.
It sprang up at **once** because the soil was not **deep**,
  and when the **sun** rose it was **scorched**,
  and it **withered** for lack of **roots**.
Some seed fell among **thorns**, and the thorns grew **up**
  and **choked** it.
But **some** seed fell on **rich** soil, and produced **fruit**,
  a **hundred** or **sixty** or **thirtyfold**.
Whoever has **ears** ought to **hear**."

Pause at the end of the narrative of the parable to mark the shift away from it. It will return later.

Jesus explains his use of parables in answer to the disciples' inquiry.

The disciples approached him and said,
  "Why do you speak to them in **parables**?"
He said to them in reply,
  "Because **knowledge** of the mysteries of the kingdom
    of **heaven**
  has been granted to **you**, but to **them** it has **not** been granted.
To anyone who **has**, **more** will be given and he will grow **rich**;
  from anyone who has **not**, even what he **has** will be
    taken away.

"This is why I speak to them in **parables**, because
  they **look** but do not **see** and **hear** but do not **listen**
    or **understand**.
Isaiah's prophecy is fulfilled in them, which says:
  *You shall indeed **hear** but not **understand**,*
  *you shall indeed **look** but never **see**.*
  ***Gross** is the heart of this people,*
  *they will hardly **hear** with their **ears**,*
  *they have **closed** their eyes,*

A quotation within a quotation—the Evangelist Matthew quoting Jesus, who quotes Isaiah at length. Take your time so that the assembly can follow.

The second part steps back from the parable as the disciples ask Jesus why he uses parables, and he answers in detail, bringing in the prophets to support what he posits.

The final part, as long as the parable itself, is Jesus' interpretation of the parable. He returns to the same narrative structure for the interpretation. So the unpacking of the actions in the first part comes in the same order: seed on the path, on rocky ground,

among thorns, and on good soil. The patterns and the repetitions in the vocabulary and structure can be used to good advantage in proclamation, especially with a parable that is familiar to many.

The two challenges for you as you prepare are the length of the reading as a whole and the familiarity of its message. To help with the latter, think about your own familiarity with the story and how, if you were the hearer rather than the proclaimer, you would enjoy hearing it and be most engaged by the proclamation.

As the notes indicate, pause after the introductory few verses and after each of the three basic parts. Although the agricultural imagery of the passage may not be universal in experience, these are accessible images, particularly in summer when some might be tending to gardens and watching their lawns grow and harvesting bountiful fields.

*lest they **see** with their **eyes***
*and **hear** with their **ears***
*and **understand** with their **hearts** and be **converted**,*
*and I **heal** them.*

"But **blessed** are **your** eyes, because they **see**,
   and your **ears**, because they **hear**.
Amen, I say to you, many **prophets** and **righteous** people
   longed to see what **you** see but did **not** see it,
   and to hear what **you** hear but did **not** hear it.

"**Hear** then the parable of the **sower**.
The seed sown on the **path** is the one
   who **hears** the word of the kingdom without
      understanding it,
   and the **evil** one comes and steals **away**
   what was sown in his heart.
The seed sown on **rocky** ground
   is the one who **hears** the word and **receives** it at once with **joy**.
But he has no **root** and lasts only for a **time**.
When some **tribulation** or **persecution** comes because
      of the word,
   he immediately falls **away**.
The seed sown among **thorns** is the one who **hears** the word,
   but then worldly **anxiety** and the lure of riches **choke** the word
   and it bears no **fruit**.

"But the seed sown on **rich** soil
   is the one who **hears** the word and **understands** it,
   who indeed bears **fruit** and yields a **hundred** or **sixty**
      or **thirtyfold**."

[Shorter: Matthew 13:1–9]

Pause again. Now we return to the parable, with Jesus interpreting.

The parable ends with the good seed bearing fruit. Have your proclamation reflect the meaning with a satisfied, positive voice.

16TH SUNDAY IN ORDINARY TIME

Lectionary #106

READING I   Wisdom 12:13, 16–19

A reading from the Book of Wisdom

There is **no** god besides **you** who have the care of **all**,
    that you need show you have **not** unjustly **condemned**.
For your **might** is the source of **justice**;
    your **mastery** over **all** things makes you **lenient** to all.
For you **show** your might when the **perfection** of your power
        is **disbelieved**;
    and in those who **know** you, you rebuke **temerity**.
But though you are master of **might**, you judge with **clemency**,
    and with much **lenience** you **govern** us;
    for **power**, whenever you will, attends you.

And you taught your **people**, by these deeds,
    that those who are **just** must be **kind**;
and you gave your children good ground for **hope**
    that you would permit **repentance** for their **sins**.

The first line reveals that the "you" is the Lord. The whole reading addresses the Lord.

lenient = LEE-nee-ent

temerity = teh-MAIR-ih-tee
clemency = KLEM-en-see

This middle section concentrates on the Lord's strength, and then focuses on the Lord's mildness.

This last section sees in the Lord's works an example for the people. Perhaps make direct eye contact in consonance with the Lord's works giving hope and repentance to the people.

READING I   Although there are a number of wisdom books in the Old Testament—Psalms, Proverbs, Job, Sirach, today's Wisdom among them—they do not often appear in the Sunday Lectionary, perhaps because they do not usually tell a story, as do most of the Old Testament readings chosen for the three-year Lectionary. (Psalms are an essential element of the Liturgy of the Word, of course, but as song, not narrative or exhortation.) The wisdom literature is important in the liturgical tradition, and it certainly contributed to the Christian traditions of the New Testament, particularly in the theology that speaks of Jesus as an all-knowing wisdom figure.

This reading is a kind of praise-hymn to the Lord. Notice that the very first line establishes you (the lector) as the speaker and God as the one to whom the praise is addressed throughout the passage. One challenge of this particular literary form is deciding to whom (or to what) physically you will direct the reading. Will you glance up toward the ceiling so that the "you" at the beginning will be directed as if toward heaven? Or will you speak the second-person "you" as if to the assembly? (Because the design of your parish church is unique, the discernment of the optimum direction is up to you as the minister of the word. If you have questions, consult the pastor or liturgy director.)

In whatever direction you aim your address physically, think of it as praise highlighting the Lord's care and mercy for believers. The attributes of the Lord in the reading—"might," "clemency," "lenience," "mastery"—are indeed wonderful qualities, so your delivery should be spirited.

Romans = ROH-munz

The reading is short, so take your time with the proclamation.

Pause between the two sentences so that the depth of the meaning is appreciable.

READING II   Romans 8:26–27

A reading from the Letter of Saint Paul to the Romans

Brothers and sisters:
The **Spirit** comes to the **aid** of our **weakness**;
    for we **do** not know how to pray as we **ought**,
    but the Spirit **himself** intercedes with inexpressible **groanings**.
And the one who searches **hearts**
    knows what is the intention of the **Spirit**,
    because he **intercedes** for the **holy** ones
    according to God's **will**.

The passage is an amalgam of several parables, tied together by the agricultural metaphors.
Here is the first parable of the passage; take a breath after it.

GOSPEL   Matthew 13:24–43

A reading from the holy Gospel according to Matthew

Jesus proposed another **parable** to the crowds, saying:
"The kingdom of **heaven** may be likened to a man
        who sowed **good seed** in his **field**.
While everyone was **asleep** his **enemy** came
        and sowed **weeds** all through the **wheat**, and then went off.

"When the crop grew and bore **fruit**, the **weeds** appeared as well.
The slaves of the householder came to him and said,
        '**Master**, did you not sow **good** seed in your field?
Where have the **weeds** come from?'
He answered, 'An **enemy** has done this.'
His slaves said to him, 'Do you want us to go and pull them **up**?'

READING II This is one of the briefest readings in the whole of the Lectionary, only two sentences. Its theology, however, is not as abbreviated as its word count, so in preparing take some time to appreciate what the apostle Paul was trying to express to the church at Rome in the middle of the first century, so that your community, like the Romans, might be built up from this theology.

The Letter to the Romans is among the last of Paul's letters, written about the year 58 or 59. Although this was written centuries before the theology of the Holy Spirit could be hammered out and the philosophical categories debated to figure out the relationship between the Father and the Son and the Holy Spirit (which we express in the Creed each Sunday), we find here one of the earliest Christian teachings about the role of the Spirit in the Church.

Paul reveals here that the Holy Spirit "comes to our aid in our weakness," so—against the culture that says that our every success depends on us as individuals—we know that in the end God's will for us will supply what we need. God's will for us is wiser than what we can discern left on our own. One of the many gifts of God in the power of the Spirit is the assembly of the Church, the body of Christ. That body helps us in our weakness.

Almost invisible in the reading is the reference to the "holy ones," sometimes translated "saints." The process for canonizing saints was not instituted until 1588, so when in the first century Paul wrote about holy ones, he was not thinking of the same

He replied, 'No, if you pull up the weeds
   you might uproot the wheat along with them.
Let them grow together until harvest;
   then at harvest time I will say to the harvesters,
    "First collect the weeds and tie them in bundles for burning;
   but gather the wheat into my barn."' "

Now the next. Pause after this one, too.

He proposed another parable to them.
"The kingdom of heaven is like a mustard seed
   that a person took and sowed in a field.
It is the smallest of all the seeds,
   yet when full-grown it is the largest of plants.
It becomes a large bush,
   and the 'birds of the sky come and dwell in its branches.' "

And the third. Pause again.

He spoke to them another parable.
"The kingdom of heaven is like yeast
   that a woman took and mixed with three measures
    of wheat flour
   until the whole batch was leavened."

Now Matthew offers a reflection on parables in general, and then the disciples ask Jesus for an explanation of the parable of the weeds.

All these things Jesus spoke to the crowds in parables.
He spoke to them only in parables,
   to fulfill what had been said through the prophet:
   I will open my mouth in parables,
   I will announce what has lain hidden from the foundation
   of the world.

Then, dismissing the crowds, he went into the house.
His disciples approached him and said,
   "Explain to us the parable of the weeds in the field."

His answer can be divided into fairly equal sections.

He said in reply, "He who sows good seed is the Son of Man,
   the field is the world, the good seed the children
    of the kingdom.

---

thing we think of. He was probably thinking of believers in Rome whom he had met. He was thinking of believers still alive and worshiping in the local community. For us, we heed the Church's teachings about the saints in the calendar, but, in line with the reading, this should not prevent us from imagining that some of the people with whom we celebrate the liturgy week after week are themselves saints, the chosen of God. After all, we are all called to holiness!

GOSPEL   This parable lets the reader and hearer know that the community of Matthew's Gospel had been in existence long enough to find out that churches could have good members and bad members, symbolized here as the wheat and the weeds. This parable is the Evangelist Matthew's way of instructing the early Church about what to do when a community realizes that there are both "good guys" and "bad guys" in its midst. Matthew's answer, on the lips of Jesus, is that the church should

do nothing: "Let them grow together until harvest," when God will sort the wheat from the weeds.

In the many centuries of the Church's long life, there have been countless saints, some of whom we know because their holiness was made public by their communities of faith, but many more whose holiness is long forgotten, or never known. This makes them no less holy, and it does not render

The **weeds** are the children of the **evil** one,
   and the **enemy** who sows them is the **devil**.
The **harvest** is the **end** of the **age**, and the **harvesters** are **angels**.

"Just as **weeds** are collected and burned up with **fire**,
   so will it be at the end of the **age**.
The Son of **Man** will send his **angels**,
   and they will **collect** out of his kingdom
   all who cause others to **sin** and all **evildoers**.
They will throw them into the fiery **furnace**,
   where there will be **wailing** and grinding of **teeth**.
Then the righteous will **shine** like the **sun**
   in the kingdom of their **Father**.
Whoever has **ears** ought to **hear**."

[Shorter: Matthew 13:24–30]

their good deeds less efficacious or less important. But there have also been many members of the Church who were far from being saints. This parable and its explanation at the end reveal that this is not a new situation for the Church, which has included a mix of good and bad from the earliest days.

This long Gospel from Matthew might also be a little frightening to proclaim: The assembly hears that in its midst are both the righteous and evil-doers, and that the evil-doers will be thrown into the "fiery furnace." For those familiar with the Gospels, this is not a great surprise, but still it is not a great consolation.

Some proclaimers think that the best way to handle a long passage is to hurry through it. It would be better, however, to proclaim it well, accessibly and engagingly, even if it takes a little longer. In this way, its length will not be apparent to your listeners.

17TH SUNDAY IN ORDINARY TIME

Lectionary #109

READING I   1 Kings 3:5, 7–12

The first verse gives us the context: the LORD's appearance to Solomon in a dream. Solomon = SOL-uh-mun

This second verse is Solomon's account of the relationship of God and Solomon's father, King David, and the people. The words of Solomon here are his prayer to God. He is already wise enough to know how much he doesn't know.

And here is the Lord's response to Solomon's humble prayer.

A reading from the first Book of Kings

The LORD appeared to **Solomon** in a **dream** at night.
God said, "**Ask** something of me and I will **give** it to you."
Solomon answered:
"O LORD, my God, you have made me, your **servant**, king
    to succeed my father **David**;
    but I am a mere **youth**, not knowing at **all** how to act.
I serve you in the midst of the **people** whom you have **chosen**,
    a people so **vast** that it cannot be **numbered** or **counted**.

"**Give** your servant, therefore, an understanding **heart**
    to **judge** your people and to distinguish **right** from **wrong**.
For **who** is able to **govern** this vast **people** of yours?"

The LORD was **pleased** that Solomon made this request.
So God said to him:
    "**Because** you have asked for **this**—
    not for a long **life** for yourself,
    nor for **riches**,
    nor for the life of your **enemies**,
    but for **understanding** so that you may know what is **right**—
    I **do** as you **requested**.
I give you a heart so **wise** and **understanding**
    that there has **never** been anyone **like** you up to **now**,
    and **after** you there will come **no** one to **equal** you."

READING I   As you prepare for this proclamation from First Kings, notice that most of this reading is an exchange between God and Solomon. First, God speaks, then Solomon responds with a humble prayer, and finally God responds to Solomon's prayer.

The narrative device of the LORD appearing in a dream is most well known from the two Josephs: Joseph of the Book of Genesis (famous in our day for his technicolor coat); and Joseph the husband of Mary, whose dreams are told in the infancy story in the Gospel of Matthew. This device appears in many stories in ancient literature.

Here the LORD encourages Solomon, "Ask something of me and I will give it to you." Solomon takes that invitation seriously, for much of the reading is Solomon's request!

Solomon's gift for leadership came not simply from his own skills but because he turned to the LORD for direction: "Give your servant . . . an understanding heart to judge your people and to distinguish right from wrong." (Would that all leaders were so humbly wise!) The "wisdom of Solomon" is almost a cliché, yet today's reading tells us how this great ruler became so wise. The ultimate source of his wisdom was the LORD's prompting, after which Solomon turned to the LORD, after which Solomon became the wise leader of the people, following in the footsteps of his father, David.

READING II   In this Year A, a big span of the Lectionary is occupied by the Letter of Paul to the Romans. We began reading through the letter on the Tenth Sunday in Ordinary Time (June 5), and we will not put it down until the Twenty-fourth

Romans = ROH-munz

This opening verse is a powerful consolation. Be clear with this opening.

Note the threefold parallel: "those he . . ." followed by "he also . . ." The second verb of the previous part becomes the first verb of the next: "predestined . . . called," "called . . . justified," "justified . . . glorified."

These parables of the kingdom are similes, each with a positive result.

READING·II   Romans 8:28–30

A reading from the Letter of Saint Paul to the Romans

Brothers and sisters:
We **know** that **all** things work for **good** for those who love **God**,
 who are **called** according to his **purpose**.
For those he **foreknew** he also **predestined**
 to be **conformed** to the image of his **Son**,
 so that he might be the **firstborn**
 among **many** brothers and sisters.
And those he **predestined** he also **called**;
 and those he **called** he also **justified**;
 and those he **justified** he also **glorified**.

GOSPEL   Matthew 13:44–52

A reading from the holy Gospel according to Matthew

Jesus said to his disciples:
"The kingdom of **heaven** is like a **treasure** buried in a **field**,
 which a person **finds** and **hides** again,
 and out of **joy** goes and sells **all** that he has and **buys** that field.

"**Again**, the kingdom of **heaven** is like a **merchant**
 searching for fine **pearls**.
When he finds a pearl of great **price**,
 he goes and sells **all** that he has and **buys** it.

"**Again**, the kingdom of **heaven** is like a **net** thrown into the **sea**,
 which collects fish of every **kind**.

Sunday (September 11). This Sunday for which you prepare is the halfway point in the proclamation of the Letter to the Romans.

This particular passage is short, only three verses, yet it is rich theologically. It is written in the first person plural, "we know . . . ," so the proclamation works both as an ancient text written by Paul to the church at Rome and as a text for the church before you as your proclaim.

For those who are familiar with this passage from Romans already, the second verse will not be hard, but on first hearing it

is fairly opaque. If you are not familiar with it, discern its meaning so that you can proclaim it with confidence rather than apprehension. Allow the passage some space for its theological heft to be appreciated, that is, proclaim it deliberately.

The last verse of the reading has three parts, each with common vocabulary and a common rhetorical pattern. The first half of each of the three parts begins, "And those God [verb in the past tense]," and ends, "he also [another verb in the past tense]." Notice

that these parts are in a logical order, with the second verb of one line becoming the first of the next line: "predestined . . . called; called . . . justified; justified . . . glorified." Practice this so that the repetitions work to the best effect for the hearers.

GOSPEL   The theological content of the reading clearly has two different directions. (Although there is the option, this Gospel reading doesn't seem long enough to warrant using the shorter version; but you know your community best.)

When it is **full** they haul it **ashore**
    and sit down to put what is **good** into buckets.
What is **bad** they throw **away**.

Pause here, for the tone shifts to judgment
and separation of the evil and the righteous.

"**Thus** it will be at the end of the **age**.
The **angels** will go out and separate the **wicked** from
        the **righteous**
    and **throw** them into the fiery **furnace**,
    where there will be **wailing** and grinding of **teeth**.

Familiar expressions from the Gospels.

"Do you **understand** all these things?"
They answered, "**Yes**."
And he replied,
"Then every **scribe** who has been **instructed**
    in the kingdom of **heaven**
    is like the head of a **household**
    who brings from his storeroom both the **new** and the **old**."

[Shorter: Matthew 13:44–46]

As you practice in preparation for your proclamation, consider the two parts separately at first. Part one contains three parables presented by Jesus to help the disciples understand the kingdom of heaven. There is some overlap and some difference among the three similes—the treasure hidden in the field (one), the merchant in search of fine pearls (two), and the net that caught fish of every kind (three). Each of the objects, the thing found or caught, is something of value. Read this part as a unit pointing toward the same issue, the kingdom, but with enough distinctiveness in each parable so that the hearers can appreciate the inventive metaphor of each.

Part two does not have the happy endings of each of the three short parables: no treasure discovered, pearl found, or fish caught here. No, in the second part of this Gospel the tone changes. There is judgment carried out by the angels who will separate the evil from the righteous and cast the former into the furnace, with the proverbial wailing and teeth-grinding. (Such a reading in the Lectionary is usually found at the end of Ordinary Time and the beginning of Advent, when Christ's second coming and the final judgment are highlighted in the readings.)

This reading, as often with proclamations, may not suit your own frame of mind and heart. But wrestle with what the Evangelist has written about judgment and separation. Proclaim it with as much clarity as you can, not to frighten those in the assembly, but to be faithful to the fullness of the Gospels even when it includes such a sober message of judgment.

18TH SUNDAY IN ORDINARY TIME

Lectionary #112

Isaiah = i-ZAY-uh

Imagine these particular elements as you prepare and as you proclaim. Perhaps if you imagine the taste of wine and milk, bread, and rich food (all for free) as you practice, your proclamation will make your hearers' mouths water.

READING I   Isaiah 55:1–3

A reading from the Book of the Prophet Isaiah

Thus says the LORD:
All you who are **thirsty**,
    come to the **water**!
You who have no **money**,
    come, receive grain and **eat**;
Come, without **paying** and without **cost**,
    drink **wine** and **milk**!

Why spend your **money** for what is not **bread**;
    your **wages** for what fails to **satisfy**?
Heed me, and you shall eat **well**,
    you shall **delight** in rich **fare**.
Come to me **heedfully**,
    listen, that you may have **life**.
I will **renew** with you the everlasting **covenant**,
    the **benefits** assured to **David**.

Pause before the last sentence, which embraces the earlier parts of the passage.

READING I Some think that easy access to the comforts of life can make people lose their faith. In that view, satisfaction makes people lose sight of the past when they did not have enough and lose sight of those for whom life is not so easy.

Christian theology and its sacramental tradition teach that the satisfaction of needs is no real satisfaction until all have their satisfaction.

The poetry of the prophet Isaiah speaks both to those who are without the necessities and to those who have abandoned those in need. You have been assigned a beautiful reading for its sharp imagery and for its social values.

Two things to bear in mind as you prepare. First, while a proclaimer often speaks in the voice of a prophet or the apostle Paul or another writer of scripture, this is different. The text is indeed from a prophet, but the prophet records the words of the LORD speaking in the first person: "I" and "me." As the proclaimer, you speak the words of the LORD.

Second, you need to find the best balance of poetic reading and social justice concern as you read to the assembly. Too much of the former and the assembly will not hear the words of the LORD about caring for those in need. Too much of the latter and the assembly will miss the beauty of compassion.

READING II   Romans 8:35, 37–39

A reading from the Letter of Saint Paul to the Romans

Brothers and sisters:
What will **separate** us from the love of **Christ**?
Will **anguish**, or **distress**, or **persecution**, or **famine**,
    or **nakedness**, or **peril**, or the **sword**?
No, in **all** these things we conquer **overwhelmingly**
    through him who **loved** us.

For I am **convinced** that neither **death**, nor **life**,
    nor **angels**, nor **principalities**,
    nor **present** things, nor **future** things,
    nor **powers**, nor **height**, nor **depth**,
    nor any **other** creature will be able to **separate** us
    from the love of **God** in Christ Jesus our **Lord**.

There are two lists in this reading. Be deliberate, clear, and measured in moving through the ingredients in the lists. (See below.)

This final verse is summary. Practice how to make its embrace felt by the assembly in which you minister.

GOSPEL   Matthew 14:13–21

A reading from the holy Gospel according to Matthew

When **Jesus** heard of the **death** of John the **Baptist**,
    he withdrew in a **boat** to a **deserted** place by **himself**.
The crowds **heard** of this and **followed** him on foot
        from their **towns**.
When he **disembarked** and saw the vast crowd,
    his **heart** was moved with **pity** for them,
        and he cured their **sick**.

The opening verses set the scene.

READING II Paul wrote his Letter to the Romans later in his life as an apostle in the early Church. Here in this passage we find echoes of Paul's experience, either direct experience or what he has heard in his years of traveling around the Mediterranean basin proclaiming the Gospel.

The passage has two basic parts, both arranged in detailed lists. Both lists contain things that might try to separate Christians from the love of Christ.

The first list contains elements that the members of the assembly can imagine easily,

tangible things that still befall people today. The second has elements that are a little more philosophical or abstract, perhaps, so consider how you can best keep the assembly attentive to that second list.

The final verse sums up the whole of the reading when it says that nothing in all creation can separate us from the love of God in Christ. Because it is not a sentence unto itself, you cannot pause before this final thought, but proclaim the final verse with conviction.

GOSPEL Here there are various things going on. Part one, the first two verses, puts the scene in context (after the beheading of John the Baptist), and mentions the great crowd there for Jesus, that Jesus felt for them, and that he cured the sick.

In the second part, the disciples want to send the people away so that they can buy food, but Jesus tells them to feed them. They respond with the crux of the problem: There are a lot of people and only five loaves and two fish, that is, not nearly enough.

Here is the link to the first reading's prophecy of food for the poor.

When it was **evening**, the disciples approached him and said,
  "This is a **deserted** place and it is already **late**;
  dismiss the crowds so that they can go to the **villages**
  and buy **food** for themselves."
Jesus said to them, "There is no **need** for them to go away;
  give them some food **yourselves**."
But they said to him,
  "Five **loaves** and two **fish** are all we have here."
Then he said, "**Bring** them here to me,"
  and he ordered the **crowds** to sit down on the **grass**.

The actions of the multiplication narrative here sound like the Last Supper: took, blessed, broke, and gave. Highlight these similarities in your proclamation.

Taking the five **loaves** and the two **fish**, and looking up to **heaven**,
  he **said** the blessing, **broke** the loaves,
  and **gave** them to the disciples,
  who in turn gave them to the **crowds**.

They all ate and were **satisfied**,
  and they picked up the **fragments** left over—
  twelve wicker baskets **full**.
Those who ate were about **five thousand** men,
  not counting women and children.

In the third part, the absence of food in the presence of the hungry people prompts Jesus to act. Notice the progression of the basic actions of the Eucharist: he took, blessed, broke, and gave. The end adds some details that will help the assembly appreciate the vastness of the multiplication miracle.

As you prepare, practice, and then proclaim, pause after each scene so that the assembly follows the narrative through its parts. There are a number of elements to be appreciated in what Matthew has done here;

he places the miracle in chronological context in relation to the death of the Baptist; he reveals Jesus' profound compassion for the sick and the hungry; he records a multiplication miracle and incorporates into it the actions of the Eucharistic tradition of the late first century; finally, he polishes the story with details about the quantity that was left over.

While this is not a difficult proclamation for its vocabulary, it is a complex narrative because of the variety of elements, some of which compete for theological emphasis. If you are also the preacher, you

might handle the proclamation so that the Christian assembly will hear most clearly the elements that will be taken up in the homily. If you are the proclaimer but not the preacher, perhaps you can find out what parts of the Gospel passage will be central to the sermon. If this is not possible, take your time preparing for the reading so that you are well rehearsed.

19TH SUNDAY IN ORDINARY TIME

Lectionary #115

READING I   1 Kings 19:9a, 11–13a

A reading from the first Book of Kings

At the mountain of **God**, **Horeb**,
   Elijah came to a cave where he took **shelter**.
Then the LORD said to him,
   "Go **outside** and stand on the **mountain** before the LORD;
   the LORD will be passing **by**."

A strong and heavy **wind** was rending the **mountains**
   and crushing **rocks** before the LORD—
but the LORD was **not** in the **wind**.
After the wind there was an **earthquake**—
   but the LORD was **not** in the **earthquake**.
After the earthquake there was **fire**—
   but the LORD was **not** in the **fire**.
After the **fire** there was a **tiny whispering sound**.

When he heard **this**,
   Elijah hid his **face** in his **cloak**
   and went and **stood** at the **entrance** of the **cave**.

Horeb = HOH-reb

Elijah = ee-LĪ-juh

This opening section sets up the rest of the reading. Pause slightly after identifying the reading, and be particularly clear with what the LORD said, "Go outside . . . for the LORD will be passing by."

Take each of these natural elements (wind, earthquake, fire, tiny whispering sound) as a short vignette, and pause slightly after each.

READING I   Of the historical books of the Hebrew Scriptures—1 and 2 Kings, 1 and 2 Chronicles—the passage that you are preparing to proclaim is one of the most well-known. Its drama and its message are striking and unique.

The dramatic elements are in the natural phenomena: the great wind, the splitting mountains, the earthquake, and the fire. Any of these would be an attention-getter, but the concatenation of them in one brief story adds to the effect.

On Sundays when you have not been serving as lector, you have probably witnessed some lectors who were too low-key for the content of a story, and some lectors who were too animated, too dramatic for the content of a story. If the personality or manner of the reader interferes with the people's ability to receive the word of God as the word of God, that is indeed too dramatic.

This reading clearly lends itself to some animation. (You cannot tell a story that includes rending mountains and an earthquake and a fire in the same tone of voice as a list of telephone numbers.) This reading might be a good opportunity to consult another skilled lector or a friend who will give you good constructive and critical feedback. You might practice the reading in a range from too low-key to too dramatic as a way of experimenting, and as a way of homing in on the best level for this proclamation.

READING II   In Paul's letters we learn a bit about his ancestry and his social and family background. We know that he was advanced in his life as a Jew (see Galatians 1:13–14) and that he was a rigorous and devoted follower of the Mosaic law. This reading you are preparing is more understandable in the context of who Paul

Romans = ROH-munz

These first lines are introductory. You stand in the apostle's shoes as you proclaim these words in the first-person "I."

Israelites = IZ-ree-uh-līts
Paul is praising his Jewish kindred according to the flesh. The Christian faith is deeply indebted to Judaism, for it is the foundation of many of our scriptural, theological, and liturgical traditions. Read this with the utmost respect.

This blessing, its with "Amen," is a fine closing at the end of the passage. Keep it buoyant.

The story has two crises (see below), with an introduction before them and a confession of faith after them. These opening verses set the context in time and place.

READING II   Romans 9:1–5

A reading from the Letter of Saint Paul to the Romans

Brothers and sisters:
I speak the truth in **Christ**, I do not **lie**;
    my **conscience** joins with the Holy **Spirit**
        in bearing me **witness**
        that I have great **sorrow** and constant **anguish** in my **heart**.

For I could wish that I **myself** were **accursed**
        and cut **off** from Christ
    for the sake of my **own** people,
    my **kindred** according to the **flesh**.
They are **Israelites**;
    theirs the **adoption**, the **glory**, the **covenants**,
    the giving of the **law**, the **worship**, and the **promises**;
    theirs the **patriarchs**, and from **them**,
    according to the **flesh**, is the **Christ**,
    who is over **all**, God blessed **forever**. **Amen**

GOSPEL   Matthew 14:22–33

A reading from the holy Gospel according to Matthew

After he had fed the **people**, Jesus made the disciples
    get into a **boat**
    and **precede** him to the other **side**,
    while he dismissed the **crowds**.
After **doing** so, he went up on the **mountain** by **himself** to **pray**.

is and of how much his own life was built on the traditions of Israel.

What we learn from Paul in this reading is not just that God called him to an extraordinary conversion, but that his call was to become one of those whom he had persecuted so fiercely. His enemies were to become his brothers and sisters in Christ. He would therefore have to abandon his family ties and social advantages by heeding the call to conversion. With this in mind, we can appreciate his turmoil here: "I have great sorrow and constant anguish in my heart."

Even though the bottom line of Paul's statement is that he has left the Jewish faith, he pays his ancestral faith great honor when he writes that to the Jews belong "the adoption, the glory, the covenants," "the law, the worship, and the promises," and the patriarchs; and from the Jews comes the Messiah. One can feel Paul's loving pride in this foundation.

From the distance of two millennia, it is hard to appreciate the huge change it was for Jewish Christians to give up their adherence to the Mosaic law. The law was all they had known of God's providence and

care, yet the spread of the Gospel depended on leaving it behind. Paul, as a faithful Jew, could lead the way because he knew of what he wrote and spoke.

Capture the noble background of the apostle in your reading, for as a baptized Christian ministering the word, you stand in his place now nearly two millennia after he wrote these words.

GOSPEL   This Gospel narrative has a number of elements that can make your proclamation of it engaging to the assembly. First, it has a clear structure

When it was **evening** he was there **alone**.
Meanwhile the **boat**, already a few miles offshore,
    was being **tossed about** by the **waves**,
        for the **wind** was against it.

During the fourth watch of the **night**,
    he came toward them **walking** on the **sea**.
When the disciples saw him walking on the sea
        they were **terrified**.
"It is a **ghost**," they said, and they cried out in **fear**.
At **once** Jesus spoke to them, "Take **courage**, it is **I**;
    do not be **afraid**."

Peter said to him in reply,
    "**Lord**, if it is **you**, command me to **come** to you on the **water**."
He said, "**Come**."
Peter got **out** of the **boat** and began to **walk** on the water
        toward Jesus.
But when he saw how **strong** the **wind** was
        he became **frightened**;
    and, beginning to **sink**, he cried out, "Lord, **save** me!"

Immediately Jesus stretched out his **hand** and caught Peter,
    and said to him, "O you of little **faith**, why did you **doubt**?"
After they got into the boat, the wind died down.
Those who were in the boat did him **homage**, saying,
    "**Truly**, you **are** the Son of **God**."

Here begins some dialogue, first between the disciples and Jesus and then between Peter and Jesus. Pause slightly between speakers so that the transitions are recognized.

The phrase "it is I" is grammatically correct and in a formal register. Don't put too much emphasis on the phrase.

This final section, with Peter's "little faith" and the disciples' confession of faith in Jesus as "the Son of God" is a strong finish to the story.

---

with a beginning, middle, and end. Second, the story can be a consolation to members of the assembly who are feeling lonely or frightened. Third, the story reveals that the disciples and we have more in common than we might think.

First, the structure. This lengthy Gospel can be considered in four parts as you prepare: introduction, disciples' thinking Jesus is a ghost, Peter's response, and resolution with their confession of faith.

The introduction sets the context in place and time, and mentions the previous

event in the Gospel. This section does not need great emphasis.

Jesus returns to the boat by walking on the sea, and the disciples are "terrified" and think he is a ghost! This is a climax in the story, so take your time in proclaiming it. That the disciples relax when they hear Jesus' words is key; there are other stories where the Lord's voice or his calling someone's name calms people's fears.

Since Peter is the leader of the disciples in the Gospel of Matthew, this third section is an important part of the Gospel story. Even the eyewitness to so many sav-

ing events can still be fearful, and this can be an important point for those who think the disciples were so much more holy than we are. Peter cries out to the Lord to save him, just as we do in the liturgy and in times of fear and need. The final section of the story tells us that the crisis is over; the wind eases and the disciples worship Jesus as the Son of God.

There are a number of elements here that can make this an engaging narrative, so take advantage of them.

20TH SUNDAY IN ORDINARY TIME

Lectionary #118

READING I   Isaiah 56:1, 6–7

Isaiah = ī-ZAY-uh

A reading from the Book of the Prophet Isaiah

Thus says the LORD:
Observe what is **right**, **do** what is **just**;
    for my **salvation** is about to **come**,
    my **justice**, about to be **revealed**.

Good advice for any time: Observe what is right! Do what is just!

The **foreigners** who **join** themselves to the LORD,
    ministering to him,
loving the **name** of the LORD,
    and becoming his **servants**—
all who keep the **sabbath** free from profanation
    and hold to my **covenant**,
them I will bring to my holy **mountain**
    and make **joyful** in my house of **prayer**;
their burnt **offerings** and **sacrifices**
    will be **acceptable** on my **altar**,
for my **house** shall be called
    a house of **prayer** for **all** peoples.

Here is the LORD's response to Gentiles who would join the Jews in service to the LORD.

READING I Since Vatican II, the Church has found new life in the witness and experience and testimony of those adults who are received into the catechumenate and initiated into the Church at the Easter Vigil. Keep your witness or experience of conversion in mind as you prepare this text for proclamation.

The prophet Isaiah makes a bold statement about "foreigners," those who are strangers to the Jewish tradition and yet "join themselves to the LORD . . . keep the sabbath . . . and hold to my covenant." These foreigners could have been an inspiration to those who had been born into the tradition.

In our own churches, many members were baptized before they could know what that meant, that is, before they chose the faith themselves. Those baptized in infancy can be complacent because the message and the traditions are the way things have always been done, with "nothing new under the sun." When new members join the Church and they testify to how the richness of the tradition inspired them to change their lives, we who were baptized as infants can ourselves be prompted to conversion and a newness of heart. Isaiah is hinting at this kind of experience in offering the LORD's testimony about the faithfulness of the foreigners.

As you prepare for this reading, perhaps you can think about people who have influenced your life in this way. Thinking of these particular people and your response to their experience as you prepare and when you proclaim will lend vigor and vivacity to your ministry.

READING II   Romans 11:13–15, 29–32

A reading from the Letter of Saint Paul to the Romans

Brothers and sisters:
I am speaking to you **Gentiles**.
Inasmuch as I am the **apostle** to the Gentiles,
    I **glory** in my ministry in order to make my race **jealous**
    and thus save **some** of them.
For **if** their rejection is the **reconciliation** of the world,
    what will their **acceptance** be but life from the **dead**?

For the gifts and the call of God are **irrevocable**.
Just as **you** once **disobeyed** God
    but have now received **mercy** because of **their** disobedience,
    so **they** have now **disobeyed** in order that,
    by virtue of the **mercy** shown to **you**,
    they **too** may now receive **mercy**.
For God delivered all to **disobedience**,
    that he might have **mercy** upon all.

Gentiles = JEN-tils

Autobiographical reflection is Paul's trademark.

**This middle sentence of the passage is the key to Paul's point: that God's gifts and calling are irrevocable. Highlight this sentence as you proclaim.
irrevocable = eer-REV-uh-kuh-b*l**

READING II In the first reading, we see that the prophet Isaiah highlights the faith and practice of the "foreigners" as a way of inspiring the Israelites. In the Gospel, we see another foreigner, a Canaanite woman, setting an example for those who witness her "great faith," to use Jesus' words. Now, in the reading from Romans that you will proclaim, we see that the apostle is "speaking to you Gentiles," that is, "foreigners" to the Jews, "in order to make my race [that is, his own people, the Jews] jealous." He is hoping that the example of those who "were once disobedient" but "have now received mercy" will inspire the Jews to richer lives of faith.

The conflict between Jews and Gentiles was a huge theological issue of the first century, between the death of Jesus and the last of the New Testament writings. Although this particular division is not central in our lives of faith today, there are always new "foreigners" approaching the Church as inquirers every year, people who deserve to be met with the welcome and hospitality that should characterize all Christian communities.

The challenge to you as the proclaimer of this passage is that its language does not make the issue as apparent as one might hope for a text with such a powerful message. His point is that God's merciful love is never-ending. All have disobeyed; all will receive mercy. With good preparation, you can make Paul's message come through.

Tyre = tīr
Sidon = SĪ-dun
Canaanite = KAY-nuh-nīt

Israel = IZ-ree-ul
Express in your tone the values of sheep and dogs so that the hearers will know from your tone what the Evangelist means by these.

Jesus' exclamation to the woman and the resolution come abruptly. Pause before you proclaim this last verse so that the closure to the story is heard.

GOSPEL   Matthew 15:21–28

A reading from the holy Gospel according to Matthew

At that time, Jesus withdrew to the region of Tyre and Sidon.
And **behold**, a Canaanite woman of that district came
    and called **out**,
    "Have **pity** on me, Lord, Son of **David**!
My **daughter** is tormented by a **demon**."
But Jesus did not say a word in answer to her.

Jesus' disciples came and asked him,
    "Send her **away**, for she keeps calling **out** after us."
He said in reply,
    "I was sent **only** to the lost sheep of the house of **Israel**."

But the woman came and did Jesus **homage**, saying,
    "Lord, **help** me."
He said in reply,
    "It is not right to take the food of the **children**
    and throw it to the **dogs**."
She said, "**Please**, Lord, for even the dogs eat the **scraps**
    that fall from the **table** of their **masters**."

Then Jesus said to her in reply,
    "**O woman**, **great** is your **faith**!
Let it be **done** for you as you **wish**."
And the woman's **daughter** was **healed** from that **hour**.

GOSPEL   This is a fascinating Gospel story. It seems at first as if Jesus is going to ignore the intercession of this foreign woman.

The animal metaphors used by Jesus and the woman are telling, for he uses "sheep," a common symbol in both the Old and New Testaments, most commonly known to Christians for the one lost sheep that the Lord goes searching for or in relation to Jesus' identifing himself as the good shepherd.

Less common in scriptural metaphor and Christian imagination is the dog. This story suggests how dogs were thought of at that time. Both Jesus and the woman mention dogs, but not as examples of loyalty or friendship. No, they are beggars, scavengers. In comparison with sheep, dogs were not well regarded. The woman trumps his animal metaphor with her own: No, you don't throw the children's food to the dogs, but they can have the crumbs that fall from the table.

Because the assembly to which you proclaim the word is not hearing the reading as listeners from the eastern Mediterranean in the first century would have, you might have your tone communicate the cultural value of the animals. The woman's sharp intelligence and great faith prompt Jesus to attend to her plea, and the daughter is healed immediately.

ASSUMPTION

Lectionary #622

READING I   Revelation 11:19a; 12:1–6a, 10ab

A reading from the Book of Revelation

God's **temple** in heaven was **opened**,
    and the ark of his **covenant** could be seen in the temple.

A great sign appeared in the **sky**, a **woman** clothed with the **sun**,
    with the **moon** beneath her **feet**,
    and on her **head** a crown of twelve **stars**.
She was with **child** and wailed aloud in **pain** as she **labored**
        to give **birth**.

Then **another** sign appeared in the sky;
    it was a huge red **dragon**, with **seven** heads and ten **horns**,
    and on its heads were seven **diadems**.
Its **tail** swept away a third of the **stars** in the sky
    and hurled them down to the **earth**.
Then the dragon **stood** before the woman about to give **birth**,
    to **devour** her child when she gave birth.

She gave **birth** to a son, a **male** child,
    destined to rule all the **nations** with an iron rod.
Her child was **caught** up to **God** and his **throne**.
The woman **herself** fled into the **desert**
    where she had a place **prepared** by God.

The reading has three parts. The first part is a short beginning.

The second part is the vision, and it occupies most of the reading. It describes the woman, then the dragon, and the woman and her son. This part will take the most practice in preparation.

As you prepare this text, you will need to decide how to handle the dramatic images in this passage.

READING I   **The Book of Revelation has been both ignored and studied too closely over the many years of Christian history. Between the sixteenth century (1570) and Vatican II (1962–1965), the book was rarely proclaimed in the Church's liturgy. Over the centuries many groups who thought the world was coming to an end have studied and interpreted each syllable of the book, often to erroneous and dangerous ends. Regular proclamation of this book** in the sacred assembly and sound preaching can keep this book from being either forgotten or misinterpreted. To this end, your ministry is central.

As you prepare for this proclamation, experiment with different styles in order to find one that suits the apocalyptic imagery. You do not want to be so dramatic as to send children fleeing to the parking lot, but you also do not want to be so understated that the terrible beauty of the passage slips away. Try out a few different methods with a fellow lector to determine the best voice for your proclamation.

The passage was not written about Mary, but through the centuries the tradition has applied the woman "with child" to Jesus' mother, Mary. That tradition is what brings this reading to the Lectionary for this day.

The last part starts in the first person. Speak with confidence. The "now" of this last verse tells us that this saving vision is not something of the past, but that the "kingdom of our God" and the "authority of his Anointed One" are still alive and at work. Bring this to life with your proclamation.

Then I heard a loud **voice** in heaven say:
"**Now** have **salvation** and power come,
and the **Kingdom** of our **God**
and the **authority** of his **Anointed** One."

READING II   1 Corinthians 15:20–27

Corinthians = kor-IN-thee-unz

You address the assembly before you as "brothers and sisters" as Paul addressed his letter to Corinth.

A reading from the first Letter of Saint Paul to the Corinthians

Brothers and sisters:
Christ has been **raised** from the **dead**,
the **firstfruits** of those who have fallen **asleep**.
For since **death** came through man,
the **resurrection** of the dead came **also** through man.
For just as in **Adam** all **die**,
so **too** in **Christ** shall all be brought to **life**,
but each one in proper **order**:
Christ the **firstfruits**;
then, at his coming, those who **belong** to Christ;
then comes the **end**,
when he hands **over** the Kingdom to his God and **Father**,
when he has **destroyed** every **sovereignty**
and every **authority** and **power**.

Key line of Paul's argument: "So too in Christ shall all be brought to life."

The reading finishes with this cosmic vision of Christ.

For he must **reign** until he has put all his **enemies** under his **feet**.
The **last** enemy to be destroyed is **death**,
for "he subjected **everything** under his **feet**."

READING II   If you have heard this passage of First Corinthians in the liturgy, it was more likely a funeral than a Sunday Mass. A number of the choices of second readings for funerals come from this chapter of Paul's well-known letter. The theological tradition of the Assumption of Mary is that Mary was exempt from death because of her holiness. For this reason, the passage is fitting for this feast because Mary, who

was without sin, was spared the wages of sin. First Corinthians supports the theological tradition even though Mary is not mentioned in the passage. This celebration is one of God's life in humanity. As Mary was saved from sin and death by God's grace, so does God rescue all baptized believers from sin.

The theology of Christian death, in which Mary is an example for all believers, is a key aspect of the Church's teaching and of your proclamation on this solemnity.

GOSPEL   This reading has three parts: an introductory narrative about the Visitation, a speech from Elizabeth about Mary and her child, and a canticle from Mary. The three parts are wrapped up in the final verse: "Mary remained with [Elizabeth] about three months and then returned to her home."

The opening narrative describes the meeting and the leaping of Elizabeth's child (John the Baptist) in her womb at Mary's

GOSPEL   Luke 1:39—56

A reading from the holy Gospel according to Luke

The opening sets two scenes; the first is Mary's journey.

Judah = JOO-duh
Zechariah = zek-uh-RĪ-uh

Mary set out
  and traveled to the **hill** country in **haste**
  to a town of **Judah**,
  where she entered the house of **Zechariah**
  and greeted **Elizabeth**.

The second, and more famous, scene is the greeting of the two women. Linger over this part, for it is a tender scene.

When Elizabeth heard Mary's **greeting**,
  the infant **leaped** in her womb,
  and **Elizabeth**, filled with the Holy **Spirit**,
  cried out in a loud voice and **said**,
  "**Blessed** are you among **women**,
  and **blessed** is the fruit of your **womb**.

This verse contributed to the traditional prayer, the "Hail Mary," so proclaim this sentence with clarity. Pause after "the fruit of your womb."

And how does this happen to **me**,
  that the mother of my Lord should come to me?
For at the moment the sound of your **greeting** reached my **ears**,
  the **infant** in my womb **leaped** for joy.
Blessed are you who believed
  that what was **spoken** to you by the Lord
  would be **fulfilled**."

Take a significant break after Elizabeth's words, for there are only three words of transition from Elizabeth's words to Mary's: "And Mary said." The next ten verses depend on these three words for the assembly to recognize Mary as the speaker.

And Mary said:
  "My **soul** proclaims the **greatness** of the Lord;
  my spirit **rejoices** in God my **Savior**
  for he has looked upon his lowly **servant**.
  From this day all **generations** will call me **blessed**:
  the **Almighty** has done great **things** for me,
  and **holy** is his **Name**.
  He has **mercy** on those who **fear** him
  in every generation.

Mary's hymn of praise is very deep in the liturgical tradition; pause before each new section.

greeting. Although this scene of Mary and her cousin Elizabeth appears in only one Gospel, it has shaped Christian tradition and theology immensely; it has been a favorite subject for artists for centuries. Few museums with sizable collections of European art would be without one or several paintings of the scene depicted in this Gospel for the Solemnity of the Assumption.

The esteem that the liturgical tradition has accorded the text here—taking one verse into the "Hail Mary" ("Blessed are you among women, and blessed is the fruit of your womb") and taking the canticle into Evening Prayer in the Liturgy of the Hours every day (the Magnificat)—cannot be overestimated.

This is a long Gospel passage. As you prepare, recognize and mark the different movements in the text. The challenge as you

proclaim is to comfort the assembly with the familiarity of the beloved story, yet also proclaim it as if for the first time. Anticipate what points in the story will move your assembly and be confident about the infancy story. That will contribute to a good proclamation. Take your time.

Israel = IZ-ree-ul

Abraham = AY-bruh-ham

Pause at the end of Mary's hymn before closing with the narrative summary.

"He has shown the **strength** of his **arm**,
and has **scattered** the proud in their **conceit**.
He has cast down the **mighty** from their **thrones**,
and has **lifted up** the **lowly**.
He has filled the **hungry** with **good** things,
and the **rich** he has sent away **empty**.
He has come to the **help** of his servant **Israel**
for he has **remembered** his promise of **mercy**,
the promise he made to our **fathers**,
to **Abraham** and his children for **ever**."

Mary **remained** with her about **three months**
and then returned to her **home**.

Lectionary #121

READING I   Isaiah 22:19–23

Isaiah = ī-ZAY-uh

The opening line identifies the speaker as the Lord; pause before this first line so that "the Lord" will be heard.
Shebna =SHEB-nah
Eliakim = ee-LĪ-uh-kim
Hilkiah = hil-KĪ-uh
You do not need to stress these uncommon names. Proclaim them smoothly and go on.

Jerusalem = juh-ROO-suh-lem
Judah = JOO-duh

The final two verses are a summary, so be clear as you finish the passage.

A reading from the Book of the Prophet Isaiah

Thus says the **Lord** to **Shebna**, **master** of the **palace**:
"I will **thrust** you from your **office**
    and pull you **down** from your **station**.
On that day I will **summon** my servant
    Eliakim, son of Hilkiah;
I will **clothe** him with your **robe**,
    and **gird** him with your **sash**,
    and give over to him your authority.
He shall be a **father** to the inhabitants of **Jerusalem**,
    and to the house of **Judah**.

"I will place the **key** of the House of **David**
    on Eliakim's shoulder;
when **he** opens, **no one** shall shut
when **he** shuts, **no one** shall open.
I will **fix** him like a **peg** in a **sure** spot,
    to be a place of **honor** for his **family**."

READING I Some of the people mentioned in this passage from the prophet Isaiah are not familiar to even dedicated readers of the Bible. The names are here as a foundation for a consideration of divine election. Here in the Hebrew Scriptures, the theology of election is tied to ancestry and family, unlike the theology of election in the New Testament or in the life of the Church.

The verses just before this in Isaiah have the Lord scourge Shebna the steward for not obeying the Lord. Because of his disobedience, Shebna is removed from his office and Eliakim put in his place.

As you prepare for this proclamation, keep in mind that the assembly has not heard why the Lord is going to remove Shebna. Pick up the chastising tone of the Lord's words in your voice. Second, keep in mind that most of these names are not familiar. The members of the assembly will recognize some—David, Judah, Jerusalem—but not others.

More secure in the imaginations of the hearers will be the domestic images of the final two verses, terms such as "key," "peg," and "place of honor." So be particularly clear here, for these two verses both sum up the earlier portion and include the sense of election—"I will place the key . . . on Eliakim's shoulder"—that is the point of the passage.

READING II Romans 11:33–36

A reading from the Letter of Saint Paul to the Romans

Oh, the **depth** of the **riches** and **wisdom** and **knowledge** of **God**!
How **inscrutable** are his **judgments** and how **unsearchable**
    his **ways**!
  *For who has **known** the mind of the **Lord***
  *or who has been his **counselor**?*
  *Or who has **given** the Lord anything*
  *that he may be **repaid**?*
For **from** him and **through** him and **for** him are **all** things.
To **him** be **glory** for**ever**. **Amen**.

Although this is a quotation, you need not make this apparent in your proclamation.

The closing verse is a doxology, a short praise that wraps up the passage nicely. End on an upbeat note.

GOSPEL Matthew 16:13–20

A reading from the holy Gospel according to Matthew

Jesus went into the region of **Caesarea Philippi** and
    he asked his disciples,
  "**Who** do people say that the **Son of Man** is?"
They replied, "Some say John the **Baptist**, others **Elijah**,
    still others **Jeremiah** or one of the **prophets**."

He said to them, "But who do **you** say that I am?"
Simon Peter said in reply,
  "You are the **Christ**, the Son of the living **God**."

Caesarea = sez-uh-REE-uh
Philippi = fih-LIP-ī

Elijah = ee-LĪ-juh
Jeremiah = jair-uh-MĪ-uh

The first part of the reading is a dialogue between Jesus and Peter. Pause slightly each time the speaker changes so that the hearers can note the switch.

READING II In antiquity it was not uncommon for an orator or letter-writer to cite a familiar passage to establish the authority of the case being made. This literary device is used in the New Testament at times, and by Paul in particular. In the middle of the passage from Romans that you are attending to there are a few lines of quoted text, familiar perhaps to the Romans to whom the letter was addressed but not to us today.

Here in the excerpt from Romans the quotations take up nearly half of the reading, so you need to consider how best to incorporate them into the passage as you proclaim it. Decide if it is best to have your voice mark the change of speaker or if you should move smoothly through the quotation because it is consistent with the rest of the text in which it appears. For this passage, the latter seems to be the best strategy, because there is no introductory phrase identifying a new source—such as "as we have heard" or "as the Lord said"—and because the rhetoric of the quotation is not too dissimilar from what the apostle himself is saying about the inscrutability of the ways of God.

The final verse is a short passage of praise to God, the source of the riches spoken of in the reading and, as it says, of all things. This is a stirring doxology (from the Greek *doxos,* "praise"), and a good upbeat close for the short reading.

GOSPEL In comparison with the other Gospels, the disciples are portrayed in the Gospel of Matthew in a most favorable light, Peter in particular. The

These two verses are a rousing praise of Peter and his role in the Church.
Jonah = JOH-nuh

Jesus said to him in reply,
"**Blessed** are you, Simon son of Jonah.
For **flesh** and **blood** has not revealed this to you,
　　but my heavenly **Father**.
And so I say to you, you are **Peter**,
　and upon this **rock** I will build my **church**,
　and the **gates** of the **netherworld** shall not prevail against it.
I will give you the keys to the kingdom of heaven.
Whatever you bind on **earth** shall be bound in **heaven**;
　and whatever you **loose** on earth shall be **loosed** in heaven."
Then he **strictly** ordered his disciples
　to tell **no one** that he was the **Christ**.

This is a summary verse, less dramatic than what preceded, in which Matthew reminds us of Jesus' desire for his mission to be secret.

Gospel of Matthew does include Peter's denial of the Lord, but on balance there are more scenes showing Peter and the disciples as heroes rather than impediments. This Gospel reading you are preparing now is one of those in which Peter is a hero. Some of the narrative is found in other Gospels, but the loftiest verses about Peter are unique to Matthew. They have been important to the theology of Church, ministry, and reconciliation in the tradition for centuries. Since these verses do not appear often yet are so important to the theology of the Church, proclaim them well.

The reading has two closely related parts. The first has Jesus asking the disciples who people say he is, and their answers. The second part of the reading is when Jesus, on hearing Peter's response, blesses Peter and promises him the keys of the kingdom. (In Christian art through the centuries, Peter always has a set of keys in his hand. This artistic symbol and tradition comes from this passage.) After this rousing revelation of Peter's role in the Church, the Evangelist reminds hearers of Jesus' desire for his messianic mission to remain secret.

This reading makes it easy for you to engage those who listen. It has a good balance of story and dialogue, of parts that advance the story and parts where someone speaks directly. Your preparation can be facilitated by marking the speeches in your *Workbook* and practicing how you will proclaim these so that the assembly will know from your voice the difference between the two kinds of text.

22ND SUNDAY IN ORDINARY TIME

Lectionary #124

READING I   Jeremiah 20:7–9

Jeremiah = jair-uh-MĪ-uh

Usually the words of prophets mediate the words of the LORD. Here the prophet is speaking to the LORD.

A reading from the Book of the Prophet Jeremiah

You **duped** me, O LORD, and I **let** myself be **duped**;
   you were too strong for me, and you **triumphed**.
All the day I am an **object** of **laughter**;
   everyone **mocks** me.

Whenever I **speak**, I must cry **out**,
   violence and **outrage** is my message;
the word of the LORD has brought me
   derision and **reproach** all the **day**.

The prophet is clearly angry at this point. Get his feeling across without being overly dramatic.

I say to myself, I **will** not **mention** him,
   I will **speak** in his name no **more**.
But then it becomes like **fire** burning in my **heart**,
   imprisoned in my **bones**;
I grow **weary** holding it in, I cannot **endure** it.

READING I   In spite of the difficulty of some of the tasks the LORD gave the prophet (earlier in the book), Jeremiah carried them out to the letter. But in the passage you are now preparing, the prophet starts to react to the difficulties. You can almost hear him saying, "No more! That's it! Enough! I can't go on!"

   It is Jeremiah's passion—for the people and for the LORD—that makes his words so stirring. The prophet's words in the passage here come just after the prophet had been flogged and locked in the stocks overnight

for his unwelcome prophecies. Knowing these details will help you appreciate just how grueling the prophet's life was.

   The ministry of the lector is not stage drama, so do not act out the part of Jeremiah as if you yourself had been flogged and locked in the stocks. But still you can communicate some of Jeremiah's anger and grief so that the assembly can appreciate the gravity of the prophet's situation. Moreover, although few in your assembly have been in similar straits, some people do feel abandoned by God at the darkest moments of their lives. This passage will touch their hearts.

Proclaim it well for those who will find consolation in the fact that even the LORD's chosen have been through very difficult times.

READING II   The passage you will proclaim this Sunday is integral to the Christian understanding of communal life, the integrity of the human body, and what we know of God's life in the world from considering the body and the relationship of mind and body. It is a very short excerpt, but

READING II Romans 12:1–2

A reading from the Letter of Saint Paul to the Romans

I **urge** you, brothers and sisters, by the **mercies** of **God**,
    to offer your **bodies** as a living **sacrifice**,
    holy and **pleasing** to God, your spiritual **worship**.
Do not **conform** yourselves to **this** age
    but be **transformed** by the **renewal** of your mind,
    that you may **discern** what is the will of **God**,
    what is **good** and **pleasing** and **perfect**.

GOSPEL Matthew 16:21–27

A reading from the holy Gospel according to Matthew

Jesus began to **show** his disciples
    that he must go to **Jerusalem** and suffer **greatly**
    from the **elders**, the chief **priests**, and the **scribes**,
    and be **killed** and on the **third** day be **raised**.

Then **Peter** took Jesus aside and began to **rebuke** him,
    "God **forbid**, Lord! No such thing shall **ever** happen to you."
He turned and said to Peter,
    "Get **behind** me, Satan! You are an **obstacle** to me.
You are thinking not as **God** does, but as **human beings** do."

its meaning is deep. A key phrase in the theology of Romans and for your proclamation in the liturgy is "living sacrifice."

As you review the passage, think about how the appreciation of the human body is ennobled by Paul's speaking of it in this way. A bridge between the two verses might come to the surface if you think about how the culture in which we live does not prompt us to think positively about our bodies. The consumer culture depends on making people feel that their bodies do not measure up somehow—not strong enough, not slim enough, not stylish enough, not *something*

enough. "Buy this," the ads tell us, "and you'll be a new person!" The Catholic view of the body provides an alternative.

Even though Paul's world was quite different from our own, the passage still challenges faith that is too comfortable in the world. We can sometimes let the ways of the world shape our thinking, feeling, and acting more deeply than our faith, and the reading from Romans is clear in prompting the members of the Church to be wary of the world when it drags them down, as it often does.

GOSPEL   This reading from the Gospel of Matthew has three basic parts: The first has Jesus predicting his Passion, the second is a dialogue between Peter and Jesus, and the third is Jesus teaching the disciples about the price of being his followers.

Each of these is a different literary form, so you might consider how you will proclaim them individually at first before you piece them together for the meaning and proclamation of the whole. The passage closes with a foreshadowing of things to come.

The remainder of the reading is the words of Jesus to the disciples, and in turn to the Church.

Then Jesus said to his **disciples**,
 "**Whoever** wishes to come after me must **deny** himself,
  take up his cross, and **follow** me.
For whoever wishes to **save** his life will **lose** it,
  but whoever **loses** his life for my sake will **find** it.
What **profit** would there be for one to **gain** the whole **world**
  and **forfeit** his life?
Or what can one **give** in exchange for his **life**?

"For the Son of **Man** will come with his **angels**
   in his Father's **glory**,
  and then he will repay **all** according to his **conduct**."

As you prepare, look at the second reading for this liturgy, where Paul commands the Romans, "Do not conform yourselves to this age." The Gospel excerpt that you are preparing confirms this suspicion about the ways of the world with its question, "What profit would there be for one to gain the whole world and forfeit his life?"

The second part of the Gospel reading is the dialogue between Jesus and Peter. As you prepare for this portion, recall that just last week the Gospel reading showed Peter in a most favorable light: "You are Peter, and upon this rock I will build my Church." This week Jesus rebukes Peter fiercely, "Get behind me, Satan!" That sounds extreme; Peter simply wanted to protect Jesus from the suffering he had predicted.

Remember as you prepare for reading this passage that Peter was just a simple fisherman at the start, he becomes the leader of the disciples once he starts putting two and two together, and Jesus entrusts the Church to him as the Crucifixion draws near.

The last section is Jesus' teaching. Be aware of that change in the character of the reading.

23RD SUNDAY IN ORDINARY TIME

Lectionary #127

READING I   Ezekiel 33:7–9

Ezekiel = ee-ZEE-kee-ul

After this first line, the remainder of the proclamation is the prophecy of Ezekiel. Therefore, be clear and direct with this line as a springboard to an animated proclamation of the prophecy.
Israel = IZ-ree-ul
Find a way to mark the distinction between this quotation within the prophecy and the rest.

The prophecy is mostly warning; but the last line has hope.

A reading from the Book of the prophet Ezekiel

Thus says the LORD:
You, son of man, I have appointed **watchman**
    for the house of **Israel**;
    when you hear me say **anything**, you shall **warn** them for me.

If I tell the **wicked**, "O **wicked** one, you shall surely **die**,"
    and you do not speak out to **dissuade** the **wicked** from his **way**,
    the wicked shall **die** for his **guilt**,
    but I will hold **you** responsible for his death.

But if you **warn** the **wicked**,
    trying to **turn** him from his **way**,
    and he **refuses** to turn from his way,
    he shall **die** for his guilt,
    but you shall **save** yourself.

READING I   Ezekiel provides some of the most beautiful and inspirational words in all of the Hebrew Scriptures, but he also captures a dark time in the history of Israel, the period leading up to the defeat and captivity of the nation. The temple was burned as the people were carried off to exile in a foreign land, and that destruction is the subject of many of the lamentations in the Hebrew Scriptures.

The prophets were not merely proclaiming consolation and hope as they mediated the words of God to the nation; they also spoke hard truths to the people about how they had broken the covenant, the law, and the word of the LORD. Both the consolations and the indictments that the prophets proclaimed were the word of God.

In our own time and place, there are those who speak the hard truths and measure human failings against the grandeur that God has granted us in Baptism. In this

they do for the Church what Ezekiel did for the nation of Israel.

Your strong proclamation here can be an occasion for the assembly to recognize the high standard by which the LORD measures people. Mere membership does not allow us to ignore our vocations to heed God's word; rather, Baptism makes us sentinels like Ezekiel. Be a brave sentinel yourself in proclaiming this word in the assembly.

The first clause of Paul's letter to the believers in Rome is key.

Practice this long sentence so that the assembly will recognize that the list of commandments is parenthetic to the point about love.

This line is the keystone of the whole reading.

This two-line explanation of the line above is important too.

READING II Romans 13:8–10

A reading from the Letter of Saint Paul to the Romans

Brothers and sisters:
Owe **nothing** to anyone, except to **love** one another;
   for the one who **loves** another has **fulfilled** the **law**.

The commandments, "You shall not commit **adultery**;
   you shall not **kill**; you shall not **steal**; you shall not **covet**,"
   and whatever **other** commandment there may be,
   are summed up in **this** saying, namely,
   "You shall **love** your **neighbor** as **yourself**."

Love does **no** evil to the **neighbor**;
   hence, **love** is the **fulfillment** of the **law**.

Proclaim this first section well and clearly. It leads to the more important second half.

GOSPEL Matthew 18:15–20

A reading from the holy Gospel according to Matthew

Jesus said to his **disciples**:
"If your brother **sins** against you,
   go and tell him his fault between you and him **alone**.
If he **listens** to you, you have won over your brother.
If he does **not** listen,
   take one or two **others** along with you,
   so that 'every **fact** may be **established**
   on the **testimony** of two or three **witnesses**.'
If he **refuses** to listen to them, tell the **church**.

READING II The passage of Paul's theology of love that nearly everyone recalls is the familiar "Love is patient; love is kind" that we hear so often at weddings. That passage from chapter 13 of the First Letter to the Corinthians is indeed a beautiful and poetic section of the Bible. Yet in the context of the apostle's Letter to the Romans, this passage on love is equally profound.

We think of the Old Testament law in its summary, the Ten Commandments. Yet there were and are more than six hundred legal prescriptions for observant Jews, so when Paul writes that "the one who loves another has fulfilled the law," he is setting out a remarkable reinterpretation of the Jewish tradition. Remember that Paul was himself an observant Jew, a Pharisee who found joy in the finest points of the law. So here after his conversion, he weighs the law and the Gospel together and this short passage is the result.

Paul sounds here very much like Jesus in some passages of the synoptic Gospels. We all know the "love your neighbor as yourself" law from Jesus in the Gospels, yet we might not realize that this passage from Paul's Letter to the Romans pre-dates the Gospels by a few decades. So Paul's words here are the first written appearance of this theology of love in relation to the law.

GOSPEL Matthew, the Evangelist most attentive to the Jewish law, concentrates here on settling difficult matters in the communal life of believers. He recommends reconciliation when one member sins against another, with the Church as

This verse provides a foundation for the Sacrament of Reconciliation. Proclaim it with clarity.

Here is the tradition's foundation for community life and communal prayer. A beloved, consoling word.

If he **refuses** to listen **even** to the **church**,
    then treat him as you would a **Gentile** or a **tax** collector.

"**Amen**, I say to you,
    whatever you bind on **earth** shall be bound in **heaven**,
    and whatever you **loose** on earth shall be **loosed** in heaven.
Again, **amen**, I say to you,
    if **two** of you agree on earth
    about **anything** for which they are to **pray**,
    it shall be **granted** to them by my heavenly **Father**.
For where **two** or **three** are gathered **together** in my name,
    there am I in the **midst** of them."

the mediator of reconciliation. For those of us who think of the "early Church" as a romantic period of peace and harmony among believers, this passage, with its testimony to disputes and disagreements in the community, should wake us up. The Church has always had and settled disputes!

The language of "witnesses" and "testimony" makes Matthew's legal concern apparent. In ecclesial life today we have canon law, which sets boundaries and settles disputes. (In the midst of these legal details, it might be a consolation to read Paul's words, "Love your neighbor," in the second reading!) This passage reveals that legal practice, language, and settlements in Church life go back to at least the late first century, when the Gospel of Matthew was written. Yet it is essential to recognize and proclaim clearly that the first step of the process is a conversation between two people.

Although the practice of the Sacrament of Reconciliation in the Church today is different from the experience of the community of Matthew's Gospel, this text provides the foundation for it. The final verse here puts a priority on communal prayer over private prayer, for the Evangelist does not offer "one, two, or three" who gather for Christ's presence, but "two or three."

Your strong proclamation of this reading is part of the work of worship where two or three or more are gathered. Appreciate the opportunity you have to proclaim God's word in this gathering in Christ's presence.

24TH SUNDAY IN ORDINARY TIME

Lectionary #130

READING I   Sirach 27:30—28:7

A reading from the Book of Sirach

Wrath and **anger** are **hateful** things,
    yet the **sinner** hugs them **tight**.
The **vengeful** will suffer the LORD's vengeance,
    for he remembers their sins in detail.
Forgive your neighbor's **injustice**;
    then when you **pray**, your **own** sins will be forgiven.

Could anyone nourish **anger** against another
    and expect **healing** from the LORD?
Could anyone refuse mercy to another like himself,
    can he seek **pardon** for his **own** sins?
If one who is but **flesh** cherishes **wrath**,
    who will forgive his **sins**?

Remember your **last** days, set **enmity** aside;
    remember **death** and **decay**, and cease from sin!
Think of the commandments, hate **not** your neighbor;
    remember the Most High's **covenant**, and **overlook** faults.

Sirach = SEER-ak

This Old Testament book is not familiar to many, so pronounce its name clearly and confidently.

The first two sentences describe, and the third is direct address: "Forgive . . ." They speak to the same issue, but notice that shift and consider how you will deliver it.

This section has three rhetorical questions. Proclaim them as questions for the consideration of those to whom you speak. Pause between the questions.

This last section is set in the imperative mood, commanding the hearers, "Remember! Think! Hate not!" The semicolons function like periods. Treat each as a new command.

READING I   The wisdom books of the Hebrew Bible do not appear often in the Lectionary, and Sirach quite infrequently.

The Roman Catholic canon of the Old Testament includes seven more books than the Protestant. This goes back to the sixteenth century, when the Church was divided, a topic too complex to take up here. But the book from which this reading comes is one of the seven that are considered inspired by Catholics and either not inspired or not as inspired by Protestants. It is usually in the theological issues of Purgatory and prayer for the dead that the difference of the canons comes up, because the scriptural foundation of the Roman Catholic theology of Purgatory is in these seven books.

The text can be considered in three parts, with the first part descriptive, the second posing questions, and the third setting out commands in response. A significant pause between each of the three different parts will help the assembly prepare for the change from one part to the next.

Each part has a number of sentences with similar structures, which you should utilize to the fullest. Take your time practicing each section by itself until you are comfortable with it and with the tone of your proclamation. Then bring them together and work on the transitions from section to section.

The passage will remain a challenge because it does not move in one direction, nor is it a narrative with beginning, middle, and end. Much of the wisdom literature consists of chains of fairly discrete aphorisms and sayings. These here are related, with a logical conclusion, but even so, proclaiming poetry can be challenging. The best proclamation will come from your familiarity with the content.

Romans = ROH-munz

Take your time with this brief passage.

Notice the repeated words, particularly "live" and "die." Be careful.

Here is the central message: "whether we live or die, we are the Lord's."

READING II   Romans 14:7–9

A reading from the Letter of Saint Paul to the Romans

Brothers and sisters:
None of us **lives** for **oneself**, and no one **dies** for oneself.
For if we **live**, we **live** for the **Lord**,
     and if we **die**, we **die** for the **Lord**;
     so then, whether we **live** or **die**, we are the **Lord's**.
For this is why Christ **died** and came to **life**,
     that he might be **Lord** of both the **dead** and the **living**.

Peter's question and Jesus' answer set up the theological and pastoral issue at the heart of the parable to follow, so be clear in proclaiming the exchange.

Pause slightly before you begin the parable of the king settling accounts.

First, the king with one of the servants who owes a huge debt.

GOSPEL   Matthew 18:21–35

A reading from the holy Gospel according to Matthew

Peter approached **Jesus** and asked him,
"**Lord**, if my brother **sins** against me,
     how **often** must I **forgive**?
As many as **seven** times?"

Jesus answered, "I say to you, not **seven** times
     but **seventy-seven** times.
That is why the kingdom of **heaven** may be likened to a king
     who decided to settle **accounts** with his **servants**.
When he began the accounting,
     a **debtor** was brought before him who owed him
          a **huge** amount.

READING II   Both the first and second readings point out the inevitability of death. This message is not often heard in our culture, which never wants to think about death. That first reading reminds the assembly: "Remember your last days," and "remember death and decay." These are not comfortable reminders, but they are important nonetheless.

This text from Paul is not quite as grim, but it too puts death front and center.

In the passage various forms of the words "live" and "die" come up repeatedly.

Don't trip over these repetitions. You can take your time with this, because the passage is very short. Pause after you announce the source of the passage ("A reading from the Letter of Saint Paul to the Romans") and pause at the end, before you start the dialogue with "The word of the Lord." (These pauses should be standard for all your proclamations.)

In addition to the repeated words, there is a parallel structure to the first two-thirds of the reading. The most fruitful proclamation will take advantage of the parallels so that attentive hearers will recognize the

point the apostle is making. You are a courageous proclaimer of the word with such a passage; proclaim it well and make the apostle proud of you.

GOSPEL   This parable from the Gospel of Matthew is not one of the most familiar, perhaps because, unlike those that end on a positive note, this ends with the wicked servant sent off to the torturers.

There are two verses that serve to set up the parable and one verse after the parable's close. The parable itself is the main

Since he had **no** way of paying it **back**,
    his master ordered him to be **sold**,
    along with his **wife**, his **children**, and all his **property**,
    in **payment** of the debt.
At that, the servant fell **down**, did him **homage**, and said,
    'Be **patient** with me, and I will pay you back in **full**.'
Moved with **compassion** the master of that servant
    let him go and **forgave** him the loan.

"When that servant had left, he found one of his **fellow** servants
    who owed him a much **smaller** amount.
He seized him and started to **choke** him, demanding,
    'Pay **back** what you **owe**.'
Falling to his **knees**, his fellow servant **begged** him,
    'Be **patient** with me, and I **will** pay you back.'
But he **refused**.
Instead, he had the fellow servant put in **prison**
    until he paid back the debt.

"Now when his **fellow** servants saw what had **happened**,
    they were deeply **disturbed**, and went to their **master**
    and **reported** the whole affair.
His master summoned him and said to him,
        'You **wicked** servant!
I forgave you your **entire** debt because you begged me to.
Should **you** not have had pity on your **fellow** servant,
    as **I** had pity on **you**?'
Then in **anger** his master handed him over to the **torturers**
    until he should pay back the whole **debt**.

"So will my heavenly **Father** do to **you**,
    unless **each** of you forgives your **brother** from your **heart**."

Then, that servant with another servant who owes a much smaller debt to him.

The one is in prison and the other handed over to the torturers.

Pause before this final verse, for it returns to the original inquiry and meaning.

part of your proclamation. For this reason, pause after the those first two verses and before the last, so that the faithful will recognize the shift to and from the parable.

You might recall last Sunday's Gospel with its description of settling disputes in the community of faith. In the Bible, this Gospel comes right after last Sunday's. The theology and practice of forgiveness have been (and truly are) essential components of Church life since the beginning.

The parable does not end with a comforting image: The unforgiving servant is not only imprisoned, but will be tortured until he repays his debt. Though this is the end of the story, the king was merciful to the servant at the beginning of the parable, and it might be that the parable is meant to shed more light on the earlier mercy of the king than on the closing torture of the servant.

The parable is a story with a beginning and ending, and between these terminal points there are a few smaller narratives, that of the servant meeting the fellow servant and of the return of the king at the end. If you've spent a lot of time with children, you might already have good story-telling skills. If not, this is a perfect opportunity for you to seek the advice of people you know who have read more children's stories out loud than they can remember. You can draw from their experience for good advice on how best to proclaim this text.

25TH SUNDAY IN ORDINARY TIME

Lectionary #133

READING I   Isaiah 55:6—9

Isaiah = ī-ZAY-uh

You stand in the place of the prophet today proclaiming what Isaiah proclaimed to the people of Israel millennia ago.

Engage the assembly with these imperatives and invitations.

The phrase, "says the LORD," as well as the first-person pronoun, "my," make it clear that this second section is the words of the LORD. There is a jump from one speaker, the prophet, to another, the LORD.

A reading from the Book of the prophet Isaiah

Seek the LORD while he may be **found**,
    call him while he is **near**.
Let the **scoundrel** forsake his way,
    and the **wicked** his thoughts;
let him turn to the LORD for mercy;
    to our **God**, who is **generous** in forgiving.

For **my** thoughts are not **your** thoughts,
    nor are **your** ways **my** ways, says the LORD.
As high as the **heavens** are above the **earth**,
    so high are **my** ways above **your** ways
    and **my** thoughts above **your** thoughts.

READING I The book of Isaiah is the basis for much of the theology of the New Testament, as the early Church tried to interpret the life of Jesus through the theological traditions of the Hebrew Scriptures. The prophecies of Isaiah contributed to the infancy narrative of the Gospel of Matthew and to the Passion narratives in all four Gospels. In particular, chapters 54 and 55 of Isaiah are at the heart of the message taken up in the Christian liturgical tradition. Each of these chapters of Isaiah is represented in the seven Old Testament readings at the Easter Vigil, equaled only by

Genesis, which also contributes two readings to the Vigil.

The prophet helped the nation recover after its return from exile, and the passage that you will proclaim is one of the key exhortations to the people, bidding them to consider how the ways of the LORD are different from their own ways.

As you can see in the margin notes above, the passage has two discernible speakers: The first half finds the prophet urging the people to look for the LORD; the second half has the words of the LORD mediated through the prophet. Although it might be a

little daunting, think of your vocation as a minister of the word as one of standing in the footsteps of the prophet. The assignment of this reading to you is not accidental, so put your reservations aside and step up to address the assembly with conviction and strength. The words of the LORD delivered to Isaiah and proclaimed from your lips have the power to change people's lives.

READING II This passage from the Letter to the Philippians was written in hope, one of those three things Paul

Philippians = fil-LIP-ee-unz

Imagine yourself standing before the assembly reading a letter written today. Though Paul's words are nearly two millennia old, they are still the *living* word of the *living* risen Lord to a *living* Church. Read it as such.

You stand in the stead of the apostle, so proclaim his first-person testimony as your own.

Speak to the believers before you as if they are the original recipients of the missive.

This is a long parable, and the opening line supplies context for the long narrative that follows. Pause after the opening line.

The first few lines set up the parable. Be clear with this, for the agreement between the owner and the various workers is necessary for the meaning at the end. There are six time checks in the story (dawn, nine o'clock, around noon, three o'clock, five o'clock, evening). Only once does the owner specify "the usual daily wage" and that is with the first group. When he hires later groups, he says at most, "I will give you what is just." These details are important.

READING II   Philippians 1:20c–24, 27a

A reading from the Letter of Saint Paul to the Philippians

Brothers and sisters:
Christ will be **magnified** in my **body**, whether by **life** or by **death**.
For to me **life** is **Christ**, and **death** is **gain**.
If I go on living in the **flesh**,
     that means **fruitful** labor for me.
And I do not **know** which I shall **choose**.
I am caught between the two.
I long to **depart** this life and be with **Christ**,
     for that is far **better**.
Yet that I remain in the **flesh**
     is more **necessary** for **your** benefit.

Only, **conduct** yourselves in a way **worthy** of the **gospel** of Christ.

GOSPEL   Matthew 20:1–16a

A reading from the holy Gospel according to Matthew

Jesus told his **disciples** this **parable**:
"The kingdom of **heaven** is like a **landowner**
     who went out at **dawn** to hire **laborers** for his **vineyard**.
After agreeing with them for the **usual** daily **wage**,
     he sent them into his **vineyard**.
Going out about **nine** o'clock,
     the landowner saw **others** standing **idle** in the **marketplace**,

---

elsewhere says will last to the end (faith, hope, and love; 1 Corinthians 13:13). Its message was hard for that original community in the Mediterranean world in the middle of the first century, and it is no less hard and no less important today. Your task is to proclaim it with boldness and conviction.

Paul trusted that ancient community of faith, and he would have thought of them as the body of Christ. We are inclined to think he means his own physical body when he writes that "Christ will be magnified in my body," but we can be sure that he is also thinking of the body that was (and is) the

Church. In 1 Corinthians 6:12–20, when he wrote of "your body," that "your" was not singular but plural; there he clearly meant the community of faith.

In this passage, then, when Paul writes about whether he is to "go on living in the flesh" or "depart and be with Christ," he is speculating about whether or not he will be physically present in the body of the Church.

In your ministry of the word, you know that you will be physically present for your reading. The Church requires physical presence for the sacraments to be celebrated. When the second reading has pronouns like

"I," "me," and "my," and pronouns like "you" and "your," these not only signify the relationship of Paul and the churches of Philippi and Corinth long ago, but the relationship of you and the church to which you minister as you proclaim the word of God. Accept your call, and deliver the word with courage.

GOSPEL   Note the direct quotations in this section, several from the owner and one from the grumbling workers. Perhaps you might stop and think about your own experience in unpleasant

and he said to them, 'You **too** go into my **vineyard**,
and I will **give** you what is **just**.'
So they went off.

"And he went out again around **noon**,
and around three o'clock, and did **likewise**.
Going out about **five** o'clock,
the landowner found **others** standing around, and said to them,
'**Why** do you stand here **idle** all day?'
They answered, 'Because no one has **hired** us.'
He said to them, 'You **too** go into my **vineyard**.'

"When it was **evening** the owner of the vineyard
said to his **foreman**,
'**Summon** the laborers and give them their **pay**,
beginning with the **last** and ending with the **first**.'
When those who had started about **five** o'clock came,
each received the **usual** daily **wage**.
So when the **first** came, they thought that **they** would
receive **more**,
but **each** of them also got the **usual** wage.
And on **receiving** it they **grumbled** against the landowner, saying,
'These **last** ones worked only one **hour**,
and you have made **them** equal to **us**,
who bore the day's **burden** and the **heat**.'
He said to one of them in reply,
'My **friend**, I am not **cheating** you.
Did you not **agree** with me for the **usual** daily **wage**?
Take what is **yours** and go.
What if I wish to give this **last** one the same as **you**?
Or am I not **free** to do as I **wish** with my own **money**?
Are you **envious** because I am **generous**?'

"Thus, the **last** will be **first**, and the **first** will be **last**."

This exchange at evening is the longest episode in the parable.

---

work situations, and how you would have felt in the place of the owner who had made the agreement and of the workers who felt cheated. Speak from these feelings so that the members of the assembly will feel the gravity of the circumstances. You are not acting, but narrating; your personal engagement with the story will be a good foundation for your proclamation.

In the centuries and millennia since this parable was first spoken and heard by people of faith, there have been fierce debates between those who think that we earn God's grace and love and those who think that God's grace and love are gifts that cannot be earned, no matter how much or how good our work. Surely, this debate about grace and works was raging in the first century or the parable would not have been told. The debate about grace and works flared again in the early fifth century, when Augustine confronted the Pelagians. And it raged again in the sixteenth century when Martin Luther called the Roman Catholic Church to amend its understanding of the relationship between grace and work. There are surely some "landowners" and "grumbling laborers" in the assembly to which you will proclaim this Gospel.

Your task is to prepare and proclaim this parable so that its "ever ancient and ever new" message for the Church in all times and places will be heard clearly yet again.

26TH SUNDAY IN ORDINARY TIME

Lectionary #136

READING I   Ezekiel 18:25–28

Ezekiel = ee-ZEE-kee-ul

The opening line identifies the LORD as the speaker. Within the LORD's words is a quote from the people of Israel, to which the LORD responds with these two questions.
Israel = IZ-ree-ul

Good people turning to bad . . .

Bad people turning to good . . .

The passage ends on a note of hope. It is never too late to repent.

A reading from the Book of the prophet Ezekiel

Thus says the LORD:
You say, "The **LORD's** way is not **fair**!"
Hear **now**, house of **Israel**:
    Is it **my** way that is unfair, or rather, are not **your** ways unfair?

When someone **virtuous** turns away from virtue
        to commit **iniquity**, and **dies**,
    it is because of the **iniquity** he **committed** that he must **die**.

But if he **turns** from the **wickedness** he has **committed**,
    and **does** what is **right** and **just**,
    he shall **preserve** his life;
    since he has turned **away** from all the **sins**
        that he has **committed**,
    he shall surely **live**, he shall not **die**.

READING II   Philippians 2:1–11

Philippians = fil-LIP-ee-unz

The first long sentence is an "if-then" proposition. It is well presented and will be accessible to the assembly if you practice it and proclaim it forthrightly.

A reading from the Letter of Saint Paul to the Philippians

Brothers and sisters:
If there is any **encouragement** in **Christ**,
    any **solace** in **love**,
    any **participation** in the **Spirit**,

READING I Nearly the entire passage is the prophet Ezekiel speaking the words of the LORD. Be clear in your identification of the prophet and in your proclamation of the first line.

Overall, the passage is not the most comforting in the Lectionary. The reading is about conversion, about people changing their ways, with a strong indictment of sinners. Ezekiel is a forthright prophet; for better or worse, he put no sugar-coating on the words of the LORD when he prophesied to the people of Israel.

As you proclaim the reading, your tone of voice should not clash with the meaning. As the reader of such a grave indictment, your voice will need to bear the gravity of what the prophet said centuries ago, both encouragements and indictments.

Overall, the reading ends on a more hopeful note. Take advantage of that ending to demonstrate that this is not the end of the story. The LORD is as infinitely merciful as just.

READING II The second half of this passage is also the second reading on Good Friday. The theology of the cross and of Christ's exaltation by God make it most fitting for the Paschal Triduum. In fact, before the reform of the liturgy, this reading was often chanted as the cross was borne into the assembly.

Scripture scholars hypothesize that the hymn (the second half of today's passage) pre-dates Paul's writing of the letter, which would make it one of the most ancient of extant Christian texts. This does not bear on

any **compassion** and **mercy**,
  complete my joy by being of the same **mind**,
    with the same **love**,
  united in heart, thinking **one** thing.
Do **nothing** out of **selfishness** or out of **vainglory**;
  rather, humbly regard **others** as more important
    than **yourselves**,
  each looking out not for his **own** interests,
  but also for those of **others**.

Have in **you** the same attitude
  that is **also** in Christ **Jesus**,
  Who, though he was in the form of **God**,
  did not regard **equality** with God
    something to be **grasped**.
Rather, he **emptied** himself,
  taking the form of a **slave**,
  coming in **human** likeness;
  and found **human** in appearance,
  he **humbled** himself,
  becoming **obedient** to the point of **death**,
  even **death** on a **cross**.

Because of this, God greatly **exalted** him
  and **bestowed** on him the **name**
  which is above **every** name,
  that at the name of **Jesus**
  every **knee** should **bend**,
  of those in **heaven** and on **earth** and **under** the earth,
  and every **tongue** confess that
  Jesus **Christ** is **Lord**,
  to the **glory** of God the **Father**.

[Shorter: Philippians 2:1–5]

Here is a transition from the life of the community to the life of Christ, and then a hymn of praise to Christ's humility, obedience, and exaltation.

The reading is lengthy, so practice to get a good balance of depth without having it feel drawn out to those listening.

its meaning one way or another, but it does help us appreciate the tradition at its earliest.

For this Twenty-sixth Sunday in Ordinary Time, you will proclaim a longer excerpt of the Letter to the Philippians than is proclaimed on Good Friday, and the added portion gives the reading a different theological emphasis. Paul gives advice to the community at Philippi, with instructions about living in community and sharing together in the life of Christ. The result of the extension is that Paul's reflection on the exaltation of the cross is juxtaposed with the "cross" of living one's life as part of a community of faith.

As a minister of the word, you may think that these hardly weigh equally in the balance as you proclaim them: belonging to the Church and Jesus' suffering on the cross. But by God's grace the Church manifests the body of Christ when it assembles, so the efforts and sacrifices that any members of the community make for the building up of the Church are tied to the Paschal Mystery of the suffering of Jesus. This is part of the gift of God's unimaginable generosity.

Your proclamation will manifest this mystery and this gift to the Church once again. Practice the two halves carefully, that on the life of the community and that on the humility and exaltation of Christ. Then bring them together for building up the body of Christ by your proclamation.

GOSPEL Although there are many people in this Gospel reading, Jesus himself is the main speaker. The point he is making has to do with consonance between words and actions.

GOSPEL   Matthew 21:28–32

A reading from the holy Gospel according to Matthew

This opening verse sets the context for
the parable.

One of the many stories from Jesus of a
father and his sons.

Jesus said to the chief **priests** and **elders** of the people:
"What is **your** opinion?
A man had two sons.
He came to the **first** and said,
    '**Son**, go out and work in the **vineyard** today.'
He said in reply, 'I will **not**,'
    but **afterwards** changed his mind and **went**.
The man came to the **other** son and gave the **same** order.
He said in reply, '**Yes**, sir,' but did **not** go.
Which of the two did his father's **will**?"
They answered, "The **first**."

After the story Jesus asks his listeners for
their interpretation of obedience.

The application of the story to the world in
which Jesus and his hearers lived.

Jesus said to them, "**Amen**, I say to you,
    tax collectors and **prostitutes**
    are entering the kingdom of **God** before **you**.
When **John** came to you in the way of **righteousness**,
    you did not **believe** him;
    but **tax** collectors and **prostitutes** did.
Yet even when you saw **that**,
    you did not later **change** your minds and **believe** him."

In presenting this the Gospel has three parts: (1) Jesus telling a short parable, (2) Jesus asking for response, and (3) Jesus' own interpretation.

The first part is the parable itself. There are three speakers in it, each of whom Jesus quotes: the father, the first son, and the second son.

In the second part, also brief, Jesus asks those present who was the obedient son, the one who gave the right words but did not follow through with action, or the one who did not answer as the father would want but who did the work that the father needed. They rightly choose the doer over the talker.

The third part is the longest, in which Jesus applies the parable to the world of his hearers. The son who helped his father is like the "tax collectors and prostitutes," who appear frequently around Jesus and in his teaching. We still have both tax collectors and prostitutes as part of our social world these many, many years later; they are probably not appreciated any more now than they were then. This reading is an opportunity for you, the proclaimer of the Gospel, to remind the assembly of Jesus' lesson here. He isn't criticizing them here; he simply notes that they believed John the Baptist and so they will reach the kingdom before the priests and elders who didn't believe the Baptist.

27TH SUNDAY IN ORDINARY TIME

Lectionary #139

READING I   Isaiah 5:1–7

Isaiah = ī-ZAY-uh

A reading from the Book of the Prophet Isaiah

vineyard = VIN-yerd

**Take your time. Perhaps imagine for
yourself what this vineyard and tower
look like so that your proclamation
will have a vibrant visibility to it.**

Let me now sing of my **friend**,
    my friend's **song** concerning his **vineyard**.
My friend had a **vineyard**
    on a fertile **hillside**;
he **spaded** it, cleared it of **stones**,
    and planted the choicest **vines**;
within it he built a **watchtower**,
    and hewed out a wine press.
Then he looked for the crop of **grapes**,
    but what it yielded was **wild** grapes.

Jerusalem = juh-ROO-suh-lem
Judah = JOO-duh

**Ask these questions of the assembly.
Think of them as the "inhabitants of
Jerusalem and people of Judah."**

Now, inhabitants of **Jerusalem** and people of **Judah**,
    judge between **me** and my **vineyard**:
What **more** was there to do for my vineyard
    that I had not done?
Why, when I looked for the crop of **grapes**,
    did it bring forth **wild** grapes?

**Picture yourself as doing these things,
perhaps in your own yard, so that your
proclamation will have a tangibility to it.**

Now, I will let you know
    what I mean to do with my vineyard:
take **away** its hedge, give it to **grazing**,
    break through its **wall**, let it be **trampled**!

READING I This reading from the
prophet Isaiah has such a
lovely opening—"Let me now sing of my
friend, my friend's song concerning his
vineyard"—that the bitter disappointment of
the ending is even more heartbreaking.

The vineyard about which the prophet
and now you sing is Israel. The hill where
the vines were growing was fertile, and the
friend did his best for his vineyard: good soil
well prepared, choice vines, a watchtower
so he could guard against vandals. There is
every reason to expect a fine harvest.

The "grapes" the vintner expected and
the "wild grapes" he got would have more
resonance in a wine-growing region, but
clearly, the prophet means that "grapes"
make good wine and "wild grapes" don't.
Perhaps you can add some of that meaning
to the words with the tone of your voice.

In the middle of the passage, the
prophet asks some rhetorical questions:
"What more was there to do . . . ?" and
"Why . . . did" this happen? Immediately
comes what will happen. Because of this
abrupt change, a pause after the two questions will give the assembly a moment to
think before they hear of the destruction of
the disappointing vineyard.

Yes, I will make it a **ruin**:
 it shall not be **pruned** or **hoed**,
 but **overgrown** with **thorns** and **briers**;
I will command the **clouds**
 not to send rain upon it.
The **vineyard** of the LORD of **hosts** is the house of **Israel**,
 and the people of **Judah** are his cherished **plant**;
he looked for **judgment**, but see, **bloodshed**!
 for **justice**, but **hark**, the **outcry**!

Israel = IZ-ree-ul

READING II   Philippians 4:6–9

Philippians = fil-LIP-ee-unz

A reading from the Letter of Saint Paul to the Philippians

Brothers and sisters:
Have no **anxiety** at **all**, but in **everything**,
 by **prayer** and **petition**, with **thanksgiving**,
 make your requests **known** to **God**.
Then the peace of **God** that surpasses all **understanding**
 will guard your **hearts** and **minds** in Christ **Jesus**.

Finally, brothers and sisters,
 whatever is **true**, whatever is **honorable**,
 whatever is **just**, whatever is **pure**,
 whatever is **lovely**, whatever is **gracious**,
 if there is any **excellence**
 and if there is **anything** worthy of **praise**,
 think about **these** things.
Keep on **doing** what you have **learned** and **received**
 and **heard** and **seen** in **me**.
Then the God of **peace** will be with **you**.

The opening two verses will be a consolation to those who live with stress or chaos. The exhortation "Have no anxiety" and the promise of "the peace of God" will help them recognize that there is a help in time of need. Take your time here.

Notice that the word "whatever" is repeated six times here. Take your time and pause between each of the three-word phrases that start with "whatever."

This final promise of "the God of peace" forms an embrace with the "peace of God" near the start of the passage.

The final verse explains the meaning of the vineyard and supplies a summary. The two-line summary looks more complex than it is. The subject and verb in the first line, "he looked for," are meant to carry over to the next line to make a parallel sentence: "[he looked for] justice, but hark, the outcry!" This is not an unusual literary device, but it is not often heard in oral proclamation.

READING II Often the second reading takes a course through a particular letter or book of the New Testament quite independent of the other two readings. This is apparent here.

The Letter to the Philippians is one of the undisputed Pauline epistles. This excerpt comes immediately after the well-known "Rejoice" passage and just before another passage of rejoicing. In the passage here we can sense the end of the letter drawing near, since Paul writes "Finally, brothers and sisters," in the middle.

You will notice here that there are a few second-person pronouns here, where Paul is addressing the Philippians directly. The Church teaches that the word is ever living and active in the assembly gathered for

GOSPEL   Matthew 21:33–43

A reading from the holy Gospel according to Matthew

Jesus said to the chief **priests** and the **elders** of the people:
"Hear another **parable**.
There was a **landowner** who planted a **vineyard**,
    put a **hedge** around it, dug a **wine** press in it, and built a **tower**.
Then he **leased** it to **tenants** and went on a **journey**.

"When **vintage** time drew near,
    he sent his **servants** to the **tenants** to obtain his **produce**.
But the tenants **seized** the servants and one they **beat**,
    another they **killed**, and a third they **stoned**.
Again he sent **other** servants, more **numerous** than the first ones,
    but they treated **them** in the same way.

"**Finally**, he sent his **son** to them, thinking,
    'They will respect my **son**.'
But when the **tenants** saw the **son**, they said to one another,
    'This is the **heir**.
Come, let us **kill** him and acquire his **inheritance**.'
They **seized** him, threw him out of the vineyard, and **killed** him.

"What will the **owner** of the vineyard **do** to those tenants
        when he **comes**?"
They answered him,
    "He will put those **wretched** men to a wretched **death**
    and lease his vineyard to **other** tenants
        who will give him the **produce** at the proper times."

The opening line of this long Gospel passage supplies context for the story.

Here is the link between the Gospel and the first reading. Review the reading from Isaiah so that you know what elements will resonate.

This middle part of the reading is bloody. Don't shrink from it; Jesus is making a point.

Note the quote within the parable, and mark this with your voice.

The same thing here.

Now Jesus turns to his listeners and asks what they think will happen next.

---

the sacraments, so you can confidently proclaim such passages to the assembly as if it were written to your community in particular.

Proclaim the reading as pastoral advice, which it was and is. Your voice should be nurturing and encouraging. The final advice, to "keep on doing what you have learned," is a comfort.

GOSPEL   This narrative passage, unique to Matthew, is one of those that sometimes makes a hearer wonder, "Did I just hear what I think I heard?" Did that story describe putting "those wretched men to a wretched death"?

Clearly, the Evangelist was drawing from the part of Isaiah that was proclaimed as the first reading. (Review that first reading so that you can build on what the assembly will have already heard.) Toward the end the story we hear a more familiar quote, "The stone that the builders rejected has become the cornerstone." But that quote is usually heard in another scriptural context.

Most of the passage is the parable told by Jesus, and within it Jesus quotes the landowner and the wicked tenants. Outside the parable, he asks his hearers a question,

Have your voice mark this quote from the Hebrew Scriptures.

Jesus said to them, "Did you **never** read in the **Scriptures**:
    *The **stone** that the builders **rejected***
    *has become the **cornerstone**;*
    *by the **Lord** has this been done,*
    *and it is **wonderful** in our **eyes**?*
Therefore, I say to you,
    the kingdom of ***God*** will be taken ***away*** from you
    and given to a people that will ***produce*** its ***fruit***."

they answer, and Jesus quotes scripture in his response to them. As you prepare for your proclamation, note how you will mark these levels of quotation so that they will be apparent to your own hearers. This is an important part of your discernment and task for this reading, and you might ask someone to help you with it if you need it.

28TH SUNDAY IN ORDINARY TIME

Lectionary #142

READING I Isaiah 25:6–10a

Isaiah = ī-ZAY-uh

The prophet is portraying a rich and detailed image for the assembly. Imagine it for yourself and it will be more vivid for those who listen to you.

As vivid as the feast is, so is the the veil covering the people. A hearer should recognize the difference between these sections by how you are reading.

God will reign, and death, sorrow, and reproach will be taken away. Have your voice reflect this consoling theology.

The phrase "on this mountain" is the opening and closing of your proclamation. This sets the a prophecy in the context of an eschatological vision. Believe it, and proclaim it for your Church.

A reading from the Book of the Prophet Isaiah

On this **mountain** the LORD of **hosts**
  will **provide** for all **peoples**
a **feast** of rich **food** and choice **wines**,
  juicy, **rich** food and **pure**, choice **wines**.

On **this** mountain he will **destroy**
  the **veil** that veils all **peoples**,
the **web** that is woven over all **nations**;
  he will **destroy** death forever.
The Lord **GOD** will wipe away
  the **tears** from every **face**;
the **reproach** of his people he will **remove**
  from the whole **earth**; for the LORD has **spoken**.

On **that** day it will be said:
"**Behold** our **God**, to whom we **looked** to **save** us!
  This is the LORD for whom we **looked**;
  let us **rejoice** and be **glad** that he has **saved** us!"
For the hand of the LORD will **rest** on this **mountain**.

READING I This is a delightful reading, a message of consolation that in the LORD's place, that is, "on this mountain" of the LORD, life will be rich and bountiful, and every sorrow and tear will be wiped away. The effectiveness of this reading depends on the proclaimer's trust that such a vision will be realized in our midst. Read the passage, and pray about it. Do you really think that what Isaiah anticipates will be realized? If so, then your proclamation of his vision will be full and appreciated.

As you prepare this reading, be mindful that such end-of-time messages operate on two levels; first, they anticipate the condition of humanity at the end of the world, when we as God's people will come to see God and the bounty promised us at Baptism, when we entered the kingdom of God. But second, such end-of-time messages also tell us about what is ours in the Church and in the sacraments. Sunday after Sunday, we do indeed meet the body of Christ, however dull or predictable you might find it. (It's wonderful if we find the Church a joy and surprise each week, but more often, our parish lives are merely comfortably predictable.)

Eschatological readings remind us that no matter how predictable we, in our limited capacity, find the Sunday assembly, the life of God is revealed therein, for better or worse, no matter how ordinary those celebrations are. So here, when you proclaim to your assembly that they will find "a feast of rich food and choice wines," believe it, for God has promised it. Imagine such a feast in your heart so that as you proclaim, what you imagine will be brought to life for those who hear you. As the reading itself assures us, "Behold our God."

Philippians = fil-LIP-ee-unz

The reading starts energetically.

The details in these two sentences are important for demonstrating his point about indifference to material things.

The central message: "I can do all things in him. . . ."

The hope and doxology of the final two verses can be proclaimed with courage.

READING II   Philippians 4:12–14, 19–20

A reading from the Letter of Saint Paul to the Philippians

Brothers and sisters:
I **know** how to **live** in **humble** circumstances;
    I know **also** how to live with **abundance**.
In **every** circumstance and in **all** things
    I have learned the secret of being **well fed** and of going **hungry**,
    of living in **abundance** and of being in **need**.

I can do **all** things in him who **strengthens** me.
Still, it was **kind** of you to **share** in my **distress**.

My God will **fully** supply whatever you **need**,
    in accord with his glorious **riches** in Christ **Jesus**.
To our God and **Father**, glory for**ever** and **ever**. **Amen**.

The opening verse sets the scene of who is speaking to whom. Since it begins the reading, take your time so that the assembly is settled in and ready to listen.

GOSPEL   Matthew 22:1–14

A reading from the holy Gospel according to Matthew

Jesus again in reply spoke to the chief **priests** and **elders**
    of the people
  in parables, saying,
"The kingdom of **heaven** may be likened to a **king**
    who gave a **wedding** feast for his **son**.
He dispatched his **servants**
    to summon the invited guests to the **feast**,
    but they **refused** to come.

READING II Saint Paul often uses the first person—"I," "me," "my"—in his letters, referring to himself, his theology, his concerns, and even his life story. The reading you prepare now has a higher amount of the first person than usual, and this is to your advantage as a reader. Such passages are engaging to the assembly.

Although proclaiming the word is not acting, it is not false to proclaim this reading as if these words are indeed yours for the adoption.

Paul's theology here appears simple, but it is no less profound. His willingness to accept what comes to him, whether that means having little or having plenty, is a serious witness for us who live in a culture in which wealth is the measure of one's worth. The Gospel of Jesus Christ and the theology of Paul in this Year A have been forming us in indifference to the world, but it is not easy to accept. Paul makes a magnificent and bold claim of Christian faith, one that we must heed so that our ministry of the word will be confirmed by our lives.

God's word is ever-inspired and ever-living in the assembly that comes to celebrate the sacraments. When you as the reader are standing in the apostle's stead as a minister of the living and active word, imagine yourself as the one who delivers the message. Although you are not the author, you are a member of the living body of Christ, that body in which God's word is efficacious and challenging.

GOSPEL This enigmatic parable from the Gospel of Matthew is unique in the Gospel tradition, not appearing in any of the other Gospels.

A **second** time he sent **other** servants, saying,
   'Tell those **invited**: "**Behold**, I have prepared my **banquet**,
   my **calves** and fattened **cattle** are **killed**,
   and everything is **ready**; come to the **feast**."'
Some **ignored** the invitation and went **away**,
   one to his farm, **another** to his business.
The **rest** laid hold of his servants,
   mistreated them, and **killed** them.
The king was **enraged** and sent his **troops**,
   destroyed those murderers, and **burned** their city.

"Then he said to his **servants**, 'The feast is **ready**,
   but those who were **invited** were not **worthy** to come.
Go out, therefore, into the main roads
   and invite to the **feast** whomever you **find**.'
The servants went out into the streets
   and gathered **all** they found, **bad** and **good** alike,
   and the hall was **filled** with guests.

"But when the king came in to **meet** the guests,
   he saw a man there not **dressed** in a **wedding** garment.
The **king** said to him, 'My **friend**, how is it
   that you **came** in here without a **wedding** garment?'
But he was reduced to **silence**.
Then the king said to his **attendants**, 'Bind his hands and **feet**,
   and **cast** him into the darkness **outside**,
   where there will be **wailing** and grinding of **teeth**.'
Many are invited, but **few** are chosen."

[Shorter: Matthew 22:1–10]

Some make weak excuses and others murder the messengers.

Notice and express this furious reaction from the king.

Slight pause before the second set of invitations.

The story is another of those that might find a person in the pew thinking, "Did I just hear what I think I heard?" Did that story just describe going out into the streets to invite everyone, good and bad, to the wedding banquet, after burning the city of the previous guests who wouldn't come? Does it not make us uncomfortable to hear about such a means of filling up the wedding banquet, which after all is a symbol of the reign of God? Will I be sharing the heavenly banquet with one of the riff-raff brought in to fill the hall? And what about that poor man who got thrown out because he didn't have the right clothes? Mysterious.

Many of the joys and frustrations of our ministry in the Church have the same source, that we are not the source of our ministry or of what we do in the assembly. The pericopes in the Lectionary do not vary according to our personal theologies and experiences. Since Vatican II, the Church proclaims far more scripture in the liturgy than for centuries previous, with the result that we find passages in the Lectionary that we might prefer to remain unproclaimed, as in the old days. Even though we as individuals might have shaped the Lectionary differently, it is the will of the Church, realizing the life of God for us the baptized, that these texts be the matter for our proclamation and for the homilists' preaching.

Such eschatological scenes, particularly with the familiar image of "wailing and grinding of teeth," strike terror into some hearts and consolation into others. Wrestle with the text and proclaim it as accessibly and animatedly as you can.

29TH SUNDAY IN ORDINARY TIME

Lectionary #145

READING I   Isaiah 45:1, 4–6

Isaiah = ī-ZAY-uh

Cyrus = SĪ-rus

This long opening verse is establishing the context for the prophecy to follow.

Pause here since the voice changes to direct address.

Israel = IZ-ree-ul

There are two iterations of the reading's basic message, here . . .

. . . and here at the end of the passage. Proclaim these clearly; take your time; be heard and understood.

A reading from the Book of the Prophet Isaiah

Thus says the LORD to his anointed, **Cyrus**,
   whose right hand I grasp,
subduing **nations** before him,
   and making **kings** run in his **service**,
opening **doors** before him
   and leaving the **gates** unbarred:

For the sake of **Jacob**, my **servant**,
   of **Israel**, my **chosen** one,
I have **called** you by your **name**,
   giving you a **title**, though you knew me **not**.
I am the LORD and there is no **other**,
   there is no God besides me.
It is **I** who arm you, though you know me **not**,
   so that toward the **rising** and the **setting** of the **sun**
   people may **know** that there is **none** besides **me**.
I am the LORD, there is no **other**.

READING I — Isaiah's courage, conviction, and mediation have shaped much of Christian theology. That message is most recognizably proclaimed in Advent (with his words about the coming of the Messiah) and in Holy Week (with the Suffering Servant songs). Now the community of faith hears the prophet in Ordinary Time.

The reading for this Sunday could not be more foundational for Isaiah's theology or, indeed, for the theology of the whole Old Testament: "I am the LORD, and there is no other."

This reading you prepare now is from Second Isaiah, whose word instructed and gave consolation to the people as they began to return to Jerusalem after their deportation to Babylon. This text is later than the prophecies of the original Isaiah, whom scholars call First Isaiah. The original Isaiah prophesied in the late eighth century BC. This message is two centuries later, 539 BC.

The basic message of this text is a reiteration of Israel's monotheism, "I am the LORD, and there is no other"; and this is tied to the prophet's word that the king of Persia does the LORD's bidding even though he does not know the LORD, for the sake of the LORD's chosen people Israel.

Notice that the passage has two basic elements. The first verse sets up the context—the LORD speaking to Cyrus, whose hand the LORD has grasped. The second element is complex. The point is the LORD's making use of the pagan king Cyrus for the sake of Israel, reinforcing the message that "I am the LORD, and there is no other." As ever, the first- and second-person rhetoric of this second part of such a prophecy—the LORD as "I" and "me," and the king who does

Thessalonians = thes-uh-LOH-nee-unz

Silvanus = sil-VAY-nus
The first three lines of identification all lean toward the greeting, "Grace to you and peace." This might have been a liturgical greeting in the ancient community to which Paul wrote, like our own liturgical greeting, "The Lord be with you." Pause after it.

Although much of the remainder of the reading is standard fare for a letter of Paul, such words of encouragement are ever needed, so proclaim them with feeling and vigor.

Take your time with the identification of "we" and "brothers and sisters loved by God."

READING II 1 Thessalonians 1:1–5b

A reading from the first Letter of Saint Paul to the Thessalonians

Paul, **Silvanus**, and **Timothy** to the church of the **Thessalonians**
in God the **Father** and the Lord Jesus **Christ**:
grace to you and **peace**.

We give **thanks** to God **always** for **all** of you,
remembering you in our **prayers**,
unceasingly calling to **mind** your work of **faith** and labor
of **love**
and endurance in **hope** of our Lord Jesus **Christ**,
before our God and **Father**,
knowing, brothers and sisters loved by God,
how you were **chosen**.
For our **gospel** did not come to you in word **alone**,
but **also** in **power** and in the Holy **Spirit**
and with much **conviction**.

not know the LORD as "you" and "your" — can be proclaimed as fresh and inspirational for the assembly among whom you minister God's word.

READING II Last week we heard what was clearly the end of Paul's Letter to the Philippians, and we could therefore anticipate that this week's second reading would be the opening of another letter. And so it is. This is the First Letter to the Thessalonians.

Scripture scholars posit that this may be the earliest extant book of the New Testament, written about the year 51, twenty years after the death of Jesus and about twenty years before the writing of what is held to be the earliest Gospel, Mark. Unlike some of Paul's other letters—Romans and First Corinthians, for example—First Thessalonians does not discuss particular theological or social or moral issues. Yet the letter reveals the intimate bond the apostle had with that ancient Greek community of faith, and these opening five verses of the letter bring this bond to light.

Once your proclamation has moved beyond the greeting, the message of the apostle is as contemporary as any Church encouragement could be. Paul is inspiringly direct in recognizing the community's election by God and the gifts of the Holy Spirit that animate its life together. As a minister of God's word nearly two millennia after Paul wrote this missive to an ancient Mediterranean community, you stand in his shoes and you, like Paul, proclaim the truth of God's word to open and eager ears. The

Pharisees = FAIR-uh-seez

The opening verses offer the familiar set-up: conflict between Jesus and those who would thwart him and his word. Herodians = her-OH-dee-unz

The narrative is punctuated by speeches. This first is the longest; the questioner first "butters up" Jesus with praise of his honesty, and then springs the trap. Pause before "Tell us, then . . ." so that the assembly will catch the question.

This final verse is the point of the text. Deliver it slowly and with conviction.

GOSPEL   Matthew 22:15–21

A reading from the holy Gospel according to Matthew

The **Pharisees** went off
and plotted how they might **entrap** Jesus in speech.
They sent their disciples to him, with the Herodians, saying,
"**Teacher**, we know that you are a **truthful** man
and that you teach the way of **God** in accordance
with the **truth**.
And you are not concerned with anyone's opinion,
for you do not regard a person's **status**.
Tell us, then, what is your **opinion**:
Is it **lawful** to pay the **census** tax to **Caesar** or **not**?"

Knowing their malice, Jesus said,
"Why are you testing **me**, you **hypocrites**?
Show me the **coin** that pays the **census** tax."
Then they handed him the Roman **coin**.
He said to them, "Whose **image** is this and whose **inscription**?"
They replied, "**Caesar's**."
At that he said to them,
"Then repay to **Caesar** what belongs to **Caesar**
and to **God** what belongs to **God**."

"we" of this reading is you, and the "you" of this reading are those to whom you proclaim. Deliver this word with "much conviction," as Paul says, "in power and in the Holy Spirit," as your vocation calls you to do.

| GOSPEL | The chief priests, Pharisees, and here the Herodians are always set up in the Gospel as the bad guys, seeking to thwart Jesus' message and trip up the Savior. Today's Gospel is the familiar story of the coin with the image of the emperor on it.

This passage shows us the relationship between faith life and civil life, and this problem is not restricted to the first century. The metaphor of the coin can stand for the many issues where Christians today might find a conflict between their citizenship and their Baptism, between what makes them a member of a nation and what makes them a member of the Church.

Your strong proclamation of this familiar reading will raise the important Church-state issue once again. Notice that the passage has a series of direct speeches, first from the opponents of Jesus, then from Jesus himself, an answer to his question by the inquirers, and then Jesus' final retort, "Repay . . . to God what belongs to God." As the reader, you will have to navigate these so that they are clear to the hearers.

Your work here is to proclaim the familiar reading anew. Pray over the text and recognize its importance to yourself as a Christian living in a culture with some values contrary to our faith. Then your proclamation will have a vibrancy for the assembly to which you deliver it.

30TH SUNDAY IN ORDINARY TIME

Lectionary #148

READING I   Exodus 22:20—26

A reading from the Book of Exodus

Here the Lord is telling Moses what to say to the people. The "you" refers simultaneously to the ancient Israelites and to the assembly to which you proclaim.

Thus says the **Lord**:
"You shall not **molest** or **oppress** an **alien**,
    for **you** were once aliens yourselves in the land of **Egypt.**
You shall not **wrong** any **widow** or **orphan.**
If ever you **wrong** them and they cry **out** to me,
    I will surely **hear** their cry.
My **wrath** will flare up, and I will **kill** you with the **sword;**
    then your own **wives** will be **widows,**
        and your children **orphans.**

The "I" is the Lord—"I will surely hear their cry," "my wrath will flare up."

"If you lend **money** to one of your **poor** neighbors
    among my people,
    you shall not act like an **extortioner** toward him
    by demanding **interest** from him.
If you take your neighbor's cloak as a **pledge,**
    you shall **return** it to him before **sunset;**
        for this **cloak** of his is the only **covering** he has for his **body.**
What else has he to **sleep** in?
If he cries out to me, I will **hear** him; for I am **compassionate.**"

These prescriptions for social and economic justice are important. Take your time in proclaiming them.

The final line—"if [your neighbor] cries out to me"—with the Lord's promise— "I will hear"—is beautiful. It ends the legal prescriptions with a reminder of the Lord's compassion, so be measured and direct as you close the proclamation so that this echoes in the minds and hearts of your assembly.

READING I   The protection of the vulnerable in ancient Israel was remarkable. Even though widows and orphans were not regarded as persons unless they were attached to an adult male, the care accorded them in the law still echoes in the Jewish and Christian traditions. The Catholic Church has a long history of thinking and writing on social issues, and scriptures such as today's passage are the source. Believers go the extra mile to care for the marginalized and the vulnerable because we are conscious of the place of the poor at the banquet table of the Lord.

Be particularly clear in the reference to Israel's slavery in Egypt, when the Israelites were "resident aliens" in a foreign land, removed from their beloved land.

The second half of the reading is far removed from the economic tenets of our culture. No interest when you lend money? Owning so little that a coat would also be a blanket? Many of us might not imagine such poverty, but in our society there are many who glean their basic necessities from the cast-offs of the wealthy. The counsels of the Old Testament to help those in need—widowed, poor, orphaned, abandoned—are more easily ignored than heeded. Your task as the minister of God's word today is to be the promulgator of the law, to announce the legal code by which we have a duty to the vulnerable in the assembly of faith and in the world. Be confident in delivering that law this Sunday.

Thessalonians = thes-uh-LOH-nee-unz

As so often in Paul's letters, the language is in first- and second-person pronouns.

Macedonia = mas-uh-DOH-nee-uh
Achaia = uh-KEE-uh
There is no need to place too much emphasis on these two places, Macedonia and Achaia. Pronounce them clearly and with confidence, but because they might be distracting from the main message, don't draw too much attention to them.

The last two verses— beginning with "For they themselves openly declare . . ." to the end—have the richest theological content. Take your time with them, and pause before the closing "The word of the Lord."

READING II   1 Thessalonians 1:5c—10

A reading from the first Letter of Saint Paul to the Thessalonians

Brothers and sisters:
You **know** what sort of **people** we were among you for your sake.
And you became **imitators** of **us** and of the **Lord**,
    receiving the word in great **affliction**,
        with **joy** from the Holy Spirit,
    so that you became a **model** for all the believers
    in Macedonia and in Achaia.
For from **you** the word of the Lord has sounded **forth**
    not only in Macedonia and in Achaia,
    but in **every** place your faith in God has gone forth,
    so that we have no **need** to say **anything**.
For they **themselves** openly declare about **us**
    what sort of **reception** we had among you,
    and how you turned to **God** from **idols**
    to serve the **living** and **true** God
    and to await his **Son** from **heaven**,
    whom he **raised** from the **dead**,
    Jesus, who **delivers** us from the coming **wrath**.

READING II Last Sunday, we heard the opening of the First Letter to the Thessalonians. Today's second reading follows immediately upon that passage. We can hear Paul establishing his audience as he praises them for the depth of their conversion.

The apostle calls us to reflect back on the past as a way of uniting us in our experience. This is the very nature of the Eucharist: We remember the past, "on the night before he died," and are united in our common experience of it, building on it to approach God in thanksgiving and interces-

sion today, "And so, Father, we bring you these gifts. . . ."

The past on which we reflect is not always the same; it may be the Lord's law-giving to Moses (as in today's first reading), or the law-giving of Jesus to the Pharisees (as in today's Gospel), or it may be the common sacramental experience we have week after week in the liturgy. Such remembering is fundamental to Christian life and liturgy, and we sense such a pattern of the past paving the way for the present and the future in Paul's rhetoric at the beginning of his letter.

The text points to the conversion of the Thessalonians from idols to "the living and true God." Such conversion is ever part of our life as community and as individuals. Your clear proclamation of this early letter will be consolation to any in the assembly who might deprecate their own experience and think that in Jesus' and Paul's times and places, people were holier. They were no holier than we are, and your good communication of the experience of Paul with the Thessalonians might contribute to their appreciation of the access we have to the life of God in the Church.

GOSPEL   Matthew 22:34–40

A reading from the holy Gospel according to Matthew

When the **Pharisees** heard that **Jesus** had silenced the **Sadducees**,
   they gathered **together**, and one of them,
   a scholar of the law, **tested** him by asking,
    "**Teacher**, which **commandment** in the law is the **greatest**?"

He said to him,
"You shall **love** the Lord, your **God**,
   with **all** your heart,
   with **all** your soul,
   and with **all** your mind.
This is the **greatest** and the **first** commandment.

"The **second** is like it:
   You shall love your **neighbor** as **yourself**.
The whole **law** and the **prophets**
     depend on these **two** commandments."

Pharisees = FAIR-uh-seez
Sadducees = SAD-y<u>oo</u>-seez

The opening sets up the lawyer's inquiry and Jesus' response.

Pause after the question, then be clear in identifying Jesus speaking.

Again, pause slightly between the first and second commandments.

GOSPEL In literary terms, this reading is mostly direct discourse. It has an introduction setting the context, a question from a lawyer, and the delivery of two commandments from the mouth of Jesus.

As we have seen throughout this Year A, the Gospel of Matthew puts a high value on the Mosaic law. To that end the first Evangelist often shows Jesus acting as Moses, the law-giver of the Old Testament, acted in the opening books of the Bible. Because of this theology of Jesus as the new Moses, the opening verse of this reading mentions Moses, and we have previously seen Jesus giving the law on a mountain as Moses did. Today's Gospel continues this narrative and theological connection between Moses and Jesus. As the law was important in ancient Israel, so it was important in the theology of the Evangelist Matthew, who saw the Church as the new Israel. The place of the law in a life of faith and community is clearly the main issue in today's first reading and today's Gospel, so it is no surprise to find that the inquirer here is a scholar of the law.

There may be great differences in the practice of law in Jesus' time or Matthew's time a few decades later and the practice of law in our own time, but the sparseness of the reading and the simplicity of the commandments that Jesus delivers are such that the use of "law" and "scholar of the law" in the passage transfers well. Proclaim the reading with strength, particularly the two commandments.

31ST SUNDAY IN ORDINARY TIME

Lectionary #151

READING I   Malachi 1:14b—2:2b, 8–10

A reading from the Book of the prophet Malachi

A great **King** am I, says the LORD of **hosts**,
    and my name will be **feared** among the **nations**.

And **now**, O priests, **this** commandment is for **you**:
    If you do not **listen**,
if you do not lay it to **heart**,
    to give **glory** to my name, says the LORD of hosts,
I will send a **curse** upon you
    and of your **blessing** I will make a curse.

You have turned **aside** from the **way**,
    and have caused **many** to falter by your **instruction**;
you have made **void** the covenant of **Levi**,
    says the LORD of hosts.
I, therefore, have made you **contemptible**
    and **base** before all the **people**,
since you do not **keep** my ways,
    but show **partiality** in your decisions.

Have we not all the **one** father?
    Has not the **one** God created us?
Why then do we break **faith** with one another,
    violating the **covenant** of our **fathers**?

Malachi = MAL-uh-kī

The reading starts out powerfully.

Here the LORD is expressing anger at the bad example of the priests. Your tone should match the prophet's indictment.

Here the speaker shifts; the prophet asks the people to remember that we are all children of the one God. So why are we faithless?

READING I   Malachi is the last of the twelve minor prophets and the last book of the Old Testament, a book only a few pages long. (The four major prophets are Isaiah, Jeremiah, Ezekiel, and Daniel; the books of the first two are longer than the whole collection of minor prophets.)

The passage you will proclaim is not an easy reading, for the LORD here is chastising the priests of Israel for their disobedience. Its words are punishing. Your job in proclaiming, whatever the reading's message, is to be faithful to the text before you as the word of God. The books of scripture are varied in their messages; most times the Lectionary serves up passages that are wonderful to proclaim (if sometimes difficult to understand!), but there are times when the scriptures and the Lectionary deliver a harsh message, as today with the prophet Malachi.

As you proclaim, know that the final verse, though continuing the LORD's chastisement, has a positive and uplifting element. The prophet asks, "Have we not all the one father?" and "Has not the one God created us?"

On the practical level, notice that most of the reading comes from the LORD, with some interjected words from the prophet. Three times the reading reminds us that the words come from God, thus "says the LORD of hosts." And the final four lines, are from the prophet to the errant priests.

In spite of the harsh message, deliver the word of God with stalwart clarity and conviction.

READING II   First Thessalonians is not only among the earliest New Testament writings—that is, the letters of Paul—but this particular letter is

READING II   1 Thessalonians 2:7b–9, 13

A reading from the first Letter of Saint Paul to the Thessalonians

Brothers and sisters:
We were **gentle** among you, as a nursing **mother** cares
    for her **children**.
With such **affection** for you, we were determined
    to **share** with you
  not only the **gospel** of God, but our very **selves** as well,
    so dearly **beloved** had you **become** to us.
You **recall**, brothers and sisters, our **toil** and **drudgery**.
Working **night** and **day** in order not to **burden** any of you,
    we **proclaimed** to you the gospel of **God**.

And for **this** reason we too give thanks to God **unceasingly**,
    that, in **receiving** the word of God from hearing **us**,
    you received not a **human** word but, as it truly is,
      the word of **God**,
    which is now at **work** in you who **believe**.

Thessalonians = thes-uh-LOH-nee-unz

This reading dives right into the heart of the matter; pause briefly, therefore, after you identify the book of the Bible so that the assembly is poised and attentive for the proclamation.

The first-person "we" here means both Paul's missionary team and the whole Church, the community of faith, both in Paul's time and today.

Pause for the transition here, for the tone changes to Paul's expression of thanks to God.

Notice the paired opposites: "human word" and "the word of God."

---

probably the earliest of Paul's extant letters. Paul wrote around AD 50–60, beginning about two decades after the death of Jesus, whom he never met, so First Thessalonians was written near 50–51.

There are two qualities of Paul's writing that often make them attractive for proclamation. First, their content can often still be contemporary, even millennia after their composition, and second, their use of the second-person voice, "you," can make them engaging to those who hear them proclaimed.

On the contemporary quality of Paul's writing: Notice that there are many verses that do not feel like they were written almost two thousand years ago: "we were determined to share with you . . . our very selves," and "you recall, brothers and sisters, our toil and drudgery," and "we too give thanks to God unceasingly." Even though Paul wrote in Greek, many centuries ago, these words could have been written today. As a minister of God's word, you are standing in the footsteps of Paul, not imitating his voice but announcing the ever-new word of the Lord to the people as he did.

This passage is about the demands of ministry, about how tiring yet rewarding it can be to work for the Gospel. Paul was driven in his ministry; as he says here, he "worked day and night." Each minister has a particular mission and task for the building up of the Church, and for you this is your service to God's word. Though you are to work at this ministry, it is a gift given to you from God, which you in turn give back to the community and to God by your preparation and dedication. Be inspired by Paul's message in this letter, and then, with conviction,

GOSPEL   Matthew 23:1–12

A reading from the holy Gospel according to Matthew

The opening line identifies those whom
Jesus is teaching.
Pharisees = FAIR-uh-seez

Jesus spoke to the **crowds** and to his **disciples**, saying,
"The **scribes** and the **Pharisees**
    have taken their **seat** on the chair of **Moses**.
Therefore, **do** and **observe** all things whatsoever they **tell** you,
    but do **not** follow their **example**.
For they **preach** but they do not **practice**.
They tie up heavy **burdens** hard to carry
    and **lay** them on people's **shoulders**,
    but they will not lift a **finger** to move them.
All their works are performed to be **seen**.
They **widen** their phylacteries and **lengthen** their tassels.
They **love** places of honor at **banquets**,
     seats of **honor** in **synagogues**,
     greetings in marketplaces, and the salutation '**Rabbi**.'

Each sentence about the scribes and
Pharisees begins in the same form: "They
do this . . . They do that . . ." Pause
after each of these so that the indictments
can be distinguished from one another
in the proclamation.
phylacteries = fih-LAK-tuh-reez

synagogues = SIN-uh-gogz

Rabbi = RAB-ī

Big pause for the switch from Jesus
speaking about what *they* do to what *you*
are to do. As before, take your time.

"As for **you**, do not be called '**Rabbi**.'
You have but **one** teacher, and you are all **brothers**.
Call **no** one on earth your **father**;
    you have but **one** Father in **heaven**.
Do not be called '**Master**';
    you have but **one** master, the **Christ**.
The **greatest** among you must be your **servant**.
Whoever **exalts** himself will be **humbled**;
    but whoever **humbles** himself will be **exalted**."

The last verse summarizes the teaching in
this now familiar saying.

proclaim the message to your community
of faith.

GOSPEL The Gospel you are preparing delivers a harsh message. Here Jesus is speaking of leaders whose actions belie their words. "Do as they say," he tells his listeners, "not as they do."

As you study this reading for proclamation, reflecting on the situation in the community of Matthew's Gospel should be a consolation. From our vantage point hundreds of years after this writing of this Gospel, we can tend to romanticize what

Church life was like among those who still had a vibrant personal memory of Jesus. Yet Gospel passages like this one remind us that the Church has always been both blessed and burdened in its leadership. Some were saints and some were sinners; most, like ourselves, were a little of both at the same time.

As you prepare, notice that all but the first verse of the passage is a speech on the lips of Jesus. That first verse identifies the context of Jesus speaking to the crowds and his disciples, so be particularly clear at the start. The remainder of the passage has

two basic parts, the first speaking about some people, the second speaking to some other people. The first is his indictment of the leaders, and in a way it takes the burden off the assembly to hear him scolding someone else. But then he turns and speaks to his listeners directly. Here the assembly might be a little less comfortable. But be bold with the Gospel and deliver it as boldly as the Evangelist wrote, for the final message about the greatest and the humble is one to be proclaimed at all times and in all places.

ALL SAINTS

Lectionary #667

READING I Revelation 7:2–4, 9–14

A reading from the Book of Revelation

Do not hasten through the passage because it is complex.

I, **John**, saw another **angel** come up from the **East**,
    holding the **seal** of the living God.
He cried out in a loud **voice** to the four **angels**
    who were given **power** to damage the **land** and the **sea**,
    "Do not damage the **land** or the **sea** or the **trees**
    until we put the **seal** on the **foreheads** of the servants
        of our **God**."
I heard the **number** of those who had been marked with the seal,
    one **hundred** and forty-four **thousand** marked
    from every tribe of the **children** of **Israel**.

This horde of 144,000 robed in white is a symbol of the Church; do not rush through the details.

After **this** I had a vision of a great **multitude**,
    which no one could **count**,
    from every **nation**, **race**, **people**, and **tongue**.
They stood before the **throne** and before the **Lamb**,
    wearing white **robes** and holding **palm** branches in their **hands**.
They cried out in a loud **voice**:
    "**Salvation** comes from our **God**,
    who is **seated** on the **throne**,
    and from the **Lamb**."

For the sake of those who know that the white robes are a sign of initiation, be clear in the three places of the passage where the white robes are mentioned.

READING I As a lector studying this passage for your proclamation, you might think that it has little relation to your own faith or life. The Book of Revelation, with its many strange and obscure symbols, can make readers of the Bible and hearers at the liturgy think it refers to a very different time and place. That is certainly true, but there are some clues to help you appreciate that this text is not as far from your faith life as you might think.

To prompt you to see the reading in a new light, consider a few of the important symbols in this passage: the one hundred and forty-four thousand, the robes of white, the blood of the Lamb.

The number twelve is a symbol of universality in much of the Bible, so when the scripture's inspired writers specified twelve tribes of Israel, for example, or twelve disciples, they meant not only the historical fact, but an embracing symbol of all. So when the author here writes of the crowd of 144,000 people, this symbol means a kind of grand ultra-inclusiveness. $12 \times 12 = 144 \times 1000 =$ the crowd; the universe $\times$ the universe $\times$ a thousand.

Now consider the white robes. When we are baptized, whether as an infant or an adult, we are robed in white, a symbol of newness and of the new life into which by Baptism we have been reborn. The white robes in this passage tell us that this is a vast crowd of the baptized, representing those

All the angels stood around the throne
and around the **elders** and the four living **creatures**.
They **prostrated** themselves before the throne,
worshiped **God**, and exclaimed:
"**Amen**. **Blessing** and **glory**, **wisdom** and **thanksgiving**,
honor, **power**, and **might**
be to our God for**ever** and **ever**. **Amen**."

Then one of the **elders** spoke up and said to me,
"Who **are** these wearing white **robes**, and where did they
come from?"
I said to him, "My **lord**, **you** are the one who **knows**."
He said to me,
"**These** are the ones who have **survived** the time
of great **distress**;
they have **washed** their robes
and made them **white** in the Blood of the **Lamb**."

The paradox of the blood-washed white robes is a brilliant literary device of the author.

who have been initiated into the community of the Book of Revelation, and indeed, believers of every nation and every time.

Finally, those robes washed in the blood of the Lamb. It was no easier then than now to get blood stains out of white clothes—what could the author mean with this paradox? The Lamb is Christ, and the baptized people wearing the robes, like the Church today, are the body of Christ. The juxtaposition of the blood and the white robes

suggests that these believers were baptized in the blood of Christ, that is, they are the martyrs. Notice that the people in white robes hold palm branches in their hands. Palm branches are a Christian symbol for martyrdom.

The details of these symbols will make the reading more engaging for you so that you, in turn, can be clear and intentional and engaging when you proclaim the reading to the assembly to whom you minister. It's a difficult passage, but don't be deterred.

Revelation is a great work, so the Bible saves it for the end, both of the Bible and the liturgical year!

READING II This is a beautiful text; take its message to heart so that you can communicate it boldly. It is quite brief, so there is absolutely no need to hurry through it.

READING II 1 John 3:1–3

A reading from the first Letter of Saint John

The passage is short, so your reading can be measured and well proclaimed. The first-person language enables you to speak to the assembly intimately.

Beloved:
See what **love** the Father has bestowed on **us**
that **we** may be called the **children** of **God**.
Yet so we **are**.
The reason the world does not know **us**
is that it did not know **him**.

Pause here so that your use of "Beloved" in addressing the assembly comes through.

Beloved, we are God's children **now**;
what we **shall** be has not yet been **revealed**.
We **do** know that when it **is** revealed we shall be **like** him,
for we shall **see** him as he **is**.

Everyone who has this **hope** based on **him** makes himself **pure**,
as he is pure.

GOSPEL Matthew 5:1–12a

A reading from the holy Gospel according to Matthew

After these opening lines, the remainder is in Jesus' words, to the end.

When **Jesus** saw the **crowds**, he went up the **mountain**,
and after he had sat **down**, his **disciples** came to him.
He began to **teach** them, saying:

Because the passage is familiar and the literary form repeated, take your time.

"**Blessed** are the poor in **spirit**,
for **theirs** is the Kingdom of **heaven**.
Blessed are they who **mourn**,
for **they** will be **comforted**.

The language of "we" and "us" is present because the author of the letter was writing to and with his faith community, and together they were "children of God." This is no different for yourself and the faith community to whom you will proclaim this passage.

Remember that when this was written the Christian movement had not yet spread far, so when the author writes that "the world does not know us," that was true. In the intervening centuries, of course, the faith has grown into one of the major world religions. The world does indeed "know us," meaning Christians, and "know him," meaning Christ, even among those who are not themselves members of the Church. Even though the world situation of Christianity has changed, you can read this directly, for in many ways the Church and Christ always need to be better known.

Pause at the end of the first section ("it did not know him"), for the word the author uses to address his community at the start of the next section—"Beloved"—is touching. If you pause slightly, the assembly will be poised to hear you address them as the author addressed his fellow believers: "Beloved, we are God's children now."

GOSPEL In the three-year Lectionary, passages come up occasionally that are traditionally beloved and well-known, and this passage from the Gospel of Matthew is among them. The

"**Blessed** are the **meek**,
    for **they** will inherit the **land**.
Blessed are they who hunger and **thirst** for **righteousness**,
    for **they** will be **satisfied**.

"**Blessed** are the **merciful**,
    for **they** will be **shown** mercy.
Blessed are the clean of **heart**,
    for **they** will **see** God.

"**Blessed** are the **peacemakers**,
    for **they** will be called **children** of God.
Blessed are they who are **persecuted** for the sake
        of **righteousness**,
    for **theirs** is the Kingdom of **heaven**.

"**Blessed** are **you** when they **insult** you and **persecute** you
    and utter every kind of **evil** against you **falsely** because of **me**.
Rejoice and be **glad**,
    for your **reward** will be **great** in **heaven**."

Pause before "Blessed are you when they insult you," for the text shifts slightly here.

This final verse is not a "beatitude" as the other verses are. But its imperatives, "rejoice," "be glad," are important.

Beatitudes are known not only by Christians, but by many non-Christians as well, for they are one of the signature texts of the faith for the wisdom and counsel they offer.

This Gospel reading is an excellent choice for the Solemnity of All Saints, for its portrait of saintliness, its image of holiness, can be seen completely in the lives of those to whom you will be proclaiming this Gospel. Many of those to whom you will proclaim this word of God are indeed "poor in spirit"; they "mourn" or have mourned; they are "meek," or "merciful," or "pure in heart"; they make peace; they "hunger and

thirst for righteousness"; they have been insulted for holding to the convictions of their faith. They, like the canonized saints, have been shaped by the Gospel.

As the proclaimer of the Gospel of the Beatitudes, you can make this familiar text a key ingredient for this solemnity. With the clarity and strength of your proclamation, let those in the assembly know that lives of holiness are not far from the lives they are living. God's grace is a free gift to all, and those who are baptized are members of a community of faith in which that grace is nurtured and encouraged.

Though it is never a good idea to presume that one is a saint, it is likely that more believers err on the opposite side—never thinking that they have any holiness at all. Your proclamation of the Beatitudes can invite members of the congregation to think of holiness as not completely removed from their day-to-day lives. Proclaim with conviction, with trust in God's grace, and knowing that God's word proclaimed by you will be efficacious.

32ND SUNDAY IN ORDINARY TIME

Lectionary #154

READING I Wisdom 6:12–16

A reading from the Book of Wisdom

Resplendent and **unfading** is **wisdom**,
  and she is readily **perceived** by those who **love** her,
  and **found** by those who **seek** her.
She hastens to make herself **known** in anticipation of their **desire**;
  whoever **watches** for her at dawn shall not be **disappointed**,
  for he shall **find** her sitting by his **gate**.

For taking **thought** of wisdom is the **perfection** of prudence,
  and whoever for **her** sake keeps **vigil**
  shall **quickly** be free from **care**;
  because she makes her own rounds,
    seeking those **worthy** of her,
  and graciously **appears** to them in the **ways**,
  and **meets** them with all **solicitude**.

Readings from the wisdom literature are lists of insights that are related, but they don't exactly build in the way that a story does.

Pause briefly after each idea from the Book of Wisdom so that each insight will be heard clearly and received.

READING I   The wisdom books can appear as a kind of ancient advice column to us today, for the authors offer maxims and sage advice about human living and particularly about human relations, about how to treat one's fellow human beings, in the faith or in the larger society.

In the context of much of sacred Scripture that draws lines between insiders and outsiders, the wisdom literature is wonderfully inclusive much of the time, encouraging readers and hearers to treat their fellow human beings with graciousness and courtesy, much on the model of God toward humanity, ever gracious, ever patient. Coming now as it does near the end of the liturgical year, the wisdom literature is, well, wise in encouraging its listeners to treat their social peers with grace, much as God treats them.

This text from the Book of Wisdom was not written in anticipation of Jesus' incarnation and birth, but the Evangelists discerned God's will for humanity by interpreting the Hebrew scriptural tradition. They applied much of that to the Savior, and from this emerged the tradition in which Wisdom and the literature about Wisdom was applied to the person, ministry, and teaching of Jesus. (This is especially so of the fourth Evangelist, John, whose prologue captures Jesus as Wisdom and whose Gospel frequently speaks of Jesus' omniscience, his knowing all things.)

Think of this as a kind of hymn of praise to Wisdom for her enrichment of human life. Each verse contributes to the hymn even if together they are not moving toward a logical conclusion. Be careful with the final

READING II   1 Thessalonians 4:13–18

Thessalonians = thes-uh-LOH-nee-unz

Proclaim the passage as if we are waiting as anxiously as Paul was.

A reading from the first Letter of Saint Paul to the Thessalonians

We do not want you to be **unaware**, brothers and sisters,
   about those who have fallen **asleep**,
   so that you may not **grieve** like the **rest**, who have no **hope**.
For if we believe that Jesus **died** and **rose**,
   so too will **God**, through Jesus,
   bring **with** him those who have fallen **asleep**.
Indeed, we tell you this, on the word of the **Lord**,
   that we who are **alive**,
   who are **left** until the **coming** of the Lord,
   will surely not **precede** those who have fallen **asleep**.

Imagine the scene to yourself so that when you proclaim, your personal engagement with Paul's scene will come through.

For the Lord **himself**, with a word of **command**,
   with the voice of an **archangel** and with the trumpet of **God**,
   will come down from **heaven**,
   and the **dead** in Christ will rise **first**.
Then we who are **alive**, who are **left**,
   will be caught up **together** with them in the **clouds**
   to **meet** the Lord in the **air**.
Thus we shall **always** be with the Lord.
Therefore, **console** one another with these **words**.

[Shorter: 1 Thessalonians 4:13–14]

sentence, which is quite long. Anticipate the best place to take a breath as you practice.

READING II First Thessalonians might be the oldest text in the New Testament. The dramatic scene depicted in this letter is not, therefore, from the latest writings included in the New Testament but among the earliest. The earlier the writing, the more dramatic the ideas about the proximity of the end of the world and about how

this would take place. This reading is vividly dramatic, and that means it is a good opportunity to use your best skills as a minister of the word.

Theologically, it is not a coincidence that we come upon these apocalyptic readings at the end of the liturgical year. The end of the liturgical year has traditionally been *the* time for thinking about the inevitability of death and the end of the world itself.

Although we are now nearly two millennia away from Paul's writing to the Thessalonians, we should not dismiss the apocalyptic images in his letter. None of us knows when the world will end or what that end will be. The end of the liturgical year gives us some lead time before the end of the calendar year, so we can afford to take a little time thinking about our own readiness for death or the end of the world.

The placement of this parable at the end of the year reflects the sense of the end of the world that is characteristic of the liturgical calendar at this time each year, as the days shorten.

Pause at the breaks in the Lectionary.

GOSPEL   Matthew 25:1–13

A reading from the holy Gospel according to Matthew

Jesus told his **disciples** this **parable**:
"The kingdom of **heaven** will be like ten **virgins**
    who took their **lamps** and went out to meet the **bridegroom**.
Five of them were **foolish** and **five** were **wise**.
The **foolish** ones, when taking their lamps,
    brought no **oil** with them,
    but the **wise** brought flasks of **oil** with their lamps.
Since the bridegroom was long **delayed**,
    they all became **drowsy** and fell **asleep**.

"At midnight, there was a cry,
    '**Behold**, the **bridegroom**! Come out to **meet** him!'
Then all those **virgins** got up and **trimmed** their lamps.
The **foolish** ones said to the **wise**,
    'Give **us** some of **your** oil,
    for **our** lamps are going **out**.'
But the **wise** ones replied,
    '**No**, for there may not be **enough** for us **and** you.
Go instead to the **merchants** and buy some for yourselves.'
While they went off to **buy** it,
    the **bridegroom** came
    and those who were **ready** went into the **wedding feast**
        with him.
Then the door was **locked**.

As you prepare, take your time to appreciate what Paul was writing to the church at Thessalonica. You can do this by stepping into his shoes in earnest and feeling what it must have been like to be a Church leader who believed that the end of the world was imminent.

| GOSPEL | You have your work cut out for you in proclaiming this parable of the wise and foolish bridesmaids. Its message might call up ominous feelings

of dread about the end of the world and its unexpected arrival.

I know that I will be among the foolish, having done my best while alert and energetic, but fading when the time for sleep arrived and the bridegroom hadn't yet arrived. Perhaps adding to my foolishness, I will trust that the Lord, at that final coming as the bridegroom, will be a little more compassionate than the parable portrays him when he says to the foolish women: "Amen,

I say to you, I do not know you." Mindful of the other parables and teachings in the Gospels in which he is far less strict, I'd ask, "What do you mean, you don't know me? We're only talking about forgetting a little oil!"

In spite of my hope that the final judgment will not be as strict as it sounds in today's reading, you as proclaimer of this Gospel reading need to trust that the parable was written to address a difficult pastoral situation in the community of Matthew's

The parable ends with the short interpretation: Stay awake!

"Afterwards the **other** virgins came and said,
  '**Lord**, **Lord**, open the door for **us**!'
But he said in reply,
  '**Amen**, I say to you, I do not **know** you.'
Therefore, stay **awake**,
  for you know neither the **day** nor the **hour**."

Gospel. For that reason, you need to proclaim it as boldly as the Evangelist has written it.

Theologically, the story of the foolish and wise women is appropriate for, as ever near the end of the liturgical year, the readings look toward the end of the world. The parable of the bridesmaids clues us in to how ill-prepared half of them were as they anticipated the end. As the second reading focused on the end-of-the-world meeting of those who are still alive and the risen Christ in the clouds, so does this reading focus on our preparedness for the end.

As proclaimer, your ministry is to deliver the word of God well to the assembly. Much of the time, this is a delightful task, delivering the Lord's words of healing, compassion, and hope. Here the Gospel is one of judgment and exclusion, not as delightful as usual. Proclaim it well so that your hearers will consider their prudent preparation for the coming of the Bridegroom.

33RD SUNDAY IN ORDINARY TIME

Lectionary #157

READING I   Proverbs 31:10–13, 19–20, 30–31

This text is best proclaimed as a series of maxims and sayings. As you practice, mark the text at those places where you feel the need for a breather or where you think the reading is calling for a pause.

A reading from the Book of Proverbs

When one finds a worthy **wife**,
    her **value** is far beyond **pearls**.
Her husband, entrusting his **heart** to her,
    has an unfailing **prize**.
She brings him **good**, and not **evil**,
    all the days of her **life**.
She obtains **wool** and **flax**
    and works with loving **hands**.

She puts her hands to the **distaff**,
    and her **fingers** ply the **spindle**.
She reaches out her **hands** to the **poor**,
    and extends her **arms** to the **needy**.

Charm is **deceptive** and **beauty fleeting**;
    the woman who fears the LORD is to be **praised**.
Give her a **reward** for her **labors**,
    and let her works **praise** her at the city **gates**.

READING I   The Book of Proverbs is just that, a collection of advice about human living and human relations. Each section brings together proverbs or maxims that are related by topic; unlike stories or narratives or prophecies, they do not usually argue toward a point. They are not trying to be persuasive, but simply illustrate how the tradition would direct one's life in a particular social setting.

This reading attends in particular to domestic life and to the role of the wife and mother in particular. You can see by the citation that these verses have been excerpted from a larger portion, and your preparation might be helped by reading the whole of Proverbs 31.

In the area of gender relations and women in society, there is a considerable cultural difference between the place and time for which this text was written and the place and time in which you are proclaiming it. Women's rights and equality were not imaginable to the author of these words. Yet even alongside the verses that might seem quaint, there are many that clearly depict the woman's role as that of strength, prudence, wisdom, and generosity to the needy.

Thessalonians = thes-uh-LOH-nee-unz

Pause after "a thief at night." There is a quotation that the faithful can be poised to hear, and the image of the pregnant woman is so wonderful at this time of the liturgical year that you need to do whatever you can to make sure the assembly is ready to hear it.

In this second half, the pairs of opposites—darkness/night and light/day—make the theology of the end of the world much more engaging for the imagination.

READING II   1 Thessalonians 5:1–6

A reading from the first Letter of Saint Paul to the Thessalonians

Concerning **times** and **seasons**, brothers and sisters,
    you have no need for **anything** to be written to you.
For you yourselves know very **well** that the day of the **Lord**
        will come
    like a **thief** at **night**.
When people are saying, "**Peace** and **security**,"
    then sudden **disaster** comes upon them,
    like **labor** pains upon a **pregnant** woman,
    and they will not escape.

But **you**, brothers and sisters, are not in **darkness**,
    for that day to **overtake** you like a **thief**.
For all of **you** are children of the **light**
    and **children** of the **day**.
We are **not** of the **night** or of **darkness**.
Therefore, let **us** not sleep as the **rest** do,
    but let us stay **alert** and **sober**.

READING II The letters of Paul have the wonderful and supremely inspired quality of timelessness. In this reading from First Thessalonians, written nearly two thousand years ago, Paul draws on the experience of "labor pains [coming] upon a pregnant woman" to tell us how the "day of the Lord will come like a thief in the night." Though our world is vastly different now than when Paul lived, many of the details that make his writing so vivid are still the same as they were in the middle of the first century, as Paul sailed throughout the Mediterranean world, spreading the Good News, founding churches, being thrown in prison, and writing letters of encouragement and support (and chastisement) to communities of faith that he had visited or would visit.

From the opening of this passage, we can detect that the believers were still part of their Jewish communities and following their customs of time-keeping. Passover and Pentecost were likely observed in this fledgling Christian community much as they were in the Jewish communities of the diaspora. (The First Letter to the Thessalonians is roughly contemporary with the meeting of Church leaders in Rome to decide on the

Each part of the Gospel reading has a beginning and an end, and each has some narrative quality of its own, apart from the whole. Consider how each part works as a story before putting them all together. Part has two set-ups: Part 1A for the context of what Jesus will say and Part 1B for the parable itself, in which the three servants are introduced.

Part 2 reveals to the hearers what each of the three servants did with their talents.

Part 3 is the reckoning, and it has three parts: 3A is the reckoning for Mr. Five-Talents; 3B for Mr. Two-Talents; and 3C for Mr. One-Talent.

GOSPEL   Matthew 25:14–30

A reading from the holy Gospel according to Matthew

Jesus told his **disciples** this **parable**:
"A man going on a **journey**
    called in his **servants** and entrusted his possessions to them.
To one he gave **five** talents; to another, **two**; to a third, **one**—
    to **each** according to his **ability**.
Then he went away.

"**Immediately** the one who received **five** talents
        went and **traded** with them,
    and made **another** five.
Likewise, the one who received **two** made **another** two.
But the man who received **one** went off and dug a **hole**
        in the ground
    and **buried** his master's **money**.

"After a long time
    the **master** of those servants came **back**
    and settled accounts with them.
The one who had received **five** talents came forward
    bringing the **additional** five.
He said, '**Master**, you gave me **five** talents.
See, I have made five **more**.'
His **master** said to him, '**Well done**, my good and faithful **servant**.
Since you were faithful in **small** matters,
    I will give you **great** responsibilities.
Come, share your master's **joy**.'

"Then the one who had received **two** talents also came forward
        and said,
    '**Master**, you gave me **two** talents.

foundational question of practices and of theologies, about the inclusion of Gentiles in the Gospel's embrace, and about how much of the ritual patterns of Judaism they would have to follow.)

The letter is in the second person, "you have no need . . ." and "you yourselves know very well . . ." and "all of you are children of light." Such exhortations are invitations for you, the proclaimer, to stand boldly in the place of the apostle and take

his words as your own, not as a dramatic reading of the words of Paul, but as the words of a committed Christian exhorting those in the community of faith to be encouraged by the gifts they have been given and to recognize their status as the "children of light" and "children of the day," for that is what you and your assembly are. Be bold; be engaging; spread the Good News.

GOSPEL   The coming of the Son of Man reflected in this parable from the Gospel of Matthew fits this time of the liturgical year very well, for near the end of the Church year we always highlight the end of the world and the final judgment.

This is a long parable, close to the beginning of the Passion in Matthew. Although the parable is familiar, its turn toward praising the shrewdness of the two servants who doubled their investment is

See, I have made two **more**.'
His master said to him, '**Well done**, my good and faithful **servant**.
Since you were faithful in **small** matters,
   I will give you **great** responsibilities.
Come, share your master's **joy**.'

"Then the one who had received the **one** talent came forward
      and said,
   '**Master**, I knew you were a **demanding** person,
   harvesting where you did not **plant**
   and **gathering** where you did not **scatter**;
   so out of **fear** I went off and **buried** your talent in the **ground**.
Here it is **back**.'

"His **master** said to him in reply, 'You **wicked**, lazy **servant**!
So you knew that I **harvest** where I did not **plant**
   and **gather** where I did not **scatter**?
Should you not then have put my money in the **bank**
   so that I could have got it back with **interest** on my **return**?
Now then! **Take** the talent from him and **give** it to the one
      with **ten**.
For to **everyone** who **has**,
   more will be **given** and he will grow **rich**;
   but from the one who has **not**,
   even what he **has** will be taken **away**.
And throw this **useless** servant into the darkness **outside**,
   where there will be **wailing** and **grinding** of **teeth**.'"

[Shorter: Matthew 25:14–15, 19–21]

Part is the maxim about what happens to those who have and have not, and describes the chilling fate of the "lazy servant."

unexpected. As Christians often mindful of simplicity of life, we would not have been surprised if the "one-talent" servant was praised, the one who hid the talent in a hole in the ground while the master was away. "Wow," we might think, "that servant did not allow himself to be distracted by worldliness. Instead, he found a safe place and returned the talent exactly as it had been entrusted to him." But this simple servant is not the one who is lauded by Christ, but the two who had ventured to gain double what had been entrusted to them. They are praised as "good and faithful servants."

The one-talent servant comes in for a serious tongue-lashing, "You wicked, lazy servant!" and is thrown out "into the darkness outside." It's not the most reassuring note on which to end the teaching of Jesus in this passage, but as proclaimers of the Gospel, we do not insert our meaning into the narrative but deliver it as clearly and candidly as we can.

The Lectionary gives the option to proclaim a shorter version. The alternate version focuses on the success of the five-talent servant. It is not simply a shorter version of the same story, for the meaning and theology of the parable is very different in the two versions. Your approach to the proclamation, therefore, will be much different because a large part of the long version focuses on the one-talent servant and the "wailing and grinding of teeth" that is his fate, while the short version focuses on the successful five-talent servant.

CHRIST THE KING

Lectionary #160

READING I   Ezekiel 34:11–12, 15–17

Ezekiel = ee-ZEE-kee-ul

The first section sounds nurturing and caring. The Lord GOD describes how He will go out to find the lost sheep.

A reading from the Book of the Prophet Ezekiel

Thus says the Lord **GOD**:
I **myself** will **look** after and **tend** my **sheep**.
As a **shepherd** tends his **flock**
    when he **finds** himself among his **scattered** sheep,
    so will I tend **my** sheep.
I will **rescue** them from every place where they were **scattered**
    when it was **cloudy** and **dark**.

The LORD will strengthen the sheep that are weak.

I **myself** will pasture my sheep;
    I **myself** will give them **rest**, says the Lord **GOD**.
The **lost** I will seek **out**,
    the **strayed** I will bring **back**,
    the **injured** I will bind **up**,
    the **sick** I will **heal**,
    but the **sleek** and the **strong** I will **destroy**,
    shepherding them **rightly**.

Pause before this final verse, for it veers from the tender shepherd to the judging. The pause will mark the shift.

As for **you**, my sheep, says the Lord **GOD**,
    I will **judge** between **one** sheep and **another**,
    between **rams** and **goats**.

READING I   Ezekiel prophesied while the Jews were being carried off into exile in Babylon, and his words often reminded the Jews of why they were in such dire straits, miserable and dejected in the foreign land.

In the Bible just before this passage, you will find the prophet's stinging indictment of the leadership of Israel: "You shepherds of Israel who have been feeding yourselves! Should not shepherds feed the sheep? You eat the fat, you clothe yourselves with the wool, you slaughter the fatlings, but you do not feed the sheep." The passage you have been assigned is more comforting. There's an element of judgment, but overall the passage offers hope and consolation to any believers who hear his words. The earlier verses will help you appreciate the context of the prophet's words. The theology of this passage circumvents the human shepherds who have abused their trust. The Lord GOD will be the shepherd, the LORD asserts, in the absence of these shepherds who have neglected their vocation.

Even if your assembly is among the many that have been well shepherded, they will have heard of situations where the flock was neglected. Proclaim the prophet's message of hope and consolation with conviction.

Corinthians = kor-IN-thee-unz

This reading considers Creation as a whole, Adam, and Christ, the "new Adam," restoring what was lost. The Church is part of this restoration and resurrection.

In Paul's view of the world, the cosmic hierarchy has been re-ordered under Christ. Death itself is an "enemy."

The final line, "that God may be all in all," is a summary of this new cosmic order.

A reading from the first Letter of Saint Paul to the Corinthians

Brothers and sisters:
Christ has been **raised** from the **dead**,
    the **firstfruits** of those who have fallen **asleep**.
For since **death** came through man,
    the **resurrection** of the dead came **also** through man.
For just as in **Adam** all **die**,
    so too in **Christ** shall all be brought to **life**,
    but each **one** in proper **order**:
    Christ the **firstfruits**;
    then, at his **coming**, those who **belong** to Christ;
    then comes the **end**,
    when he **hands** over the **kingdom** to his God and **Father**,
    when he has **destroyed** every **sovereignty**
    and every **authority** and **power**.
For he must reign until he has put **all** his **enemies** under his **feet**.
The **last** enemy to be destroyed is **death**.

When everything is **subjected** to him,
    then the Son **himself** will **also** be subjected
    to the one who **subjected** everything to him,
    so that **God** may be **all** in **all**.

READING II Anniversaries, the turning *(-versary)* of a year *(anni-)*, are more striking than the turning of a week or a month, for of those we have many, but of years we have fewer. New Year's Eves and birthdays are marked with public, social events for this reason.

Like these other turnings of years, the end of the Church year is a traditional time for the Church to focus on the end of time, the end of the world. None of us knows whether the end of the world or the end of our own individual life will come first, but from the point of view of faith, our preparedness would be the same. So the prescription of this reading from Paul's First Letter to the Corinthians suggests the same, that the end of the liturgical year is a time for believers to think about dying and death.

As you prepare for a strong proclamation about this inescapable topic, keep in mind that the figure of Adam plays double duty in the writings of Paul, referring of course to the first human being and also to the whole of humanity. So when Paul writes that "for just as in Adam all die, so too in Christ shall all be brought to life," the present tense of "all die" lets us know that as Paul wrote he was not thinking *primarily* of the Garden of Eden and Adam, but of what has been passed down to us from Adam. Christ is the new Adam because he reversed the debt of sin that we inherited from Adam and from our parents, and all humanity

GOSPEL   Matthew 25:31–46

A reading from the holy Gospel according to Matthew

Jesus said to his **disciples**:
"When the Son of **Man** comes in his **glory**,
    and all the **angels** with him,
    he will **sit** upon his glorious **throne**,
    and all the **nations** will be **assembled** before him.
And he will **separate** them **one** from **another**,
    as a **shepherd** separates the **sheep** from the **goats**.
He will place the **sheep** on his **right** and the **goats** on his **left**.

"Then the **king** will say to those on his **right**,
    '**Come**, you who are **blessed** by my **Father**.
Inherit the kingdom **prepared** for you
        from the **foundation** of the **world**.
For I was **hungry** and you gave me **food**,
    I was **thirsty** and you gave me **drink**,
    a **stranger** and you **welcomed** me,
    naked and you **clothed** me,
    ill and you **cared** for me,
    in **prison** and you **visited** me.'

"Then the **righteous** will answer him and say,
    '**Lord**, **when** did we see you **hungry** and **feed** you,
    or **thirsty** and give you **drink**?
When did we see you a **stranger** and **welcome** you,
    or **naked** and **clothe** you?
When did we see you **ill** or in **prison**, and **visit** you?'
And the **king** will say to them in reply,
    '**Amen**, I say to you, **whatever** you did
    for one of the **least** brothers of mine, you **did** for **me**.'

between the two. For this reason, the Church claims that Baptism removes original sin, for we are brought into the body of Christ, the new Adam, when we are initiated into the Church.

GOSPEL   Every year on the final Sunday in Ordinary Time, the Solemnity of Christ the King (the Thirty-fourth Sunday in Ordinary Time), the issue of the last judgment is the heart of the matter.

It is fitting that on this last Sunday of the liturgical year in which the Gospel of Matthew has been our guiding text we have a mixture of consoling social justice and chilling final judgment. It is a familiar text, but do not let the familiarity prompt you not to practice your proclamation; passages that we *think* we know by heart can often surprise us with a new insight. Take the opportunity to study this Gospel. If you find it engaging, so will the assembly to which you proclaim it.

In spite of the brilliance of Matthew's Gospel, we know from our work as Church, local and universal, that such discernment about God's presence is not a once-for-all happening. Part of the vocation of being Church is a continual process of discerning who is *in*, and who is *out*, and such a process does not lead to easy questions or answers. The members of that ancient Church, like us, probably had some social justice enthusiasts, wanting to find the risen Christ in the poor; they, like us, probably had

"Then he will say to those on his **left**,
  '**Depart** from me, you **accursed**,
  into the eternal **fire** prepared for the **devil** and his **angels**.
For I was **hungry** and you gave me no **food**,
  I was **thirsty** and you gave me no **drink**,
  a **stranger** and you gave me no **welcome**,
  naked and you gave me no **clothing**,
  ill and in **prison**, and you did not **care** for me.'

"Then they will answer and say,
  '**Lord**, **when** did we see you **hungry** or **thirsty**
  or a **stranger** or **naked** or **ill** or in **prison**,
  and **not** minister to your **needs**?'
He will answer them, '**Amen**, I say to you,
  what you did **not** do for one of these **least** ones,
  you did **not** do for **me**.'
And **these** will go off to eternal **punishment**,
  but the **righteous** to eternal **life**."

Peace and all good things to you and your ministry of proclaiming the Gospel of the Lord.

some worship enthusiasts, wanting to find the exact ritual prescriptions for the realization of Christ's presence in their midst; they, like us, probably had some theological absolutists, certain that God acts *this* way and not *that* way; they, like us, probably had some members who were satisfied with leaving things as they had always been; and they, like us, probably had some eager members whose interests changed with each new idea or interest that passed by.

The Evangelist Matthew captured this variety of Christ's body in the metaphor, employing "the sheep on his right" and "the goats on his left." But he did not leave it in metaphor; he concretized it and highlighted the ministry to the hungry, thirsty, stranger, the naked, ill, and imprisoned. The metaphors and symbols of the worshiping community are not ends in themselves, but means to the end of saving God's people, of the Body of Christ changing the world and realizing God's kingdom. Proclaim this beautiful reading to further the work and realization of the Gospel.